VERNACULAR RELIGION

NORTH AMERICAN RELIGIONS

Series Editors: Tracy Fessenden (Arizona State University), Laura Levitt (Temple University), and David Harrington Watt (Haverford College)

Since its inception, the North American Religions book series has steadily disseminated gracefully written, pathbreaking explorations of religion in North America. Books in the series move among the discourses of ethnographic, textual, and historical analysis and across a range of topics, including sound, story, food, nature, healing, crime, and pilgrimage. In so doing they bring religion into view as a style and form of belonging, a set of tools for living with and in relations of power, a mode of cultural production and reproduction, and a vast repertory of the imagination. Whatever their focus, books in the series remain attentive to the shifting and contingent ways in which religious phenomena are named, organized, and contested. They bring fluency in the best of contemporary theoretical and historical scholarship to bear on the study of religion in North America. The series focuses primarily, but not exclusively, on religion in the United States in the twentieth and twenty-first centuries.

Books in the Series

Ava Chamberlain, *The Notorious Elizabeth Tuttle: Marriage, Murder, and Madness in the Family of Jonathan Edwards*

Terry Rey and Alex Stepick, *Crossing the Water and Keeping the Faith: Haitian Religion in Miami*

Isaac Weiner, *Religion Out Loud: Religious Sound, Public Space, and American Pluralism*

Hillary Kaell, *Walking Where Jesus Walked: American Christians and Holy Land Pilgrimage*

Brett Hendrickson, *Border Medicine: A Transcultural History of Mexican American Curanderismo*

Jodi Eichler-Levine, *Suffer the Little Children: Uses of the Past in Jewish and African American Children's Literature*

Annie Blazer, *Playing for God: Evangelical Women and the Unintended Consequences of Sports Ministry*

Elizabeth Pérez, *Religion in the Kitchen: Cooking, Talking, and the Making of Black Atlantic Traditions*

Kerry Mitchell, *Spirituality and the State: Managing Nature and Experience in America's National Parks*

Finbarr Curtis, *The Production of American Religious Freedom*

M. Cooper Harriss, *Ralph Ellison's Invisible Theology*

Ari Y. Kelman, *Shout to the Lord: Making Worship Music in Evangelical America*

Joshua Dubler and Isaac Weiner, *Religion, Law, USA*

Shari Rabin, *Jews on the Frontier: Religion and Mobility in Nineteenth-Century America*

Elizabeth Fenton, *Old Canaan in a New World: Native Americans and the Lost Tribes of Israel*

Alyssa Maldonado-Estrada, *Lifeblood of the Parish: Masculinity and Catholic Devotion in Williamsburg, Brooklyn*

Caleb Iyer Elfenbein, *Fear in Our Hearts: What Islamophobia Tells Us about America*

Rachel B. Gross, *Beyond the Synagogue: Jewish Nostalgia as Religious Practice*

Jenna Supp-Montgomerie, *When the Medium Was the Mission: The Religious Origins of Network Culture*

Philippa Koch, *The Course of God's Providence: Religion, Health, and the Body in Early America*

Jennifer Scheper Hughes, *The Church of the Dead: The Epidemic of 1576 and the Birth of Christianity in the Americas*

Tisa Wenger and Sylvester Johnson, *Religion and US Empire: Critical New Histories*

Deborah Dash Moore, *Vernacular Religion: Collected Essays of Leonard Norman Primiano*

Vernacular Religion

Collected Essays of
LEONARD NORMAN PRIMIANO

Edited by Deborah Dash Moore

Foreword by Judith Weisenfeld

NEW YORK UNIVERSITY PRESS
New York

NEW YORK UNIVERSITY PRESS
New York
www.nyupress.org

© 2022 by New York University
All rights reserved

References to Internet websites (URLs) were accurate at the time of writing. Neither the author nor New York University Press is responsible for URLs that may have expired or changed since the manuscript was prepared.

Library of Congress Cataloging-in-Publication Data
Names: Primiano, Leonard Norman, author. | Moore, Deborah Dash, 1946– editor.
Title: Vernacular religion : collected essays of Leonard Norman Primiano / edited by Deborah Dash Moore.
Description: New York : New York University Press, [2022] |
Series: North American religions | Includes bibliographical references and index.
Identifiers: LCCN 2022001956 | ISBN 9781479818662 (hardback) | ISBN 9781479818679 (paperback) | ISBN 9781479818686 (ebook) | ISBN 9781479818693 (ebook other)
Subjects: LCSH: Catholic Church—United States—Customs and practices.
Classification: LCC BX1406.3 .P75 2022 | DDC 282/.73—dc23/eng/20220225
LC record available at https://lccn.loc.gov/2022001956

New York University Press books are printed on acid-free paper, and their binding materials are chosen for strength and durability. We strive to use environmentally responsible suppliers and materials to the greatest extent possible in publishing our books.

Manufactured in the United States of America

10 9 8 7 6 5 4 3 2 1

Also available as an ebook

For
Leonard Norman Primiano
PEACE

CONTENTS

Foreword   x
   Judith Weisenfeld

Preface: A Labor of Love   xiv
   Deborah Dash Moore

Introduction: Vernacular Religion and the Search for Method in Religious Folklife   1

PART I. RELIGIOUS MATERIAL CULTURE

1. Textures of a Religious Life: The Vernacular Religious Art of Sister Ann Ameen   17

2. The Vow as Visual Feast: Honoring St. Joseph in Sicilian American Homes   31

3. Postmodern Sites of Catholic Sacred Materiality   41

4. Artifacts of Belief: Holy Cards in Roman Catholic Culture   57

5. Catholiciana Unmoored: Ex-Votos in Catholic Tradition and Their Commercialization as Religious Commodities   75

PART II. DIGNITY IN PHILADELPHIA

6. The Gay God of the City: The Emergence of the Gay and Lesbian Ethnic Parish   105

7. What Is Vernacular Catholicism? The Dignity Example   123

8. "I Would Rather Be Fixated on the Lord": Women's Religion, Men's Power, and the Dignity Problem   131

PART III. FATHER AND MOTHER DIVINE

9. "The Consciousness of God's Presence Will Keep You Well, Healthy, Happy, and Singing": The Tradition of Innovation in the Music of Father Divine's Peace Mission Movement — 145

10. "Bringing Perfection in These Different Places": Father Divine's Vernacular Architecture of Intention — 169

11. "And as We Dine, We Sing and Praise God": Father and Mother Divine's Theologies of Food — 195

12. "As a Living Shrine I Came": Remembrance, Creativity, and Paradox in God's American Tomb — 217

Coda: Encountering the Female Divine . . . Literally: Ethnographic Writing about Mother and Father Divine's Peace Mission Movement — 241

Acknowledgments — 251

Notes — 259

Further Reading — 303

Index — 307

About the Author and Editor — 325

Color illustrations appear as an insert following page 200.

FOREWORD

JUDITH WEISENFELD

On a wall near the desk where I am writing, in a black frame, hangs a list of the rules and regulations for guests of hotels owned by followers of Father Divine, mostly in New Jersey and Pennsylvania. At the top of this broadside, which was posted in each hotel room, is the word "Peace," Father Divine's preferred greeting, and in the body of the document is the declaration, "It is our desire to be a blessing to everyone who avails themselves of the facilities we offer. This can only be made effective to you by your willingness to cooperate in maintaining the standard of Americanism, Brotherhood, Christianity and True Judaism that FATHER DIVINE dedicated these hotels to exemplify."[1] These rules and regulations emphasize the Peace Mission's recognition of "only one race, the human race," and the consequent refusal of racial segregation in assigning shared rooms. The group's practices of celibacy and sex-segregation led to the posted requirement that women and men be accommodated on separate floors and interact only in the lobby or dining room. The commitment to modesty shaped the hotel's directive that guests dress in "evangelical" attire, and the insistence on honesty and independence guided rules about prompt payment of rent, all in the service of "the upliftment of mankind in general."

This artifact arrived in my office mail several years ago, a gift from Leonard Norman Primiano in recognition of our shared scholarly interest in Father Divine and the Peace Mission. That Leonard rescued this discarded object from the trash following the closure of one of the group's Philadelphia hotels reflects not only his long-term commitment to understanding the Peace Mission but also his endless wonder at the materiality of religious expression in the many communities to which he turned his eye over years of research, writing, and teaching about religion. Indeed, Leonard declared, in his essay on collecting Catholic ex-votos, that he was attracted to religious material because he had "directed the energies of my career to unlocking the mysteries of why people are religious in their everyday lives."[2] Those who knew him knew that these energies were considerable and that his interest in people was deep and joyous.

Those of us similarly interested in why and how people are religious in their everyday lives are immensely fortunate to have Leonard's essays collected in this posthumous volume. It is a remarkably interdisciplinary assemblage, grounded in his training in folklife studies, his expertise as an ethnographer, and his interest in religion, featuring essays that were published in journals or edited volumes focused on a range of topics—architecture, magic and ritual, folklore, material religion, religious studies, ethnography. Taken together, these essays offer resources for scholars in a variety of fields to understand the religious experiences, identities, and expressions of people embedded in social contexts and communities. In one essay, Leonard remarks that, "being trained in the folklife studies approach," he "recognized that attention to the nuances of everyday life is a singularly important contribution that ethnographic work can make to understanding religious culture. It encourages emphasis on aesthetic or artistic creation, historical process, and the construction of mental, verbal, or material forms."[3] The volume is brimming with insights about method and marked by rich descriptions of the experiences that motivated Leonard to pursue certain topics, sites, and questions in his research. We can accompany him through the aisles of the St. Jude Shop outside Philadelphia and learn from his analysis of the meaning and merchandizing of Catholic sacred items, follow the path that led him to become a collector of Catholic ex-votos, observe with him the religious and social negotiations that Dignity members made in living as gay and lesbian Catholics, and join him in moving through Peace Mission spaces to understand the rich "artistry and aesthetics of [individual members'] everyday lives" as expressed in foodways and devotional music.[4]

The core contribution of Leonard's work collected here is his offering of "vernacular religion" as a methodological tool "for studies at the intersection of religion, folklore, and folklife."[5] At stake for Leonard is the search for a method of understanding how people live their religious lives that does not draw a distinction between "official" and "elite," on the one hand, and "folk" or "popular" on the other. Making such a distinction, he insists, confers authenticity on those religious beliefs, forms, and sites that scholars characterize as "official" and devalues those designated as "unofficial" or "popular." Vernacular religion, as Leonard develops, elaborates, and applies that concept in these essays, involves examining the religious lives of individuals as they carry them out in social contexts that produce "creative self-understanding, self-interpretation, and negotiation by the believing individual." These social contexts can include religious institutions and official dogma, ethnic, racial, and sexual identity, and elements of local community life, for example, that shape religion as it is lived. "From this context," he writes, "the beliefs of individuals themselves radiate out and influence the surrounding environments."[6]

Two words appear repeatedly in Leonard's elaboration of vernacular religion: *creativity* and *negotiation*. We see creativity and negotiation as the hallmarks of vernacular religion in all the case studies featured in this volume, from the creative vernacular religious art of Sister Ann Ameen to the negotiations of individual spirituality and official theology in practices of Catholic sacred materiality and in participation in Dignity, an organization of gay and lesbian Catholics. The creativity and negotiation so central to Leonard's framework of vernacular religion come out most profoundly in the set of essays focused on his extended ethnographic work with the Peace Mission. No scholar spent more time with the members of this movement, was more familiar with its history and development over time, or was more attuned to the dynamics of change and adaptation in the group's vernacular religious expressions than Leonard. In contrast to the many studies that have characterized "sectarian movements" like the Peace Mission as static and their followers as unthinking adherents to the founder's official theology, Leonard's empathetic and careful ethnography shows both members and leaders adapting, creating, and transforming in relation to their social and material environments and to each other, including in response to the death of the founder. Throughout this volume, we see Leonard's own ethnographic and interpretive creativity, his negotiation of research ethics and his position as a scholar in different contexts, and the transformation of his questions and approaches over the course of his career. The concluding essay, in which he reflects on his years of fieldwork in the Peace Mission and his practice of "reciprocal ethnography" with Mother Divine, returns to the consideration of the stakes of scholarship and the value of the method of vernacular religion that opens the volume.

As I neared the end of my research on the Peace Mission in 2014, I visited Woodmont, the group's "Mount of the House of the Lord" in Gladwyne, Pennsylvania, on a Sunday when the property was open to visitors. I am not an ethnographer and did not visit as a researcher; I wanted to experience something of the sounds, tastes, and sights of the current vernacular religion of the group that I had spent so much time pursuing in archives and historical records. The member who greeted me at my car, an elderly woman wearing the uniform of the Rosebuds choir, looked me up and down to affirm that I was dressed modestly in a skirt or dress and a top with sleeves. I passed the test, despite her hesitation at my open-toed sandals. She asked what brought me to visit, and I told her of my longtime interest in the group. She was pleased to learn that I was from Queens, which she referred to from that point on as "Queens, Long Island," connecting me to the story of the Peace Mission through a reference to the group's time in Sayville, Long Island, in the 1920s. She was similarly pleased when I mentioned that I knew Dr. Primiano, and the regard that he had earned from his years of respectful presence and recognition of their vernacular religious world was clear to me. Escorting me through the house, she stopped before a door and knocked, telling me that she hoped we would be able to enter. She put her ear to the door for a moment and then opened it to usher me into an entirely unexpected and quite intimidating audience with Mother Divine, who was seated with her secretary in an office I recognized from photographs. "She's from Queens, Long Island," my guide informed Mother Divine, "and she is a student of Dr. Primiano's." I saw no need to correct her because, indeed, I have been his student. Through this collection of essays, we can all be. Later, in time for the Holy Communion Banquet Service, Leonard appeared. We smiled and greeted one another. "Peace," he said.

PREFACE

A Labor of Love

DEBORAH DASH MOORE

This volume of essays by Leonard Norman Primiano is rare and precious, a true labor of love. Its roots reach back to the 1990s, when a group of "young scholars in American religion" joined me in Indianapolis for a series of weekend sessions designed to encourage their scholarship, teaching, and the study of religion in the United States. Ava Chamberlain, Tracy Fessenden, Kathleen Joyce, Laura Levitt, Elizabeth McAlister, Leonard Norman Primiano, and Jennifer Rycenga ended up naming themselves "the Creoles" in a gesture reflecting their commitment to embrace religion in all its multiplicity. Periodically we would meet to share scholarship and friendship. The last time was in Philadelphia in 2018, when we all enthusiastically encouraged Leonard to complete the book that he wanted to write.

It was not to be.

After his untimely death in 2021, we took up the task to finish the project and present between two covers Leonard's brilliant interpretations of vernacular religion to a wide audience.

Everyone—Ava, Tracy, Kate, Laura, Liza, and Jennifer—pitched in and made this volume a reality.

In addition, we had superb editorial assistance from Sara J. Arnold, encouragement from Jennifer Hammer at New York University Press, wonderful suggestions from two anonymous reviewers, and excellent photography from John Chew, Don Dempsey, Katie Reing, and Joseph Sciorra. We are grateful to the journals and publishers who gave permission to publish Leonard's previously published work. We want to thank Greg Garrity, Laura Sauer Palmer, Katie Reing, Clara Saraiva, Joseph Sciorra, and Matt Slutz for their help. We greatly appreciate the financial support from David Harrington Watt and the Quaker Studies program of Haverford College, Philip Goff and the Center for the Study of Religion and American Culture, the University of Michigan, and the estate of Leonard Norman Primiano.

As Judith Weisenfeld wrote in her foreword, now we all have the opportunity to be Leonard Norman Primiano's students, to learn from him, and to be inspired.

Ann Arbor, Michigan, October 2021

....

Vernacular religion is more than a purely conceptual term, a methodological abstraction without any practical utility. Full understanding of this term establishes a methodological foundation from which the vernacular study of religion will grow as a method of practice, a way of doing ethnography that has not been considered before.

....

INTRODUCTION

Vernacular Religion and the Search for Method in Religious Folklife

The relationship of reflexivity to the study of religious folklife is of great significance not only to fieldwork methods and ethnographic work but also to the very conceptual methodological core upon which folklore and folklife studies is predicated and which continues to influence the way folklorists study and analyze lived religion. By methodology, I mean here the conscious activity of disciplinary and multidisciplinary theoretical self-criticism. This term should stand juxtaposed to "approach," which includes conceptual "theory" and practical "method," specific disciplinary tools of analysis.

When the word "theory" is employed, it can sustain several levels of meaning. Theory may refer to a specific analytical concept that can then become a technique or tool, as in "Freud's theory of psychoanalysis." Theory may also be used to indicate the meta-inquiry of methodology, in which case it is the analytical umbrella under which all methods and individual theories can be viewed and discussed. Theory as methodology is often a reflection on the integrity and self-critical trends within a discipline, but it can also indicate theoretical considerations that transcend individual disciplines and find utility in multidisciplinary contexts, as in "postmodern theory." Focusing on religion as it is lived calls for the development of a reflexive "methodology" regarding the ethnography of religious folklife—that is, the interdisciplinary examination of such ethnography's theoretical foundation.[1]

Folklore as a scholarly discipline is not only about doing ethnography, and ethnography is not only about work in the field. Although our discipline is based in fieldwork, there is, after all, more to doing fieldwork

---

Originally published in 1995.

than just doing it. There is also more to the changing patterns of scholarly usage than mere academic politics or fashion. Changes in choices of terminology reflect substantive shifts in our perceptions of human realities. Questions need to be asked and then re-asked about those basic theoretical perspectives, including the words, terms, and meanings that are freely taken from received scholarly traditions even before we have had our first interactions in the field.

Folklorists often encounter religious belief in their fieldwork and engage with its expression in their capacities as researchers, teachers, museum administrators, archivists, and workers in a variety of public-sector positions. When the folklore-folklife scholar begins to analyze data, no conscientious member of the discipline would choose to do violence to the emic perspectives that have been expressed by informants. Yet every time a folklorist encounters religion and designates it "folk religion," he or she has done that religiosity an extreme disservice.[2]

Scholars may not intend to residualize the religious lives of believers, but their insistent acts of misnaming constrain the way they study and interpret their informants and negatively influence how the scholarly and nonscholarly worlds view these people. The book of Genesis in the Judeo-Christian Bible contains a well-known passage (2:19) in which Adam, the creation of God, is given the privilege of naming every living creature. Scripture scholars inform us that this act of assigning names to the animals signifies the dominion or power that humanity has over these creatures. Scholars share with the biblical Adam that same power to name—to signify, to classify—people, ideas, and behaviors around them. Through such naming in their writings and teaching, scholars can influence, even control, the perceptions of their fellow scholars as well as the non-academic public regarding particular subjects of interest. That kind of power is a privilege that some scholars have used with insufficient methodological self-criticism.

Religious folklife as a scholarly discipline, as opposed to a subject matter, has been guilty of such a misuse of power. Scholars within the discipline have consistently named religious people's beliefs, in residualistic, derogatory ways, as "folk," "unofficial," or "popular" religion, and have then juxtaposed these terms with "official" religion, as a two-tiered model. When folklorists discuss "folk religion" or "religious folklore" in the context of a "religious folk group," they imply that religion somewhere exists as a pure element that is in some way transformed, even contaminated, by its exposure to human communities. This tendency is emblematic of how folklorists have consistently devalued "folk religion" by assigning it unofficial religious status.

Folklorists have maintained an interest in the reality of religion as it is lived, and they must be credited for their sympathetic engagement with religion as it is expressed in everyday life. Unfortunately, folklorists have also maintained a problematic terminology for and conceptualization of the religion they study. Folklore and folklife's terminological and conceptual considerations of "folk" religion are represented significantly in the work of Don Yoder. Yoder mentions that the term *religiose Volkskunde*, according to German scholarship, was in fact coined by the Lutheran minister Paul Drews in 1901 to prepare young seminary graduates for the radically different religious ideas of their rural congregants.[3] For Yoder, folk religion can be thought of primarily as unofficial religion. In this regard, Jeff Todd Titon has remarked that Yoder's definition remains closely aligned with the "official" church-centered orientation of Ernst Troeltsch.[4] Yoder, in personal communication, does not agree that his concept of folk religion has any relationship to Troeltsch's division of religion into church and sect types. In Yoder's view, folk religion does not oppose a central religious body in an organized form, as would Troeltsch's conception of a "sect," but represents unorganized practices and ideas that have a dynamic relationship to official religion.

Folklorists have followed the two-tiered model employed by historians, anthropologists, sociologists, and religious studies scholars that creates distinct categories separating the "folk" or "popular" religion of the faithful from "official" or institutional religion administered by hierarchical elites through revealed or inspired oral and written texts. This practice both residualizes the religious lives of believers and reifies the authenticity of religious institutions as the exemplar of human religiosity. The Yoder definition illustrates that this residualism is a problematic but extremely influential idea that has long affected the scholarly description, conceptualization, and analysis of folk and popular religion. Put simply, Yoder's conception of folk religion is residualistic in its reliance on a two-tiered model for dichotomizing "official" and "unofficial" religiosity.[5]

Religion as it is practiced and perceived necessitates an inductive approach that provides an alternative to this inadequate two-tiered model. An inductive approach does more than simply extrapolate general principles from data; it generates a theory of and method for the study of religion based on criteria of religious validity established by the inner experience and perception of the believer. Scholarship on lived religion is, however, never a purely objective undertaking but rather a subjective composite of various analytical vantage points. A presentation of the beliefs of others occurs always through the filter of the empathetic perception and interpretation of the scholar. The inductive process balances the scholar's own knowledge and perspectives with that scholar's empathetic understanding of the individuals being studied. In this sense, the concerns of an inductive approach are oriented toward the attempts of scholars to interpret cultural data in a way that is meaningful to their informants as well as theoretically rigorous and responsible. As sociologist of religion Pieter H. Vrijhof asserts, "Socio-religious research needs an inductive approach to religious phenomena with sensitizing concepts. By this inductive approach, popular religion can become disentangled from Christian concepts and interpretations."[6]

One of the hallmarks of the study of religion by folklorists has been their attempt to do justice to belief and lived experience. Folklorists may have not yet challenged basic terminological designations, but they have done much to open scholarly eyes to the experiential factors behind many human belief systems. They have done this not by psychologizing beliefs and believers but by taking seriously what people say, feel, and experience.[7] This respect for the integrity of individuals' sometimes wonderfully unique, sometimes wonderfully ordinary religious lives is what should set folklorists and, especially, religious studies scholars apart from other students of human culture. However, such a sensitivity to religion has never been distilled into a mutually cross-pollinating theoretical and methodological approach. What is often the case is that folklorists have been insufficiently attentive to theoretical reflection and analysis, and religious studies as a discipline has been interested more in the historical processes and linguistic products of religious institutionalization than in the way people actually live their religious lives.

In an effort to initiate such a cross-disciplinary approach to understanding and studying religion, one that transcends a consideration of religion as only a manifestation of and within institutions, I offer the term "vernacular religion."[8] When I speak of "vernacular religion," I am not simply substituting the word "vernacular" to avoid the connotations that I do not like in "folk" or "popular." I am, rather, attempting to redress a heritage of scholarly misrepresentation in the ethnographic process through what I see as a necessary methodological reflexivity. Understanding religion as "vernacular religion" does justice to the variety of manifestations and perspectives found within past and present human religiosity.[9] It also provides a methodological tool for studies at the intersection of religion, folklore, and folklife.

"Vernacular" is an especially appropriate word to use in this context. The *Oxford English Dictionary* gives two relevant definitions, both distinct from the word's usual meaning as writing, using, or speaking the native or indigenous language of a country or district—the meaning that is applied in sociolinguistic usage of the term to refer to "the indigenous language or dialect of a speech community." "Vernacular" can also be defined as simply "personal, private," or it can mean "of arts, or features of these: native or peculiar to a particular country or locality."[10]

A further application of "vernacular" can be found in Margaret Lantis's early discussion of "the vernacular aspect or portion of the total culture." Lantis does not conceptually equate vernacular culture with subculture or terminologically equate it with folk culture, or the culture of folk groups, because in her opinion vernacular culture is "not held by an organized group." It is a way of communicating, thinking, behaving within, and conforming to a particular cultural circumstance.[11]

The notion of vernacular as "that which is common or native in a given area" or "indigenous, used by the people" has been applied by some folklorists and architectural historians to designate various built environments as "vernacular architecture."[12] Alan Gowans, in a volume of readings on vernacular architecture, has provided the following assessment of the word: "A vernacular style in building or speech (whence the word was originally borrowed by architectural writers, Sir George Gilbert Scott being the first to use it, apparently, in 1857) is flexible in meaning according to situation. Essentially it means an unaffected, unselfconscious way of building (speaking)."[13]

Other scholars have debated and explored the term's usefulness, expanding its applicability beyond the categorization of certain kinds of buildings. Dell Upton prefers to see "vernacular architecture" used in reference to an inclusive way to observe and study all architecture. He has specifically complained that the term is currently inadequate because it has come to represent so many "disparate kinds of buildings"; his inclusive approach to the study of all architecture eliminates the exclusivity of the label.[14] Henry Glassie also emphasizes that the study of vernacular architecture should not concern itself with specific kinds of buildings. Since all architecture can be classified as vernacular, Glassie sees such a study as encompassing the personal, aesthetic, cultural, and social investment of the designer and builder of a structure as well as the ways that individuals privately and creatively adapt such built environments to their specific life needs.[15]

My conception of the term "vernacular religion" shares some of the qualities associated with such a multivalent understanding of the "vernacular" in architecture. The need to do justice to the experiential component of people's religious lives can only be satisfied through use of a term that specifically addresses the "personal" and "private." Equally significant is the relationship of "vernacular" to the "arts" manifested in the creativity and artistry expressed in the human drive to interpret religious experience. Personal religious interpretation, as lived, involves continuous and various negotiations of belief and practice, including, but not limited to, original invention, unintentional innovation, and intentional adaptation. This human artistry is as meaningful as the creation, performance, and communication of any number of folklore genres that have interested folklore and folklife scholars for generations.

Vernacular religion is, by definition, religion as it is lived: as human beings encounter, understand, interpret, and practice it. Since religion inherently involves interpretation, it is impossible for the religion of an individual not to be vernacular. Vernacular religious theory involves an interdisciplinary approach to the study of the religious lives of individuals, with special attention to the processes of religious belief, the verbal, behavioral, and material expressions of religious belief, and the ultimate objects of religious belief.

The phrase "processes of religious belief" refers to the complex linkage of belief acquisition and formation that is accomplished through conscious and unconscious negotiations of and between believers. It is important to acknowledge within these processes of believing the presence of bidirectional influences of environments upon individuals and of individuals upon environments. Manifold human factors influence the individual believer, such as physical and psychological predispositions, the natural environment, family, community affiliations, religious institutions, the socialization process, tradition, education and literacy, communication media, and political and economic conditions. All of these elements interact with the individual mind to form what Don Yoder has called "a unified organic system of belief."[16] This unified system of possibly disparate feelings and ideas also forms a context of its own. This context is the content of religious belief, resulting from the continuity of creative self-understanding, self-interpretation, and negotiation by the believing individual. From this context, the beliefs of individuals themselves radiate out and influence the surrounding environments.[17]

The verbal, behavioral, and material expressions of religious belief generate a wide variety of instruments and occasions of expressive culture, which can be categorized under the rubric of visual or performed arts, public and private cultural performances, and individual acts. By "visual or performed arts," I do not imply a conventional, secular understanding of visual art or performance art as entertainment; rather, I mean that religious expressions involve creative enactment and reaffirm the idea that ordinary people's everyday lives are both religious and artful. Such expressions include the following, though the list is not exhaustive: speech, music and song, dance, mime, ritual and drama, bodily communication, myriad uses of writing, foodways, costume, culturally encoded architecture, and the permanent and ephemeral objects within domestic and public environments.[18]

"Official religion" as a Western scholarly concept has been sustained partly out of deference to the historical and cultural hegemony of Christianity, which has set the dominant tone for Western culture.[19] Through a process of reification, "institution" has become equated, for both believers and scholars, whether lay or clerical, with "Church"/"church," with "valid," and with "official." Religion as institution has been mistakenly identified as religious reality itself and not as an ideal type. We must be aware that this process of reification has taken place when we consider the concretization of the human religious impulse. Religious studies scholar Wilfred Cantwell Smith makes the point that the very concept of "religion" in the West has evolved through a lengthy reification process of "mentally making religion into a thing, gradually coming to conceive it as an objective systematic entity." This development has also included "the rise into Western consciousness in relatively recent times of several so conceived entities, constituting a series: the religions of the world." Smith prefers to speak of "an historical 'cumulative tradition,' and the personal faith of men and women," as more dynamic conceptions of human religiosity.[20]

In fact, there are bodies and agencies of normative, prescriptive religion, but no practice objectively expresses "official religion." No one—no special religious elite or member of an institutional hierarchy, neither the pope in Rome nor the Dalai Lama of Tibet nor the patriarch of Istanbul nor the chief rabbi of Jerusalem—lives an "officially" religious life in a pure, unadulterated form. The members of such a hierarchy are themselves believing and practicing vernacularly, even while representing the most institutionally normative aspects of their religious tradition. There is always some passive accommodation, some intriguing survival, some active creation, some dissenting impulse, some reflection of lived experience that influences or directs these individuals' religious lives.

Scholars have studied and keep studying institutional religion as "official religion," maintaining it as the standard against which the varieties of people's religious impulses are measured. To continue to compare the vernacular religious ideas of people of any culture to the construct "official religion" is to perpetuate the value judgment that people's ideas and practices, because they do not represent the refined statements of a religious institution, are indeed unofficial and fringe. This attitude is particularly faulty because it is the ideas of individuals that inspired the formation of institutional religion in the first place and that maintain its authority. Vernacular religion takes into consideration the individual convictions of "official" religious membership among common believers, as well as the vernacular religious ideas at the root of the institution itself. Individuals, as believers, feel their personal belief system to be "official," and they also, at the same time, feel the belief system disseminated by the agencies of the institutional hierarchy to be "official religion." Elaine J. Lawless notes that within the American context of small religious congregations, there exists an internal notion of their own oral traditions serving as "official religion" within that community.[21] In such contexts, the concept of vernacular religion can highlight the creative interpretations present in even the most ardent, devout, and accepting religious life while also being sensitive to the power and perceived validity of "official" religion.

Vernacular religion, in relation to a class-structured view of society, is not to be equated with popular religion as a religion of the masses, nor should it be juxtaposed to the religion of social leaders or intellectual cognoscenti. The power relations inherent in social divisions of class, economics, race, ethnicity, gender, and sexual preference do profoundly influence communities of religious individuals; these divisions, in fact, are mirrored in, and often formed by, the politics of religious institutions in their internal relations of power. But vernacular religious creativity finds fertile ground in all social and political environments. In this sense, vernacular religion can develop to contest unequal power relations, to affirm the existence of inequality, or simply to confirm the social status quo.

The folkloristic study of religious belief and believers should emphasize the integrated ideas and practices of all *individuals* living in human society. Indeed, while such an interest in the individual would seem to be a major concern of the scholar of religious folklife, it has, in fact, been the least examined element.[22] What has prevailed in the discipline has been the notion of individuals communicating with or relating to other individuals within specified social units.[23] This perspective has included an orientation toward generic categorizations and sociocultural identifications based on group affiliation or regional association.[24] Religion, however, is a far more dynamic phenomenon than such a limited notion can capture.

Folkloristic scholarship on religion needs to transcend the accepted parameters of the inherent relationship of social groups to folklore. Folklore, in general, must enlarge its focus to emphasize the individual as the creator and possessor of a single folkloric worldview who constantly interprets and negotiates his or her own beliefs. This does not imply that an individual is not influenced by several physiological, cultural, social, and environmental forces; it recognizes that, given the human capacity to interpret these influences, people develop their own folklore within as well as around themselves. This idea is apparent in the explorations of folklorists as they reduce the number of people they consider necessary for folkloric processes to occur.

This can be observed in work on the folklore of intimacy by Regina Bendix, in which she continues a discussion of the importance of "dyadic idioculture," relating it specifically to heterosexual couples. She notes that it is Gary Alan Fine who "suggests the term 'idioculture' to characterize small-group culture, defining it as 'a system of knowledge, beliefs, behaviors and customs particular to an interacting group to which members can refer and employ as the basis of further interaction.'" This culture can be represented by dyadic folklore, such as playful nicknames or turns of phrase, and personal traditional behaviors, such as physical routines that develop between two people.[25]

Bendix further reports on a paper given by Jay Mechling at the 1986 meeting of the American Folklore Society in Baltimore. In this paper, Mechling "posited that, based on his interactions with his dog, dyadic folklore exists between humans and their pets."[26] This is a fascinating insight on Mechling's part, but if we are giving worthy consideration to folklore as artistic communication between such parties, is it not also about time to recognize the existence of "uniculture" to characterize the personal discourse that we all carry on with ourselves as self-aware beings?[27]

An expanded, published version of Mechling's paper offers a provocative reevaluation of the boundaries of folklore by emphasizing the broader context of human interaction in which folklore occurs. Not only can folklore be observed in the interaction of individuals within small groups, but, from Mechling's vantage point, the folkloric context of human interaction must be redefined to emphasize the systemic nature of all human interactions, including "folklore between people and pets, between people and things, and between people and imaginary others."[28] His inclusion of individual interaction within the contexts of play (e.g., solitaire) and fantasy (e.g., an imagined relationship with a celebrity) does usefully extend accepted folkloristic parameters, but his dependence on the systems-centered epistemology of Gregory Bateson does not allow him to take a balanced view of the reality of the individual in addition to the systems that constitute that individual.

In the end, Mechling surrenders the autonomy of the folkloric world of the individual because he judges folklore to be "a feature of systems, and we ought not let our human hubris make us forgetful of this fact."[29] The individual is indeed constituted within various internal and external systemic relations, but Mechling's view does not give proper credence to the multitude of ways that an individual interacts with himself or herself. Individuals, even the most physiologically and emotionally impaired, have a relationship with their own thoughts, feelings, and bodies that is always developing, from their earliest consciousness until their death. Uniculture could thus be defined as a processual system of conscious and unconscious knowledge, beliefs, behaviors, and customs particular to the individual to which he or she refers and which she or he employs as the basis of everyday living. Such a folkloric understanding of uniculture would allow room not only for play and fantasy, as in Mechling's dyadic conception, but also for a much wider range of interactions with the self. Belief, be it religious, political, health-centered, or of another kind, is one such context of interaction within the autonomous self that we cannot ignore when considering the culture of the human individual. This point does not negate the importance of received elements from other individuals or communities and their transmission, but it recognizes that unicultural folklore is a product of the personal creativeness of our own daily lives.

The creativity of uniculture is particularly manifest in the parallel creative activity of vernacular religion.[30] Several instances gleaned from my own fieldwork illustrate the processes of belief inherent in vernacular religious life. Human beings do not always communicate what they believe to others, because their individual beliefs can be substantially different. This fact is especially true as it concerns religious beliefs. A good illustration can be found in the Roman Catholic experience of going to a confessional to confess one's sins. An individual is supposed to tell all, but does one ever? Many American Catholic informants tell me of the importance of their own personal, solitary confessions to God, especially if they happen to find incompatible priest confessors in their parish or locale.[31]

Individual belief does not need to be founded in or based on ideas and practices emanating from a group-oriented and structured religious institution. A less familiar example of personal creative spirituality would be the individual religiosity of solitary practitioners of Wicca, one of the names for contemporary Witchcraft, a variety of eclectic networks of life-affirming religious beliefs and practices combining elements of nature magic and earth-oriented Goddess worship.[32] Solitary Wiccans do not consistently receive or transmit their understanding of their religion within the constraints of the small group, or coven, community. Although they receive collective materials from sources that might be deemed part of popular culture, such as mass-distributed books and periodicals, as well as from more conventionally folkloric sources such as inherited traditions within a family of Witches, as solitaries they formulate their interpretations of their religious paths and the methods of their practice on their own.

Religious belief takes as many forms within a tradition as there are individual believers. A final relevant example is the religiosity of members of Dignity Philadelphia, a chapter of the national organization of gay and lesbian Roman Catholic men and women.[33] These individuals have joined together to be living, worshipping witnesses to their belief that God creates good things and God created them with their homosexual orientation, so, therefore, their sexual acts are good and they as sexual beings are worthy of inclusion in the Church. Still, many of them are also active members of traditional parishes. Such individuals have obviously altered their beliefs to accommodate not only their subculture but also their religious roots and sacramental sensibilities.

Vernacular religion, as an approach embracing theory and method, incorporates attention to such ongoing interpretations and negotiations of religion within groups and institutions by applying theoretical awareness and ethnographic reflexivity to the study of such individual creations of religion. "Vernacular religion" is more than a purely conceptual term, a methodological abstraction without any practical utility. Full understanding of this term establishes a methodological foundation from which the vernacular study of religion will grow as a method of practice, a way of doing ethnography that has not been considered before. If all religion need be traditional, inherited, group-oriented, deliberate, and involved in performative verbal art to be considered "folk religion," then folklorists, even though they have made an effort to study such religion in the context of holistic systems, have neglected a considerable amount of potential religiosity. Vernacular religion, as an approach to understanding religion as it has been lived in the past and is lived today, emphasizes the study of the *belief* systems of religious people. This means a consideration of the contents and motivations of the actual beliefs of individuals. Folklorists have, in their tendency to "genrify" religious folklore, left out the religious contents and implicit or explicit objects of belief that are arguably the most important concerns of all. The intersection of folklore and religion should be about not only *how* and *what* people have said, sung, or expressed religiously but also the substance and objects of those beliefs in and of themselves, whether natural or supernatural. In addressing the fullest range of conscious and unconscious human belief and practice, vernacular religion offers the resources to realize this unfulfilled scholarly potential.

Vernacular religion challenges religious studies to incorporate the interdisciplinary strengths of folklore/folklife in the study of the religious individual and the significance of religion as it is lived in contemporary contexts. Vernacular religion challenges all of folklore to extend ethnographic reflexivity into the interdisciplinary domain of methodological reflexivity. In this way, present and future folklorists may properly inform and direct their ethnographic practice, with theoretical rigor, in the study of the contents, expressions, and objects of human religiosity.

PART I

Religious Material Culture

Ann Ameen's art is the material expression of her vernacular religion, religion as she interpreted, negotiated, and created it. She took a traditional Newfoundland craft, the hooked mat or rug, and transformed it into a religious object. Sister Ann is not merely a Newfoundland vernacular religious artist, nor even a Canadian one, but the epitome of the vernacular religious artist within the North American context. Her art expresses her religious encounters, contacts, and exchanges—ultimately, her understanding and negotiation of religion as lived and practiced in her everyday life.

1

Textures of a Religious Life

The Vernacular Religious Art of Sister Ann Ameen

As the days went by I longed to do something for Jesus in the mission field. One afternoon, I was looking out the window watching a young man building a house. He had it all sheeted up with black Donna Kona [tar siding]. As I looked, a man's hand appeared. It moved across the [surface]; and as it moved, a beautiful picture began to take shape. There was sky, sea gulls, a duck pond, trees, flowers, and an old fashioned cottage. The sunset was crimson. Oh, what colours, what beauty. I heard myself saying, "Why that is hooked." The hand held a rug needle like grandmother used to use on her rag mats but this looked like yarn. I kept looking at this beautiful picture until it faded away as if it had never been. The soft voice spoke. "Child, you can do that." But I would need a frame, mat needle and burlap yarn to do it. The soft voice again spoke, "I will provide." I walked away from the window wondering how these things would be.
—Sister Ann Ameen

But they keep stable the fabric of the world, and their prayer is in the practice of their trade.
—Ecclesiasticus, or the Wisdom of Jesus the Son of Sirach

The workings of the mind and the touch of the hand live eternally in artifacts.[1]
—Henry Glassie

This essay introduces to the public a significant vernacular religious artist, Sister Ann Ameen (1908–1998).[2] Little known outside her home region of Newfoundland, Canada, she combined a sensitivity to her

---

Originally published in 2002.

community's traditions of art and craft with her own unique vision of the divine.³ As a longtime resident of both Newfoundland and the United States, Ameen was a uniquely North American religious artist who negotiated her knowledge and experience of both Canadian and American Christianity. Her distinctive "picture rugs" and "scripture rugs" embody her understanding that these mundane objects can function as didactic religious art, expressing her own Christian beliefs while working to transform the beliefs of those who behold them. I had the opportunity to know Sister Ann Ameen personally during the last five years of her life. In the summer of 1995, she even allowed me to live in her home for several days and photograph many of her hooked "mats."⁴

Sister Ann Ameen died in 1998 at the age of ninety. She described herself in the second of her three self-published spiritual autobiographies as "the little woman who lived very plainly so that souls across the sea could learn of Jesus."⁵ Married multiple times, Annie Francis Sharpe Hansen Ameen Brown called herself "Sister" not because she was a Roman Catholic "woman religious" but because she was a sister in the Lord Jesus Christ, dedicated to spreading the message of evangelical Christianity to anyone who would hear it.

Sister Ann Ameen was born in 1908 in the rural community of Shearstown, Conception Bay, in the eastern part of Newfoundland.⁶ Her father, Martin Sharpe, was a sea captain and an Anglican. Her mother, Elizabeth Snow, was a Methodist. There was a singular and insular homogeneity to Newfoundland's primarily English and Irish population at this time. In many ways, this insularity persists into the twenty-first century. The restrictions of living in an isolated "outpost" disturbed this spirited and attractive teenager. The occasion for Annie Sharpe's escape came in the form of an advertisement from a Rhode Island dentist for a mail-order bride. His positive response to her letter presented the opportunity to leave Newfoundland, and so began Sister Ann's noteworthy and colorful life in the United States. This departure was only the first of many for Sister Ann. After a short time, she left this first marriage, due to, in her own words, "sexual incompatibility" with her older spouse. She then enjoyed some success as a ballet dancer and chorus girl in the New York burlesque circuit, but this career was cut short because of a toe injury, as well as a scandal: Sister Ann, posing as British royalty, had an affair with a married member of New York society. When the man's wife sued Annie Hansen to cease and desist, her deception was uncovered, and, after a suicide attempt, she was taken to Bellevue Hospital for psychological evaluation. These details were reported in the December 7, 1928, edition of the local Newfoundland newspaper, the *Bay Roberts Guardian*, no doubt to the embarrassment of her family in that close-knit community.[7]

It was after these tumultuous episodes that she had a conversion experience and began, in her own words, "fifty-five years knowing Jesus." Accompanying her through at least ten of those years was her second husband, the Reverend Kattar Ameen, a Lebanese Christian she met in Florida. They both attended a Church of the Nazarene Bible school in New York State, and they then proceeded to establish an evangelical ministry in Danbury, Connecticut, along with a home for the elderly. Ann returned to Newfoundland in 1958 after the death of her husband, closing the American chapter of her life. There she began a forty-year private and public odyssey of moving from house to house, promising to complete buildings, self-promoting her various projects for charitable contributions, and creating a Christian cottage industry by hooking mats to gain financial support for everything from mission activities in Asia and Africa to her Newfoundland "homes for wayward girls" to her small Bible study classes. In 1982, her seventy-fourth year, she traveled to Bangladesh for five months to visit the people to whom she had consistently sent contributions and many King James Version Bibles.

During one of my extensive interviews with her from 1994 to 1997, I asked, "What is your theology—are you a premillennial or a postmillennial Christian?" She responded, "I'm sure Jesus didn't use those words." I then asked, "And Sister Ann, are you a folk artist, a Canadian artist, a Newfoundland artist, or a religious artist?" "A Christian artist," she replied. "That's how I would describe myself."

Trained in the early decades of the twentieth century, first in the Church of England in Newfoundland and then in the Methodist and Holiness traditions of the American denomination known as the Church of the Nazarene, she was a painter who occasionally used oil-based and acrylic paints but who most frequently used wool and acrylic yarn to communicate, in a painterly way, a message of fidelity to and love of God through the art of hooking rugs. These "paintings in wool," as she called them, were inspired by her religious and cultural background and the actual voice of her God consistently telling, commanding, prompting, and urging her to express her Christian beliefs.

Ann Ameen's religious beliefs can be placed within the very broad category of Protestant Evangelical Christianity—encompassing those churches, like the Church of the Nazarene, that emphasize the teachings and authority of the scriptures, especially of the New Testament, as opposed to the institutional authority of the Church itself, and that stress as paramount the tenet that salvation is achieved by personal conversion to faith through the atonement (that is, through the life, suffering, and death) of Christ. As a corollary to this faith, believers are required to spread the gospel as a part of their expression of belief in God. It is, however, inaccurate to think of Sister Ann as having any denominational affiliation. Her lived religion, like her hooked rugs, illustrates a belief system influenced by and interpreted through her many contacts with religion in North America.

It is vital to remember when documenting and analyzing the material expression of religious belief in general that it is not sufficient merely to study a static religious object among many objects; it is essential to attempt to understand a context of meaning and the use of religious artifacts for individuals and their communities.[8] Verbal, behavioral, and material expressions of belief are a part of community and individual religious culture and can be found in formal or informal art forms. By the material expression of religious belief, I mean artifacts, interior and exterior environments or landscapes, and forms of architecture that are individual and communal expressions of religious belief, affiliation, or faithfulness. Such religious material culture can be further delineated using sacred, decorative (or aesthetic), and functional categories. The material expression of religious belief can be specifically observed in paintings, drawings, prints, sculpture, photography, books, foodways, clothing, bodily alterations and adornment, architecture, agriculture, town planning, furniture, furnishings, and even machines and devices. Religious material culture can include anything from a statue of Saint Joseph in a contemporary Catholic kitchen placed in a location of honor because of a promise made to the saint[9] to the festive foodways of holiday occasions, and from the aesthetic of plainness in a colonial Puritan or Quaker home to the display of colorful hooked rugs emblazoned with religious images and words in a home or church.

Scholars who study the visual production of artists like Sister Ann have fashioned terms to classify such creatives and their work, including "primitive," "naive," "self-taught," "folk," "outsider," "visionary," "idiosyncratic," "found," "grassroots," "isolate," "intuitive," and "art brut."[10] Folklorist Terry Zug offers a solid scholarly description of the folk artist as acquiring "knowledge and skills through a long-standing, informally transmitted, regional tradition." The work of the "outsider artist," for Zug, might draw on past experiences, but the "artistic impulse comes from deep within and is intensely personal in form, execution, and meaning."[11]

The deficiency of all such concepts is that they do not leave sufficient room for understanding the nuanced relationship between individual creativity and community influence. In the case of Sister Ann, she is not adequately described by either category of "folk" artist or "outsider" artist. Her rugs are both regionally traditional and deeply personal. Her output as a religious artist emerged from a craft tradition transmitted to her by family and community. Ameen created her rugs to sell to a community that would immediately recognize and understand the form she was using. Her work, however, is completely individualistic, even idiosyncratic; this is evident in her treatment of the hooked rug as a religious object, in her use of color, and in the subject matter of her creations.

What, in the end, is so distinctive about Sister Ann's "paintings in wool"? Ameen's art is the material expression of her vernacular religion, religion as she interpreted, negotiated, and created it. She took a traditional Newfoundland craft, the hooked mat or rug, and transformed it into a religious object. One of the standards of the hooked and sewn rug genre has been that "religious themes, although common in other household handicrafts, are hardly ever found in hooked rugs. As these rugs were made to be walked on, religious subjects were probably considered inappropriate."[12] Ann Ameen's rugs, her vernacular religious art, are the exception to this rule. By her own estimation, Sister Ann Ameen hooked over twelve hundred mats—everything from small mats in the traditional "welcome" size (20" × 34") to medium size (28" × 56") to what can be called her "monumental" mats (the largest of which, *The Rapture*, measures 79" × 142"). For a woman only four feet ten inches tall, hooking this rug when she was over eighty years old, such production was a remarkable physical as well as artistic accomplishment.

Residents of St. John's recall seeing her in the window of her various shops in the city in the 1970s and 1980s, hooking hour after hour, day after day. She developed a technique that allowed for swift rug production. Such speed could account for her enormous output.[13] To create the pile surface, Sister Ann usually used not torn rags but acrylic yarn (which she called wool), positioned below the stretched burlap. She would insert the hooking tool (a bent nail driven into a wooden handle, with a "vee" notch filed into the edge of the rod at the tip) between two strands of the weave, engage the yarn, and bring it above the surface of the burlap, where a loop was made.[14] She would repeat the process in the same spot, making a second loop, then move along several spaces in the weave and repeat the steps.

Sister Ann's linear process of hooking made for an impressive visual impact, but her "lower loop density" did not result in a durable product.[15] Her textiles are not thick and heavy like typical hooked rag rugs. They could not be put in a washing machine; if soiled, they have to be washed by hand in cold water, like a wool sweater. Still, there was a justification for Sister Ann's technique: these textiles were made to be placed not on the floor but on the wall. Such treatment was Sister Ann's response to the tradition of not walking on religious rugs. Her art had a pedagogical as well as a mnemonic purpose. She believed that all her rugs were religious rugs, though some had no overt message or orientation (either people requested them or they simply sold well to tourists): "I was praying while I was hooking [it], that's what makes it religious."

Unlike other Newfoundland artists (for example, Gerald Squires) who incorporate the stark beauty of the province's gray, dark, cold, harsh vistas, Sister Ann's view of the Newfoundland landscape in wool and acrylic is of her own invention.[16] Her colors are vibrant, even effervescent, like the public face of her personality and her effusive belief in the glory of God and the wonder of creation. "I loves [sic] bright, cheerful colors," Sister Ann noted, "whites, light pinks, light blues." She also often hooked her vision of the landscape where Jesus lived. In countless instances, she created a terrain that combined both places: Newfoundland as Holy Land and Israel as the land of Atlantic fishing ports. This vision meant the presence of both palm trees and lighthouses, of seabirds on the coast and angels around the tomb.

Canadian art writer Peter Gard has described Sister Ann's use of color as "outrageous." He has written that "they are as bright as a kid's toy and as subtle about faith as a Jehovah's Witness at the door."[17] When I wanted to understand her use of color and why her mats were so bright, she pointed me toward the vivid flowers and weeds growing outside her front door. "Look at their color," she explained. "They are bright like all of God's creation." Her hooked rugs or mats attempt to mimic the radiant, sunny colors of that creation and, naturally, could never be dour or dull. In her personal diary, Sister Ann specifically addressed the colors of nature and how God presented them to humanity:

> What a wonderful Heavenly Father we have to give us the Beauty of His Colours. Summer the Beautiful flowers. Autumn. The crimson and gold on His trees. Winter the snow in all its glistening white, and the spring with its soft green grass and Lilac trees . . . yes we have a very great and very Holy God and I wonder how many of us looks [sic] up toward Heaven in the run of a day and whispers thank you Dear God.

In the final years of her life, Ann Ameen lived in Bay Roberts, a community about an hour outside St. John's, in buildings she called her Beacon Light Bible School and Bethany House. This complex consisted of the remnants of a restaurant, a store, and a central two-story structure by the bay, in which she occupied the only heated room. She hoped that the structure named Bethany House would be the location of a "home for wayward girls" that she had spoken about for thirty years but which never came to fruition. For the most part, she lived alone in Newfoundland after her return to the province from the United States. She said that she accepted a life of loneliness and solitude as a part of her duty as a missionary of Jesus's message, and this motif of waiting alone for someone to come and for something great to happen is also found in her art.

A reading of Sister Ann's three-volume collection of writings, which mentions in some detail her activities with Reverend Ameen, could lead one to assume that her return to Newfoundland occurred as she mourned the death of her beloved husband. I confidently thought that the mats she created in the first years after her return were, in the words of Barbara Kirshenblatt-Gimblett, "objects of memory" of her beloved spouse and their many years of devoted marriage and work together.[18] Her dead husband, however, never appears in her mats. When I asked to see a picture of him, she could not or would not provide me with one. There were no images of him in her living quarters. She told me, during my stay with her in 1995, that their marriage, in fact, dissolved in the United States when her husband fell in love with another woman, Ruth, a nurse who worked in one of the couple's nursing homes in Connecticut. Sister Ann returned to Shearstown, her birthplace, to escape the bad memories of her husband's infidelity, his divorce of her in Mexico, and, finally, his unfortunate death along with Ruth in a Florida automobile accident.

Her creations are still memory objects, though—if not of her husband, of her life as a child waiting for her seaman father to return, of the stern discipline and religious nurturing of her Methodist mother, and of the special attraction that Newfoundland itself holds for natives as a place they long for after they leave it. This intrinsic connection to the windswept island is the reason why Newfoundlanders become teary-eyed when they sing their former national anthem, "The Ode to Newfoundland." "The weather is beautiful [here]," Sister Ann told me, "if you like fog, rain, and wind. . . . Our Newfoundland is a good tyrant." It is therefore possible to see in Sister Ann's mats correlatives of memory[19]— that is, images from everyday life that correspond to another person or thing in the past: a lighthouse, a church, a ship, scripture passages, and other subjects that are central to her life. Of course, the challenge is trying to figure out what images fit which memories and experiences, and when and if these things actually happened to her.

Sister Ann acknowledged that a reason she lived such a solitary life was that people shied away from her constant attempt to engage them in conversation about religion. Following an impulse that was part evangelical and part self-serving, she would press visitors to talk about their religious lives, simply to allow herself an opportunity to give her own life history. She did this when conversing with strangers, individually or in group settings, through an outpouring of continuous narratives—many of them exquisite memories, personal tales of supernatural encounters, and stories about how God constantly touched her life. She spoke of how Jesus, in the form of a little boy, visited her in her garden when she was a young girl; about her own healing from cancer through a vision; about how God provided her with bags of money when she needed it for a project; even about how God told her not to eat the inside of bananas.

These narratives represented, like her rugs, a significant display of her religiosity. Their enactment, in fact, was in obedience to what she perceived to be the voice of God. Therefore, when she gave her testimonials to visitors, she employed two voices: her own and the voice of God, her "heavenly Father." Her performances of these personal religious narratives were the oral explications of her material paintings in wool, and her hooked mats were the materialization of her individual religious beliefs. The irony of the way she turned local inhabitants away from her in the last ten years of her life was that she desired an audience for her stories. For this reason, she especially enjoyed first-time visitors: such occasions gave her the chance to conjure the miraculous story of her life again. The opportunity to tell such spiritual narratives anew is an important expressive mode for elderly religious individuals and communities because it allows them to both relate the central beliefs important to their lives and situate themselves within larger religious narratives.[20]

Sister Ann never connected herself to a specific congregation or denomination in Newfoundland, such as the Pentecostal community or the Salvation Army. She deliberately remained outside such affiliations to retain her independence. She loved the attention that the media could give to her and her Christian message, and she maintained a very public profile, appearing on local radio broadcasts, in public settings, and even on television. Still, she enjoyed living on the margins and being a woman of mystery. She shared few private confidences with friends, neighbors, or other Christians. To spend time with Sister Ann was also to witness how she engaged in not just telling her story to others but consistently reinterpreting her autobiography for her listeners. Like any competent and sensitive performer, she altered her stories at each telling so that they would have the greatest effect on her listener. This habit of consistently editing her life led one artist, who curated a 1995 exhibit on her hooked mats at the Art Gallery of Newfoundland and Labrador, to note that Sister Ann was "the ultimate post-modernist, her life is a novel, and she rewrites, re-presents, and revises it daily."[21]

It is often assumed that mothers pass the techniques of hooking rugs on to their daughters, but Sister Ann indicated that her mother never actually gave her instruction in the technical method for creating a rug. She did, however, grow up in a household where both her grandmother and mother were active rug hookers, and she observed them in their craft.

Ann Ameen did not actually begin hooking mats until she was in her midfifties in Newfoundland, with her period of greatest production coming as she grew older. What her mother did teach her was that hooked rugs could be aesthetically pleasing and that they were objects to be respected. It was Ameen's understanding that, just as these simple objects expressed beauty and commanded respect, they could also convey powerful messages about life and God. As noted in other folkloristic perspectives on elderly men and women, Sister Ann Ameen "proudly [took] credit for her personal discovery of a medium and form for recasting" her life. As Kirshenblatt-Gimblett has observed, Sister Ann "forged distinctly individual solutions to common needs: in the process . . . [affirming] the creative potential in the expressive culture of the elderly and the centrality of life review in this period in the life course."[22] Steeped in paradox, she credited both God and herself for the creation of the rugs.

The artistic output of Newfoundland women and their hooked rug traditions suggest both a received style, based in the consistent use of geometric designs, and a personal and innovative style, drawing on a diversity of designs from outside the community's repertoire. In terms of the latter, any model might be borrowed, from a pattern in another textile to a scene from a printed source. Folklorist Gerald L. Pocius, writing on Newfoundland hooked rugs, notes that "even printed words could serve as a design source. . . . The highest degree of innovation with design sources involves the mental assemblage of ordinary objects into an image to be used specifically for a rug, and not merely an attempt to copy a concrete holistic model."[23] Sister Ann Ameen rarely produced geometric designs. Out of forty mats in her home that I once had the opportunity to examine and photograph, I found only one with geometric design elements. Her mats were intended for the wall, not the floor. She learned from her mother that picture rugs are special—not typically to be used in the kitchen—and Newfoundlanders would customarily not step on special rugs. Her paintings in wool would teach their owners about Christianity; these rugs deserved the same respect that one would give to the Bible or some other religious object, such as a chromolithograph of a religious subject in one's home.[24] Her rugs are personal and innovative in style and pattern because they are religious—as she would say, "God inspired." Considering her use of religious words and/or images as well as very bold colors, Sister Ann's creations not only follow a tradition of design innovation within the

Newfoundland aesthetic but represent the highest degree of innovation within that tradition.²⁵

One of the noteworthy themes of twentieth-century Christian iconography has been the way that radical individuality and political environments have inspired artists to integrate local or indigenous forms into Christian visual culture. The art tradition of African American Christians in the United States has produced dark-complected figures of Jesus, and the "liberation theology" of Latin and South America has been expressed visually in paintings of scriptural passages using images from everyday life in Nicaraguan base communities.²⁶ As already noted, Sister Ann's rugs represent her personal negotiation of local and universal subjects and sites serving as Christian symbols—from blue shorelines with geese to the fires of hell with ominous blackened birds. What is particularly dramatic about them as integrative artifacts of belief is how these objects are a testimony of her journey through North America's religious cultures.

Religious studies scholar Catherine L. Albanese, in her assessment of the way scholars have formulated consensus histories of American religion, has suggested that the religious identity of Americans bears "the signs of contact with those who were other and different. . . . The shape and operation of American religious life—all of it—is best described under the rubric of religious combination."²⁷ Sister Ann Ameen, daughter of Newfoundland, longtime resident of the United States, producer of artwork of such multisource richness and spiritual vitality, offers an intriguing bicultural example of North American religious contact, combination, and exchange—a natural extension, it seems, of Albanese's thesis.²⁸

Sister Ann's orientation—the eventual style and form and character of her art—can best be understood within the context of religion in Newfoundland. At the turn of the twentieth century, when Ann Ameen was born, religious life on the island was both restrictive and segregated. One lived in distinctive Roman Catholic, Church of England, or Methodist Christian communities.²⁹ In Conception Bay North, where Sister Ann was raised, settlement patterns marked religious affiliation geographically. Newfoundland remains to this day a land where people can identify the religious affiliation of individuals and where they once lived on the island simply by hearing their family name. The separation between the Christian denominations was well understood by inhabitants. Interaction between Roman Catholics and Protestants was strained, and marriage between them was socially unacceptable. Sister Ann's mother was a Methodist and her father an Anglican, and her home of Shearstown lay in the staunchly Protestant community of Conception Bay North. It is quite possible that she had little contact with Catholics or even other Protestant groups in her formative years.

Her arrival in the United States was undoubtedly a shock to her religious sensibilities. She experienced there something unique to her: the plurality of American religion. Eventually she would even marry a Lebanese Christian man, and together they would seek out evangelical forms of Christianity. Such contact deeply influenced her visual expression of religion. From the deeply pluralistic American environment, she drew an imaginative religious vocabulary that made space for a variety of Christian iconographic forms.

Ameen's designs, which all combine the color and energy of American culture with traditional elements of Newfoundland craft, can be divided into three categories. In the first are those that incorporate the conventional Newfoundland hooked rug subjects or modes, such as a flower, a welcome mat, or a geometric design; as Sister Ann told me, "anyone can do a flower in a mat." These mats are religious because she willed them to be so. In the second category are her "paintings in wool"—that is, pictures without words, or with only a few words: ideal, ordered, perfectionist landscapes populated by seabirds and palm trees, lush foliage and explosive sunsets. She felt that these rugs, collectively, were her most significant creative contribution because of their effect: "Naturally [these rugs] are religious. . . . Looking at it puts you in the mind [of religion]."[30] Many of these feature overtly religious motifs, such as doves, churches, and angels, and, though her proportions sometimes distort reality, she felt she was offering a realistic rendering of her chosen subjects. Most importantly, in these cases, she was painting the "concept" that Jesus Christ is always among us; she tried to place Christ within the context of people's everyday lives (plates 1 and 2).

The third category is what Sister Ann referred to as her "blackboards," each a choreography of words and images amounting to a visual religious text. These mats interpose words and images, integrate words into images, and surround script with colorful borders or backgrounds accompanied by representational figures. Serving as Ameen's tools for teaching scripture, they also represent her embodiment of scriptural words as images—her own hooked illuminated manuscript art. The words or phrases in these mats are usually from the New Testament, but without the biblical citations; Ameen assumed that the viewer would recognize the biblical source text. Related to this category are her monumental rugs, which can be six feet tall and sometimes eight feet across, containing script and/or images, each of which took her up to six months to complete. A continuation of her practice of transforming Christian words into Christian images, these rugs were created for sale and display in public settings such as churches, schools, and even government administration buildings.

Ann Ameen took a traditional understanding of the design and production of hooked rugs and shifted the function of this artistic form to carry a religious meaning and purpose rooted in what was important to her conception of a religious life. Sister Ann, both insider and outsider, combined her Protestant evangelical sensibility, with its emphasis on biblical text, her Christian iconophilia, her American Holiness training, her cultural knowledge as a Newfoundlander, and all the various influences she absorbed as a religious "American" to create individual objects of vernacular religious belief. Sister Ann is not merely a Newfoundland vernacular religious artist, nor even a Canadian one, but the epitome of the vernacular religious artist within the North American context. Her religious art expresses her spiritual encounters, contacts, and exchanges—ultimately, her understanding and negotiation of religion as lived and practiced in her everyday life.[31]

During the last five years of her life, when I would go to visit her cold, dusty home by the bay, Sister Ann would speak of her intention to hook more mats and to teach the technique to others. Such crafts, she felt, could be used to support the missionary work she saw as so essential. Alone and seemingly abandoned by all but a few visitors, she on several occasions pulled, from a book that kept it flat, a color photocopy of an image of Jesus from either a magazine or a religious mailing. "I would love to hook this picture," she would tell me. Sister Ann engaged in copy work, but she was never much of a copyist; it is anyone's guess how her interpretation of this image of Jesus would have finally materialized. Independent to the end of her life, she lived in that private residence as long as she could before entering a nursing home in 1997. There she died surrounded by some of her rugs. These individual expressions of religion reflected the multitude of environments influential to their creator's process of believing. Like Sister Ann Ameen herself, they embody the textures of a religious life.

The religious lives of the Sicilian American women encountered here are bound up in a complex, negotiated ethnic religious sensibility filled with devotionalism, belief in the efficacy of religious healing, and a worldview open to communications from dead relatives in a series of visionary dreams and signs. In this vernacular Catholicism, vows to dead relatives and powerful saints remain a significant means of communicating love and respect, and the communion of saints is not simply a theological construct but a living reality. Representations of biological and sacred families are interwoven within these altars through the careful placement of photographs of family members and petitionary letters among blessed candles and the multitude of saints' statues of various sizes. Here, images and words stand side by side, interacting, alive, and open for sacred intervention concerning a family's problems; the secular family items are sacralized by their contact with the holy objects and their position inside this altar of vows.

2

The Vow as Visual Feast

Honoring St. Joseph in Sicilian American Homes

I always like to present a visual feast in my religious studies courses at Cabrini College by bringing into the classroom a variety of objects of religious material culture to challenge the students and teach them something about creativity and religious expression. Recently, as a part of my undergraduate course on vernacular religion, I brought an object to class to help illustrate my lecture on visual traditions of the human body in everyday religious practice. This charm or talisman, a representation of a single open eye affixed to a circular dark-blue disc of blown glass, is meant to protect one's person, family, and home against the "evil eye." It was purchased for me by a student at a market in a village outside Istanbul. Though the object is illustrative of Turkish religious culture, four of my North American students immediately related it to their own lives, referencing contemporary Italian American traditions about the evil eye, known as the *malocchio* or *gettatura*, in their families, including the training received from Roman Catholic grandmothers concerning a variety of protections and cures against negative vibrations and intentions possibly caused by its assaults. Such classroom experiences remind me that traditional religious beliefs and practices can still be found among contemporary American Catholics, even in the face of secularization and an increased illiteracy concerning institutionalized religious traditions.[1]

Many of these practices involve the home and the use of objects in it, as in the case of the Italian American Christmas Eve custom of serving a meal of "seven fishes," or the Polish American blessing of Easter tables filled with holiday foods, including dyed eggs and butter in the form of

---

Originally published in 2007.

a lamb symbolizing Jesus. Secular objects such as foods can be given a religious purpose, and religious objects might be used for public display, such as when palm crosses are hung on doors, Marian holy corners are set up in prominent spaces, or religious statues or images are arranged in windows. The elaborate home altars of Sicilian Americans living in Gloucester, Massachusetts, typically dedicated to Saint Joseph or Saint Anthony, offer a compelling example of such a living vernacular religious tradition. These feasts for the eyes of color, spirit, and creativity, rooted in the religious tradition of making vows to God for the granting of some blessing or healing, are at the ethnographic center of this essay.

My study of Sicilian American home altars in Gloucester is informed by the work of folklife scholar Gábor Barna, who has chronicled the challenges of studying domestic religious objects such as statues, prints, holy cards, and rosaries in his native Hungary.[2] Barna notes that historical studies of the presence of such religious material culture in the home are difficult because of the paucity of relevant available data, especially from the Middle Ages or the early modern period.[3] In terms of contemporary analyses of religious objects in the home, few ethnographic studies exist concerning their use or even the sources and distributors of such objects.[4] Based on data from estate inventories and available photographs of Hungarian peasant homes, as well as ethnographic work within particular communities, Barna finds that the Catholic Church has been a significant influence in the dissemination of relevant devotions and associated objects (as in the case of the Sacred Heart of Jesus and the apparitions of the Virgin Mary at Lourdes or Fatima). He is also attentive to pilgrimage sites, with their own unique vernacular religious ecology, as sources for such objects.[5] Barna reflects on what I call "vernacular Catholicism" when he considers how contemporary personal decisions about religious objects, such as using them as home furnishings or wearing them as dress accessories, reveal a transformation and negotiated flexibility of everyday religious practice.[6] This practice is influenced by institutional models and ideals of orthodoxy and orthopraxis. It is also formed by powerful community and individual spiritual traditions of interpreted belief and practice that exist alongside organized religious idealizations.

Issues of power (institutional Christianity's influence over individual and community beliefs and practices), aesthetics (what is considered beautiful, artful, or even visually appropriate within a particular ecclesiastical, domestic, or personal context, and how such ideas can shift over centuries and generations), and secularization (the loss of understanding, appreciation, respect, and sensibility for religious ideas and meanings) lie at the root of Barna's research about present practice and the use of religious material culture. He therefore poses a very postmodern question: Are these items "objects of popular devotion or only objects of decoration"?[7]

Another way of posing Barna's important question, or perhaps a way to extend it, is to ask whether some vernacular religious displays are both decorative and devotional at the same time. Furthermore, is there a basic set of characteristics or qualities of vernacular Catholicism that might be helpful to folklorists working in government and nonprofit organizations as well as in academic teaching and research contexts—a framework that would assist in answering this question, in identifying particular relevant expressions, and in linking diverse traditions under a broader umbrella of recognizable qualities? For public-sector folklorists, such characteristics would offer a language for communicating and explaining the quality, history, aesthetics, creativity, and meaning of an object or practice, not only to their colleagues but to believers themselves, as well as to government administrators and funders. For folklorists involved primarily in scholarly work, such a synthesis would provide cognitive constructs for the identification of relevant material and a better understanding and appropriate contextualization of a practice or artifact and its communicative and creative aesthetic. To work toward such a framework, I will examine the practice of building home altars and conclude by offering a basic set of characteristics of vernacular Catholicism drawn from my own research on religion, material culture, and the senses.

In 2003 I was introduced to a vibrant Sicilian American tradition that astonished me—namely, the construction of home altars in Gloucester, Massachusetts, dedicated to Saint Joseph, the foster-father of Jesus and husband of the Virgin Mary. I knew, from my familiarity with the work of folklorist Kay Turner, that such altars remained a living tradition in the United States in Sicilian American communities in Texas and New Orleans.[8] I had also been informed of isolated examples elsewhere, such as those specially constructed in church basements in New York, New

Jersey, California, and Kansas City. But I was not aware of a contemporary proliferation of domestic altars to this extent in one community on the East Coast of the United States.

Starting in 2003, I traveled to Gloucester to witness for myself these altars, which had been assembled as part of the March 19 feast day of Saint Joseph. I was immediately struck by the quantity of altars created in the community. On the eve of the saint's feast, I participated in car caravans that drove around Gloucester neighborhoods, visiting six different homes, each decorated with large altars filled with statues, flowers, family photos, and candles—an assemblage surrounding a large statue of Saint Joseph, carefully layered and color coordinated (plate 3). Alongside these displays were stacks of lemons, oranges, and specially shaped breads, some marked with crosses and others formed into staffs. After songs, prayers to the saint, and recitation of the rosary, the people who were gathered stopped for coffee and tea and a few pastries—actually, an explosion of zeppole, or cream-filled fried dough balls traditionally eaten as part of this feast-day celebration, as well as cannoli. These altars were but a small fraction of the total number on display across the homes participating in the tradition: between thirty-five and forty families built large and small home altars in 2003.

As I spoke to the women who had designed these domestic shrines, all Sicilian Americans, many the wives of fishermen or individuals employed in that industry, ranging from thirty-five to seventy-five years old, it became clear that the common element in their decision to participate in this tradition was the powerful religious practice of making a "vow" to holy figures. These altars were votive offerings to Saint Joseph, as vibrant as any *retablo* painting or cast tin *milagros* of bodily organs, thanking the saint for a favor received or a blessing granted due to his intercession. With the exception of the work of Robert Teske and Joseph Sciorra, little scholarship has been done on vowing within American vernacular religion.[9] When making a "vow" to accomplish something, an individual dedicates himself or herself to a task completely, unequivocally, and passionately. Religious vows affect a person's entire being.[10] They are personal promises to Jesus, Mary, and the saints; moreover, such vows establish a substantial bond between giver and receiver. A religious vow thus both creates and solidifies, simultaneously, a sacred partnership based on reciprocal giving. A vow is not a pledge to the past but to the future. Vows support efforts to fulfill obligations and accomplish certain tasks.[11]

The Gloucester home altars of March 19 can best be understood as visualized narratives for the community of altar makers, relatives, visitors to the altars, the healed, and those praying for healing. The altars are materialized vows of gratitude for recovery from life-threatening illness, financial instability, emotional trauma, and a multitude of other individual and family problems. To appreciate the nature and power of these vows, one needs to understand something about this community, its people, and their working lives, centered around a hazardous industry that has been dominant there for 375 years. Over this period, more than five thousand Gloucester fishermen have died at sea. In February 1879, fifty-three local women became widows in a single storm. For this Gloucester community, economic survival has been based on fishing, and family survival has been based on the resilience of women—mothers and daughters who live for long periods, sometimes weeks at a time, without their husbands and fathers. Wives' responsibilities have included managing homes, shore businesses, and other needs of the community. They have often raised their children alone. They have prayed that their men would come back to them, and that their husbands and sons would not drown or lose fingers or limbs at sea. They have lived with a sense of fear and a need not for saintly role models but for saintly patrons and protectors to guide their men home.

Italian fishing families have established themselves in Gloucester since the 1920s, coming especially from small towns in Sicily. They gradually saved money and purchased their own boats. By the 1970s, Sicilians made up three-quarters of the four hundred men who fished out of Gloucester. In 1994 and 1995, federal fishing regulations curtailed massive fishing activities. As retraining programs started for some of these men, the community's concerns widened beyond fears about the dangers of fishing to include worries about their very economic survival. In the face of such challenges, these women did not lose their Catholic faith. Instead, they maintained their traditional understanding of death, sickness, unemployment, and other troubles not as a sign of God's abandonment of them but as a manifestation of both divine attention and the sacred mystery of life. Katie Fontana, whose Saint Joseph's Day festivities include making sixteen pounds of fresh pasta to feed family and friends, as well as distributing four cases of oranges and two cases of lemons to visitors to her altar, noted to me, in an expression of both her relationship to the saints and her fatalism about that interaction, referencing the saints themselves, "You never know what they're going to do to us."

The individual vows that keep the Gloucester altar tradition alive are embedded in the social environment of a local religious and ethnic organization called the Mother of Grace Club. The existence of the club is itself the result of a vow that three sisters, Katie Fontana included, made to their powerful Sicilian American mother to keep the club alive. The Mother of Grace Club currently comprises sixty-three women of Italian and Portuguese descent, all wives of Gloucester fishermen. Dedicated to the Virgin Mary, the club originated when its founding women came together during the early 1940s to pray for the safety of their fathers, husbands, sons, and brothers who were going off to fight in the Second World War. In response to such anxieties, the women regularly gathered to pray, recite the rosary, and sing hymns. The focus of their petitions to Mary and the saints was the safe return of their men. Their meetings created a network of support and friendship at a time of isolation and loneliness. After they prayed, the women would eat pasta and enjoy pastries and coffee. At the conclusion of the war, all their loved ones returned home to them. Their devotion had worked; their prayers had been answered. The women decided to maintain their meetings, and they approached the city of Gloucester about purchasing an abandoned building downtown to serve as their clubhouse.

These women, with the assistance of their husbands and network of relations, restored the building on Washington Street. The club's location makes it central to a variety of Italian American parades, pageants, feasts, and novenas that take place in the city. Within the constellation of religious activities that club members participate in is the tradition of building domestic shrines. The home altars to Saint Joseph represent a direct transplant of a Sicilian tradition, but they are refashioned for their North American context. I have been privileged to meet the women who belong to this club, see their altars, and enjoy their endless hospitality on several trips to Gloucester. This vibrant practice of vow making and vow fulfillment that surrounds the design, construction, and maintenance of their altars continues—as a vow to a saint made by a mother continues to be kept by her daughter, in fulfillment of a vow made to the dying matriarch, in the case of the continuation of this club.

This cycle is ongoing as the granddaughters of the original Mother of Grace Club members step up to build altars to honor Saint Joseph. In my favorite example of that continuity, the daughter of Mrs. Margaret Giacalone, after her mother's death and her assumption of the family altar-building tradition, had her home remodeled to include two Corinthian columns framing a permanent space to accommodate her mother's six-foot Saint Joseph statue. The altar, with this plaster figure, now remains visible and partially decorated throughout the year.

The religious lives of the Sicilian American women encountered here are bound up in a complex, negotiated ethnic religious sensibility filled with devotionalism, belief in the efficacy of religious healing, and a worldview open to communications from dead relatives in a series of visionary dreams and signs. In this vernacular Catholicism, vows to dead relatives and powerful saints remain a significant means of communicating love and respect, and the communion of saints is not simply a theological construct but a living reality. Representations of biological and sacred families are interwoven within these altars through the careful placement of photographs of family members and petitionary letters among blessed candles and the multitude of saints' statues of various sizes (plate 4). Here, images and words stand side by side, interacting, alive, and open for sacred intervention concerning a family's problems; the secular family items are sacralized by their contact with the holy objects and their position inside this altar of vows.

These saints, devotion to whom has been transferred from Sicily to America, include such well-known international Catholic saints as Saint Joseph and Padre Pio as well as more localized figures such as the regional Sicilian Black Madonna. Indeed, some of these statues themselves have made the trans-Atlantic journey, purchased in European centers of pilgrimage such as Rome, Fatima, and Lourdes, with the sacredness of those places adding to the authenticity and increased possibility of the power their depicted intercessor might wield.

The day-to-day relationships between believers in this community and a saint like Saint Joseph, whose image is central to these domestic shrines, are complex. In the case of Saint Joseph in particular, his petitioners sometimes see him relationally, as a miracle-working friend of the family, not as a hierarchical holy figure. At other times, the capriciousness of his decisions makes him appear cold and forgetful of his faithful. Thus, they tend toward a feeling of divine fatalism, a vernacular interpretation that all events are subject to fate or are somehow predetermined. These women of Gloucester demonstrate and articulate their belief that, as with the variability of the weather, the sea, or the moods and personalities of family and friends, one never has total control: life means submission to God's will. The saints, as their divine relations, can bring joy or suffering—and yet, paradoxically, very significantly, there remains the possibility for negotiation, for the transformation of negative outcomes or experiences through intercession, miracle, and vow.

Such sacred relationships are the foundation for these community altars, the motivation and meaning behind them, and choices about both altar appearance and vow dedication are made only after serious consideration. The fabrics covering an altar's surfaces are carefully selected, as are the colors of the candles and even flower arrangements. The length of time to be dedicated to the fulfillment of a vow to a saint, a short or extended plan of commitment, is decided on with the same degree of care.

In a rich and illuminating way, this altar tradition expresses and exemplifies, in the communicative and creative aesthetics of belief and practice it represents, nine fundamental characteristics of vernacular Catholicism. I have crafted this list based on my ethnographic experiences in Gloucester and work with other Catholic individuals and communities over time.[12] Importantly, these characteristics are often observed as central principles of normative Catholic theology, but it is in vernacular religious belief and practice that they achieve a particular, subtle, dramatic, erratic, touching, engaging, colorful, and paradoxical vitality and reality. In this sense, these are characteristics drawn from "the practice rather than the recognition of the Church."[13] The nine fundamental characteristics of vernacular Catholicism, then, are the following:

- Sacramentality: the understanding of all reality as potentially or actually bearing and expressing the sacred presence of God—the conviction that the created world not only embodies the sacred but can itself serve as a sacred, divine, or ultimate source

- Mediation: the principle that the deity works through secondary phenomena, objects, or facts to achieve both divine and human ends
- Communion: the idea that the purpose of all religious activity, both institutionally sponsored and vernacularly conceived, is the union of self, family, and community with God
- Imitation: the notion that an individual or community can create a new atmosphere by repeating acts of devotion and bringing their power to bear on the intended
- Objectification: the concept that one can take ideas and actions and make them significant holy things; that is, the idea of the holy as a transferable quality
- Historicization: the relation of the history of the present to the sacred history of the past
- Universalization: the internationalization of local religious ideas, practices, and figures
- Parochialization: the localization of internationally recognized religious ideas, practices, and figures
- Negotiation: the personal interpretation of normative Catholic belief and practice, expressed in both dramatic and subtle ways by believers as a natural part of their religious lives

These characteristics have been framed within the worldview of the traditional belief system known as Roman Catholicism, but they could, of course, be applied to other systems of religious belief and practice. Even if, as Gloucester consultant Katie Fontana put it, we may never know what the saints are going to do to us, we as folklorists can appreciate the beauty and creativity in the myriad creative religious forms that the expression of that anticipation may take. The Gloucester altars, built organically in the service of sacred vows, are as much celebrations of the joy of visual, tactile, auditory, and gustatory creativity and display as they are feasts of fatalism. As bounties of vernacular Catholicism, they are indeed both decoration and devotion.

Christians continue to integrate into the mundane world material culture expressing Christian imagery and symbols. From handcrafted items to printed media and mechanically produced objects, religious material culture has been and continues to be purchased and given for placement in the home, in workplaces, in modes of transportation, or on the person. This study is concerned with how religious objects enter into the everyday lives of North Americans; which Christian traditions and ideas about the material world are expressed by these sites; and how retail stores stimulate the negotiation between Roman Catholic tradition and the vernacular creativity of contemporary Catholics.

3

Postmodern Sites of Catholic Sacred Materiality

A few years ago, I received a telephone call from a former student living in the city of Corner Brook in western Newfoundland. He had taken my course on folk religion when I was a visiting professor at Memorial University of Newfoundland's Department of Folklore. Remembering my discussion of the contemporary veneration of Catholic saints, he had a request for me: Could I purchase and send him an inexpensive statue of Saint Joseph, patron saint of workers and the family?

Even though he was residing in the province's second-largest city, and the island has a large Catholic community, he was having difficulty obtaining this Catholic religious object that his father believed was crucial for the selling of their home. My student told me that his father had heard that individuals were having success in selling commercial and residential real estate in the difficult economic times of the early 1990s by burying a statue of Saint Joseph in the backyard of the building or home in question. The method for burying and preserving the saint's statue (upside down or right side up, left in its box, in the back or front of the house, facing the house or facing the street, or next to the "For Sale" sign) had been transmitted and interpreted to this student's father in several variants, but it always included the ritual of digging up the image when the property was sold and installing it in a place of honor in the newly acquired home or business.

This homeowner became convinced of the efficacy of this practice and wanted to apply it to his own personal circumstances.[1] He was, in fact, following an ancient Christian tradition of taking holy things such as the relics of the martyrs and saints and using them to transform or "sacramentalize" everyday life.[2] Christians continue to integrate into the mundane world material culture expressing Christian imagery and symbols. From handcrafted items to printed media and mechanically

---

Originally published in 1999.

produced objects, religious material culture has been and continues to be purchased and given for placement in the home, in workplaces, in modes of transportation, or on the person.[3] One can readily observe this tradition when doing ethnographic work with religious individuals and regional or ethnic communities in North America.[4]

My student's request to purchase a statue of Saint Joseph prompted me to reflect on several interrelated folklife questions concerning religious material culture in the United States.[5] At the end of the twentieth century, what were the possible sites for the purchase of such religious objects in an urban American context, such as the city of Philadelphia, where I was living? What did such an availability of religious materials for purchase by the contemporary audience say about the personal religiosity of Americans? In an ethnographic context, how do the individuals who purchase such articles make use of religious objects within their lives? This study is a response to the first two queries. It is concerned with how religious objects enter into the everyday lives of North Americans; which Christian traditions and ideas about the material world are expressed by these sites; and how retail stores stimulate the negotiation between Roman Catholic tradition and the vernacular creativity of contemporary Catholics.

I choose to emphasize religious material culture because it is still possible to study American religious history and never touch any artifact, see any image, or even visit a site that relates to the lived religion of the people who are the subjects of discussion. It is also quite possible to read texts on American religion and never see a religious object pictured or even discussed within its narrative. American ecclesiastical art and architecture are, on the other hand, the two components of material culture study and American religious creativity frequently considered by scholars.[6] Such studies present an excellent foundation for understanding the material expression of religious institutions in America, but they present the material face of normative religion, not expressions of the people's belief. Only recently have some historical studies of American religious material culture and lithography been published that discuss the religious objects used or created by Americans.[7] In *Material Christianity*, Colleen McDannell discusses Protestant catalogs and bookstores selling religious goods in America from the perspective of "Christian retailing," but she does not consider in much detail stores that sell Catholic religious articles.

My interest in Catholic imagery in general and Saint Joseph in particular took me to several retail establishments in the city of Philadelphia. I visited museum and church shops selling gothic-style Christian artifacts, everything from medieval gargoyles, Renaissance angel figurines, and kitchen magnets to stained-glass replicas of great cathedral art. I discovered folk art stores selling authentic Mexican, New Mexican, and Puerto Rican *santos* (antique and contemporary carved wooden statues of the saints or the crucified Christ), *retablos* (tin votive or devotional paintings of saintly subjects and personal miraculous events), and contemporary religious art produced for the tourist trade (plaster, clay, or papier-mâché images of Our Lady of Guadalupe, patroness of the Americas, for example, resting in tin or wooden shrines).[8] There were also retro-Catholic stores that specialized in selling mass-produced Catholic-inspired items such as "NunZilla," a wind-up toy image of a nun that "breathes fiery sparks as she walks," or "the Punching Nun," a nun puppet wearing boxing gloves, and, more significantly, Catholic devotional objects from the first sixty years of the twentieth century, including plaster reproductions and statuary of Marian apparitions at Lourdes and Fatima.

I also found Afro-Caribbean botánicas selling candles marked with many images of saints, statuary of plastic and plaster, and magical oils, sometimes also offering the opportunity for a session with a reader and adviser in a back room.[9] Often overlapping with botánicas in both materials and clientele are New Age/pagan/Wiccan shops or stores. These usually offer a wide selection of material representations (Neolithic goddesses of old Europe, Druidic and Celtic symbols, the ancient Greek and Roman pantheon, Native American totems, Hindu and Buddhist statues, Roman Catholic iconography, and Afro-Caribbean votive images). They also stock candles, oils, stones and crystals, and devotional books and periodicals, as well as drums and rattles, chalices and vessels, pentacles for ritual use both for wearing on the person and for placing on an altar, and meditative and ritual music.[10] The general public visits botánicas and these metaphysical centers out of curiosity, out of general interest, or out of a syncretic desire to tap into the belief systems they represent.

The same could be said about traditional Roman Catholic religious goods stores, where it is possible to see the full spectrum of contemporary Americans who identify with the Roman Catholic tradition. Traditionalist, restorationist, and progressive Catholics may visit such stores, as well as Catholic-influenced or interested peoples, such as adherents of Vodou or Santería.

My quest for an inexpensive statue of Saint Joseph finally led me to the St. Jude Shop in Havertown, Pennsylvania, advertised in the archdiocesan newspaper the *Catholic Standard and Times* as "the largest religious goods store." This store is located in a middle-class suburb of the ethnically diverse city of Philadelphia, known still for its conservative brand of Catholicism. The shop is the main branch of six sites under the corporate title St. Jude Shop Inc., which was described to me by one of its family owners, Mark G. DiCocco, as "a corporation whose principal operation is the whole[sale] and retail sale of religious articles, books, and church goods." This store had run out of inexpensive statues of Saint Joseph, and it was necessary for me to return later to make my purchase. Further visits to this shop piqued my interest in such a thriving contemporary source of religious goods—and in the place of these objects and stores in the total lifeways of contemporary Catholics.

Students of contemporary American religion frequently encounter examples of such "sacred materiality" in their fieldwork not only within Christian and Christian-influenced communities but among non-Christian individuals and groups as well.[11] These groups include but are not limited to Roman Catholics, Eastern Orthodox, Lutherans, Mormons, Pentecostals, Evangelicals, Afro-Caribbeans, Jews, Muslims, Buddhists, Native Americans, Neo-Pagans/Wiccans, and New Age believers. Researchers might recognize that the blessedness of material objects is a potent force within religious belief systems, but they do not know what to call it. Each culture and religious tradition articulates its own beliefs about sacred materiality and the form that it takes.

Within Roman Catholicism, the unique theological term used to express the relationship of the sacred and the material is "sacramentality."[12] Sacramentality has been described as the "notion that *all* reality is potentially and in fact the bearer of God's presence and the instrument of divine action on our behalf."[13] The principle of sacramentality "affirms that the invisible and spiritual God is present through the visible and the material, and that these are in turn made holy by that presence."[14] For believing Catholics, a unique religious material culture exists, one that reinforces the Catholic attraction to sacramentality and the Catholic taste for sacramentals or material objects that assist worship or devotion.

Which kinds of sacramentals interest individual Catholics depends on their personal belief and practice, the type of family or ethnic Catholicism within which they have been raised, how they have been educated about Catholicism, and the locale or region of the country in which they live. The term "sacramental" is employed by Catholics to designate individual creations in a church: liturgical art objects (such as altars, chalices, vestments, monstrances, paschal candles) or church decorations (such as statuary, murals and frescoes, stained-glass windows). "Sacramentals" are also the objects used in daily liturgies (such as sacramental wine, candles, incense). The term can also describe material culture used as a part of the personal devotional life of Catholics (paintings or statues for the home and articles for use on the person, such as relics, rosaries, medals, scapulars, crucifixes, holy cards, religious jewelry).

The history of the first religious goods stores to open in America, dispensing objects imported from Europe or made in this country, has yet to be written. It is, however, known that missionaries and European-trained clergy brought religious objects with them from the stores and monastic workrooms of Europe. An example is the holy cards that Bishop John Neumann, now canonized as a saint and buried in Philadelphia, brought with him to North America from Bohemia. American religious historians Ann Taves and Colleen McDannell have noted that for an American Catholic prior to the Civil War, canvassers or peddlers, some of whom were Jewish, were the major source of devotional books and religious objects such as rosaries, scapulars, statues, and holy pictures; they "made the rounds of Catholic homes, schools, and churches."[15] As the Catholic population grew, in the 1890s, established Catholic book publishers, who had been distributing religious goods to the peddlers and parish missions, expanded, and newer businesses opened. Companies such as D. and J. Sadlier's and P. J. Kenedy and Sons in New York City, Benziger Brothers in Cincinnati, Krieg Brothers in Indianapolis, and the Herder Company in St. Louis offered a variety of Catholic materials for distribution to local stores. The manufacture of many forms of religious goods also expanded, as a result of the increased personal piety endorsed by the institutional hierarchy, such as devotions to the Sacred Heart of Jesus and the rosary.[16] It was also stimulated by the growth of the American Catholic parochial school system, with its need for books and objects to reinforce catechism lessons and the life of faith for Catholic immigrant children. The Victorian interest in filling the American home with material objects that nurtured Christian beliefs and values was another contributor to this process.[17] Such practices were also a natural transplantation and evolution of the devotionalism of European Catholic homes, which had their "holy corners" for centuries.[18]

One of the oldest religious goods stores in Philadelphia was Kilner's Church Goods, which opened in 1888 on Market Street and closed on Arch Street in June 1986 because of changes in urban buying patterns. Its Arch Street location was by that time surrounded by shops selling pornography. Founded by Isaac Kilner as a business that published mostly religious literature in Baltimore, this was eventually the last of the religious supply houses in an area that once contained five such stores. Kilner's even had its own relic of Saint Anthony of Padua, a signed and sealed document from 1953 certifying the relic's authenticity, and a statue of the saint marking its entryway. Here individuals would occasionally kneel and say a prayer or leave a written petition in the hand of the statue. Religious goods stores such as Kilner's, as money-making enterprises, would not typically offer relics, as the shop connected to Philadelphia's National Shrine of St. John Neumann does (there, the saint's body is honored by the faithful, who view his body in a glass altar).[19] In the case of Kilner's, placement of the relic at the entrance to the store was in response to a vow to the saint for a new Arch Street location. The presence of this relic (referred to in the tradition as a "first-class relic," a remnant of the body of the saint) gave visitors a special feeling that the store itself was a sacramental.

I myself recall entering this shop as a child in the late 1960s, with its wooden floors and neatly displayed articles and books. The store reminded me of a church sacristy, with an atmosphere I recognized from service as an altar boy, and I was quite careful about what I touched inside. Its musty smell and dim lighting added to the sensation of entering one of Philadelphia's many functioning turn-of-the-century churches, and the store was adorned with objects the way the city's churches were: a relic, statues, cards for the altar, candles. The only element missing was the flowers.

The back of Kilner's Church Goods contained the "Sisters Lounge," which included a small kitchen, a few sofas, a refrigerator, and a restroom, in an era when nuns did not enter public bathrooms. This lounge was one of the few areas in the Archdiocese of Philadelphia where sisters could go and comfortably socialize with each other, as well as take their visiting nieces and nephews on Saturdays, the free day outside their teaching duties. The store owner would provide coffee, tea, and soft drinks for the women religious, and they would bring their own food. Though sisters from different orders did meet and converse as teachers in Philadelphia's parochial high schools, these women sometimes sought the opportunity for respite and conversation in an environment of sacred materiality within a non-diocesan building, away from the public and the institutional Church.

Kilner's Church Goods could be described as one of many establishments in the first half of the twentieth century selling objects called "Barclay Street art." The term refers to the Manhattan district housing French and other importers and producers of religious materials. This designation actually became "a derogatory term for books and objects that were cheap, vulgar, and pretentiously pious."[20] Women religious whom I have interviewed, however, recall Barclay Street fondly as a culturally iconic place. It was appreciated not simply as the name of a street or a source of Catholic consumer goods. This collection of businesses represented the existence in America of a thriving culture of Catholicism, the power of Catholic devotions and schools, and, with so many sisters in habit, the significant presence of women religious in America.

As Kilner's and the stores on Barclay Street in New York City did in the past, the St. Jude Shop continues to serve both the liturgical needs of the institutional Church and its functionaries (priests, deacons, sisters) and the needs and wants of the public. Considerable space in this retail establishment is devoted to the laity's desire for religious items. After opening the store in 1965, co-founders Louis and Norma DiCocco gradually established other similar stores, as well as wholesale and retail catalog businesses. At the end of the 1990s, St. Jude's was one of the top ten dealers of Christian religious materials in the continental United States. The circulation of its five-hundred-page wholesale catalogs exceeded ten thousand, predominantly in churches and schools on the East Coast. They distributed an equal number of retail catalogs. Since Louis DiCocco's death in 1993, the business has expanded even further to include Internet marketing and sales.

The Havertown St. Jude Shop is in a former supermarket that was renovated in 1981 into twelve thousand square feet of retail space. This main store is attached to the more modest stone shop that housed the original business and now sells First Holy Communion dresses, veils, and suits as well as special-occasion dresses. A cream-colored stucco facade and large windows reframed in gothic style were added to the exterior of the spacious showroom in 1996. From their positions along the sills, statues, such as a five-foot Saint Jude, gaze through these clear windows onto the outside world. Instead of a shrine to Saint Anthony at its entrance, a marker to the right of the main exterior door bears a bronze plaque with an image of the entrepreneurial founder of the store. The inscription reads, "In Loving Memory of Louis R. DiCocco, Jr., Co-Founder of the St. Jude Shop, When Through One Man A Little More Love and Goodness, A Little More Light and Truth Comes Into the World, Then That Man's Life Has Had Meaning."

The large retail space, with its plaster ceiling, exposed fluorescent lights, and worn tan carpet, occupies the front section of the store; storerooms and small offices are hidden from view in the rear. A central island on a raised platform allows cashiers to observe aisles lined with glass shelves, where merchandise is displayed, and glass cases, where more expensive items are visible. Above this central station, punctuating the otherwise smooth expanse of the ceiling, is an illuminated dome covered with gold wallpaper. Future plans call for this dome to be fitted with stained-glass panels, creating a skylight. These features seem to suggest a post-Vatican II sanctuary, where the congregation sits around a centrally located liturgical space.

The St. Jude Shop lacks the sacramental ambiance of the old-style religious goods stores I had visited as a child. Still, when I entered the building, I knew immediately that I was in a Catholic site: the store is jammed with all manner of sacred things, religious objects, Catholic stuff. I encountered there a veritable explosion of Catholic sacramentals, from the small image of Saint Jude on the metal entry door, screwed in above the handle, to the First Holy Communion paper plates in a display to the right of the front windows. The St. Jude Shop is a center for the observation of both past and present-day material expressions of Catholic personal piety, as well as of the Catholic communities that use them. Myriad forms of sacred materiality can be found there, objects deliberately made to complement the sacred mission of the Church as well as normally secular objects that have been given a specifically religious reference.

Objects for personal use or for gift giving are positioned in the front of the store, and church goods are placed in the rear. As you enter, you immediately find yourself before multiple images of the Virgin Mary in plaster, ceramic, and wood, as well as in framed prints. A variety of angel figures also inhabit the store's front section. In their diverse forms—dolls, ceramics, framed images—they pay tribute to the American fascination with these spiritual beings at the end of the millennium. Family-themed collectibles such as German Hummel figurines join other secular gift items, such as plates, stuffed animals, and picture frames.

As you move through the aisles, you observe displays organized around particular themes: angels, Confirmation, First Holy Communion, saints, rosaries, Marian apparitions. Here one can find objects made to commemorate both Catholic sacramental rites of passage and events in an individual's life, such as First Communion and Confirmation certificates and "First Penance" rings, as well as guardian-angel medals for a newborn's bed, crib, or carriage. Wherever you turn in the St. Jude Shop, hundreds of pairs of eyes peer back at you, a reminder that you are not alone. In a colorful display near the central cashiers is a multitude of statues of saints of every imaginable size and variety, from Saint Patrick and Saint Frances Xavier Cabrini to Saint Peregrine and Saint Martin de Porres. Nearby is a generous assortment of inexpensive three- to five-inch statues of holy figures, what can be called Catholic plasticiana. Displayed on the right wall are images of the Infant Jesus, Jesus within the Trinity, the Suffering Jesus, the Sacred Heart of Jesus, and several variants on what could be called the Second Vatican Council Jesus: the "laughing" Jesus, the bohemian Jesus, and my personal favorite, Jesus playing ice hockey. Next to these prints stands a row of plaster statues in all sizes portraying Jesus as the child king, an image known in Catholic tradition as the "Infant of Prague." One or two regal outfits for devotional dressing of the royal image by the faithful normally accompany these statues, but most of them are dressed only in white ceramic gowns.

Throughout the showroom, one can find a multitude of crucifixes, crosses, scapulars, candles, vestments, and images of the heavenly pantheon represented on medals of gold and silver, as plaster statuary, on small holy cards of paper or encased plastic, and on iconographic plaques laminated with a passion. In their variety, the rosaries make for a colorful display: there are "egg" rosaries (i.e., a rosary enclosed in a tiny plastic egg), large and small wooden rosaries, crystal rosaries, one-decade (i.e., one ten-bead section) hand rosaries, pink, black, white, blue, and glow-in-the-dark plastic rosaries. Holy water fonts, angelic hook racks to hang keys, and guardian-angel light-switch plates are all available for purchase, as are kitchen magnets with the Madonna glued on (as well as lightbulb magnets proclaiming "Jesus Power and Light") and Saint Jude keychains. The traditional patron for safe travel is remembered here in the form of Saint Christopher magnetic plaques for the car, the boat, and the bicycle. I found 1960s printed blessings of Saint Clare of Assisi, patron saint of television, to be placed on top of the set; Blessed Virgin Mary lamps and night-lights; and even $1.50 "Marian Shrines" that feature the Blessed Virgin Mary encased in a plastic torpedo and are something of a Freudian analyst's dream.[21] A few objects look carefully handmade, but most are obviously mass-produced.

Objects specifically related to the pro-life movement are gathered together in a display closer to the center of the store. A graphic reminder of how traditional images can be freshly negotiated by contemporary forces is the multitude of images of Our Lady of Guadalupe, sold under the designation "the Virgin of the Unborn." This Marian icon, so significant to Hispanic Catholics in this hemisphere, has been appropriated by pro-life anti-abortion Catholics as a symbol of their cause based on the traditional interpretation that Mary, in this image, appears pregnant.[22]

Eventually, the store even stocked a contemporary commercial response to property owners' interest in Saint Joseph's intercessory powers. Designated the St. Joseph Home Sale Practice, this prepackaged kit includes printed instructions, petitionary prayers with a printed image, and a small plastic statue of Joseph holding bread and a jug. On the reverse of the package is a drawing of a man either burying or digging up something at the back of his home.

The store sells objects to be used for prayer and objects to make everyday living a constant devotion. Materials for the sanctuary, the parochial schoolroom, the catechetical class, and the Catholic home are all available. Recordings of religious music, greeting cards, and games, as well as video documentaries of saints' lives and classic films such as *The Song of Bernadette*, are found in the second half of the store. The rear of the room is reserved for vestments, chalices, patens, cruets, flagons, and bells.

Books are also displayed beyond the central cashier station: Bibles, lectionaries, sacramentaries, aids for religious education classes, coloring books, missals, prayer books, devotional literature, and a few scholarly texts by conservative Catholic authors. This is not, however, a book store that also sells some religious articles; it is a religious goods store that stocks books and devotional pamphlets. One can find the documents of the Second Vatican Council, works of Thomas Merton and Pierre Teilhard de Chardin, and papal encyclicals, but there are also many popular devotional books on apparitions of the Virgin Mary at Lourdes, Fatima, Garabandal, and Medjugorje, though Our Lady of Bayside is excluded.[23]

The store is representative of a general material culture of American Catholicism, which has incorporated older ethnic devotions and images. The St. Jude Shop relates to Catholics as a generic American ethnic group rather than a particular group of ethnic Catholics. It reflects the homogenization and nationalization of Catholicism, especially after the Second World War, when prosperity and the breakup of ethnic neighborhoods caused a change in the Catholic evaluation of place and self.[24] The acceptance by Catholics of material culture associated with Protestantism or nondenominational Christianity is also evident here in the presence of certain images, such as *Praying Hands*, the "Good Shepherd," or Warner Sallman's *The Head of Christ* or *Christ at Heart's Door*, as well as word-centered plaques and other objects.[25]

Objects adorned with an appropriate inscription, prayer, or scriptural passage are part of the Christian practice of transforming words into images. The embodiment of scriptural words as images and the enhancement of word-centered documents has been cultivated by various denominations—for example, by the Pennsylvania Germans in their illuminated manuscript art called "fraktur." Considering this tradition, one might ask, Which is primary for a particular religious group or individual believer, the words or the images generated from them? Catholics and Protestants have their own sensibilities when it comes to religious imagery. In his assessment of the popular Protestant religious art of Warner Sallman, David Morgan points to American Protestant memorates (first-person accounts of the supernatural) that report miraculous experiences concerning the artist's famous *Head of Christ*.[26] He also stresses that it was Sallman's intention to "verify the literal character of the biblical text."²⁷ Morgan observes, "The character of mechanical reproduction" of the New Testament stories in Sallman's work "serves to textualize the sacred image and therefore to make it acceptable to the Protestant community. . . . Protestant believers feel safe *reading* the image of Christ."²⁸

Catholics, however, feel safe *seeing* the image of Christ, and the Virgin Mary, and the saints. The fact remains that images are the foundation of the St. Jude Shop. This store represents a pre-Vatican II Catholic understanding of sacramental culture, centered on the visual, the sensual, and the innate association of these with the supernatural and the sacred. When individuals possess such a sensibility, they do not read an image—they *feel* it. This idea of "feeling" an image, of responding to it emotionally, is a way of articulating Catholic sensibility, or the affective component of Catholic experience.

It is perfectly understandable that someone who is not familiar with Catholic culture would ask about such a setting as St. Jude's, What exactly is going on here? What is this store all about? What does it all mean? The store as a site carries complex, "multiple layers of meanings, uses, symbolisms, and connotations," like the objects it displays.²⁹ As one looks at all these objects of devotion and artifacts of belief, it is possible to see, come to life, the Reformation controversies over mediated grace, purgatory and indulgences, and justification by faith and works. The store also signifies the tension between the individual orientation of vernacular devotionalism, with its stress on personal salvation, and the communal sensibility of the institutional Church, an important principle of Catholic theology and practice. Considered within the study of vernacular religion, particularly American vernacular Catholicism—by which I mean not the multitude of ethnic, regional, or cultural expressions of Catholic faithful, but the religious lives of the individual Catholic believers within such contexts—the St. Jude Shop is a significant postmodern Catholic site.³⁰

This space presents a notable opportunity to view an example of virtually every kind of devotional item used by or popular with Catholics, both pre- and post-Second Vatican Council. Researching the National Shrine of Saint Jude Thaddeus, which opened in Chicago in 1929, Robert Orsi has noted that "devotionalism reached its peak in the 1950s, just prior to the Second Vatican Council."³¹ The "popular devotions" of which he writes were stimulated especially by devotional periodicals, as well as by "pastors and prelates of the airwaves, Catholic fiction, catechisms, sermons, religion classes, book clubs, moral handbooks, and so on."[32] These devotions included expressions of both an immigrant piety and a "modern, indigenous post-immigration piety" that "reflected the different experience of space and time among the immigrants' children; it did not simply replace the older devotional forms, but extended, supplemented, and (in some cases) reimagined them."[33]

A mark of the postmodern American Catholic community is its division over the necessity of employment of devotional objects to enhance personal piety. Starting with the liturgical movement of the twentieth century[34] and especially since the reforms of the Second Vatican Council,[35] the institutional Church has made a concerted effort to stop paraliturgical activities during the celebration of the liturgy by the congregation (such as praying the rosary or other devotions). The goal is greater participation in the reformed Mass of Paul VI, which is said in the vernacular language of the region.[36] The use of such personal sacramental objects as rosaries, prayer books, and holy cards during Mass or at other times has likewise been de-emphasized. Sacred materiality, of course, has not been dismissed in Roman Catholicism, but its position within Catholic devotionalism has been questioned by the institutional Church.[37] Council documents and later institutional writings direct clergy and laity to see the function of sacramental objects as expressions of the sacredness and holiness of a particular ritual action or occasion but not as sacred objects in and of themselves. So, for example, it is not the incense, candles, vestments, monstrance, or white Communion wafer as objects that are important but rather how they work holistically to enhance the significance, solemnity, and prayerfulness of the liturgy. These items should be of fine quality because they are being used in important sacred ceremonies, not because they are significant in and of themselves. The same thinking relates to personal piety: it is not the saint's statue or relic or holy card that is the center of attention in an act of prayer but how these sacramental objects serve the goal of aiding in the quality of an occasion of prayer to God.

Contemporary American Catholics are split in thought and action over the treatment of religious objects. Traditional and restorationist Catholics retain a more object-oriented, subjective sacramentalism, while progressive Catholics support a more holistic and relational attitude toward religious objects. It is impossible to consider post-Vatican II American Catholicism and not recognize the differences in the traditions, quality, and style of both institutionally sponsored and lay practice in various regions of the United States. For example, parishes in dioceses of East Coast cities maintain a more traditional and conservative demeanor of Catholicism than do parishes in the Midwest. This phenomenon may be related to the general relative cultural formality of the East, or to the specific ethnic Catholic groups who settled there. For progressive Catholics, the St. Jude Shop, filled as it is with religious articles, is an anachronism of the devotional past, the public face of the tradition that communicates nothing of its contemporary reality. For other communities, such as traditionalist Catholics or members of Afro-Catholic syncretic religions of the Caribbean, including Vodou and Santería, the store and its contents represent what it means for them to be Catholic: participating in a magical, mysterious religion according to which objects reflect and manifest the power of the sacred and the supernatural. Ironically, at any given time, there might be in the store a remarkably disparate assembly of shoppers, all representing constituencies of the late-twentieth-century American Catholic Church: parish priests and campus ministers purchasing their church goods, housewives preparing for their own home liturgies, mambos buying some necessity for a Vodou ceremony not available at a local botánica, and grandmothers shopping for First Holy Communion gifts. The store services the contemporary American Catholic community in all of its surprising diversity.

The St. Jude Shop embodies passive accommodations, intriguing survivals, active creations, dissenting impulses, and reflections on lived experience that mark the vernacular religion constantly emerging in everyday life.[38] The items sold there have been flexibly employed both by a powerful, directive Church to create a compliant community of believers and by equally resourceful individuals who have negotiated their own creative and personal experiences of God.

Many of the objects for sale in this store might be classified by observers, even by Catholics, as nothing more than Catholic kitsch: religious-themed junk or knickknacks with little or no spiritual value. Such a classification, however, passes judgment on the beliefs of the individuals who buy from this shop. Given the sacramental nature of Catholic culture, all objects have the potential to become objects of belief. Such material culture forces scholars to reconsider the limiting designation of "kitsch," defined as "false art . . . often devised for mass consumption . . . meant to offer instant satisfaction of the most superficial aesthetic needs or whims of a wide public."[39] The term "Catholic kitsch" encompasses the complicated amalgamation of affection and joy at the absurd or outrageous aspects of the ethnic, regional, and national expressions of the tradition within the American context. To appreciate why such things as, for example, images of Saint Lucy holding plates with eyeballs, copiously bleeding stigmatics, or the mummified bodies of "incorruptible" saints kept in sitting positions at side altars for centuries are affective and meaningful, one has to participate in some way in the values and culture that they represent. This applies whether such objects or expressions are categorized as folk art, popular representation, fine art, or kitsch. Stores like the St. Jude Shop offer the opportunity for a rich exposition of American Catholic religious folklife in the form of an ethnography of the senses of American Catholicism. They mark the change—some might say rupture—in the visual, tactile, auditory, and olfactory experience of Catholics pre- and post-Vatican II.

When I look at this repository of Catholicism, I see not only institutional sanction for theological principles of intercession, mediation, and sacramentality but also a deeper meaning, a vernacular religious sanction of the way ordinary people themselves continue to sacramentalize even the most humble or everyday parts of their lives. Passing time in the St. Jude Shop means not only encountering statues of Saint Joseph, the Virgin Mary, and other Catholic friends but immersing oneself in a multitude of expressions of an ancient human impulse to objectify our gods and to seek a blessing for ourselves and the created world around us.

I did purchase an inexpensive statue of Saint Joseph and mail it off to my student's father. He buried it as he had been instructed, and six months later his house was sold. That plastic statue that I searched for all over Catholic Philadelphia is currently enshrined in the dining room of his next Newfoundland home.

Within the constellation of paper ephemera—including calendars, Mass/memorial cards, large devotional prints, scapulars, parish bulletins, parish collection envelopes, and devotional letters/donation appeals sent through the mail—associated with the visual culture of North America's Roman Catholic population, "holy cards" remain one of the most enduring religious "things" characteristic of everyday religious life into postmodernity. A traditional Catholic conception of sacred ephemera perceives certain pieces of printed paper to be more than something beautiful to look at or significant as the communication of a feeling or lesson. They are "sacramentals," representing a Catholic belief about the potential utility of all creation to bring the faithful closer to God. Holy cards, a prime example, are paper cards printed with images and words that are made holy by their religious subject matter, intention of use, and, at times, the blessing of the institutional Church. Observing these objects from the perspective of visual piety as alive with their sacredness, believers have therefore sensed holy cards as anything but ephemeral. This chapter introduces the uninitiated to this visual, tactile, and resilient Roman Catholic sacramental tradition, stopping to consider holy cards' history, usage, and artistic influence in North America.

4

Artifacts of Belief

Holy Cards in Roman Catholic Culture

Within the constellation of paper ephemera associated with the visual culture of North America's Roman Catholic population—including calendars, Mass/memorial cards, large devotional prints, scapulars, parish bulletins, parish collection envelopes, and devotional letters/donation appeals sent through the mail—"holy cards" remain one of the most enduring religious "things" characteristic of everyday religious life into postmodernity.[1] A traditional Catholic conception of sacred ephemera perceives certain pieces of printed paper to be more than something beautiful to look at or significant as the communication of a feeling or lesson. They are "sacramentals," representing a Catholic belief about the potential utility of all creation to bring the faithful closer to God. Holy cards, a prime example, are paper cards printed with images and words that are made holy by their religious subject matter, intention of use, and, at times, the blessing of the institutional Church. They exemplify the "sacramental imagination," a way of seeing, feeling, and experiencing God in all things. To believers, they are alive in their sacredness; they are anything but ephemeral. I offer this exploration of holy cards' specific history, usage, and artistic influence in North America as an illustration of the visual, tactile, and resilient Roman Catholic sacramental tradition.[2]

The Holy Card as Artifact of Belief

Holy cards (plate 5) are small, illustrated, and most often printed pieces of paper that Catholics have employed in their religious lives in myriad ways for many centuries, especially since advancements in printing technology in the nineteenth century. Roman Catholic "holy cards," "devotional

---

Originally published in 2016.

images," "holy pictures," or "prayer cards"—as these objects are variously referred to in contemporary American culture—are pieces of paper containing both a printed image and, on the reverse, words centered around a religious theme, such as a prayer. A recently published scholarly assemblage of "key words in material religion" offers an opportunity to see holy cards in light of a number of relevant phenomenological categories: "Belief," "Display," "Icon/Image," "Ritual," "Sacred," "Sensation," "Sign," "Space," "Thing," "Touch," "Words."[3] For many believers, the classification of these pictorial objects the size of playing cards, once a vibrant part of vernacular Catholicism and still in continuous use, is exuberantly fluid. Though the use of holy cards by the faithful has declined within post-Vatican II Catholic culture, and the cards are now less elaborately designed and produced, these small color printed-paper images of Jesus, Mary, the saints, or sacred texts remain important objects that people—both Catholic and non-Catholic—use to sacralize religious, secular, mundane, and specially created spaces, places, and even persons. They evoke a blessing, whether taped to the cash register at an ethnic bakery, positioned under the glass counter of a convenience store, distributed at a saint's procession, hung to adorn a vernacular religious shrine, left near a department store escalator, tucked in a prayer book, carried in a wallet or purse, or hidden from view under a family's mattress. Furthermore, in an era when older holy cards have become valued as collector's items and even sometimes exhibited as objects of graphic and devotional art, they are also exemplars of "Catholiciana," or "the material world of Catholic culture and tradition."[4] Holy cards are also one of a number of religious items that have been unmoored from their contexts and put up for sale on online auction and shopping platforms such as eBay.

Given what they can convey about the complex relationship of aesthetics, design, and belief/faith, it is surprising that holy cards in America have gone unstudied and often even unacknowledged. Even a text as definitive as the *Encyclopedia of Ephemera*, "a guide to the fragmentary documents of everyday life for the collector, curator, and historian," fails to devote a separate article to these objects.[5] Scholar of Catholicism Richard McBrien uses holy cards to depict various sacraments in his illustrated book introducing Roman Catholicism, but he never offers an explanation in his text or glossary of exactly what these objects are.[6] Yet these small, popular religious prints have played, and continue to play, innumerable roles through their everyday use, mirroring a Catholic worldview, representing and reinforcing powerful beliefs about the sacred and the dead, and expressing visual, consumer, and spiritual traditions as old as Christianity itself.

Holy cards both illuminate the Catholicism of the past and, as folklife scholar Don Yoder has noted about Pennsylvania German ephemera, offer a "window into the culture" of the present.[7] Indeed, these cards accompany the individual Catholic's life from one rite of passage to the next: from birth and baptism to school and First Holy Communion to death and burial. Their persistence and significance, therefore, within the culture of contemporary American Catholicism warrants greater scrutiny and more careful inquiry. Holy cards may not be handcrafted objects of religious art, "a unique creation by an individual," to recall the words of Swiss folklife scholar Robert Wildhaber and a rather dated perspective on folk art.[8] Though eBay has listed for sale some holy cards described as "handcrafted," they have in fact most often been mass-produced, mass-marketed products. Still, their special place in the spectrum of religious material culture emerges not only from the beauty of their design and the ubiquity of their production and distribution in Catholic culture but also from the nature and variety and meaning of their use. Whether they are functioning as sacramental rites of passage, blessings, collectible commercial objects, memorials, or artistic inspiration, these artifacts of belief still mark the everyday experience of many Catholic Americans, even those who consider themselves neither devout nor practicing.

Holy Card Production and Efficacy

For Roman Catholics educated in American suburban parochial schools in the late 1960s and early 1970s, the years just following the Second Vatican Council, who experienced both traditional and reform-minded expressions of American Catholicism, holy cards were a natural part of everyday life and development as a Catholic. Those who are unfamiliar with the holy card tradition within Roman Catholicism—including, it appears from my interactions with contemporary college and university students, a substantial population of younger American Catholics under thirty years of age—will ask, What exactly are these cards, and what is their relationship to Catholic devotional culture?[9] The term "holy card" can be applied to several different types of religious and artistic objects within Roman Catholic culture, from fifteenth-century images made from wood blocks to seventeenth-century two-color engravings; from eighteenth-century hand-painted cut-outs and parchment to nineteenth-century lace-bordered lithographs; and from twentieth-century colored and gilded chromolithographs to the digitally designed and laminated cards of the twenty-first century. Separate centers of holy card production could be found at various times throughout Europe, in Switzerland, Spain, Italy, France, Germany, the Netherlands, and the former Czechoslovakia.

It is possible to identify the producer of some holy cards by examining the printed trademark that appears on the card's bottom quarter.[10] It is uncommon, however, to find an actual printed date of manufacture, and it is even more difficult to locate the artists who originally created most of these images.[11] Naturally, it is easier to identify the iconography of cards that feature images taken directly from known works of art, such as Michelangelo's *Pietà* or Leonardo da Vinci's *The Last Supper*.

The cards are referred to as "holy" cards because they carry religious images and texts, are used in Catholic devotions, and have for centuries been employed by the Church as promulgators of an institutionally sanctioned proper piety and spiritual attitude in everyday life. In a more general theological sense, they operate under the principle known as "sacramentality." Richard McBrien eloquently explains this Catholic sensibility and understanding of the "really real":

> Simply put, the principle of sacramentality means that there is more to human life and cosmic reality than meets the eye. There is a "beyond" in our midst. There is a deeper, unseen reality—Being itself—that is in fact more "real" than all the beings that we take to be real. A sacramental perspective, therefore, is one that "sees" Being in beings, the divine in the human, the infinite in the finite, the spiritual in the material, the supernatural in the natural, the holy in the secular, the eternal in the temporal. For Catholicism all reality is sacred, or sacramental, because all reality is but a visible expression of invisible Reality itself: which is God.[12]

Within institutional Roman Catholicism, as previously mentioned, holy cards belong to the specific category of religious objects known as "sacramentals." A contemporary definition of sacramentals views them as sacred signs or actions instituted by the Church to prepare for and prolong the sanctifying effects of the sacraments. The name *sacramental* signifies that the sign has some resemblance to a sacrament, inasmuch as it is a means of grace, but a sacramental differs from a sacrament in that a sacrament always produces grace directly (when there is no obstacle on the part of the recipient), while the sacramental produces it only indirectly by generating devotion in the mind of the receiver or user. The old Roman Catholic Code of Canon Law classifies sacramentals as either *acts* or *things*. An example of sacramental acts would be the blessing of persons or places, and in some cases of objects that are used for a nonreligious purpose, such as one's car. Sacramental things fall into two categories: those articles used during church services, such as holy water, blessed candles, blessed ashes used on Ash Wednesday, and blessed palms used on Palm Sunday, and those items used in churches and by private individuals, such as crucifixes, images of Christ, Mary, or the saints, and medals, rosaries, and scapulars, which may or may not be blessed by a priest. Holy cards are an obvious addition to this list.

Holy Cards and the Production and Distribution of Christian Imagery

In his study of historical and contemporary American religious devotions in the home and their relation to Christian imagery and material culture, visual piety scholar David Morgan has observed that "the evidence is clear that people invest rich personal, familial, and communal meanings in very common, mass-marketed objects like religious pictures.... This is especially the case among those who attest that mass-produced religious images participate in the formation of Christian identity in the home."[13] Admittedly, Morgan is assessing the importance of larger-format printed images of Jesus, such as the famous portrait *The Head of Christ* by the American artist/illustrator Warner Sallman, often found in American Protestant church and domestic environments.[14] Nevertheless, small devotional images such as Roman Catholic holy cards have likewise played a meaningful and distinctive, if sometimes subtle, role in the establishment and affirmation of Catholic religious and cultural identity. They have marked the parochial school experience of Catholic children, the faithful's visits to Catholic holy places such as shrines, and even the liminality of the death rituals of Catholic family and friends. Such use of the imagery of Catholic holy persons as personal and domestic markers of Catholic affiliation and devotion should be observed in the context of the creation and availability of such images and within the larger narrative of Christian art.

The history of the holy card is linked to both the history of the use of Christian images and the history of techniques for printing, engraving, and mechanically reproducing graphic art and design in Western Europe. While early Christianity generally prohibited artistic representations of holy personages, widespread desire among the faithful for the visualization of important Christian personalities soon convinced the Church to support such interests, a development that emerged within the first three centuries of its existence. Indeed, a tide of Christian art on church walls became a flood as religious art and architecture flourished over the course of the fourth century. Small, hand-produced religious pictures or miniatures appeared as early as the beginning of the seventh century and were used for pedagogical purposes by the Church in catechisms for instructing converts to the faith.

From 726 to 843 CE, the period of the Christian iconoclastic controversy, imagery was disallowed for theological reasons. Imagery broke the Jewish Bible's prohibition of idolatry, and more broadly it was felt that it was simply impossible to represent Jesus Christ accurately in icons because these presented only the human and not the divine nature of the Second Person of the Trinity. Pictures thus threatened to divide or separate the two natures of Christ, the unity and distinctiveness of which had been decided in the fourth and fifth centuries at the Councils of Nicaea I (325 CE), Constantinople I (381), Ephesus (431), and Chalcedon (451). Such prohibitions were nullified first in 787, at the Second Council of Nicaea, the seventh Ecumenical Council of the Catholic Church and the last such meeting to be recognized by the Eastern Church. The Council declarations affirmed belief in the intercession by saints and restored the practice of icon veneration, recognizing not only their significance but also their pedagogical value. Iconoclasm was revived in 813 by Emperor Leo V, but it was short-lived. Empress Theodora finally settled the controversy in 843 with an imperial edict in favor of icons.

From the ninth century onward, then, Christian art was firmly embedded within Christian doctrine and worship, both in ecclesiastical settings and in private devotion. It was created and used differently in the different regions in which Christianity held sway, but the idea that religious images were generally both permissible and desirable was not to be seriously or universally challenged again.[15] By the fifteenth century, holy pictures were in circulation in a variety of ways: as objects of admiration by women; on display alongside relics; kept in little pouches with herbs; as decorative elements on kerchiefs, combs, spoons, and little knives; and on the packaging of powders with healing properties or edibles such as cheese, gingerbread, and cakes. Painted on parchment or paper or sometimes on material, particularly silk, holy cards became a common gift from nuns to others in the high and late Middle Ages. The custom of pasting the pictures onto the inside of the covers of books or on the text itself promoted the preservation of holy pictures from the fifteenth century and the start of the sixteenth. Following the example of French and Dutch prayer books, writers of such texts began to leave empty spaces so that the purchaser could either have new small pictures painted or paste existing painted pictures there. Because of this custom, "a lively miniature trade [has] flourished in Flanders since the fourteenth century."[16]

The first small religious prints were engravings, which appeared around 1400, fifty years before the invention of printing. Printing of such images over the next five hundred years would include several fundamental processes: xylography, or relief engraving of woodcuts; intaglio engraving, or incised work on metal such as copperplate; flat-surface engraving on stone or metal, or lithography, and its color counterpart, chromolithography; and offset mechanical printing, in the period of industrialization. However, it is the grainy, rather velvety process of lithography and its color co-process, chromolithography, which both emerged in the nineteenth century, that are particularly relevant to the development and popularization of holy cards in Europe.[17] European firms established an international market for Catholic imagery in the form of popular religious prints, seeing South American and eventually North American Catholics as eager consumers of the global visual culture these businesses published.[18]

A specific example of the growth of European design and production of holy cards and other popular religious prints is found in the history of the well-known firm Benziger Brothers. Joseph Charles Benziger (1762–1841), the founder of the Catholic publishing house that bears his name, was born in 1762 in Einsiedeln, Switzerland, the location south of Zurich of a famous medieval Benedictine abbey that incorporates within its church a Marian shrine. Pilgrims have journeyed to Einsiedeln for a thousand years to see a miraculous statue of the Virgin Mary brought by Saint Meinrad to his original hermitage in the ninth century and now found in the Lady Chapel built within the shrine sanctuary. The interior of this church—itself a baroque masterpiece of gold- and pastel-painted walls, frescoes, and white marble putti, with light streaming through clear glass windows—undoubtedly influenced the Catholic aesthetic sensibility of the Benziger family, inspiring the color, texture, and drama reproduced in their holy card designs. By 1835, in addition to their book publishing business, the firm began lithographing religious pictures, coloring them by hand before the introduction of chromolithography. By 1853, the two brothers had built up a publishing business in Catholic books and prints that was the largest and most distinguished in Switzerland and known throughout the Catholic world.

Holy Cards in the Americas

The development of numerous industrial methods and processes for image reproduction, including photography, photogravure, collotype, and silkscreen painting, facilitated the production of holy cards, which became available from both European and North American sources. The first American chromolithograph of any kind was printed in 1840 in Boston by the English immigrant William Sharp. It was shortly followed by chromos produced by German-, French-, and Russian-born printers in Philadelphia and New York. By the end of the century, the progeny of these printers were operating multimillion-dollar businesses.[19]

The movement of German-speaking Catholics in the mid-nineteenth century to the East Coast, midwestern cities, and rural areas of the United States gave businesses such as Benziger Brothers the opportunity to expand their sales to much larger markets. Soon, as their website proclaimed at one point, "the Benziger sales wagon brought a welcome supply of books—including Bibles and prayer books [and holy cards]—to communities up and down the Ohio River." The first Benziger sales office opened in 1853 to sell books in German, English, and Polish to resettled Catholic immigrants in America, and in 1860 it began its development into a publishing house.[20]

As the Catholic population in the United States grew throughout the nineteenth century, other established Catholic book publishers, who had been distributing religious goods to a variety of canvassers or peddlers, some of whom were in fact Jewish, expanded, and newer businesses opened. Companies such as D. and J. Sadlier's and P. J. Kenedy and Sons in New York City, Krieg Brothers in Indianapolis, and the Herder Company in St. Louis offered a variety of Catholic materials for distribution to local stores, which then sold them to homes, schools, and churches (plate 6). Benziger Brothers opened branches between 1860 and 1888 in Cincinnati, St. Louis, and Chicago. In her history of Roman Catholic devotions during this period, religious scholar Ann Taves notes that, second to peddlers, publishers in the antebellum period made the greatest number of sales not through bookstores but through large urban parishes. The opportunity for such transactions often occurred at parish missions, which were organized Catholic revivals of faith led by order priests, such as the Redemptorists and the Jesuits, who visited parishes to preach and officiate at various mission liturgies and devotions for days or weeks at a time. "Although intended primarily as a means of deepening the piety of the laity, parish missions also provided a source of income for the parish and a major sales outlet for Catholic publishers through the sale of books and religious artifacts promoted as essential to the devout Catholic life," Taves explains.[21]

In the city of Philadelphia, one business with origins in this era was Kilner's Church Goods. Kilner's opened in 1888 on Market Street and closed in June 1986 on Arch Street because of changes in the urban environment and Catholic buying patterns.[22] The parochial school system, established in Philadelphia in the 1850s, grew exponentially for the next one hundred years. To market their goods to the teaching sisters who staffed these parochial schools in the twentieth century, Kilner's sponsored a "Sisters Lounge" in the back of the store, which contained a small kitchen, a few sofas, a refrigerator, and a restroom, in an era when Catholic women religious did not enter public bathrooms or even congregate comfortably or socialize together outside the confines of institutional Church structures. Stores such as these became major suppliers of pedagogical tools to teaching sisters in the parochial school system, especially catechism books and, of course, holy cards, which they distributed to their students. Holy cards, it was thought, would fulfill two important Catholic institutional objectives: the retention of faith and the increase of personal piety.

The retention of the faith by immigrants was an obvious hierarchical priority for the Church, but the language in which the faith would be retained became a significant question. English-language educational and devotional materials were naturally geared toward the Irish immigrants who arrived in America en masse in response to the deprivations of the potato famine in Ireland, especially from 1845 to 1850. Throughout the mid-nineteenth century, German American members of the Catholic hierarchy argued forcefully for the retention of the German language among immigrants and their descendants. They believed that this linguistic connection to belief and practice was critical for the continuation of religious affiliation. German Catholic bishops especially emphasized German literacy in catechetical teaching of the faithful. This language-specific emphasis was taken up by Polish immigrants in their ethnic parishes at the turn of the twentieth century, during a period of mass Catholic migration. Up to the Second World War, for example, Polish ethnic or national parishes in Philadelphia taught catechism exclusively in Polish and distributed only Polish-language devotional objects, particularly holy cards. In South Philadelphia's Italian ethnic neighborhood, Italian national parishes and local religious goods stores made holy cards available in the Italian language.

A second objective fulfilled by holy cards was the increase in personal piety sought by the institutional Church hierarchy, such as more frequent and widespread incorporation of devotions to the Sacred Heart of Jesus and the rosary into the daily lives of the faithful.[23] The French devotion to the Marian apparition at Lourdes and the Portuguese devotion to Our Lady of Fatima were undoubtedly popularized through the mass production of postcards and holy cards relating to the sites.[24] In America, Chicago's St. Jude League literally built a devotion to Saint Jude, patron of impossible causes, not based on physical visits to a church or shrine but by creating a "national shrine" through mass mailings of millions of printed holy cards with images of the saint.[25]

Prior to establishing American outlets for devotional lithograph prints, European commercial printers had been exporting great quantities of images to the Latin American (especially Mexican Catholic) markets for decades. Industrialization naturally brought an increase in the quality of prints available. The artistic and social impact of the influx of these prints to Latin America and New Mexico has been studied by the folklorist, art historian, and museum administrator Yvonne Lange. Tracing the influence of small devotional images from Europe on forms of religious material culture in the Americas was Lange's scholarly passion. She enthusiastically studied "popular prints as prototypes for religious folk art in the New World," specifically the influence of lithographic and chromolithographic prints on the tin devotional paintings called *retablos*. Concluding that "the influence of the ubiquitous lithographic print" was profound, Lange believed that these images influenced everything from those New Mexican painted tin images to Puerto Rican wood carvings of holy persons called *santos*.[26]

While Lange acknowledged the individual creativity of New World religious painters and sculptors, Claire Farago has expanded on Lange's work by taking seriously the artistic and creative hybridization that she sees as evident in the artistic and religious creative output of the people of the Southwest. Citing not only the likely influence of chromolithographs and other devotional prints, large and small, on New Mexican Catholic worshippers and artists—from *santo* carvers and painters to tinsmiths creating various frames—Farago sees the introduction of the global visual culture of European Catholic prints as having provided an opportunity on a local level for "modernity and tradition" to intersect rather than stand mutually exclusive.[27] The active reception of chromolithographs and their various applications, as expressed in Farago's New Mexican examples, reflects the vitality of vernacular Catholicism. The faithful of the region have long accepted and renegotiated new technologies and products, including painted or printed religious images, for their own use, generating their own religious expressions in the context of their daily lives and local communities. Such vernacular usage occurs regardless of whether the institutional Catholic Church approves of those interpretations or acts of consumer and spiritual enterprise.

Both Lange and Farago present valuable work on the influence of holy cards, as religious material culture from Europe, on the shape of religious artistic tradition in the New World. Lange employed the patience and technique of an art historian and cultural detective to trace the influence of the smallest pictorial elements of a holy card or larger lithograph on the folk art traditions she studied in the Americas, pausing to ask larger questions, for example, about the impact of lithographs in disrupting *santo* creation in a place with such a rich tradition of folk creativity as New Mexico. It is through the overlay of Farago's perspective on postcolonial Catholic paper culture and Catholic folk creativity in the Southwest, however, that one begins to gain a sense of the religious flavor—and fervor—of the reception and use of such outside objects as holy cards within an established regional population of fully engaged Catholics. This is apparent in New Mexico throughout the eighteenth, nineteenth, and even twentieth centuries; in Haiti in the 1950s, as expressed in spectacular sequin-covered *drapo Vodou*;[28] and in contemporary New York City in memorial walls, murals painted for victims of urban tragedies.[29] While Lange offers an astute study of the material culture involved and calls attention to the evocative ways that objects of art influence each other, reading Farago leaves one with a fuller understanding of the impact that printed religious images like holy cards have had on the Catholic sacramental imagination in art and everyday life.

Holy Cards within North American Life: A Quebecois Example

French Canadian Catholics present an excellent opportunity for the study of the place of holy cards within an entrenched Catholic population, and their vernacular religious traditions are among the best documented, due to extensive research conducted by Pierre Lessard in French Canada in the late 1970s.[30] Lessard's work focused on cards archived in the Larouche-Villeneuve Collection of small Catholic religious objects at the Université Laval in Quebec City, a collection carefully overseen for many years by folklorist Jean Simard.

The majority of these cards date from 1860 to the 1970s, and Lessard notes that his 1981 study *Les petites images devotés* therefore emphasizes "the pious mentality of the last 125 years." Lessard pays particular attention to the "iconographic themes borne by the small images" and "the study of the printed texts," but he also draws on rich fieldwork among older Catholics regarding the ways holy cards functioned in their lives.

What results is an affirmation "that the contacts between people and small images were frequent, constant, and sustained." Holy cards in this period "circulated abundantly in Quebec," Lessard explains, acknowledging that the small-image format served as an instrument of communication between its distributors and users—that is, between the institutional Catholic Church and faithful French Canadian Catholics. These images reflected the desire of spiritual leaders to "educate and edify the faithful," as well as manage the content of their beliefs and the direction of their devotions. To that end, holy cards featured images, printed texts, and handwritten "marks of all sorts." They served as presents, souvenirs, and messengers. Often, these pieces of religious ephemera were the only tangible remembrances of occasions of personal significance that mark everyday life, such as a First Communion or Confirmation, a scholastic achievement, or a birthday, or they represented a gift from grandparents, a good word from a childhood friend, or a purchase made when visiting a center of devotion.[31]

In addition to an analysis of these objects as visual and verbal texts, both printed and handwritten, Lessard complements this study with ethnographic work within the French-speaking Catholic population of Quebec. Interviewing more than thirty individuals about their memories and religious practices, he chronicles within a traditional Catholic community the variety of functions of the holy card in the pre-Vatican II era. These small objects were used as *l'image protectrice*, carried for individual protection in a pocket or change purse in the same way a religious medal or small pocket shrine might be used. When automobile travel became more commonplace, individuals placed small religious objects and images inside their cars, often in full view, to protect them as they traveled. In a time of intensive Catholic devotional observances such as attendance at "first Friday of the month" Mass, regular devotions to the Virgin Mary, and weekly confession, Lessard notes, "small-format images were thus utilized as amulets." He quotes a 1930 folklore study of religious images that arrived at a similar conclusion: "Domestic images, whatever their origins—pilgrimages, monasteries, personal acquisitions—most often played the role of Christian talisman."

Lessard's ethnography reveals that holy cards were likewise used for *la protection des biens matériels*, the protection of material goods. To preserve their homes, possessions, and loved ones (from immediate relatives to pets), believers relied on an entire constellation of religious material culture and related kinesic and proxemic religious practices. Religious objects came in all shapes, sizes, and variety for placement in the home and on the person, from images large and small, medals, and statues and statuettes to palms, crucifixes, crosses, lamps, candles, and waters (holy water, Easter water, Pentecost water, May water), and these were complemented by all sorts of special acts and prayers. But there was a hierarchy to all this in which small-format images occupied a privileged place. They were considered, at that time, along with some other artifacts and certain acts that were accompanied by rites and prayers, to be powerful talismans that protected people, animals, and material goods against fire, lightning, and vermin.[32]

The institutional Church, of course, has long been wary of the use of religious objects by the laity. The 1967 *New Catholic Encyclopedia* article on "amulets" goes to great pains to distinguish the use of these charms or other objects worn for magical purposes from the Christian use of sacramentals. In a classic explanation of the difference between religious and magical practices, the article assures the reader that the sacramental "is primarily efficacious through promoting in the user a religious habit of mind and personal piety, which in themselves may have a decided influence upon Christian manner of life. On the other hand, an amulet in pagan belief possesses powers that are valid whether or not the one using or handling it is aware of them."[33] Almost thirty years later, the 1994 *Catechism of the Catholic Church* likewise made note, in its discussion of sacramentals, that "forms of piety and popular devotions among the faithful" relating to the Church's sacramental life extend, but do not replace, the actual sacramental life of the Church. The text elaborates: "Pastoral discernment is needed to sustain and support popular piety and, if necessary, to purify and correct the religious sense which underlies these devotions so that the faithful may advance in knowledge of the mysteries of Christ. Their exercise is subject to the care and judgment of the bishops and to the general norms of the Church."[34] Such statements of right practice are a direct acknowledgment by the Church of vernacular religious beliefs and practices among the faithful—and of the fact that some individuals have treated sacramentals as powerful talismanic or luck-producing tokens or otherwise made use of religious objects in ways that Church documents might either condone or discourage.

Lessard's inventory of images highlights how the quality of information and iconographic themes transmitted by this multitude of illustrations assisted in the formation of a Catholic literacy all its own.[35] Holy cards taught a language of symbols and imagery that brought the faithful closer to understanding approved aspects of institutionalized Christianity—a religious material culture that served the Church's evangelical, educational, and even pastoral agendas, with these objects acting as visual Bibles, hagiographies of saints, and catechisms. Moreover, holy cards emphasized and taught proper individual prayerful behavior at Mass, as well as the latest officially approved devotions from the Church, such as the Immaculate Conception or Assumption of the Virgin Mary. In the hands of the faithful who intrinsically negotiate what the Church presents them with, just as functionaries and leaders within the institution do themselves, holy cards also taught and transmitted a powerful vernacular Catholicism in Quebec. Holy cards allowed for a vibrant fluency and freedom in the traditional daily practice of Catholicism—from the choice of where to hang images in the home for the greatest blessing to when to kiss a sacred image and which cards to slip under pillows or even swallow as small rolled-up pills during times of illness. For many of the Catholics Lessard interviewed, holy cards represented a vestige of an age of devotionalism now gone. Holy cards had often served as partners "in the daily prayer of the individual" and were "most truly distinguished by [their] regular, frequent, everyday use."[36] For ethnographers of vernacular religion, Lessard's Quebec example represents, as does the New Mexican study, an illuminating instance of the negotiation of religion in everyday life—but one from which the question nevertheless emerges of whether these objects of material religion remain relevant in the post-Vatican II era.

Conclusion: The Decay of the Holy Card?

Graziano Toni observes that the twentieth century represents, in the opinion of historians, collectors, and lovers of material culture, "the century of decline," but he notes that "if we want to speak of a decline of the holy card in our opinion, we must restrict the period from the '70s on."[37] He cites changes in traditional piety and habits of use among Catholics as the reason for this waning: "Perhaps the decay of the holy card is really due to the fact that it has lost the function for which it was born: a bookmark for the prayer-book or a prayer in itself on which to meditate, but also an image to keep on the bed-side table to which to recommend oneself before falling asleep."[38] He suggests that a decline in religious use has led to a dilution of the religious aesthetic of Catholic objects, including their imagery, text, artistry, and perceived power. For readers of David Morgan, such fluidity and fluctuation in the use and appreciation of a religious "thing" such as a holy card should come as no surprise: "Culture enables the recognition of a thing, but can also disable it," he argues. "The instability of specification is well illustrated by a historical example of objects passing through several successive frameworks of interpretation, showing how objects are culturally constructed from the march of things over time."[39] The reality of post-Vatican II spirituality, with its changed emphases regarding devotionalism, does prompt the question, Has the age of the holy card passed, and will religious paper ephemera be superseded, for example, by digital images of the holy or even digitized expressions of prayer texts, allowing the electronic object to serve as the vehicle for transmitting particular religious beliefs and forms of piety?[40]

Despite the lack of written or otherwise documented histories of individual holy cards, it is easy to recognize that they have figured prominently in people's religious lives from their bent corners, broken lace, and worn edges when they are discovered in such resting places as old family Bibles, Catholic missals, shoeboxes, contemporary believers' prayer books, or eBay listings. Since the tradition of printing holy cards to mark the experience of death for Catholics is still practiced, holy cards as ephemeral objects with a unique spiritualized half-life remain viable, if perhaps repurposed, within contemporary Catholicism. They have become less prayer devices, or reminders of the existence of purgatory and the need for prayer for the deceased, and more spiritualized objects of memory. Their attachment to saints, especially newly beatified or canonized saints, does remain—as does their association, as object, image, text, or memory, with a feeling of the sacred.

Holy cards persist as one of any number of devotional paradoxes in Catholic life. Like parts of the bodies of the saintly dead that are saved and honored as precious relics of a figure's continuing holiness, intercessory power, and life in heaven, holy cards retain their paradoxical aura as "holy" ephemera that are not quite ephemeral. Holy cards continue to be used to adorn vernacular religious spaces and places such as grottos, processions, yard shrines, and private chapels and are also left in institutional spaces such as churches.[41] As David Chidester and Edward Linenthal have noted, a "sacred space is not merely discovered, or founded, or constructed; it is claimed, owned, and operated by people advancing specific interests."[42] It is important to recognize that people still make spaces in their lives for holy cards. Taped onto another object or slipped in a corner of life here and there, these objects subtly sacralize secular spaces and landscapes with a heavenly image. Funeral holy cards, frequently found in storage spaces, still retain a relationship to memory, custom, religion, death, and the afterlife.

Like the older Catholic notion that prohibited placing blessed sacramental objects in the trash, pouring consecrated altar wine down a municipal drain, or throwing unconsumed or spoiled consecrated hosts out with the waste, holy cards represent a fascinating way that many Catholics still respect sacred materiality, associate it with their lives, and employ it in a multiplicity of forms. The question remains: Do these cards, as religious objects, especially when used in relation to the occasion of death, retain a power that will sustain their significance even for a younger generation whose factual and visual religious illiteracy is growing more profound and pronounced?

I think the answer is yes. The resiliency of religious material objects through centuries and across cultures suggests that individuals and communities will continue to use the holy card within the context of everyday life. Lavishly created or inexpensively produced, this kind of sacred ephemera endures by making manifest beliefs about the efficacy of the sacred and the agency of religious people to call upon the "holy" for assistance, protection, and care. The unique nature of the holy card for Catholics is undoubtedly associated, to borrow from Robert Maniura, with the "very ambivalence of the image, its manifest status as an artifact alongside its unsettlingly vivid evocation of a sacred presence, which is crucial to its role in religious practice."[43] It is this ambivalence and ambiguity, alongside the multivocality of holy cards as objects, images, texts, and manifestations of presence, that have sustained their resilience, their power, their beauty, and their aura into the twenty-first century.

The term "ex-voto" represents a constellation of prayerful thoughts, devotional systems, artistic craft production, meaningful materials and symbols, ritual contexts, and social interactions. When a Catholic prays for the intercession—the personal attention and demonstrated action—of a holy person to respond to human requests for assistance in daily life (to alleviate economic problems, attain a position of employment, maintain a relationship, or grant a healing), he or she can make a vow as part of that plea for intercession. An ex-voto is the visible commemoration of the fulfillment of that request by the believer in gratitude to Jesus, the Virgin Mary, or a saint. Taking the form of an object of devotion, remembrance, declaration, or gratitude related to that prayer, it is the materialized expression—on painted metal or canvas, from hammered silver, tin, or gold, or in molded wax—of obligation or thanks to a saint or holy figure for a miraculous intervention, whether in the form of money, healing, or protection in the life of an individual. It can also be the commemoration of a battle during times of war or, equally serious, salvation from accidental injury or imminent death when, perhaps in a moment of desperation, a loved one has called on a holy patron for assistance.

Bearing these definitional foundations in mind, this essay places ex-votos into historical and contemporary perspective within Christian spirituality and art, and especially as manifestations of Italian Catholic personal piety. To this end, I also explore how these expressions of vernacular Catholicism have been recontextualized in the digital age not as offerings or artistic expressions of personal faith but as objects detached from a ritual or devotional context and redefined as electronic auction items, coveted collectibles, or "charming" handcrafted art.

5

Catholiciana Unmoored

Ex-Votos in Catholic Tradition and Their Commercialization as Religious Commodities

Offer to God a sacrifice of thanksgiving, and pay your vows to the Most High. Call on me in the day of trouble; I will deliver you, and you shall glorify me.
—Psalm 50:14–15

An ex-voto is a voluntary offering to a saint or divinity. It is undertaken, performed, or dedicated in fulfillment of or in accordance with a vow and given in gratitude for a favor, blessing, or healing received. Synonymous with vow making, "ex-voto" is a Latin term, short for *ex voto suscepto*, "from the vow made" or "according to the promise that was made." The literal translation of "ex-voto" breaks down as follows: *ex* = from, in accordance with, or on account of; *voto* (the ablative form of *votum*) = vow, votive offering, prayer, desire, or hope. "Ex-voto," therefore, is most accurately translated as "in accordance with a vow or prayer."

In the material culture of Christianity, ex-votos can take various forms, including carved or molded objects or painted panels. The destination of an ex-voto offering is a church, chapel, shrine, or oratory where the worshipper seeks grace or wishes to extend public gratitude. Ex-votos have had wide appeal for centuries among many Christians throughout the world, specifically Roman Catholics and Eastern Orthodox, especially in Europe (e.g., Germany, Greece, Italy, Poland, Spain, Switzerland), parts of Asia (e.g., the Philippines), and Latin America (e.g., Bolivia, Brazil, Guatemala, Mexico, Peru, Puerto Rico).[1] Sites of Roman Catholic pilgrimage frequently contain any number of forms of

---

Originally published in 2012.

ex-voto: text-centered plaques, miracle paintings, floral arrangements, crafted wax or wooden correspondences of body parts cured or protected by a saint, silver hearts honoring the Sacred Heart of Jesus.[2] Ex-votos can take the form of wooden houses, paintings of ships saved, or even models of ships themselves. Jewelry or precious gems can be offered as ex-votos—as in the case of the icon at the shrine of the Black Madonna at Jasna Góra Monastery in Częstochowa, Poland, where mounds of amber necklaces adorning the walls of the chapel of the revered image are so resplendently abundant, they resemble folds of orange fabric. In the last fifty years, the Catholic ex-voto tradition has changed to include more cost-effective means of vow fulfillment: mass-produced paper-ephemera images of Jesus, Mary, and the saints, photographic portraits, and the handwritten notes of those who need or were granted heavenly intercession.[3]

The term "ex-voto" represents a constellation of prayerful thoughts, devotional systems, artistic craft production, meaningful materials and symbols, ritual contexts, and social interactions.[4] When a Catholic prays for the intercession—the personal attention and demonstrated action—of a holy person to respond to a human request for assistance in daily life (to alleviate economic problems, attain a position of employment, maintain a relationship, or grant a healing), he or she might make a vow as a part of that plea. An ex-voto is the visible commemoration by the believer of the fulfillment of that request, in gratitude to Jesus, the Virgin Mary, or a saint. Taking the form of an object of devotion, remembrance, declaration, or gratitude related to that prayer, it is the materialized expression—on painted metal or canvas, in hammered silver, tin, or gold, or in molded wax—of obligation or thanks to a saint or holy figure for a miraculous intervention in the life of an individual, whether in the form of money, healing, or protection. It can also be the commemoration of a battle during times of war or, equally serious, salvation from accidental injury or imminent death when, perhaps in a moment of desperation, a loved one has called on a holy patron for assistance.

Bearing these definitional foundations in mind, this essay places ex-votos into historical and contemporary perspective within Christian spirituality and art, and especially as manifestations of Italian Catholic personal piety. To this end, I also explore how these expressions of vernacular Catholicism have been recontextualized in the digital age not as offerings or artistic expressions of personal faith but as objects detached from a ritual or devotional context and redefined as electronic auction items, coveted collectibles, or "charming" handcrafted art.

Historical Developments

The practice of making and offering ex-voto objects is ancient and goes back at least as far as the Etruscans, the precursors of the Romans. While small offerings were sometimes made in response to requests concerning health and fertility, votive offerings were offered for other purposes as well. As far back as the Greek Geometric period (ca. 900–700 BCE), small bronze figures of gods, animals, and people were made to be left as offerings in temples. It was also common practice among the Romans for military generals to vow to build or rebuild an entire temple in return for victory on the battlefield.[5]

Within Christianity, there is a rich historical connection between the practice of ex-voto offerings and the rise of the cult of the martyrs and saints—that "spiritual elite whose holiness was recognized posthumously"—including the tradition of saintly relic and tomb devotion and the concept of the patron saint and the human client/saintly protector relationships that developed in late antiquity.[6] One of the most vivid expressions of the Christian saint cult was the honor paid to the miracle-producing physical remains, literally the sanctified bones, of these holy men and women. What made this belief in saints even more powerful was the sense that, as redeemed personalities in heaven, they remained in communion with their Christian brethren on earth, which complemented the miraculous nature of relics—their bodily remains. The apostle Paul had noted, in his Epistle to the Romans (12:4–8), "so we, though many, are one body in Christ, and individually members one of another." It only seemed reasonable that, if living Christians prayed for each other, those individuals redeemed in heaven would do the same.[7] It was the duty of patron saints to act as heavenly intercessors at the time of an individual's judgment before God the Father or Jesus, as well as to manifest earthly protection from the vicissitudes of a potentially violent and disease-filled world. The saint, however, expected in turn the loyalty of his or her charges, which by the Middle Ages "was promised in a vow (*votum*) consummated in the form of a commendation," some formal act that served to express the bond between patron and loyal follower. In his rich discussion of relics and their veneration in medieval Europe, Arnold Angenendt further explains:

> In general, a gift of thanks for being saved was recommended, at least the gift of a candle, with the utterance of certain prayers, or the celebration of masses, at most a pilgrimage. ... The formula for this was: *votum fecit—gratiam accepit*—the one who was saved has made a vow, and the saint has accepted it. Often one made votive offerings: an image of the person saved or of a healed body part; then objects associated with the rescue or images of them. In the ancient church, votive offerings had been forbidden; instead, a gift to the poor was expected. In the Middle Ages it had to be an offering to the saint. ... The figures of persons and their parts not only illustrated their healing, but also represented a "speaking" gift of thanks.[8]

By the late Middle Ages, votive images took on a familiar visual pattern of communication, including depiction of the dangerous circumstance below on earth—whether serious accident/situation or deadly illness—and the miraculous intervention, marked by the presence of the saint or Virgin Mary above in the heavenly clouds.[9]

Within the Italian ex-voto tradition and in the Italian language, the common term for "object" ex-votos is *ex-voto oggettuale* or *miracolo* (miracle). The most common form of such an object resembles a piece of human anatomy: the anatomical ex-voto or *ex-voto anatomico*.[10] In Italian, an ex-voto "painting"—that is, the illustration in paint of a miracle story on a particular material/surface—is referred to either as *ex-voto* or *tavoletta votive*.[11] In the specific case of Italian painted ex-votos, Mariolina Rizzi Salvatori offers a hierarchical explanation of their social origin and appeal. The tradition originated in the commissions of paintings from artists by wealthy patrons in the fifteenth century, she writes: "According to a patron's wealth, the painting would then be hung in a church, private chapel, or home. When the tradition spread to the less wealthy, it fell out of fashion with the upper classes. From Italy the tradition spread to Europe, and eventually in the colonial period to Latin America, reaching its height in Mexico during the middle of the nineteenth century."[12]

In the Americas, especially Mexico, the most widespread and frequently found examples of such humble religious paintings are the small tinplate pieces known as *retablos* and ex-votos. Gloria Fraser Giffords notes that within traditional Mexican Catholic piety, "retablos were images of individual saints painted to adorn home or workplace altars, while ex-votos were images of miraculous intercessions, each of which included the interceding sacred personage, the incident, and the date of intercession."[13] These Mexican paintings follow a visual typology similar to that of Italian votives. Salvatori explains:

> The spatial configuration of Italian painted ex-votos, often measuring twelve inches in height and twelve to twenty-four inches in width, marks two distinct and uneven parts: the smaller part, usually but not always the left upper corner, is dedicated to the heavenly figure or being, often floating on luminous clouds. The Madonna, Jesus, or a saint's gaze or outstretched hand occasionally reaches out to the supplicant, shortening "the invisible thread" between them. The rest of the space, the larger portion of the painting, is taken up by the human, and the visual representation of the miraculous event from domestic interior sickbed scenes of illness or recovery to outdoor natural weather disaster, household or work accidents or crime. At the bottom individualizing inscriptions: the name of the supplicant, the date of the event, only occasionally the name of the painter; votive acronyms (*P.G.R.*, Per Grazia Ricevuta [for grace received]; *E.V.*, Ex Voto; *V.F.G.R.*, Voto Falto Grazia Ricevuta [vow completed for grace received]); and/or brief written accounts of the specific miracle, often misspelled and grammatically fractured.[14]

All such paintings allow space for the communication of a supernatural narrative and, very significantly, a sense of perspective that positions the observer of that visual or verbal account as an audience member viewing the unfolding of an individualistic, private, miraculous human drama.[15]

Ex-Votos as the Visualized Art of Supernatural Narrative

Christianity has exerted a tremendous influence on Western art, architecture, and crafts over the last two thousand years. As Rosa Giorgi writes, "Much of the history of Western art coincides with the history of the Christian Church, and much of its iconography depends on and derives from the specific events, doctrine, influential figures, devotional movements, and trends of the Roman Catholic Church."[16] Christian art in its most traditional sense has taken a variety of forms, from sculpture and manuscripts to paintings and frescoes, from icons and fabrics to stained glass and ex-votos.

"Ex-voto," then, is both a term in the history and spirituality of Christianity, particularly Roman Catholicism, and a term found in art history, archaeology, folklore and folklife studies, and religious studies designating a particular type of religious and artistic expression: a piece of material culture produced in response to a vow made to a member of a sacred pantheon. Intrinsically, ex-votos are not domestic religious material culture, but when expressed as paintings, they often depict dramatic domestic situations. Votives are public religious objects that share a kinship with the experiential narratives that folklorists call *memorates*, or private first-person accounts of encountering the supernatural through miraculous events; in this sense, ex-votos evoke that quality from the Middle Ages of being "speaking" gifts of thanks.[17]

If a memorate is generally understood as a first-person account of an experience with the supernatural, whether that be a ghost, a demon, a god, or a saint, then an ex-voto is the objectification of that first-person encounter with the supernatural told as a visual narrative. Each ex-voto, therefore, is an individual object that itself communicates a story about such direct interventions of God in the everyday life of the particular Christian believer. What the ex-voto does not communicate is the scene of an immediate actual apparition of the holy, even when a painted votive portrays the supplicant gazing ardently and directly up to a blessed figure hovering above. This gaze represents prayerful vision, as opposed to visual intercessory interaction.

This idea of objects and images being associated with and relating narratives is intrinsic to the function of imagery in Christian art. Within institutional Catholicism, the potency and efficacy of religious imagery employed for didactic purposes can be observed historically in a letter from Pope Gregory the Great (590–604) to the iconoclastic Bishop Serenus of Marseille in which he reflects on the importance of images in teaching the illiterate faithful about the scriptures and generally enabling them to keep religious thoughts in their minds.[18] Such intentions helped to establish the practice of decorating and ornamenting Christian churches with visuals of the heavenly community, both for their beauty and for pedagogical purposes. This imagery was thought to teach the faithful about aspects of the Christian tradition from important texts that they did not know about or understand, while also reminding them about those aspects of the faith that they had previously learned. Ex-votos, too, worked in this way, instructing and reminding the faithful about the very presence of Jesus, Mary, and Catholic saints in their lives. Ex-votos complemented the primacy of text with the supernatural reality of action. They demonstrated belief through practices, specifically inclinations to prayer and requests for intercession.

Ex-votos reinforced Christianity's developed cult of the saints—a public cult—as a private devotion, and then re-presented it as examples of performed belief and community display. As it emerged from the Middle Ages, "for the mass of its practitioners, Christianity became a visual and oral culture"—and ex-votos, as they developed, meshed seamlessly with such an apprehension of the tradition.[19]

The Ex-Voto as Vow and Prayer

The appeal of ex-votos as objects of religious material culture is not limited to believers from particular social, economic, or educational ranks or levels of literacy. When reflecting on the influence of Christianity on artistic representation, we must consider not only subject matter, features, and symbols emanating from the exclusive institutional Church, its hierarchical functionaries, and its secular governmental associates but also the inclusive, non-elite vernacular traditions of creative religious negotiation at the heart of the religious practice of all Christian believers themselves. The ex-voto is an exceptional expression of such creativity inspired by belief and how it vivifies the vernacular religious life of Christians. As acts of vernacular religion—that is, religion as it is lived, interpreted, negotiated, and created by individual believers—ex-voto offerings, and most certainly votive paintings, are in no way prescribed by the institutional Catholic Church.[20]

Votives are, by their very nature, multivocal. They are voluntary offerings and occasions for the creative expression and negotiation of belief in the literal assistance of holy figures like the saints in everyday life, and associated concepts such as heavenly intercession. Votives are representations of the religious aesthetic of believers integrated with the sensibilities of trained and untrained artists. Ex-votos are expressions of individual religiosity and, therefore, fall outside the Catholic Church's theological perspective that one's spiritual relationship with God is best lived within the Christian community as guided and *mediated* by the institutional Church. Individual religion has historically made the institutional Church uneasy because it eliminates this theologically and institutionally important principle of mediation. For this reason, ex-votos are rich examples of vernacular religion existing "apart from and alongside" the institution.[21] In the case of ex-votos, whether object or painted, they are inspired by personal belief, created by artistic negotiators of the various traditions, and then assembled and housed around altars within the administrative or normative framework of an institutionally sanctioned Church building.

The act of making a vow to God, committing to perform a particular action at a future time, is an important component of the prayer lives of many Christians. In Roman Catholic religious communities, individuals joined in fellowship make vows of poverty, chastity, and obedience as indications of their membership and commitment. Such "public vows," legislated within the documents of particular religious orders of men and women, are "recognized as public in Church law and are regulated not only by the law of a given religious community, but also by the general [Canon] law of the Church." Institutional Catholicism supervises such vows and how they are observed during everyday activities. These public vows are distinguished in the language of the Roman Catholic tradition from "private vows," which are "promises made to God singly and privately by individuals and [unlegislated] promises made within the context of a community."[22]

The term "ex-voto," a complex concept within Christian spirituality, relates to this ancient Christian practice of intimate or private vow making to God, the Virgin Mary, or the saints, proffered within a variety of contexts, from lengthy prayerful reflections to immediate moments of concern or even fright or exasperation. Within the history of Christianity, one of the perhaps more famous examples of spontaneous vow making can be found in the biography of the Protestant reformer Martin

Luther. When, as a young law student in June 1505, he was caught in a severe rainstorm and almost struck by lightning and knocked to the ground, Luther's ardent religious response to this traumatic situation was to make a vow. He begged a saint to help him survive the furies of nature, petitioning the mother of the Virgin Mary, the patron saint of the miners of his youth: "St. Anne, help! I will become a monk!" The rest, as they say, is religious vow-making history: "Approximately two weeks later, in obedience to his vow, he entered the Augustinian monastery in Erfurt."[23]

For the American Roman Catholic practitioner, vow making as a part of asking for divine intercession is certainly not an unusual practice. To mark a prayer, prolong it, or thank or ask the divine for intercession, the customary physical or bodily action is to enter a church and light what is called a "votive" candle—whether by illuminating a wax candle in a glass container among many other such candles or by switching on a small lightbulb in a similar arrangement (a mark of contemporary fire and insurance concerns and regulations). Here is mental prayer, expressing a vow, wish, or desire, being embodied by the performance of a physical action. Calling up this tradition of candle lighting accompanying prayer on the occasion of an American exhibition of a sample of mariners' votive offerings from the Montenero Sanctuary in northern Central Italy, Michel Mollat du Jourdin reflected a European sensibility and expectation that ex-votos are part of commonly held knowledge, practice, and cultural recognition in asking,

> Is it necessary to recall that an ex-voto offering is an object offered to God or to one of those, such as the saints, who can intercede with Him, and that its purpose is to express faith, and gratitude for a favour asked for and obtained? The ex-voto object, whatever it is, is also intended to express by its particular nature a commemoration of that especial act of grace, and to be the representative within the chosen sanctuary of the individual donor—and here we encounter a repetition of the universal symbol of the candle and the light it provides.[24]

Ex-votos add valuable dimension to an understanding of how Catholics have actually prayed and what is designated within Christian spirituality as "petitionary prayer." In her discussion of prayer, Margaret Dorgan offers this definition: "The basic sense of the word 'prayer' as entreaty, supplication, and petition is the introductory phase of approaching the One who is infinite power and limitless goodness. In addition to petition, prayer is also intercession, thanksgiving, repentance, adoration, and praise."[25] Ex-votos, as expressive examples of devotionalism and vernacular religiosity no matter what the social station of the vow maker, can imply and include all of Dorgan's qualities of prayer.

The Collectible Sacred: Ex-Votos in the Postmodern World

Having reviewed the general history of ex-votos and established a definitional understanding of the form, let us turn now toward more current developments in the cultural life of Catholic things. Considering Italian painted ex-votos through the collection and practices of one contemporary individual—a methodology called "auto-ethnography" used by folklorists, anthropologists, and other scholars of daily life—can fruitfully enhance such a larger endeavor.[26] I have been personally collecting ex-voto paintings since 2006 and offer here the lens of my auto-ethnography and personal narrative to view and explore this facet of religious material culture. I use this method to address several key and compelling aspects of the ongoing ex-voto tradition. First, and more generally, my collection dovetails with the twenty-first-century phenomenon of the digital sale and transfer of religious objects and is representative of the material practice of vernacular religion in that context. Second, and more specifically, I speak reflexively about the very process of collecting: how I began my own collection of Italian ex-votos, especially Italian votive paintings, what I know of their sources, the experience of collecting these objects via the Internet, and why their appeal remains powerful to me.[27]

In her catalog description of an enormous, unsigned Mexican ex-voto oil painting on canvas (*Ex-Voto to the Virgin of the Rosary*) owned by the Wadsworth Atheneum Museum of Art in Hartford, Connecticut, Clara Bargellini notes, "Painted ex-votos are today usually thought of as small works by untrained artists, but some of the most important works in the history of art, including buildings and major paintings, have been created as acts of gratitude for miraculous interventions in human affairs."[28] Certainly, Titian's *Pietà* (ca. 1576), at the Venice Gallerie dell'Accademia, and Philippe de Champaigne's *Ex-Voto de 1662*, at the Musée du Louvre, are additional exemplars of ex-voto paintings by respected, formally trained, and readily identifiable artists.

My first encounters with the concept of ex-votos—as an action or object thanking the sacred forces following a promise made and a requested favor received—were not as either large or small painted forms. In fact, I had neither heard the term "ex-voto" nor known of painted votives prior to taking a "folk religion" course from American folklife studies scholar Don Yoder as a University of Pennsylvania undergraduate. Yoder liked to illustrate his lectures with slides, and I was immediately entranced by the anatomical figures and painted miraculous dramas that he used to illustrate relevant dimensions of German and Austrian "folk" religion and religious folk art. I connected with Yoder's pedagogical point that a European folklife-studies sensibility could most certainly be applied to the study of the culture of everyday life in America. As I reflected on Yoder's lectures and applied them to my own experience of the culture of Catholicism, I realized that the concept of ex-voto was, in fact, familiar to me in countless expressions. I considered, for example, such forms as the novel *The Song of Bernadette*, by the Jewish writer Franz Werfel, centered around the Marian apparition at Lourdes, France; the once-a-decade Passion Play performances at Oberammergau in Bavaria, in southern Germany; the chapel and shrine to the Marian devotion Our Lady of Perpetual Help appended to Old St. Peter's Church above the shrine of St. John Neumann at Fifth Street and Girard Avenue in Philadelphia; and the Lebanese American comedian Danny Thomas's St. Jude Children's Research Hospital in Memphis, Tennessee.[29] All of these creations are the result of religious vows; they are all ex-votos—expressions of a promise made and fulfilled in architectural, literary, institutional, and dramatic form.

Yoder often spoke in his courses of his research trips to Europe and South America, and as I went on to serve as his teaching assistant as a graduate student, I saw how he complemented his time spent in archives and libraries in Austria, Germany, Italy, and Switzerland with excursions to antique shops, book dealers, and flea markets—as he did when at home—looking for religious ephemera and material culture. Yoder used his collection of American and European religious material culture, both Protestant and Catholic, in his teaching and research.[30] He paid especially close attention to the context of Pennsylvania German history and culture and its paintings; *fraktur*, or illustrated manuscript art; medical, song, and ballad broadsides; political and military broadsides; sale bills; posters; and house blessings, "letters from heaven," and other forms of paper ephemera. Through his example, I decided to begin such an assemblage, but one that emphasized the culture of American and European Catholicism with as much devotion as Yoder had shown to European, and especially American, Protestant materials.

The major difficulty that I perceived in achieving my European collection goals through the 1980s and 1990s—beyond financing such an interest as a student and then a young professor—was that, other than by traveling to Europe or elsewhere myself, I had no access to the European objects that I wished to collect. In addition, I knew few American dealers in Catholic material culture other than local Catholic religious goods retail stores, which were filled with inexpensive crafts and mass-produced Italian-made and Chinese-made import items.[31] Those American sellers that I encountered asked such exorbitant prices that I grew less hopeful about the possibility of ever finding such examples of objects from Europe or America. My first trip to Germany in 1989 did bring me to some antique shops near the great cathedrals in cities such as Munich, where I saw eighteenth-century holy cards and sterling silver ex-voto body parts. Since I was still a graduate student with a modest income, I could not purchase such items, but I returned home resolved to continue collecting more modest American Catholic devotional artifacts such as missals used to follow the order of the Latin Mass, holy cards, prints, and the like when I found them, and to do so with greater attention. In the 1980s and 1990s, the preservation of such objects was only beginning (especially at the libraries and archives of such Catholic institutions as Boston College and Notre Dame); they were not widely appreciated in America and were often being disposed of from people's homes or cleared out among the personal effects of deceased Catholic relatives.

Collecting American materials, to me, meant including American-made Catholic objects as well as the European examples that had been continuously transferred to North America—including French Canada—following the major periods of European Catholic immigration. It was the small paper-ephemera Catholic object known as the holy card that caught my initial enthusiastic attention, because I already possessed a collection given to me by my grandmother.³² My attraction to anatomical ex-voto forms was occasionally satisfied by folklorist colleagues purchasing examples for me in Europe, or even in Philadelphia. These were not silver antiques but newly molded tin examples. All such items were valuable to me because of their usefulness as illustrations in the classroom for my lectures on religious folklife. My own searches led me to unexpected sources of supply. One of my favorite sites, where I uncovered an astonishing cache of inexpensive Mexican votive paintings, was, of all places, a Mexican restaurant supply warehouse in North Hollywood, California, where a literal heap of ex-voto *retablos* lay in a corner, available for purchase at very reasonable prices along with strings of molded red chile peppers and animal-form piñatas.

Beyond such occasional examples from Latin America, however, I had no access to European votives, especially ex-voto paintings, which I had seen in abundance at religious folklife collections in 1989 in Germany (especially in the Rudolf Kriss Collection and the Gertrud Weinhold Collection, both owned by the Bavarian National Museum in Munich). Italian examples were simply not available to me. My interest in Italian "votive figures" as collectible items was further piqued by a 1989 *New York Times* "shopper's world" article written by a Rome resident. Louis Inturrisi offered an explanation concerning their availability at that time:

> Gradually the custom of purchasing ex-votos as thank-you offerings went out of fashion—due no doubt in some part to the temptation to thievery the silver figures afforded, but also due to their replacement with monetary donations. Where did all those ex-votos—the legs, hearts, heads, et cetera—that once shimmered on the walls of the great baroque churches in Rome and Naples go, once they were removed? Lately, they have been cropping up in antique stores in Italy and America and collectors have been combing flea markets in Rome and Naples to snatch up the best of what has become a new collectible.³³

This article from the travel section included names and locations of shops and flea markets in the Italian capital for prospective collectors, mentioning that buyers should also be aware of wooden "plaques in primary colors in a primitive style . . . that are harder to come by, but they are easy to carry." It was on a trip to Rome for the canonization of

Philadelphia's Mother Katharine Drexel in 2000 that I purchased from an antique shop my first Italian ex-voto: a silver nineteenth-century heart (plate 7).

I had to wait until I was introduced to eBay, the online auction and shopping website founded in 1995, to more easily and frequently search for and procure a variety of Catholic objects, eliminating the cost of travel as well as language barriers for asking questions about dates of creation and even price.[34] As I became familiar with eBay's departments and procedures, I was soon astonished by the assortment of Catholiciana—the material world of Catholic culture and tradition—available for bid and purchase in this digital context. It has always seemed an ironic twist that, for many decades, Americans have raided the treasures, humble and grand, of Catholic Europe—for, in the words of University of Chicago literary and critical theorist Bill Brown, "Just as the Old World has considered the New World a vast geographical field for imperial expansion, so the New World came to consider the Old a vast cultural field for expropriation."[35]

The variety of such items available for digital auction was and is in large part a reflection of the seismic institutional shifts and changes in Catholic devotionalism, spirituality, and ritual promulgated by the Second Vatican Council, the reforming meeting of the Roman Catholic Church (1962–1965) championed through the pontificates of Popes John XXIII and Paul VI. Beginning in the mid-1960s, clergy and laity began to discard traditional sacramental objects such as relics, Tridentine-style vestments, and saints' statues, since they were no longer seen as complementary to the *Novus Ordo,* or the revised form of the Roman Rite Mass, also called the Mass of Pope Paul VI, promulgated by the Council's liturgical reforms. Changes in personal attention to material objects of devotion in Catholic sanctuaries dovetailed with suggested transformations in personal devotions during Mass. During the liturgy, the congregants were now requested to participate in the ritual as a community. Mass was to be offered in the language of the local congregation for greater understanding and participation and no longer in ecclesiastical Latin. Personal devotions, such as the rosary, prayers on the backs of holy cards or contained in prayer books, and missals—the hallmark of the liturgical experience of earlier generations of American Catholics attending Tridentine Masses (that is, the liturgy developed following the Catholic Reformation's reforming Council of Trent, 1545–1563)—were de-emphasized in what is now commonly referred to as the post-Vatican II period, when the unifying Eucharistic life of the Church family was stressed as the proper focus of worshipful attention. Catholic laity were challenged to be not merely ritual observers but ritual participants in the liturgy.

Liturgical transformations, starting in the mid-1960s, brought about changes to or the elimination of parish-sponsored saint and Marian devotions, resulting in the subsequent release of many associated objects, such as relics or statuary, from Catholic sanctuaries.[36] Religious objects were then disposed of as trash or made available to the public in sales. The wide availability in North America and Europe of "vintage" (to use an eBay term) Catholic objects is also a reflection of the closing of many Catholic churches in the post-Vatican II decades—especially in larger cities—for lack of congregations. Such closures came about for various reasons, from changing urban/suburban Catholic demographics in America to loss of faith among congregations in Canada, Europe, and the United States. Shortages of priests to staff American parishes also in some cases necessitated their closing.[37] Even with the institutional Church being careful to provide its own newly built suburban parishes with architectural and devotional elements from older closed parishes—such as stained-glass windows, statues, and baptisteries—a veritable marketplace of Catholic sacramental items became available to those interested individuals (devotees, collectors, decorators, secularizers) who would seek them out.

In the United States, the first decades of the new millennium saw another reason for church closings. It became necessary to sell off church properties and, therefore, transfer their contents to other local churches or even churches in other dioceses to assist in the payment of financial settlements and legal fees resulting from lawsuits against the Church in cases of child sexual abuse by priests.[38] An archdiocese such as Philadelphia would have a building filled with former decorative sanctuary ornaments and devotional objects for churches from across the country to take and reuse. Occasionally, these storehouses or even closed sanctuaries would have discreetly announced sales of stained glass and other remaining items.[39]

A contemporary examination of the eBay website illustrates the remarkable quantity of Catholic-themed material available as a result of these causes and from many of these sources. Under the category "Catholic Collectibles," for example, there might be between fifteen thousand and twenty thousand items available for inspection and bidding on any given day, a number that increases around the time of Christian holidays. This category includes postcards, comics, lapel pins, keychains, and tobacciana (ashtrays, cigarette cases, lighters, and such, in this case with Catholic themes). It is under the "Religion and Spirituality" subcategory that one can locate previously used icons, prints, votives, relics, rosaries, holy cards, medals, statues, crucifixes and crosses, "bears and dolls," holy water fonts, stained glass, thuribles, tabernacles, monstrances, jewelry, and charms. The eBay website includes what could best be described as a disclaimer to educate and assist those who lack clear knowledge about the Christian tradition: an institutional statement about the Catholic material the site carries, or what an eBay representative referred to as a "dictionary for sellers that gives meaning to what Catholicism and its related items are all about."[40] What is striking about this declaration is how lacking in nuance it is, misrepresenting Catholic history, sacramentality, and practice with a curious mélange of subjects and objects:

> There are different categories of Christians such as Protestants, Catholics, Greek orthodox, and Russian orthodox. Catholicism is generally associated with the religious beliefs, and practices of the Roman Catholic Church. The word *Catholic* is adopted from the Greek adjective *katholikos*, which literally means, "general," "universal." It is most commonly used to refer to Christians in general as part of one church. The believers have accepted the pope who resides in the Vatican City, Rome, as the head of the church. There are various sacred objects that are connected to the practice of Catholic faith, such as vintage, relics, apparels that are used in the religious sacraments, and rituals. Believers in Christianity use common objects of faiths, which may include crucifix, scapular, chalice, etc. Many believers in this faith generally have "Sacred Heart," a framed picture of Jesus Christ, which they believe to be a source of protection. These objects of faith inspire them in their devotion to the lord and are also a source of positive energy. There are numerous collectibles available that the believers can own. Such pieces of faith objects includes the catholic dictionary, lamps, sacred heart badge "Pieta" statue, scapular sets, old Catholic Encyclopedia book set, Archbishop Francis Spellman, statue of

"Kneeling Madonna and child Jesus," prayer book, statues of saints, and many other antiquities. One such antique object is the Holy Communion Charm catholic jewelry, which is made of 14k gold. These faith collectables and memorabilia help to create a sense of devotion.[41]

Again, this statement is noteworthy for its informal style and lack of precision in describing the Christian tradition and especially Catholic devotionalism. It can certainly be described as a vernacular religious description and assessment, as well as a rather remarkable example of the control that eBay allows its own users in creating explanatory text within the site itself.

Such an approach by the company is obviously quite appealing to its broad base of sellers. Indeed, through eBay, I located some excellent examples of American Catholic paper ephemera, and even Mexican *retablos*, but it was late 2006 before I actually encountered European ex-voto paintings on the site. The first source was an antiques dealer in Florida, and the second opportunity originated in Italy itself. Looking back on the experience now, I feel as if a vortex had opened allowing me specifically to build a collection during a three-year period from 2006 to 2009. During this time, I had access to beautiful examples of what I felt were authentic older painted and silver votives being offered at auction (plate 8). I relied mostly on an American expatriate couple living in Italy who uncovered these pieces in various markets and antique shops as they traveled throughout the country, especially in Northern Italy. Posting their latest offerings of a dozen or more items, including many heart-shaped and painted ex-votos, they carefully described each item to the best of their ability and in personal context, as can be seen in the following example:

> As we continue our travels around Italy searching for special treasures to bring you on eBay, we are always looking for one of our particular favorites—the Italian Hand Painted Ex-Voto. We view them as one of the most beautiful and fascinating of the Italian Religious Art forms. Painted ex-votos have a long rich history here in Italy going back to the 15th Century.
>
> These painted images are offered to God, the Blessed Mother or a Saint as a form of prayer, and are created as a thank you for prayers answered.

They tell a very personal story which is what makes them so interesting. They most often deal with illness, accidents and disasters. We are always captivated by the different artistic styles that have been created by the Artists from the various regions of Italy.... IN THIS AUCTION we are pleased to offer this wonderful Italian painted Ex-voto of a man seeking help for his cattle from Saint Chiaffredo, the Roman Soldier and Martyr. This enigmatic and devotional piece will hold a special place in your collection of antique religious artwork....

In case this is the first time you are checking with us, we are Americans currently living and traveling in Italy searching for unique items, which are designed and created here in Italy to present to you on Ebay. Please be sure to check out our other Auctions for Painted Ex-Votos, Hanging Sanctuary Lamp, Chalices, Incense Holder (Navicella), Ciborium, Statue Crown, Altar Vases (Portapalme), and a Wax Infant Jesus of Prague Statue, and many more treasures from Italy.[42]

As I began to win many of these ex-voto auctions, I grew to know these sellers via email correspondence and would inquire as to the sources of these pieces and their Italian region of origin. I also asked repeatedly whether the sellers were certain of the authenticity of these votives, especially in light of the conspicuous contemporary production of fake *retablos*, crafted to resemble older paintings, in the Mexican market.[43] The couple assured me of the authenticity of the paintings based on location and context of discovery, as well as their own knowledge from experience. I, and many other individuals, obviously believed their authentic provenance, because at times the bidding for the particularly unique votive paintings—which could cost as little as $300 or exceed $1,000—grew quite heated.

The 2008 economic downturn in the world economy played havoc on the amounts that eBay sellers could achieve in their auctions, and I began to win the auctions of the Italian ex-voto paintings at ever more reasonable prices (between $250 and $350). Soon, the couple emailed me to say that they had decided to give up selling on eBay for lack of sufficient profit. Delivery of my last ex-voto paintings from them occurred in 2010 when, on a trip to the United States, the couple brought the last vestiges of their flea-market finds to New York City and dropped them off with my colleague, folklorist Joseph Sciorra, at the John D. Calandra Italian American Institute in New York City. Sadly, but lending the episode an intriguing tinge of mystery, I never had the opportunity to meet or speak with my sources of this vernacular religious art. After 2010, my major contacts for Italian ex-votos were solely folk-art dealers who would occasionally consign pieces from various collectors who contacted them. There remains a real appetite for things Catholic, and not even resourceful eBay sellers can continuously fulfill the desires of every collector.

Catholiciana Unmoored

The last twenty-five years have seen a growing interest by religion scholars in how believers and even, at times, nonbelievers encounter, understand, use, create, and re-create material culture to mark or imbue ecclesiastical and domestic spaces and places within their everyday religious lives with a sense of the sacred.[44] Religious studies, therefore, has joined folklore and folklife studies in emphasizing the importance of such sacred materiality and how objects relate to the performance of religion.[45] David Morgan, whose scholarship on the "material practice" of religious belief and the power of visual media to inform and help mold the sensibilities of religious Americans has led the field of American religious studies in important new directions, argues that "the study of the material cultures of religions is not the study of objects per se, nor a neurological approach to belief. . . . Instead the argument is that the study of religions will benefit from an approach that undertakes an abundant account of social life mediated in feelings, things, places, and performances . . . framed by the social construction of the sacred."[46]

Influenced by anthropologist Arjun Appadurai's discussion of the "social life of things," Morgan's 2007 text *The Lure of Images* is especially useful for its treatment of American practices of consumerism, consumption, and display related to religious images. Morgan offers a story about the use of non-Catholic religious objects outside their traditional religious context that is especially relevant to my discussion of the life of Catholic ex-votos once they depart from their original shrine or church contexts. The case that he puts forth is the appropriation of the religious culture of Native Americans in the United States and its application to New Age religion, which fabricates its own mythology "as an avenue to lucrative non-Indian interest in self-help, therapeutic spirituality." Kachina dolls and sand paintings have been particularly popular in this context as "mass-produced versions of authentic Indian artifacts... widely collected as *objets d'art*, as genuine artifacts, as high-grade simulacra, and as inexpensive tourists' souvenirs. In fact, many are made and sold by Native American artists or artisans, available on the internet no less than at reservations, national parks, and in tourist shops along interstate highways throughout the West and southwest." Morgan explains that Navajo weavers and sand-image makers, upon realizing the interest of collectors and the opportunity to benefit financially, negotiated their own sanctification traditions. With regard to sand paintings, they deprived the images of "the right details" to render them "impotent and safe for commodification and public display." Such decisions about world religious objects used as *objets d'art* outside the context of their original religious purpose have wide implications—and a bearing on the life of Catholic ex-votos in the twenty-first century.[47]

Commodification and consumption of religious images are phenomena that cut across traditions, as Roman Catholicism faces a similar state of affairs concerning its own myriad sacramental objects. There exists today a wide range of expected and unexpected sites for the sale and purchase of Catholic religious objects, including church and shrine stores; lay-owned religious goods shops, some specifically for Roman Catholic, New Age, Gothic, or African-based religions; secular establishments such as corporate book purveyors (for example, the now-defunct chain known as Borders); and web-based outlets such as eBay.[48] The variety of religious and secular sources of Catholic religious material culture of every sort in post-Vatican II and postmodern contexts has led to an abundance of objects in circulation that are unmoored from their ritual or sacramental foundations and re-presented as collectibles and art. Religious objects such as ex-voto paintings have thus journeyed from materialization of memorate to biddable auction items in an international sacramental marketplace. Depending on the buyer and their understanding, inclination, and faith, the Catholic objects sold on eBay and other online outlets might be consumed with appreciation—seen as the sacramental presence of saintly holiness—or in an ironic mode of incredulity at owning articles of material belief still fostered and represented by what, for some, is a fading religious institution (or, perhaps, both of these attitudes at once).[49]

The auctioning on eBay of particular items of Catholiciana has naturally been a source of concern for some Catholics. A writer for the Philadelphia archdiocesan weekly newspaper, the *Catholic Standard and Times,* opened her report on the threat of a Catholic eBay boycott in 2006, due to the auctioning of relics, with the following exclamation: "The flesh and bones of our canonized saints are being auctioned off to the highest bidder every day on the popular on-line auction site, eBay, and some Catholics think the only way to stop the practice is to boycott the site."[50] In 2008 the sale of relics even drew a negative public response from Cardinal José Saraiva Martins, C.M.F., Vatican Prefect of the Congregation for the Causes of Saints, who vigorously castigated eBay for selling saints' relics, calling it "totally unacceptable business."[51] The response by eBay to such complaints has been to strengthen its policy on trafficking in human body parts. The website statement "Human Remains and Body Parts Policy" reads:

> We don't allow humans, the human body, or any human body parts or products to be listed on eBay, with two exceptions. Sellers can list items containing human scalp hair, and skulls and skeletons intended for medical use.... What are the guidelines? Items that contain human scalp hair (such as lockets or wigs); Clean, articulated (jointed), non-Native American skulls and skeletons used for medical research are allowed. If you are selling a first-class relic, you must state in the item description what the relic is made from. If it's a human remains it can't be sold if it's made from any body part except human scalp hair. What you cannot sell, according to eBay—even if the seller states that these items are used for medical research—are Native American grave-related items, including skulls and skeletons intended for medical research; Tibetan prayer skulls; organs; bones; blood; waste products; body fluids; sperm; eggs; any of these items included as a gift, prize or giveaway in connection with another item listed on eBay.[52]

Official eBay policy aside, auctions on the site continue for relics of Catholic saints and Christian martyrs that, to anyone familiar with the culture of Catholicism, are obviously what the tradition has considered "first-class"—that is, relics that are actual fragments, usually the bone, of a holy person. The irony of the reaction of some Catholics to this issue is that relics have, of course, been trafficked within the tradition since their recognition as important presences of the sacred within Latin Christianity in late antiquity.[53] Further, it is fascinating that there has been no outcry from the Church about other religious objects sold via eBay, given that the eventual purpose for all purchased items is ostensibly unknown and quite possibly secularized. Ex-votos, in particular, as vernacular religious material culture with a distinctively religious purpose, seemingly do not interest the institutional Church when used in a nondevotional way—for example, as Mexican restaurant decorations. Certainly, as any pilgrim to Vatican City's crowded and at times raucous religious goods shops can attest, the institutional Catholic Church cannot control what imagery and objects associated with the tradition are sold, let alone how they might be used.

Religious objects can certainly take on lives of their own even after being discarded, sold, or possibly stolen from churches and holy places. Sociologist Michael P. Carroll indicates that, in the case of painted ex-votos, older examples in Italian sanctuaries "were routinely discarded to make room for new ex-voto." Some were also lost due to deterioration from lack of care, and many votives were stolen.[54] Sociocultural anthropologist Allen F. Roberts is not surprised that such objects have a life when separated from their original context: as he puts it, "Devotional images cannot sit still. . . . Religious . . . images float or seem to sometimes possess an uncanny ability to get up and go, drifting off in startling new directions to fulfill astounding new purposes. . . . Devotional images not only permit but provoke re-signification." It is the ambivalent nature of such images to sustain many "expressive journeys" of use and relevance in various religious traditions, he notes, that makes them so powerful. Roberts specifically cites the use of chromolithographs—printed color images—in Haitian Vodou, a distinctive religion that is a hybridization of African religiosity and French Roman Catholicism, as one example of imagery translated to a new sacred space and made ready for new religious performances. In this case, of course, though the traditional images of Catholic saints, Jesus, and the Virgin Mary in a variety of devotional forms are recontextualized and shifted, they are based in a shared system of sacred meaning about the holy personages and their material visualization. There is also a shared tradition between Roman Catholics and Vodou practitioners concerning the affectionate domestic and ritual display of these sacred images.[55]

What about those commodified, commercial contexts in which religious objects move more fully beyond the boundaries intended by those who originally created them and the audience for which they were originally meant?

One example that comes to mind is the selling of Catholiciana in mass-market bookstore chains, where I have observed Catholic plastic statues of the Virgin Mary and the Sacred Heart of Jesus made into banks and painted with loud colors and glitter. Who is the intended audience here, and which corporate executive thought it was appropriate to mass-produce in China "Jesus Money Box Purple" for the American market? What sort of enterprising decorator decided that displaying Mexican *retablo* paintings in a book of interior design among other "tribal" arts was "a powerful source of inspiration," and it was therefore appropriate to objectify them along with so many other international forms of art—in this case, as "charming hand-painted . . . local miracles" hung "above the cupboards" of a model kitchen? In such examples of commodification and commercial enterprise, these devotional images have had the "holy" deconstructed right out of them. At least in the eBay universe, Catholic objects retain some of that value via their commodified descriptions as "vintage," "old," "antique," "rare," "unique," or "authentic."[56]

The possibility of individuals standing in the presence of material dimensions of Catholicism that mark significant performative expressions of everyday life and "gazing" upon them with a complete lack of appreciation *or* understanding—or even, perhaps, with disdain for their cultural significance and for the people engaged with them—has been explored by folklorist Joseph Sciorra in his ethnographic work on the experiences of contemporary Italian American Catholics. In what he describes as the "super-gentrification" that has transformed the physical, economic, and cultural landscapes of Williamsburg in Brooklyn, power relationships, local identity, and public life have been transformed as "bohemian hipsters" seeking more affordable housing outside Manhattan have entered the once multiethnic, working-class neighborhood in greater numbers. The shift in power relations, Sciorra observes, is richly apparent when the local Italian American Catholic community holds annual religious processions—a tradition since the 1880s—with their colorful statues of saints decorated with flowers boosted into the air on the shoulders of festival workers and devotees, adorned with ribbons filled with cash votive offerings. At such events, the images and their votive accompaniments are now often observed more as props in a filmed re-creation of a distant American world than a sincere display of public ethnic American Catholic religiosity: "The hipsters, for instance, have no desire to be part of the Catholic community—they snap photographs of processions like they were visiting Disneyland—and they equate the tradition of donating money during the processions with public panhandling."[57] There is little doubt that Catholic sacramental objects will continue to be bought, sold, traded, appreciated, gazed at in disbelief, and disdained in the twenty-first century, in the same way that saints' relics were "translated" from place to place almost from the beginning of the Christian system of belief.[58]

Collecting . . . Yourself

In his provocative assessment of objects, collectors, and the act of collecting, cultural theorist Jean Baudrillard offers the notion that individuals have passion for "things," and that collectors are passionate about objects removed from their original functional contexts. For Baudrillard, object collection is itself a form of the expressive culture of the abstract self: "For what you really collect is always yourself." While I do not accept Baudrillard's neo-psychoanalytic take on collecting as the "joy of possession" related to "a powerful anal-sadistic impulse" producing "the urge to sequester beauty," I do see much of myself in the time and care and pride I take in locating and acquiring Catholic ex-voto paintings—finding and owning these expressions of vernacular religion. Since I have directed the energies of my career to unlocking the mysteries of why people are religious in their everyday lives, it is not surprising that art visualizing the drama of desperate need, religious consolation, and miraculous intervention—expressed in a form accepted, but not prompted, by the institutional Church—would interest me. These paintings are the visualized expressions of vernacular religion, and vernacular

Catholicism, in action, the unspeakable dramas of religious life shedding light on otherwise muted mysteries.[59]

One of the hallmarks of twentieth- and twenty-first-century scholarly work on material culture or the study of objects in everyday life in folklore, anthropology, archaeology, art history, classical studies, religious studies, literary criticism, and critical theory has been to open the conversation to include not only how individuals make and influence the shape of things but also how things influence the shape of individuals.[60] Emerging from these studies of the production, distribution, and consumption of objects has been a reflection on the culture of collecting objects and the implications of the passionate collection of things by individuals.

As this essay reveals, the phenomenon of collecting religious "things" has a vital life of its own, into which commercialism, art, curiosity, and faith are mixed. Bill Brown, developer of the concept called "thing theory,"[61] working on the "mania" of collecting in the United States,[62] has mused that acts of collecting "generally depend on a form of consumption, but a form in which the product is carefully preserved, not used or used up; on the other hand, they are clearly acts of production, the making of the collection per se, the creation of a certain order."[63]

It was my decision to "order" the ex-voto paintings in my collection by framing each of them in consultation with framer Art Forster of Wayne, Pennsylvania. We carefully examined each piece and decided on the style of frame, grouping certain paintings together for stylistic or aesthetic reasons by placing them in matching frames. Given the tendency for folk art to be seen as aesthetically primitive, limited by its subject matter, and not as valuable and appealing monetarily, visually, or socially as so-called "fine art," I made the decision to frame all the vernacular religious art I acquired, especially ephemera and paintings, just as fine art is framed.[64] Since each object has already been plucked from its original aesthetic, functional, performative, crafted human context of use and/or appreciation, I feel that the presentation of these objects of everyday life as framed art can teach viewers about how important, beautiful, and useful such objects were and are.[65] Furthermore, as I am especially interested in using these objects for classroom instruction, lectures, or exhibition, framing them also struck me as the most practical, most protective, and most aesthetic approach.

One additional quality of my experience of ordering these votives purchased via eBay is worth noting. I have always been conscious of the capacity of objects to generate narratives about their acquisition for later communication to family, friends, colleagues, students, and other audiences. Such objects are reflectively ordered and framed in personal experience narratives that can become performative items themselves in a collector's repertoire. Perhaps this essay is a perfect example of just that creativity in written form, invoking folklorist Susan Stewart's thought that "the collector constructs a narrative of luck which replaces the narrative of production."[66] Because I can typically recall where I purchased a particular object, in what setting, and at what cost, it has struck me as unusual that my eBay auction purchases have not generated these kinds of specific tales or lasting memories for each of my ex-voto paintings. I suspect that it may have something to do with the significance of space and place in the experience of such procurement. As exciting as the moment of bidding in an eBay auction can be, it does not become a lasting memory. There is a blandness and sameness to the auction process and even to the achievement of securing the object at hand. I do, however, have very distinct memories of the personal interactions involved in receiving gifts of Catholiciana from students, purchasing pieces of pottery, and procuring ex-votos directly from folk art dealers. As grateful as I am to have eBay as a source for my collection, perhaps I am now working to detach and unmoor these Catholic objects from their cold digital and commercial captivity and restore to them a version of their value and place as individual articulations of Catholic belief and practice.

What, then, will become of the resilient ex-voto? I find this question especially captivating considering that these objects of belief have endured and kept their place in succeeding cultures and religions for thousands of years. Georges Didi-Huberman's poetic essay on the ex-voto observes,

> Votive images . . . cut across time. They are common to highly disparate civilizations. They disregard the cleavage of paganism and Christianity. . . . Votive forms are capable of both disappearing for a very long time and reappearing when one least expects it. They are just as capable of resisting any perceptible evolution. . . . They are not initially very easy to discern: the history of art ignores them and ethnology scarcely professes

to analyse them formally. They are there, however, in us and around us, ghosts returning, surviving or living on.[67]

Thus, the power of the ex-voto as a devotional object and image—whether a wax or silver piece of anatomy or a painted drama—endures in its melding of the mundane and the sacred, in its compelling visuality, and in its humbly beautiful expression of the drama of the human experience.

PART II

Dignity in Philadelphia

LGBTQ Catholics of Dignity/Philadelphia, often the progeny of Philadelphia's Irish, Italian, German, and Polish immigrants of a century or more ago, may not feel entirely at home in the churches built by their ethnic forebears, yet they still seek out the religion of their childhood. They have created in response their own vernacular parish. The God of the Catholic immigrants has been transformed into their sexually inclusive God, the gay God of the city.

6

The Gay God of the City

The Emergence of the Gay and Lesbian Ethnic Parish

> We attempt, I guess, in our worship life to—I hate to say it this way—to function as a parish.
> —President of Dignity/Philadelphia, 1988

During the closing decades of the twentieth century, lesbian, gay, bisexual, and transgender (LGBT) Roman Catholics in the United States desiring to practice their religion faced choices about where and with whom to worship. Should they remain members of the traditional parishes where they had always been present, some actively serving on parish councils and liturgy committees, without publicly expressing themselves as gay or lesbian? Should they seek out the gay Roman Catholic affinity group known as Dignity, the "national lay movement of lesbian, gay, bisexual, and transgender [Roman] Catholics, their families and their friends"?[1] Should they affiliate with Dignity and maintain a connection with their local parish? Dignity, which began in 1969 in California and gradually spread across the country, has played a significant part in the history of post-Vatican II American Catholicism.[2] The members of Dignity retain their traditional Catholic faith and practice as they seek to transform the Church's sexual morality to become inclusive and affirming of their experiences as LGBT Catholics.

This chapter addresses the making of the Philadelphia chapter of Dignity (Dignity/Philadelphia) as a "gay ethnic parish." For readers who are unfamiliar with the congregational life of American Catholicism, I begin this discussion by explaining what a parish is, why some are considered "ethnic" or "national" parishes, and how parishes still mark Catholic life in the city of Philadelphia. A parish itself is a defined com-

---

Originally published in 2005.

munity of Catholics established within the specific geographic boundaries of a diocese. The pastoral care of the parish is the responsibility of a priest called its "pastor." The pastor, who is to collaborate in his duties with "parishioners and ministers,"[3] is appointed by the diocesan bishop. Historically, priests always led parishes, but in contemporary America, priest shortages have resulted in non-clerical parish administrators.[4] Parish membership within institutional Catholicism is not meant to be the decision of an individual or family, as for Protestant Christians. The Church essentially preassigns Catholics to membership in the parish closest to their place of residence.[5]

To meet particular pastoral obligations, a diocesan bishop may request and appoint members of a religious order or congregation to administer a parish. If warranted, diocesan bishops may therefore "organize parishes nonterritorially, in accordance with special religious or sociocultural needs, like rite, nationality, or language."[6] Such was often the practice in the late nineteenth and early twentieth centuries in the United States.[7] Specific "ethnic" or "national" parishes were developed during this period. In response to the tremendous influx of non-English-speaking European immigrants in cities like Philadelphia, New York, and Chicago, churches were built within ethnic neighborhoods to serve these local communities directly.[8]

Immigrants at such churches heard relevant sections of daily masses said in their native European language and were welcomed into a constellation of culture-specific paraliturgical and social activities. Reflecting on the creation of nonterritorial parishes based on language and ethnic origin in nineteenth- and early twentieth-century America, Don Brophy notes that the Church "recognized that religious experience is mediated through culture and that people should have opportunities to encounter God in ways that are culturally meaningful to them."[9] As Catholics began moving away from their old ethnic neighborhoods after the Second World War,[10] families and individuals were permitted to retain their ethnic parish affiliation even though they no longer resided in the geographical area served by that particular church. This tradition remains intact in older ethnic parishes in cities like Philadelphia.[11]

Dignity/Philadelphia was formed as a Catholic congregation with no institutional Church sponsorship and no Church-appointed pastor or chaplain and was never permitted to hold its services in a Catholic sanctuary. This is because the Roman Catholic Church teaches that while homosexual orientation in itself is not considered intrinsically bad or evil, an active homosexual lifestyle is morally unacceptable.[12] The Roman Catholic Church's pastoral "solution" to the issue of homosexuality is for the individual to develop self-control through the practice of celibacy. Members of Dignity take a different view.

Since it is impossible for a "gay and lesbian" parish to exist with institutional sanction, the pairing of the terms "gay" and "lesbian" with "Catholic" might seem like an oxymoron. But anyone who knows Catholics and is familiar with Catholic culture is well aware that the tradition, like many others, includes a significant homosexual membership. While a parish of LGBT Catholics might seem contradictory in the abstract, in reality it is not.[13] All that is necessary is for one to maintain a flexible notion of "parish" as a congregation of a church, in this case "apart from and alongside"[14] a diocese and under the charge of a concerned laity rather than priests or ministers. Creating a congregational setting that would attract people not only from the gay neighborhood of Center City in Philadelphia but from other parts of the city, as well, Dignity Philadelphians drew from the model of an ethnic parish with which they were quite familiar.

In October 1986, a "Letter to the Bishops of the Catholic Church on the Pastoral Care of Homosexual Persons" was promulgated by the Congregation for the Doctrine of the Faith, headed by Cardinal Joseph Ratzinger, later Pope Benedict XVI. This Vatican missive was a direct response to the existence of Dignity in the United States. It was anything but pastoral, for it led to Dignity chapters being ordered by bishops to leave Catholic parishes.[15] Undaunted, Dignity continued activities, often within the confines of friendly Protestant sanctuaries. While Dignity/USA membership declined from 5,000 to 3,800 in the beginning of the 1990s,[16] the organization continued to attract new members and witness to full Christian acceptance of a gay sexual life. From the mid-1980s to 2000, Dignity/Philadelphia maintained a membership in the 200s. At the beginning of the new millennium, Dignity had 2,500 dues-paying members nationally.

In an age when many individual Catholics viewed the tradition as irrelevant and easy to abandon, these gay and lesbian Catholics felt that it was necessary and desirable to retain their affiliation, and that they deserved to do so. These were Catholics, and they would not allow anyone, especially the functionaries of institutional Catholicism, to tell them they were not. "We are the Church" was a common battle cry heard during confrontations between Dignity and the Catholic hierarchy. Ironically, these functionaries in the Catholic hierarchy were often known or assumed by Dignity members to be homosexual themselves but unwilling, for the sake of their careers, to either publicly admit their orientation or support other LGBT Catholics in their quest for understanding, acceptance, and legitimacy.

The 1986 Ratzinger letter spoke of the homosexual orientation as being "ordered toward an *intrinsic* moral evil."[17] But if there was something *intrinsic* to many Dignity members, it was their Catholicism, which they experienced as an innate part of who they were as human beings. According to Jeffrey, one of my interlocutors at Dignity/Philadelphia, "Catholicism is in my blood." Jeffrey and others felt a strong cultural attachment to Roman Catholicism and a strong spiritual commitment to the Catholic faith as they personally interpreted it. As former Dignity/Philadelphia chaplain Father Jake noted to me, those born and raised in the faith felt that Catholicism belonged to them, as "birthright" and "roots." "I am a *Roman* Catholic," Jake said. "I believe what I was brought up to believe." Dignity was Debra's "Catholic community," and her religion was "cradle Catholicism." As Greg put it, "I grew up in this church. I love the church for whatever abstract reasons." John, too, spoke of being born into Catholicism: "In my personal case, it's the tradition I grew up in, my family is all Catholic, my friends are all Catholic. And although I disagree with a lot of what they say, somebody has to stay in and say something." I asked John, who later became a president of the Dignity/Philadelphia chapter, to characterize the membership of Dignity. He explained: "The majority of its members are from the Catholic tradition and still consider themselves members of the Catholic family, and we reserve the right to remain in that family and respectfully, but purposefully, disagree with teachings on sexual ethics and morality. The majority of people who go there really do subscribe to most of the theological principles and are more steeped in the tradition, involved in it."

Members would refer to Dignity as "Church" with a capital C, meaning a part of the larger Catholic tradition, but also as "church," with a small c, meaning their local place of worship. "Oh, that's across the street from church," they might say, meaning across from the Episcopal Church of St. Luke and The Epiphany, where Dignity ran its Mass and weekly social hour. "Look at the information table at church," one member would say to another.

Insofar as Dignity assumed for many of its members the status of their church, it became Philadelphia's first gay ethnic parish. As the president of Dignity said in a radio interview in March 1986, "We attempt, I guess, in our worship life to—I hate to say it this way—to function as a parish."[18] However uneasily the chapter's officers made the identification of Dignity as a parish, the parish was the congregational model they knew best. A former officer of the chapter and former Philadelphia archdiocesan seminarian told me he knew that St. Peter Claver Catholic Church, about six blocks from St. Luke and The Epiphany Episcopal Church, "is geographically my parish church, but Dignity is really my parish church."[19]

Dignity/Philadelphia still holds its weekly liturgies on Sunday evenings at 7:00 p.m. in the basement of the Episcopal Church of St. Luke and The Epiphany in Center City, as it did in the late 1980s, when I did intensive interviews with Dignity members. They moved to this location from another Episcopal Church property in 1986.[20] The group, founded in 1973, has continuously advertised its presence in the local gay and lesbian newspaper. Its Masses are well known among the LGBT community as gay-lesbian-bisexual-transgender-affirming Catholic liturgies at which all are welcome. Dignity allows individuals who are "there for Mass" to fulfill the Sunday Mass obligation and keep a connection to organized religion. This Mass, however, is not the first of the day for some Dignity members but rather their second Mass, and usually also their second reception of the Eucharist. These members fully support the mission of Dignity but still desire the connection to a recognized Catholic parish.

At an after-Mass dinner to which I was invited during the period of my fieldwork at Dignity, I took special note of a conversation among my companions. One asked the others whether they kept up contacts with their old family or neighborhood parishes. "I go to church here. Dignity is my church," was one response. "Yes, I only go to Dignity, not my parish church," said the other. "Really?" the questioner replied. He was quite surprised that this other member did not retain an affiliation to a parish, as he did, often attending Mass twice on Sundays. In some ways, the Church's exclusionary position on homosexuality made Dignity members *more* conscious of their status as ethnic Catholics. As this man put it, "I wouldn't be a Catholic [today] except for the fact that I was raised as one." Another man at the dinner reported having tried other Christian churches but said he kept returning to Catholic Mass at Dignity. "It's in my blood," he said, "and I have explained it to people that way. I guess I really wouldn't go to church anymore, if it weren't for Dignity." I offered the observation that I found it striking that so many people would go to Dignity Mass on Sunday evening rather than to social events, particularly if they had already attended Mass that day. My companions knew that some viewed Dignity Mass as a social occasion rather than a strictly spiritual one, and they took this in stride. I was told, "Some go to check out the new meat. Others come regularly. You can tell who they are. [Still, many people] are really there for Mass."

Since the Dignity liturgy began at 7:00 p.m., and the Sabbath traditionally lasts from sunset to sunset, Dignity Mass did not fulfill the Sunday obligation in the technical sense set forth by the institutional Catholic Church. Nor were priests officially allowed to say Mass at Dignity without the permission of the local bishop. In fact, Cardinal John Krol, the archbishop of the city at the time of my fieldwork, ordered Philadelphia diocesan priests not to say Mass for Dignity at all. The chapter therefore depended on unique clerical resources: Philadelphia priests who belonged to religious orders less fearful of the cardinal's wrath, priests from other dioceses who traveled to the city to preside at Dignity's Sunday liturgy, and priests who had broken with the hierarchy and now lived in the city. For this reason, Dignity/Philadelphia's priest presiders included parish and religious order priests, as well as men who were on personal sabbaticals from the priesthood and active ministry.[21] As far as Dignity members were concerned, the powers bestowed at priestly ordination were all the legitimacy Dignity's priests needed. For Dignity members, what gave the liturgical acts of these priests further credibility was the personal courage and determination they showed in ministering to gay and lesbian people against the wishes of the hierarchy.

While the great majority of those present at Dignity's Masses had come from traditional Catholic families and diocesan schools in the Philadelphia and southern New Jersey area, there were also non-Catholic Christians in attendance, as well as some Jewish visitors.[22] One Jewish man not only attended the Mass but sang the hymns and knew the words to the prayers, reciting the Sanctus, Agnus Dei, and Our Father along with the congregation. He did not attend every week, but he was more than a casual visitor. He did not receive Communion, but other non-Catholics did.[23] After his day of work with his own congregation, a United Church of Christ minister would secretly come to the Dignity Mass. He noted that he was "liberal in policies and conservative in theology," preaching strict Reformed theology in his sermons. He did not like what he called the "wishy-washy theology" of the gay denomination, the Universal Fellowship of Metropolitan Community Churches (UFMCC), that he had attended in Philadelphia. He felt that because the Metropolitan Community Church tried to please many gay Protestant constituents, its overall theology was weak and undefined. "I don't agree with the Catholics altogether," he told me, "but at least this organization always presents a single [orthodox] view of theology, Church, and sacraments." He did feel a sense of community at Dignity. "They don't ask questions. There's a good feeling here," he said. He enjoyed the fellowship of these gay Christians and was hopeful of developing a possible romantic relationship.

Dignity, like any social group, had its ephemeral elements: the "drop-ins" and "tourists," as a Dignity member named Don described them. For them, Dignity's Masses were the gay Catholic equivalent of the services in the great Catholic cathedrals of Europe during the tourist season, when visitors, usually Catholic, stop in to connect with a larger Catholic community. Dignity member Jeffrey described the community to me as being "like the early Christians hiding away there, celebrating their own beliefs."[24]

One man I spoke to raised money for Dignity's treasury by selling lavender-colored T-shirts and buttons with Dignity/Philadelphia's logo for people to wear during an upcoming Gay Pride weekend. We conversed as he and a friend walked down Thirteenth Street after the Mass, carrying the shirts in a shopping bag. Periodically, they hugged men they knew, tried to sell them shirts, or simply talked openly about which men they thought were attractive. It was against this backdrop, in a neighborhood full of gay bars coming to life at 8:15 on a Sunday evening, that we talked about institutional Catholicism in Philadelphia. The man who designed the T-shirts complained that Cardinal John Krol would not attend a recent ecumenical prayer service for people with AIDS, though the archdiocese did send a representative. "Every Catholic diocese in America had at least an outreach for AIDS victims, and Philadelphia is the only one which doesn't because of Krol, that twisted little bitch," he said. I remarked on this man's depth of involvement with Dignity. "Yes," he answered, "as a regular Catholic, I didn't do much of anything. Now, as a gay Catholic, I'm doing everything . . . selling T-shirts, saying rosaries in public, everything."

Roman Catholic members of Dignity/Philadelphia manage to combine their active homosexual lifestyles with an active commitment to the Roman Catholic faith. This negotiation of Catholicism proceeds in part by means of distinctive understandings of their ethnicity. The Dignity members I came to know were ethnic Catholics by way of nationality; they were ethnically Catholic by their common association with and knowledge of the American Catholic tradition; and they were sexually ethnic Catholics by way of their self-identification as gay, lesbian, bisexual, or transgender people.

Dignity members represented diverse ethnic Catholic backgrounds as the descendants of nineteenth- and early twentieth-century immigrants from Europe (mostly Irish, German, Italian, and Polish). Those traditions remained with them, and, as Dignity member John acknowledged to me, their Catholicism was tied to ethnicity. The depth of cultural sharing they experienced went beyond specific nationalistic commonalities to the level of being "ethnically Catholic" in the United States. That is, as it is for many contemporary American Catholics, their Catholicism, rather than being a particular ethnic heritage, was their specific point of cultural reference.[25] Catholic beliefs, ideas, values, and sensibilities constituted an essential part of their personal identities. They felt a strong attachment to and acceptance of the basic liturgical, theological, sacramental, even ecclesiastical elements of the Catholic tradition. These individuals, many of whom were between thirty and fifty years of age in the late 1980s, had experienced both the unquestioning legalism of pre-Vatican II American Catholicism, communicated to them during their Catholic parochial school education (or Catholic religious instruction), and the unbinding of such strictures in the years following Vatican II.

The connection to Catholic culture for Dignity members naturally extended beyond institutional dogmas, hierarchical activities, and authoritative texts to the social, individual, customary, and material expressions of the religion of American Catholics. These Catholics shared a cultural knowledge that included pre-Vatican II references to holy cards, pagan babies, limbo, mortal sin, Saint Christopher medals, neighborhood parochial schools, and the wearing of white at First Holy Communion. They also shared a post-Vatican II knowledge set that included liturgies in the vernacular, Bible reading, nuns without habits, priests being called by their first names, the placement of Holy Communion in the hand, and the option to drink consecrated wine directly from a chalice. Many recalled parish bingo and altar boy service. Dignity Catholics easily related to each other through the culture of latter twentieth-century American Catholicism, a familiarity of worldview, shared experience, and personal beliefs.

What remained unique about these individuals was their expression of their Catholicism in light of their sexual lives and relationship to gay and lesbian culture. Casual observers might notice that a Dignity liturgy is gay before even noticing that it is Catholic. What has attracted its ecumenical congregation, people unaffiliated with any religion as well as Catholics of every description, is the gayness of the community. Unlike the churches filled by the ethnic European forebears of these men and women, Dignity is not based on nationalistic ties. Rather, Dignity congregations emerged from the desires of these faithful Catholics to live as sexually active gays and lesbians. Reflecting their experience of living in a city of ethnic neighborhoods, many Dignity/Philadelphia members saw themselves not only as part of a "culture" but as a separate ethnicity. This ethnicity, as they defined it, was not constructed, contingent, or fluid; it was a salient feature of their humanity, unifying them through a common biological predisposition. The members of Dignity I conversed with or interviewed explained that they were born "congenitally gay."

Furthermore, they understood this biological reality to be a creation of God, which is crucial to understanding their spirituality as Dignity Catholics. Dignity members would never deny that "gayness" could be traced as a historical construct or a product of culture, but their religious beliefs cemented their feeling of being "born gay" to their perception that God creates all things for a specific purpose. As Jackie, a convert to Roman Catholicism, succinctly explained, "I guess I do think that God created me as gay. I see my being gay as an expression of God's will . . . whether He created it in the womb or before my conception." And to take this point to its theological conclusion, John asked the question, "If God created us gay, did He really create us gay and not expect us to be loving human beings in the full potential that we have . . . ? No God would create you to be not loving."

A feeling of community was built atop an edifice of Catholic and sexual familiarity at Dignity. This intentional community forged a sense of belonging, which many of these Catholics had not felt from a religious group since coming to know themselves as lesbian or gay. Some had left their neighborhood parishes because they felt no support there for themselves as homosexual persons. As Stephen said, "I don't believe that the Catholic Church includes me when they say 'family.'" He added that he was talking about "just the way the Church looks on gay people, which is the way most society looks on gay people: at best pitiful and at worst as criminals and degenerates." Dignity was for many members their only supportive environment for remaining practicing Roman Catholics. "If it wasn't for Dignity," said John, "I'd probably be Episcopalian or Quaker or something. . . . If it wasn't for that I probably would not have this outlet to get in touch with the spiritual side of my being, which helps me." Jeffrey recalled, "Here was this thing you'd grown up with, you've been Catholic for twenty-odd years, and all of a sudden you don't feel like you belong to it anymore. Then you find this group of people who are saying it's okay to be Catholic, it's okay to be gay, come and celebrate with us, and it really felt good."

The intrinsically Catholic appeal of Dignity extended to the membership's recognition of the chapter not as a Catholic club, or even as a movement within the Church, but as a parish. Speaking broadly about American Catholic congregations in the Northeast, Joseph Casino comments that the parish community, as a form or concept, "has been and will be" a "mirror and an example to a constantly changing American society."[26] Beginning in 1969, Dignity became that mirror for gay and lesbian Roman Catholics.[27] During the 1980s, with gay Catholics decimated by AIDS and disconsolate from what many experienced as a complete lack of pastoral regard for persons with AIDS, Dignity grew in strength and solidarity. Dignity openly mourned the dead, prayed for the ill, and publicly acknowledged the suffering and ravages caused by the mysterious disease. And in the worst of the AIDS years, there were actual priests at Dignity giving homilies that said there was nothing wrong or shameful about being gay—even that gay love and gay sex were a normal, natural part of God's creation.

Whether acting as supplement or sole source of Catholic liturgy and community for its members, Dignity assumed as much of a parish role as a lay organization could. In the 1980s there may not have been children running down the aisles, babies crying, or wedding banns being read. A Dignity service was a Mass said in a Protestant church basement. Yet the textures of parish liturgical life were found there: the Sunday Mass, the priest, the homily, the collection basket, and that most essential element, the Eucharist. The makings of a social life were there, as well: dances, socials, and the after-Mass gathering. While Dignity lacked many of the traditional services of a parish, it took on the role of a parish for the gays and lesbians who referred to it not as "Dignity, the special interest organization," or "Dignity, the base community," but simply as they would the parishes of their youth—as "church." Davis, a chapter officer, longed for the day that the liturgical responsibilities of Dignity could be assumed by a "local parish" and Dignity would become "social, a support group." Until then, he said, Dignity "is serving the parish need for me personally." As Loretta perceived it, "one of the reasons Philadelphia's Dignity chapter thrived was because the city was so Catholic, that people transferred the allegiance they felt for their parish into another organization, and also because there is an adversarial position that exists with the archdiocese. And that can be a very strengthening factor to an organization, and that shouldn't be overlooked."

Dignity officials were typically careful not to refer to the organization as a parish for fear of antagonizing the Philadelphia archdiocese. By its very existence, Dignity challenged the Church and its authority. Also by its very existence, it desired to be in union with that institution.

Stephen, a Dignity officer, voiced the contradiction of relating to Dignity as a temporary refuge within the Roman Catholic Church while actually relating to it as his parish:

> Dignity is a group of Catholics, I never say a Catholic group, working within the gay/lesbian community. We have roots here that go back.... We hold weekly Mass. We do much that a regular parish does. If it looks like a duck and walks like a duck . . . We look and act and breathe like a parish. We are a temporary pressure group, but we work as an ethnic parish for gay and lesbian people. That's a distinction that I have to make.

The priests who said Mass at Dignity acknowledged both the Catholic and the ecumenical or community-wide appeal of these services by including a religiously diversified audience in their prayers and homilies. They cooperated with other Philadelphia gay religious groups and invited their ministers or rabbis to preach at or attend Mass on special occasions. The chapter took no measures to enforce the Catholic Church's rule that only Roman Catholics receive the Eucharist. Non-Catholics were permitted to be lectors as well as Eucharistic ministers. In the latter capacity, they assisted with the distribution of the consecrated bread and wine and consumed the remaining uneaten elements.[28] More traditional Catholics who might have dissented from this ecumenism were also quite aware that the organization and its liturgy were completely illicit in the eyes of the institutional Roman Catholic Church.

Members could have their confessions heard at Dignity; they could have their spiritual director at Dignity; they went to Dignity Mass on Sunday and, if desired, on holy days of obligation; they had their throats blessed at Dignity on the feast day of Saint Blaise; they attended midnight Christmas Mass at Dignity; they received blessed palms from Dignity on Palm Sunday; they went on retreats sponsored and organized by the chapter; they went to AIDS memorial services there; they were sent special Christmas and Easter envelopes for their holiday donations to Dignity; they were lectors or Eucharistic ministers at Dignity; they sang or played an instrument in Dignity's music ministry; they could travel to Lourdes or the Vatican on Dignity tours. Like any other Philadelphia parish, Dignity was a social organization as well as a spiritual one. Dignity sponsored seasonal dances, parties, book discussions, CPR training, and bake sales. Members could go jogging with each other. They met and dated people from Dignity. They had dinner and visited the bars with friends from the chapter. I was frequently told that, outside of a bar, Dignity in the 1980s was the largest meeting place for gay men in Philadelphia. One member ventured that "a third of the gay population has been to a Dignity service in Philadelphia."

In any parish context, most members participate in its spiritual or social life and leave committee work and decision making to a smaller group. Dignity was no different. When it came time to nominate officers to run the chapter, there were few people willing to invest the time such offices demanded. In his "Officer's Message" from 1986, then treasurer Mark Ratkus sounds like any pastor calling his flock to more committed participation in parish life:

> Do I assume that Dignity will always be around? I pose this question to myself and to each of you because the vitality and longevity of our Chapter depends on my and your personal response to it. . . . At first glance, the state of our Chapter appears to be superior. However, other considerations about our Chapter temper my optimism. For example, it was difficult recently to elicit willing nominees for Chapter offices and all offices were uncontested. Also, while our weekly offerings have held steady, this is because some members are extremely generous—the implication is that some donate little or nothing. Further, I hear some very active members express the sentiments of "burn-out" or the occasional feeling that their efforts are being taken for granted. How then can we build on Dignity's accomplishments and be confident about the future? Paul speaking to the Church at Ephesus reminds us as well: "Your mind must be renewed by a spiritual revolution so that you can put on the new self that has been created in God's way" (4:23–24). An increase in our *active* community and its membership would extend our ministry of promoting God's way in a truly revolutionary manner. So let's put on our "new selves." Let's stop feeling free to contribute and begin to feel obligated to do so. Let's not just assume that "Dignity will always be around." Let's make sure that it is![29]

Later that year, then executive secretary Kevin Davies sounded a similar note:

> Do you want Dignity to continue as a viable force in the community? Do you enjoy attending Dignity's mass and social hour? Do you appreciate the alternatives Dignity provides in meeting people? Are you able to relate more to the scriptures, teachings and priests by attending Dignity? Do you find the people at Dignity a basically friendly group? Do you want Dignity to continue to grow? Do you want to help Dignity help yourself? Do you feel better about yourself after attending Dignity? Do you think Dignity will be here in ten years? five years? next year?[30]

The questions asked in these 1986 statements can be answered now. Dignity has persevered through attacks from the institutional Catholic Church and indifference and even scorn from members of the LGBT community. Most of the Dignity members I met in the mid-1980s have moved on: to spiritual but not institutionally religious lives; to relationships with other, more accepting Christian denominations; to Catholic parishes with more accepting pastors and congregations; and from this life, sometimes after battling HIV/AIDS, and in more recent years from natural causes. For many of them, Dignity was a stopping-off point of a few weeks, a few months, or a few years in order to affirm and make sense of their identities as both gay and Catholic. A core group of about fifteen members remains from the days of my most intensive fieldwork. Approximating the fluidity of leadership of an archdiocesan parish, Dignity has had several generations of leaders and supporters.

Is Dignity still experienced by its members as an ethnic parish? Two particularly helpful recent responses illuminate how Dignity members view themselves and the chapter they developed. Loretta, who attends Dignity Masses a few times a year, says she conceives of Dignity not so much as an "ethnic" parish but as a "parish":

> There is squabbling within Dignity in Philadelphia. Yet, there is always the sense that you could go there week after week after week, the way you would to your parish, with its own sense of traditions. . . . And when you enter the worship space now, the first thing you notice are a series of ban-

ners with the names of the people [Dignity members] who are deceased. That is very, very powerful. So there you are worshipping with people you may have known for years. Some of whom you do not know.... You also have the sense of the past. That's so clearly right smack in front of you. Almost like you're in a church that has crypts, like down in [Old] St. Mary's where you walk through the crypts to get into the church. It's a very Philadelphia development.... Again... every Dignity chapter takes on the character of the city in which it is located.... Dignity to me right now feels very much like a [Philadelphia] parish.

Stephen remembered telling me that Dignity was his parish. Noting that the chapter is now graying and has difficulty attracting young people, Stephen nevertheless feels quite satisfied with what Dignity/Philadelphia has accomplished. While he hesitated to describe Dignity as an ethnic parish, he could not help but return to familiar images:

It is politically incorrect then and now for me to say that Dignity is a gay ethnic parish because we really are a support group for gay people within the Catholic Church.... I know Dignity/Philadelphia has grown up as a gay ethnic parish.... I think out of necessity we have become a gay ethnic parish. It's not what we were there for, and it's not what we are supposed to be.... Yes, I still think we are.... It's not Dignity's mission to form a parallel church. It is to work with the hierarchy and with the people in the Church to diversify themselves to get rid of their homophobia, to get rid of their sexism. We are to teach them by our lives. We believe the spirit is diverse. We believe the Holy Spirit wants this. We are going to work through the Holy Spirit with our church.... We're not supposed to be a gay ethnic parish, but we've grown into one.

The American Catholic Church of the middle decades of the twentieth century, historian John McGreevy points out, was notable for the crucial role it played "in molding the world of its communicants. At no point before or since have the connections between the Church and its members been as dense; at no point the Catholic culture so cohesive."[31] Dignity members in the 1980s were very much products of that cohesive Catholic culture. As much as they felt demeaned, disdained, and rejected by the institutional Church throughout the 1980s, many gay and lesbian Catholics refused to leave their tradition. These Catholics wanted their Church to accept, embrace, and absorb them and their uniqueness as gays and lesbians. They turned to an ecclesiastical form that they knew, the parish, to model their community. By the new millennium, Dignity/Philadelphia had developed additional parish services, among them inclusive-language hymnals, ceremonies of marital union, and baptisms of children. At a Dignity Mass now, one is likely to find children who run between chairs and fall asleep on the shoulders of their parents.

Gods of the City, a volume of essays edited by Robert Orsi, presents a useful tableau of religious communities that came to populate the spiritual and physical spaces of urban America, including Italian Catholics, Japanese Presbyterians, followers of Yoruba-based Caribbean religions, and members of the Salvation Army. "In the intersection of different cultures on the urban landscape," Orsi writes, "new and interesting cultural forms have taken shape."[32] For generations, gay, lesbian, bisexual, and transgender members of these traditions simply existed within their religious communities, worshipping "alongside" the rest but afraid to express themselves in any public way. Empowered by the sexual revolution and the gay liberation movement of the 1960s, LGBT congregants increasingly claimed a public place in churches and synagogues, some of which might have closed without their presence and support. Dignity became such a religious space for LGBT Roman Catholics.

Against the backdrop of widespread parish closings in cities like Philadelphia, New York, Chicago, and Detroit since the late 1980s and 1990s,[33] Dignity's resilience shows that a dynamic population of practicing Catholics does indeed persist in urban contexts. Catholics in the wake of Vatican II have tended to be more discriminating about their parish membership and to search out a parish community suited to their needs and interests.[34] Many pastors in twenty-first-century America accept the reality of such fluid parish affiliations and are often pleased to be attracting new parishioners, even at the expense of another parish. "Magnet churches," writes Don Brophy, "draw members from territorial churches that lack personality or a distinct culture."[35] Dignity/Philadelphia is such a magnet church, drawing LGBT Catholics from their neighborhood churches in Philadelphia and its suburbs.

These Catholics, often the progeny of Philadelphia's Irish, Italian, German, and Polish immigrants of a century or more ago, may not feel entirely at home in the churches built by their ethnic forebears, yet they still seek out the religion of their childhood. They have created in response their own vernacular parish. The God of the Catholic immigrants has been transformed into their sexually inclusive God, the gay God of the city.

Dignity Catholics are interpreting institutionalized religious beliefs, attitudes, images, and rituals to suit the way they want to express their personal relation to the sacred. Their expressions of personal faith reflect their experience of a religion that both disempowers and empowers them. Their empowering expressions of faith reflect a creativity and artistry of religious expression and self-interpretation that are integral to the negotiations of vernacular religion.

7

What Is Vernacular Catholicism?

The Dignity Example

Although the documents of the Second Vatican Council emphasize the need to understand the Church as inclusive of both the clergy and the faithful, many Catholics continue to assume a dichotomy between a clerical elite maintaining rules and a practicing laity absorbing them. Of course, these members of the hierarchical elite, even in the performance of their sacerdotal functions, are also creatively negotiating their understanding of Catholicism. The creativity of the hierarchy differs from that of lay Catholics in its normative effects. But it is not different in kind from the creative negotiating that takes place throughout the Church.

An example of such negotiation within the Church that I have researched extensively is the Philadelphia chapter of Dignity, the "national lay movement of lesbian, gay, bisexual and transgendered [Roman] Catholics, their families and their friends."[1] While countless gay and lesbian Catholics worship in traditional parish settings, members of Dignity have banded together as witnesses to their belief that God created them in the fullness of their embodied, relational being, and that they as gay and lesbian Catholics are worthy of recognition and equality as members of the Church. Dignity's activities predate the Stonewall riots by a year and the emergence of "queer theology" by some two or three decades. Around the time that I began my research, in the late 1980s, Dignity described its aim as "working within the Church for the development of its sexual theology, for the acceptance of gay and lesbian persons as full and equal members, and to elicit responsive approaches both inside and outside the entire Roman Catholic Church."[2]

Dignity/Philadelphia, the organization's Philadelphia chapter, traces its origins to a series of home liturgies that began in 1973. Its existence

---

Originally published in 2001.

has never been sanctioned by the Archdiocese of Philadelphia, and Dignity's liturgical or business activities have never been permitted to take place on Church property. For most of its existence, the chapter has rented space in Episcopal Church halls and sanctuaries. Yet although it has of necessity carved out separate physical space from which to affirm and minister to gay and lesbian Catholics, Dignity has never broken from the institutional Church. It has retained an allegiance to Roman Catholic dogma and tradition. At the same time, Dignity maintains the central principle that it is not immoral for a gay or lesbian Catholic to live an actively homosexual life.

How do these gay and lesbian Catholics reconcile themselves, as believers, to the traditions, teachings, and practices of the institutional Church? They have consciously added to or subtracted from the Catholic faith as they understand it, and to their satisfaction. One Dignity member described this action, what he called "rationalizing" the diverse elements of his "lived experience," as the "gymnastics of faith." Others described their practice in the familiar language of "á la carte," "cafeteria," and "pick-and-choose" Catholicism, but without the implication that there was anything wanting in such an approach. This was the case with Father Jake, the undesignated chaplain of Dignity/Philadelphia, with whom I spoke about the decisions he made about his religious life.

> LEONARD NORMAN PRIMIANO: Now, what would you say if someone said to you that you're involved in a theological cafeteria?
> FATHER JAKE: That may be true, [but] what is theology? Maybe that's where it needs to be done, [in] some cafeteria. Because we are talking about food and drink, whether it be intellectual or spiritual or pastoral. We're talking about feeding: take and eat, feed my sheep . . . the food of life, the source of life. OK, I am [choosing] food in a cafeteria.
> LNP: At the same time, you're deciding that sometimes what the chef serves, you don't have to take.
> FJ: And I don't have to.
> LNP: Because you're very perfectly nourished by the foods that you're able to choose from the line yourself?
> FJ: Yes, because they have all been produced by the chef. I don't have to eat everything that the chef puts out. Nor do I have to be goggle-eyed

over his special dish; I might get sick. Yes, since the chef brought this out, if I was present when he produced this fantastic thing and I said, Could I . . . have the recipe for that? And he said: Oh sure, here. And then next week he decides that never ever will this food be served again, and I'm over here with the recipe saying: Tough, I liked it. And I have a good reason [for this thinking], and that is theology. We must make a distinction between theology and authority, and maintain the authority of theology.

The vernacular religious life is influenced by any number of available resources, and for Catholics, the multitude of beliefs and practices represented within institutionalized and non-institutionalized Catholicism offer rich sources of inspiration. Dignity Catholics have found support for living gay and lesbian religious lives in the documents of the Second Vatican Council, which underscored for the faithful the importance of the primacy of conscience. Like other American Catholics who disagree with the Church's stances on sexual morality (from artificial contraception to divorce to abortion), Dignity Catholics appeal to what Father Jake described as "the ultimate right of the individual's conscience," which "has really been maintained by the Church throughout the ages." The authority of theology he referred to in our conversation was the primacy of his own reflections and conscience in achieving a satisfying religious life. He felt a sense of creative control over his own religious destiny, and he had no intention of relinquishing that personal responsibility. His keen understanding and interpretation of how Catholic theology worked allowed him to use the hierarchy's own instruments of doctrinal order and control to define his religious life. With learning and theological sensitivity nurtured in Catholic contexts, Father Jake transformed an "official" concept of Church into an experiential model suited to his spiritual, psychological, and social needs.

Like other Roman Catholics, Dignity members find inspiration for their religious lives in the sacred sources, traditions, and history of the Church, and in their lived experiences. Those I came to know saw their identities as religious men and women, and homosexual men and women, fulfilled in their own understanding of the Catholic faith and Catholic community. This is why they could remain within a religious tradition whose public face so often regarded them with scorn. For the same reason, both extreme traditionalists and extreme liberals, all actively gay, all Roman Catholic, all vernacularly Catholic, could be found worshipping together at Dignity.

Vernacular Catholicism is the uniquely Catholic formulation of the vernacular religious impulse shared by all religious people. It is the way a Catholic individually expresses his or her understanding of the Catholic tradition, including the history, structures, laws, customs, beliefs, and practices of its people. Vernacular Catholicism involves absorbing, learning, accepting, changing, denying, embellishing, and appreciating the spiritual and cultural parameters of Catholicism in one's life. It is manifested by Catholic believers and evidenced within the widest range of Catholic institutions: the Vatican hierarchy; the vast system of clerical functionaries throughout the universal Church; sacred environments and objects; scripture and interpretation; dogmatic pronouncements and doctrinal explanations; liturgy and paraliturgical practices, including the Mass, the sacraments, pilgrimage, and devotions; the monastic communal and religious life; educational organizations, including seminaries, the parochial school system, and missions; the parish system; Christian base communities; lay social and spiritual organizations; religious festivals and public celebrations; private belief, devotionalism, and religious practices; and the individual uses of sacramentalism. Expressions of vernacular Catholicism among members of Dignity, as within the Catholic community at large, can be observed via two specific contexts: the religious beliefs and practices of the individual Catholic, and the vernacular religion of the group. I focus here on the vernacular religion of the individual because it is there that vernacular religious creativity can be seen most vividly.

At the individual level, the Dignity members I came to know manifested the same kind of traditional piety, creative devotionalism, and individual flourishes one finds at any other Catholic home, parish, or gathering. Such expressions could be observed in specific ways, among them gestures, lay theologies, material culture, habits, and ways of socializing. At a Dignity Mass in New York City, I recall seeing a man holding the hand of the statue of the dead Jesus as he placed the Communion wafer in his mouth. An informant related to me a complex spiritual insight about Jesus's Sacred Heart and the Real Presence. Mass-produced religious ephemera, such as holy cards and inexpensive prayer books, were often found at the Dignity information table before and after Sunday liturgy. A Dignity prayer group met weekly for the recitation of the rosary. Like many American Catholics, some members of Dignity rushed to exit the Mass immediately after the distribution of Communion. Some attended morning Mass at local archdiocesan parishes as well as the evening Dignity service.[3]

Of course, such expressions of piety and belonging had the additional quality for Dignity members of being filtered and negotiated through their unique perspective as gay Catholics. During the time of my fieldwork in the late 1980s, the weekly recitation of the rosary by more traditionalist members was specifically intended as a prayer for those suffering from AIDS. The prayers they voiced for the Church's hierarchy were often directed against its refusal to acknowledge or support its gay flock. This is not to say that Dignity members could never relate to their religion without a gay reference. But they did possess a strong sense of themselves as gay Catholics, and they used their time at Dignity gatherings to affirm their sense of gay Catholic community.

When these Catholics meditated on Christ, they were thinking of him as a single man among other men, and, for some, as a man who had a special friendship with his apostle John. When they thought of the Virgin Mary, they personalized that devotion by thinking of her as their own mother, the mother of a son who never married and who did not fulfill the heterosexual expectations of his day. My informant who told me of his supernatural insight about the mysteries of the Sacred Heart of Jesus took Communion at daily morning Mass at his local parish. In his relationship with Jesus in the Eucharist, he explained to me, he experienced a personal meshing of his Catholic and gay sensibilities:

> Communion kept me together, and every day I felt like this unconditional love had loved me and then I'd go off to my dark night of confusion and misery [as a gay man]. But I always felt that for this early morning hour, this love had come and really loved me, and that was really great, and I felt the Sacred Heart of Jesus was for me all the intensity of love I could have ever wanted to experience from a human person. It was like this man came to me every day and he loved me every day, and Jesus was his name.

Vernacular religious negotiations like this man's have been in evidence throughout the history of the Roman Catholic tradition, influencing everything from personal practice to the codification of belief within institutions. From the rise of the cult of the saints in early Latin Christianity to post-industrial Marian pilgrimage, from the formation of Dignity Masses to the unwelcoming writings of Cardinal Joseph Ratzinger about homosexual people, vernacular religious expressions involve believers in personal acts of interpretation and practice. The vernacular process begins with the synthesis of an original vernacular religious insight with the social interaction of family, community, and tradition. The original vernacular creations of individuals most certainly will be lost over time, but a rich process of vernacular interpretation continues, whether it involves a believer in acts of preservation, innovation, or radical change. Through the agreement of a community of like-minded individuals, interpretations can be preserved and concertized as religious institutions. While the vernacular religious voices of the original innovators may be obscured, the creative action of the constant negotiation of religion remains a consistent quality within those institutions.

In 1985 Dignity embarked on an ambitious plan to present its own statement on sexual ethics "to our brothers and sisters in the lesbian and gay community, and to the wider Church."[4] It was the desire of Dignity's leaders that this document would complement the organization's mission as a support group and community of resistance. Dignity's core members wanted to be more than simply a movement on the defensive. What these individuals desired was for Dignity to behave like the institutional Church and theologize, but to do so from the foundation of their lives as gay Catholics. A Dignity chapter president explained to me that this was because "up until now Dignity has been trying to, as it were, defend its existence; once we get beyond that point of no longer having to fight for survival, then we can begin to discuss principles like genital activity, and promiscuity, etc."

For Dignity members, incorporating the voices of the faithful into theological statements concerning them was felt to be a style of theologizing that followed the documents of the Second Vatican Council both in spirit and letter. The act of preparing a statement on sexual ethics, as much as its content, represented a challenge to the authority of the Catholic hierarchy. It said, in effect, that the faithful, and not only the hierarchy, could and would provide theological direction and policy about sexual ethics in general and about the sexual morality of gays and lesbians in particular. Jake, who was a member of the Sexual Ethics Task Force, noted, "We are beginning to move into that area of a self-reflection or a self-examination in light of Gospel values as they apply to our lifestyle, rather than to justify our lifestyle in light of Gospel principles for somebody else."

Dignity as an organized group wished to represent the lived experiences and personal negotiations of its members in its own statement of sexual theology. Formally completed in 1989 and published as "Sexual Ethics: Experience, Growth, Challenge," the statement was a work of theology by a community of North American Catholics who wished, based on their experience, to challenge the traditional Roman Catholic understanding of who speaks with authority on the issue of morals. Here, Dignity Catholics were interpreting institutionalized religious beliefs, attitudes, images, and rituals to suit the way they wanted to express their personal relation to the sacred. Their expressions of personal faith reflected their experience of a religion that both disempowered and empowered them. Their empowering expressions of faith reflected a creativity and artistry of religious expression and self-interpretation that are integral to the negotiations of vernacular religion.

Dignity members have brought what they have felt and learned as gay people to their experience as Roman Catholics. Their ability to sustain and nurture religious belief, and to deepen association with the Church in the face of rejection and exclusion, points to religious motivations intrinsic to their Catholic lives. Their integration of gay and Catholic identities, validated by both individual and communal experience, is exemplary of vernacular Catholicism. Their example helps us, in turn, to apprehend vernacular religion as the practiced religion of all believers.

If the remarkable faith of Dignity/Philadelphia's gay Catholic men allowed them to negotiate the demands of their homosexuality with the challenges of participation in the life of the Church, then the faith of the chapter's lesbians was even more extraordinary. These women negotiated their own sexual orientation and Catholic faith not only within the male-dominant Church but also within the male-dominant climate of Dignity.

8

"I Would Rather Be Fixated on the Lord"

Women's Religion, Men's Power, and the Dignity Problem

My study of the Philadelphia chapter of Dignity was based on fieldwork completed during the years 1986 and 1987. As in all folklife studies of contemporary religion, my work was informed by the perspectives of my interlocutors, in this case the Dignity members themselves. My goal, however, was not merely to look at the beliefs and practices of gay and lesbian Roman Catholics as contesting the Church's moral and hierarchical positions.[1] I desired to focus on Dignity members' vernacular religion, religion as it is lived.[2] While learning about these individuals' lived systems of belief, I was privy to their personal critiques not only of institutional Roman Catholicism but of Dignity itself as a spiritual and social community. The women of Dignity, although small in number, had a unique perspective on Catholicism and on Dignity itself. These women are the focus of this chapter.

During my fieldwork, I was surprised to discover a distinctive lack of female presence at the group's liturgies. At a typical Sunday Mass with 235 individuals present, perhaps only ten would be women. The number of women who were dues-paying members of the chapter was only slightly higher. How and why did this most marginalized of religious groups, homosexual Catholics, itself marginalize the community of homosexual Catholic women? Why was Dignity, a self-described "community of gay and lesbian Catholics and their friends," so unappealing, alienating, even repulsive to lesbian Catholics? This is the "Dignity problem" of my title.

Dignity/Philadelphia, like other metropolitan chapters of Dignity, represented a new configuration within the context of American Catholicism and American religious history. It came into being as an

---

Originally published in 1993.

urban, ethnic parish, like those formed by the institutional hierarchy to accommodate masses of immigrant Catholics to America many decades earlier. However, it was based not on ties of national origin or neighborhood and geographical boundaries but on sexual orientation. It was not a creation of institutional directives but of the desires of these faithful believers. Among those desires was the right to live as a homosexual person in a community that defined itself as affirming of sexual activity. My research revealed that Dignity members identified themselves as a separate ethnic community and lived the culture of gayness as a new form of ethnicity. Their sexual identities transcended any loyalty to geography of origin. Theirs was an ethnicity by way of biological predisposition. They were born "congenitally gay." As one informant told me, "I consider it [homosexuality] the way I was born. If one thing made me homosexual, it was God."[3] Another explained that while being gay was for him a choice, his homosexuality was not:

> Being homosexual, and I'll speak for the male gender, is where one man is erotically aroused by another man and possibly although not necessarily chooses to act out on that and have genital relationships. Being gay adds to that an identity of, Yes I am attracted to men, Yes it's good. I'm going to identify myself with other men who are like that. I'm not going to be clandestine about that. . . . I don't feel that homosexuality is a matter of choice. It is something you are or are not, it is a given. Being gay is a matter of choice because you have to choose whether or not you're going to make that proclamation of self-identification.

There is among most Dignity members a strong sense of gay and lesbian culture and community as a matter of chosen affiliation, and of homosexual desire as God-given and innate. In this regard, it could be said that Dignity does express a spiritual, not only a psycho-social, dimension of gay existence.[4]

The singular characteristic of the chapter's gay identity must be explained. In this context, I use the term "gay" to specify male homosexuality. I specifically mean that Dignity represented a culture of men, and a gender-conservative culture that distinctly excluded lesbians.[5] It was not that the men of Dignity made women unwelcome in word or even in deed. The problem was the pervasively gendered atmosphere of Dignity itself. To begin with, there were just so many men there. In one sense, it was quite stirring to hear the combined sonority of so many male voices reciting the liturgical responses and bellowing out the evening's hymns. Such unity of expression was emblematic of the enthusiasm bred by strength in numbers that these men felt while at Dignity. But as one woman I brought to the service told me after Mass, the exclusively male nature of the gathering made the experience intimidating to her from the moment she entered the door of the Episcopal church basement where the chapter held its Sunday services.

Apart from there being so few women congregants, the Dignity Masses I attended were characterized by a lack of female presence in the liturgy itself. While some women took part in the weekly liturgy as lectors, Eucharistic ministers, and even the occasional invited homilist, there were no women celebrants of the liturgy. As much as Dignity questioned the Church's male hierarchy on issues of sexual morality, it wished to remain in some way aligned with the institution that male hierarchy administered. The illicit celebration of Mass by female clergy would separate the group from the institutional Church. Such an action would defeat the whole purpose of Dignity's existence. Many men felt that battles could be fought over female participation in the clergy only after the present hierarchy could be convinced that there was nothing immoral about being a sexually active gay Roman Catholic.

I do not want to give the impression that the men were oblivious to the chapter's dearth of women members. Its administrators tried hard to attract women to the chapter by changing the liturgy's sexist language and by urging its visiting priests and congregation to include women and their concerns in their general attitudes. Dignity nevertheless styled itself an enclave of male culture in a male environment. Dignity gatherings presented an occasion and a setting outside the bar scene for men to assert themselves as gay and to revel in a gay institution of their own creation. No matter how conscious the men of Dignity/Philadelphia were of the undesirability of excluding women from this setting, the enjoyment of their own groupness within the perceived legitimate context of a religious organization was too powerful a cultural stimulant to resist.

The folklore of the group—its humor, metaphors, and personal experience narratives, as these were expressed at its Sunday liturgies in homilies, voiced intentions of the congregation, post-Communion remarks, and announcements—centered almost exclusively on the male experience of being gay, the male body, and male sexuality. I recall the remark made on November 23, 1986, by a man who normally expressed sympathy for the cause of a greater female presence within Dignity. The chapter was planning a bus excursion to New York City to visit a gay club. "If you want a hot, throbbing time in New York City," the man said, "you've got to get to it by Greyhound." It was not surprising to hear a priest tell the congregation about his own interest in men and his own sexual desires. From the very first Mass I attended on February 2, 1986, I noticed that the celebrant's attempts to relate to the congregation using empathy and humor excluded the women present. Remarks in the homily, such as "the real sticky issues of sexuality, and I hope you grasp the full meaning of that," were greeted with laughter by most of the men in attendance. Most but not all: Jackie,[6] a member of Dignity who described himself as "conservative at least theologically," told me that he personally found it inappropriate to a religious setting when at the end of Mass a priest commented on a Dignity social function in another city: "He was talking about [attending] a party . . . and he just said it's going to be on Easter and we're going to experience everything from erections to resurrections."

It was not that lesbians drawn to Dignity were incapable of being openly erotic or pornographic on their own behalf. The point is that the eroticism stressed by the group was so exclusively male: defined by the male body and male sexual needs. For example, over a series of Sundays between November 1986 and January 1987, graphically illustrated "Safer Sex Comix" were distributed to the congregation. These were produced by Gay Men's Health Crisis Inc. of New York City to educate gay men on how to avoid contracting and transmitting the AIDS virus. When the group was cautioned about the sexually explicit nature of the "Comix" by an officer during the post-Mass announcements, the reaction of the majority of the assembled was knowing laughter. Again, the problem was not that overtly sexual material was offensive to the women at Mass but rather that the focus of the sexuality presented was entirely on men.

Within the chapter, a Committee for Women's Concerns did meet to discuss relevant issues and hold separate paraliturgies. Still, when women approached the liturgical and social center of Dignity/Philadelphia, their lesbian and female sexuality was ignored or dismissed.

While the humor, metaphors, and narratives of Dignity during the period of my fieldwork may have been aimed at a critique of the values of heterosexual culture, they did more than simply exclude women. They often derided women. In her July 6, 1986, announcement of an upcoming chapter trip to Washington, DC, a woman on the Education Committee said that her visit to the capital might be an occasion to meet "a nice woman." A male officer spoke immediately after her in a joking tone: "With my luck, I'll meet a nice woman in Washington, too." His disappointing luck, in other words, would be to meet a nice *woman*, a person who would not interest him sexually, whatever her qualities as a potential friend or ally.

How comfortable were the women of Dignity, I wondered, with the predilection of gay men in the chapter for expressing their sexual identity through the use of camp?[7] Don, a male informant, volunteered that "we [gay men] don't often know how to talk about our sexuality other than in sleaze terms. Because for so long we were inculcated with the belief that our sexuality was sleazy. And so that's how we joke about it: we camp up as 'sluts,' as 'whores.' We don't necessarily mean it, but that's the way we viewed it." Men in the Philadelphia chapter of Dignity referred to each other as "Dignettes," and some called each other by women's names or slipped into the use of feminine pronouns when speaking of one another. When a social function such as a party or the chapter anniversary dinner dance was coming up, an officer might tell the congregation at the weekly announcements to "get your ball gowns and beauty shop reservations." Whether the "camping" of female qualities by gay men aims to contest traditional male values and qualities, traditional female values and qualities, heterosexual culture, or even homosexual culture is a question of some scholarly debate. In any case, the concentration of humor in the caricaturing of women might well have been experienced by the women of Dignity as dismissive. The men of Dignity made women's sexuality into an object of humor. And as the perceived referents of such humor, women were excluded from taking part in it.

The larger question for women drawn to Dignity/Philadelphia was whether they could ever feel comfortable in general within a setting so clearly maintained as an outpost and haven of gay male culture. Loretta, reflecting on her experience as a member of the Dignity community, offered this insight:

> Think about the conditioning that the gay men have done to themselves about what it means to be homosexual. You know the emphasis is on the sex part of it, so if the only way they've ever been social with other gay men is in the context of the bar, in the context of a place where it is clearly the idea to meet someone, then what makes you think that they are going to radically alter their behavior? And is it legitimate to expect it?

Debra, an otherwise devoted member of Dignity, found it difficult even to attend on certain weeks. She told me,

> There are both feminist lesbians and non-feminist lesbians at Dignity. You'll laugh—and Nancy knows this (Nancy is my lover)—I really have to get myself psyched up to go to Dignity because I know sometimes I will be the only woman there. Sometimes I'm going to be offended by the language or I'm going to be offended by the body language of some of the men, and I have to almost put myself in a frame of mind that [I am] willing to go down there and deal with that. Now I've made conscious decisions: when I'm tired I don't go down there because I'm quick to shout out and react to that. And so I prepare myself; it's a conscious choice for me to be at Dignity on Sunday nights, where I never take it for granted that, well, if I'm not ready to receive some of these overt masculine things, I choose not to go down. I just see that as long as . . . I feel there's hope . . . I can also put those blinders on, as long as I see people trying.

Some lesbians, like Debra, fought gay male dominance at Dignity but remained there. Debra found that Dignity affirmed her Catholicism more than it did her lesbianism. Another woman, Joanne, did not experience the same discomfort. This singular informant was a non-lesbian who attended Dignity because of her own critical opinions of the institutional Church, and because she liked the chapter's Masses. She recognized that many men, including the undesignated chaplain of the chapter, did not like women. Her vernacular spirituality, however, allowed her to overlook this failing. When asked about such issues at Dignity, Joanne said that these were not her concerns. She remarked, "I would rather be fixated on the Lord," and she felt that Dignity *was* a comfortable place to follow her beliefs.

Of all the men at Dignity that I spoke to concerning the paucity of female participation, only one member, Greg, associated the difficulty for women at Dignity with the group's very association with the Catholic Church. He linked the liturgical setting of the Episcopal church basement of St. Luke and The Epiphany to a feeling of solidarity among the congregation: "When you're downstairs, it feels like a lot of people, and it feels like, 'Oh, aren't we strong!' You're a little bit dwarfed by the structure upstairs . . . you get swallowed up upstairs." Obviously, many women had the opposite feeling. Their lack of presence indicated that they experienced being "swallowed up" no matter what liturgical space the Philadelphia chapter occupied, and they did not find it very comforting or rewarding. As Greg explained,

> GREG: [The women] feel outnumbered, and you walk in and all you see is men. And the biggest problem with the Church is how patriarchal it is, and to them *we* probably look like the embodiment of that. We bend over backwards to use the right language and to get women involved. In fact, they are probably overrepresented proportionally on committees and boards just because we are desperate to get as many involved as we can. There are so *few* of them. The few we have are involved in everything, which I don't have a problem with. It's just an interesting note. I don't know what *we* could possibly do to get them in. *We'd* have to change the Catholic Church first and start ordaining women, get a female Pope. I just don't think I'll *see* that in my lifetime.
> LEONARD NORMAN PRIMIANO: Is it because of the environment of the Catholic Church that women don't come or is it because of the environment of this chapter? Is there something in the environment here that doesn't feel good for women?
> GREG: Yes, because even though we are very different from the Church, we are also very much like the Church. We are a reflection of the Church. Our liturgy is virtually identical except for some word changes, some slightly different thinking in terms of sexual issues, so we're not that different from the Church. . . . So I don't think it's a flaw in the chapter, there's nothing more we can do than what we're doing to get them in. . . . There is male innuendo because it's the men doing it.

Women like Loretta eventually found Dignity so stultifying that they discontinued their affiliation with the chapter. It was Loretta who offered me the clearest explanation for why Dignity marginalized women. In her view, it was the fact that the men there failed to realize that lesbians did not express their sexuality in the same way as men. As Loretta said,

> Yes, I happen to be a lesbian, and the way in which my lesbianism affects my life is sometimes extremely important. But in the scheme of things, my sexuality itself, the amount of time I am a sexual person, intimate with another person, is minimal. The problem with society is that by focusing on the word "sex" in homosexuality, there is an assumption that sex is a dominating definition in a person's life. For most of us, it isn't that way at all. I personally believe that women are raised to think of themselves as sexual in the context of a relationship, whereas men are raised to think of themselves as sexual. Period. So that sex is something that can occur many, many times with many different people. And it's an aspect of you that's constantly present. Whereas women become sexual once they're involved with another person. If I am sounding critical of men, it's not just gay men; I guess I'm critical of the fact that we have different ways of viewing sexuality in our culture.

A message dramatically preached by a visiting priest on Sunday, February 23, 1986, highlighted the sexual nature of the spirituality being forged at Dignity. The point of his homily was not only that gay people deserve fulfilling sexual lives; as the special people of God, they represented a new understanding of the relationship between the sex act and love.

> Gay men and lesbian women must cultivate positive ideas now, when the vector forces are trying to destroy our hard-earned moment of love. The Kingdom of God is a kingdom for gays, transsexuals, transvestites, and maybe straights [*laughter*]. For our own meaning and for our gay children—metaphorically speaking—we must believe that God loves us. . . . There is a danger to internalize that gay is second best, that gay love is not God's plan. I hold a diametrically opposing view. If the Christian believed in the love of Jesus, there would be more gay love, not less of it. All forms of love would be accepted. We want to return the compli-

ment to God for being made in his image. We believe God is good and we must say this. We believe we deserve sex, and we do, but [for some reason] not love. God challenges, calls, and seduces us into love. Jesus allows me to transfigure your self-negating doubt. I am yourself in body and blood and you deserve nothing better than me, the crucifixion. God transforms what we crucify into love. We can only be gay and conquer AIDS in God. I know I shall see all those young men who proceeded [sic] us into eternal life.

This priest was addressing a new dynamic between sex and love championed by the gay community. The old heterosexual stereotypes and prohibitions were being broken down by gay people. He did not choose to say that these formulations were the result of an impotence among gay men to love, to be faithful, to have stable, lasting relationships due to years of sexual repression and lack of role models. The message of this homily was that the new definitions and relationships of sex, love, monogamy, and marriage were blessed by God. The Dignity community, though in a period of doubt caused by the AIDS crisis, needed to be reminded that their public representation of private values challenging the Catholic Church's sexual morality made them a prophetic institution. They were the truth-seekers and truth-speakers within the Church as they fought for a greater understanding of human sexuality and its relationship to God, the God who created the reality of gay and lesbian sexuality and love in the first place. They deserved the expression of the sexuality that is a part of their created nature. The free expression of that sexuality in the homosexual sex act was a sign of their redemptive role in creation. This is the role that they were created to fulfill, having been made in the image and likeness of God. God's creation would only be fulfilled on earth when homosexual love was accepted and celebrated as another discovery in the wonder of God. Dignity, the innovator, was celebrated in this homily, as well as Dignity, the rebel.

As a dissenting voice, Loretta used her feeling that she was innately homosexual to criticize this entire idea, present at Dignity in homilies like the above and often in personal remarks, that Dignity members, by right of their homosexuality and attendant suffering, were a special people of God:

> I do believe that homosexuality is congenital. I do believe that I was born a lesbian. There was a wonderful old joke that actually was kind of stupid: "My mother made me a lesbian." "Oh, if I send her the wool, would she make me one too?" . . . I don't think that people raise their children to be homosexual. Everybody raises their children to be heterosexual. So that when I use the word *raised*, "the way men or women are raised," I'm just talking about the cultural influences. I do think our sexualities are established, who knows why, before birth. . . . God created me, I happen to be gay. Why should I emphasize, at this point in my life, the gayness over the femaleness, or the Irishness, or any other aspect? [When I was in Dignity,] I was more caught up with my lesbianism at that point, but I don't think I was any more deserving of God's love because I'm lesbian, or any less deserving, and that's really more to the point.

Here, Loretta is reflecting on the perception of some men in Dignity of being part of a moral elite, a chosen people. The notion that one is "congenitally gay" is, in a way, connected to the Christian ideal of the imitation of Christ in his passion and martyrdom, aspects of his life that were out of his control in the same way that gays and lesbians believe that their sexual orientation is out of their control. A part of their role in creation is to suffer and be persecuted like Christ because of their sexual identity, and in that suffering they achieve a status of a moral vanguard in relation to the rest of the Church and to the non-gay and non-Catholic majorities in society.

Loretta did not accept such interpretations within her own religious worldview. The spirituality that emerged from Dignity was unsatisfactory, in Loretta's view, because it was too centered on sexuality. For her, sexuality was an aspect of one's life, not the center. It was a male idea, she felt, to associate sexuality and identity that way. The whole meaning and purpose of Dignity's existence, in Loretta's experience, was a masculine interest in having gay sexuality blessed by the Church. She told me,

> It's such a narrow thing on which to pin your spirituality, isn't it? . . . [Especially] if we have a hard time with the Roman Catholic Church zeroing in on sexuality as the be-all and end-all of morality, which is one of the big problems, in my opinion, with the Roman Catholic Church, and it's not only with the question of homosexuals. It's far greater with the

question of women and the role of women and the purpose of women. It hinges on sexuality. If we have a hard time with that, then it seems to me that we have to evolve beyond that. And to stay in Dignity, and keep Dignity as your main focus, is doing the exact same thing. It's retaining the emphasis on your sexuality as a way of identifying yourself as a Catholic. For me, it's sensible that you evolve out of that.

For Loretta, Dignity stood as a metaphor for men's preoccupation with sexuality, no matter their sexual orientation or religious identity. In this sense, it had more in common with the hierarchy and agenda of the Roman Catholic Church than it did with the spiritual lives and social needs of Catholic lesbians. For Dignity/Philadelphia, the problem had no resolution. Despite the best intentions of Dignity's liberal membership and its nonsexist constitutional statements, Dignity's sexual climate caused most women who joined to eventually depart. Sentiments aside, women were not honored at Dignity. My research with the Dignity community has shown me that it was not a friendly place for women. It was not an inviting setting for women to come and laugh with the men about the absurdity of living as sexual beings. It was a place where women experienced the same frustrations and anger as they did elsewhere.

If the remarkable faith of Dignity/Philadelphia's gay Catholic men allowed them to negotiate the demands of their homosexuality with the challenges of participation in the life of the Church, then the faith of the chapter's lesbians was even more extraordinary. These women negotiated their own sexual orientation and Catholic faith not only within the male-dominant Church but also within the male-dominant climate of Dignity. Dignity, at this period, faced the continued challenge, if it wished to achieve the sexual ecumenism it claimed for itself and demanded from the Church, of creating a gender-inclusive climate of both homosexual and Catholic belief and practice.

PART III

Father and Mother Divine

In August 1942, at a Philadelphia service, using the performance of a song as the foundation for his message, Father Divine reminded his followers about the creative meaning of their song and music traditions and how sincerity should be at the center of any such outward spiritual expression. Today, in 2008, such "inspirations" exist in abundance and are an example of a living tradition of American religious song located within the still-active remnant of the Peace Mission found in Philadelphia, under the leadership of an ever-robust Mother Divine. The musical tradition of this intentional community encompasses a repertoire of thousands of songs, with hundreds in active use.

9

"The Consciousness of God's Presence Will Keep You Well, Healthy, Happy, and Singing"

The Tradition of Innovation in the Music of Father Divine's Peace Mission Movement

I first read Arthur Huff Fauset's account of Father Divine in the 1980s, as a doctoral student at Fauset's alma mater, the University of Pennsylvania. Don Yoder, the dean of American folklife studies, liked to use *Black Gods of the Metropolis* in his classes, including "Sects and Cults in American Religion." The text spotlighted groups Yoder felt were extremely important for understanding the full picture of religion in America. Fauset's descriptions of the believers he encountered mirrored the ethnographic work that Yoder had done since the late 1940s with the Pennsylvania Germans, another understudied American sect. Yoder's admiration stemmed from Fauset's attempt to create a historical and contemporary picture of American religiosity based on fieldwork—direct contact with believing men and women. Furthermore, to his enormous credit, Fauset was one of the first scholars of American religion to take seriously the study of "sects" and "cults," and especially African American sects and their leaders, including Father Divine. Fauset did not write derisive exposés on Father Divine's sexuality, money, or possessions but rather worked to achieve what he felt was a dignified analysis through ethnographically based research.[1] The fact that Fauset's research was primarily centered in the city of Philadelphia and that a Peace Mission hotel, the Divine Tracy, along with its public cafeteria, could be found only a few blocks from Yoder's Penn classroom in West Philadelphia satisfied him even more, because the students could experience at close range at least one of the communities that Fauset had studied.

Originally published in 2009.

Being trained in the folklife studies approach by Yoder, I recognized that attention to the nuances of everyday life is a singularly important contribution that ethnographic work can make to understanding religious culture. It encourages emphasis on aesthetic or artistic creation, historical process, and the construction of mental, verbal, or material forms. Furthermore, such ethnographic work can illuminate the relationship and balance of utility and creativity in such forms within particular contexts.[2] As a budding folkloristic ethnographer especially interested in the expressive culture of religious movements, I was therefore delighted that Fauset opened his discussion of Father Divine's Peace Mission Movement not with a portrait of Father Divine, as so many other authors had done, but with the moving account of the conversion of a male follower named Sing Happy.[3] Fauset offered a portrait of this man, including Sing Happy's powerful testimony of how Father Divine helped him gain stability in his life and robustness in his health during seven years of committed belief in this religious leader, thought to be an incarnation of God on earth. Fauset also thoughtfully included an explanation of how this follower received his spiritual name. Sing Happy made a public testimony with his name every day, conveying the importance of the tradition of singing in the lives and rituals of the Peace Mission membership. Fauset's approach to studying this man and his religious community can be viewed as folkloristic in nature, as he was mindful of this religion's rhythms of work, play, eating, and ritual, as well as the powerful familiarity of the musical and lyrical soundscapes that accompanied those occasions. Throughout his study, Fauset was particularly attentive to the music and songs of the Peace Mission, noting how, in the case of one female follower, the rhythm of life was best described through song.[4]

In paying attention to the beliefs and practices of such followers and by giving attention to how they expressed themselves—privately, publicly, ritually—Fauset both challenged and reassessed the scholarly and popular impression of the stiffness and rigidity of the members of so-called sects and cults.[5] Still, many questions appear to have been left unasked by Fauset. How, for example, did the variety of songs fit into the lives of followers and connect to Father Divine himself? What was it about the expressive culture of the Peace Mission that prompted a child of Father Divine to "sing happy" and experience such improved health?

Fauset, of course, was trained as a traditional sociocultural anthropologist of his time. Thus, while attentive to the worldview of members of African American sects, especially in such symbolic forms as their expressive arts of song, testimonial, and costume/dress, he tended to emphasize these groups in the chapters of *Black Gods* as social institutions relating to African American and non–African American society. After the opening sketch of Sing Happy, Fauset assumes in this text a rather conventional anthropological stance of using the testimony of this man as a springboard for a discussion of the structure, social and hierarchical organization, finances, membership, history, and rituals of the Peace Mission. As sensitive as Fauset was to his fieldwork informants and their expressive culture, therefore, the beliefs and practices of everyday practitioners were added for illustrative purposes but were obviously not perceived to be as worthy of analysis as the activities and writings of the religious leaders or more public figures in the movement. Still, Fauset's text demonstrates his dedication to the idea that one could ascertain significant data about an American religious group by interacting with its ordinary believers. In terms of an approach to data collection and analysis of material relevant to the study of American religion, then, Fauset's approach was revolutionary, was highly unusual for its time, and remains enormously useful.[6]

Undoubtedly, followers such as "Father Divinites" presented unique fieldwork challenges for the young anthropologist because, quite simply, these members did not want to be observed and interviewed.[7] They were resistant and cautious in their approach to this fieldworker, both, I imagine, to test whether he wanted to become a follower (as they were responding to his questions about prayer and baptism and generally "enlightening him a bit") and to determine whether he was yet another reporter or writer.[8] Given their theological perspective on self that deemphasized aggrandizement of the individual personality in public and even private ways, individual members did not seek to state their opinions in any public forums such as books, magazines, or dissertations.

This reticence is evident in the notes Fauset provides on "Four women in a Father Divine Peace Mission dress shop" in appendix A, "Selected Case Materials."[9] Fauset notes here that his attempt to consult the women for information led to a discussion "among themselves [of] the worthwhileness of talking with the interviewer."[10] In addition, Fauset asks these Peace Mission sisters questions that appear to insult them, and he acknowledges this fact to his readers. What is wonderful in this account of the interview is how reflexive and frank Fauset is about the fieldwork experience and that he uses this example to inform and teach his readers about how asking wrong or inappropriate questions of believers in the field can prompt critical responses from them. While he does not specifically state it, the need for researcher sensitivity toward informants/consultants is obviously of great concern to him. Fauset's approach, however, while attentive to some of the nuances of community religious life, missed details of his informants' mercantile, artistic, and religious lives that could have fleshed out the culture of the International Peace Mission Movement in the 1930s and 1940s: Where exactly was this dress shop? What were the women making? Who would wear these dresses? Who made decisions about style and design and color? Did they make dresses for followers within their own community? It is into such gaps that the present chapter steps, building on Fauset's initial insights while further contributing to an appreciation for the nuanced process of working with religious groups and to contemporary readers' understanding of the Peace Mission's creative and adaptive worldview.

The Peace Mission: Contemporary Ethnographic Opportunity and Challenge

The challenges of ethnographic work with the followers of any religious community, especially within one's own society, are enormous. Ethnographic work within the Peace Mission Movement, a community that has wished to be noticed and appreciated but not necessarily studied or analyzed in publications by scholars, comes with additional demands and layers of complexity. Some relevant issues that need attention when considering contemporary religious ethnography are "the problem of subjectivity; the insider/outsider problem; the question of researcher identity; and issues of power."[11] I myself had none of these concerns in mind when I first encountered, over twenty years ago, the Peace Mission members that I had only read about in Fauset's work. I never decided to "study" the Peace Mission per se, but only gradually fell into a relationship of trust with the followers and Mother Divine that eventually allowed me to begin a research process that has included formal interviewing, photographing, videotaping, and much time dining, singing, and otherwise interacting with the members.¹² But, as my twenty-year association with them demonstrates, it is time that builds a relationship—a resource that ethnographers sometimes do not have in abundance—and it often takes much patience to abide and to absorb the culture.

My relationship with the Peace Mission thus began quite innocently about five decades after Fauset concluded his research and writing. It began easily and tastily—without any intention whatsoever on my part of mounting such a study—over lunch. This inexpensive service was provided throughout the 1980s and 1990s at the mission's Keyflower Dining Room in the previously mentioned Divine Tracy Hotel, adjacent to the University of Pennsylvania campus. Throughout many years of eating in the dining room, I naturally spoke with the staff, all "co-workers" in the Peace Mission, whom I saw several times a week. I read through, and sometimes took with me and filed, Peace Mission literature that was placed on an entrance table for the curious. One day, I was invited to a Holy Communion Banquet Service during the celebration of the wedding anniversary of Father and Mother Divine, an event still commemorated, even though Father Divine "voluntarily threw off his body" (that is, died) in 1965. It took me ten years of eating the wonderful food of the Peace Mission in the Divine Tracy Hotel cafeteria before I even contemplated a study of the members whom I was encountering. My course on American religious movements prompted me to begin a relationship with Mother Divine and her followers, but it would be fifteen years from the time I first brought students to the hotel until I felt comfortable enough to appear at Holy Communion Banquet Services by myself, and then to bring guests of my own to special and weekly rituals. (Many members of the American Academy of Religion and the American Folklore Society have been my guests at these occasions.) Attention to proper demeanor, daunting to outsiders in many Peace Mission contexts, was a trait that I developed by attending Philadelphia parochial schools for twelve years, and this has been absolutely essential to carrying out my work with the community. Gradually, through persistence and by showing knowledge of Father Divine's teachings, a willingness to learn more, and an appreciation for their community and years of service in Philadelphia, I was allowed to do ethnographic work within the Peace Mission. The followers knew I was a researcher—and a practicing Roman Catholic—but they also perceived that I had tremendous respect for their unique American religion.

I have been attentive over the years to the structure of their lives and organization, but, as a folklorist also trained in religious studies, I have been most attracted to the artistry and aesthetics of their everyday lives, as well as to the richness of these individual members' uses of architecture, foodways, testimonial, photography, and singing traditions. In addition, I have appreciated not only the community as a structure containing individuals but also the community as a culture of individuals— men and women united in belief but not homogeneous drones of allegiance; men and women who share a code for living but who, if one takes the time to know them, offer distinctive expressions and reflections of that religious system. Initially, this interest in the expressive culture of the Peace Mission led me to consider their "vernacular architecture of intention," that is, how they reused and restored buildings for their own theological, social, and economic purposes without the need to design and build new structures.[13] The present chapter works to illuminate another of those traditions, one that Fauset noticed as important but did not stop to consider in any detail: namely, song and music within the Peace Mission. As I explore here, intentionality and creativity similarly operate in this particular form of expression.

Speaking with authority about the musical culture of the Peace Mission would not be possible without the assistance of the followers themselves and their great generosity in sharing their personal and spiritual lives and thoughts with me. One such account was given to me by Miss G, a follower from Australia.[14]

It is 1931. In a house at 72 Macon Street in Sayville, New York, on Long Island, a crowd of people are gathered in a dining room around a special T-shaped table. They are sharing a meal consisting of many courses, but this is not a dinner where conversation is the central activity. Instead, it is a religious service, the Holy Communion Banquet Service of the Reverend M. J. Divine, also known as Father Divine (plate 9). The assembled are serving themselves from large platters of food passed out by Father to the diners. Some people testify about Father Divine's positive influence on their lives; others occasionally shout ecstatic praise. Still others dance in the spirit. The expressive forms that dominate the service and carry it along for over three hours, however, are music and song: melodies played on a piano accompanying congregational singing. The crowd sings loudly and with confidence:

Now isn't this a happy day
We've reached the Promised Land.
We will not be divided
One holy, happy band.
To Be with one another
Forever More to Stay.

Oh, Sing and Praise Him
Sing and Praise Him,
Sing and Praise Him
For the Glorious Work He Has Done

On this day, the Browns, an Australian couple, are present among the worshippers. Introduced to the ideas of the Peace Mission in New Thought discussion groups in New York City, the Browns had decided to come to Sayville to experience Father Divine for themselves. And they were convinced, like many others present, that this diminutive, charismatic African American preacher and healer and exponent of New Thought ideas was the incarnation of the Creator God. Though they wished to remain with Father, as foreign nationals they were forced to leave the United States during the Great Depression.

Back home in Australia, the Browns visited meetings influenced by the Unity School of Christianity and Christian Science in Melbourne and elsewhere, and there they recounted their personal experiences with Father Divine on Long Island. In Sydney, they influenced a recent university graduate, Miss G, a gifted modern dancer and student of Mrs. Brown's, who herself had traveled to New York to study with Martha Graham. In recordings and films brought back by the Browns, Miss G heard Father Divine's voice as he preached and observed his movements as he served the banquet table. For the first time, she also experienced Peace Mission songs sung by Mr. and Mrs. Brown. As Miss G explained to me, "They heard them from Father in Sayville. He sang them himself. Beautiful, simple songs. So metaphysical."[15]

Miss G would not actually meet Father Divine until she traveled to the church's headquarters in Philadelphia in 1953 as a Fulbright scholar. Now a forty-year resident of the city, Miss G, in an interview with me, emphasized the centrality of songs and the act of singing for followers—

how "prayer and praise are synonymous": "We [in the Peace Mission] don't pray together, but . . . when we get together . . . we sing." Singing, she explained, allows you to "take your mind off of other things and place it on a focal point. It then remains in your subconscious and heart through repetition."

Miss G invoked a theology about song creation articulated by Father Divine himself, who composed some songs for his community back in the movement's formative years in Sayville.[16] In fact, during Holy Communion Banquet Services, it was singing and songs that frequently motivated his sermons and always preceded them. Often referring to songs as "inspirations," he identified a spiritual center and focus of all such artistic expression—namely, himself. For example, on January 19, 1936, at an afternoon Banquet Service, he stated,

> Oh, it is a privilege to realize that the artistic stream from the mystery of God's Presence is in the undercurrents of your sub-consciousness waiting to be awakened by the spirit of My Presence, to inspire you with Wisdom, Knowledge, and Understanding, that you might be honest—scientifically honest from the art of singing, the art of playing, the art of drawing, and everything, for you have contacted this artistic stream. If you think on ME vividly and harmoniously, I will quicken that something within your sub-consciousness, and cause you to be inspired with an inspiration that will teach you wisdom, knowledge, and understanding, and you will come to be poetically inclined, as well as inspirationally inclined.[17]

Almost a decade later, in August 1942, at a Philadelphia service, again using the performance of a song as the foundation for his message, Father Divine reminded his followers about the creative meaning of their song and music traditions and how sincerity should be at the center of any such outward spiritual expression:

> Peace, Everyone: That little inspiration as a composition just sung is well worth considering if you stop and consider what you sing and realize it is a prayer in itself. If you will make such a request, your prayer will be heard and answered speedily, for you will find a closer walk with God. We do not believe in merely singing to be singing—to make music, but we believe in singing with all sincerity and whatsoever your desires may

be, when you sing or when you make a request, it be with all sincerity, even if you are speaking it in poetry; God knows the sincere desire of the heart; your prayers are heard and answered speedily and all will find that long-sought-for Something that will satisfy every desire.[18]

Today, there are abundant examples of such "inspirations," which amount to a living tradition of American religious song located within the still-active remnant of the Peace Mission found in Philadelphia and New Jersey, under the leadership of an ever-robust Mother Divine, Father Divine's Vancouver-born, "light-complected" (using their terminology) second wife.[19] The musical tradition of this indigenous American intentional community encompasses a repertoire of thousands of songs, with hundreds in active use.

In keeping with the Peace Mission community's corporate sense of ownership, these songs, though internally created, are never reproduced with personal attributions or credits to their composers. Most songs are learned orally and remain alive only through repeated use, for followers eschew hymnals or printed text and most do not read music. Individual songs often contain repetitive lines or verses, which are typically sung by followers with increased gusto at every repetition, the musical expression deepening spiritual focus and impact. Some lyrics, and many melodies, moreover, were never written down, and thus words and music of older (and now unused or forgotten) songs have been lost to memory: "Well, the music goes back where it came from, back into the infinitude," says Miss F, a longtime member.[20] Songs are understood as sacred inspirations reserved for community religious occasions. I was told that they are rarely discussed or recalled outside the contexts of creation, practice, or ritual use. As followers explained, the spirit inspires both the songs' creation and their performance; it follows that one therefore needs a spirit-filled context for the songs to emerge. I have been present in more mundane contexts with members, however, such as performing secretarial tasks or driving a car, when taped choral singing was played in the background to "contagionize," or fill, the atmosphere with Father and his words, which in such cases take the form of sung scriptures.

Like other religions that allow for both general and special ritual occasions, the Peace Mission follows a liturgical calendar, and there are a range of corresponding songs to complement and lift the spirit. There are patriotic songs sung to celebrate God having come to America, American independence, and the creation of the United States Constitution; love songs to express the devotion of members to Father and Mother Divine; marriage songs to celebrate the various wedding anniversaries of Father to his "spotless virgin bride"; Woodmont songs to mark September 10 as both the dedication of Father Divine's seventy-three-acre Gladwyne, Pennsylvania, estate as "the Mount of the House of the Lord" and his "supreme sacrifice" of dying (that is, "giving up his life") in 1965. There are even Christmas songs that do not celebrate the birth of Jesus Christ—since no such holiday is celebrated in the Peace Mission—but rather the "American Christmas," noting the positive nature of the season and the birth of America, the New Eden, a country blessed by God's actual presence. In the words of Miss K, a pianist at Banquet Services: "We have a song for everything, we have a song for every occasion, for every calamity, we have a song for everything we do. . . . I think we just like to sing."[21] Indeed, the songs resonate personally with members' individual and spiritual experiences and also relate to communal experiences of racism, prejudice, and injustice, and to efforts to achieve economic "victory" under Father Divine and the cooperative work of the Peace Mission.

Songs were composed both for congregational singing and for three choral groups that developed within the Peace Mission: the Rosebuds (a choir of "young virtuous women"), the Lilybuds (previously married women), and the Crusaders (the men's chorus). From the 1940s through the 1980s, these groups presented at a variety of weekly programs, from Monday Righteous Government Meetings and Wednesday Devotional Hours to weekend Holy Communion Banquet Services. The Rosebuds who today gather around Mother Divine are the only chorus to still sing on a regular basis at spiritually significant occasions.

The everyday lives of followers of Father Divine still balance two components of their communitarian and celibate tradition: the formality of structured living and a celebration of the freedom of the spirit. All co-workers, for example, adhere to the formal administrative structure of the various Peace Mission churches and carry out set duties, whether managing the Divine Tracy Hotel or cutting vegetables for Banquet Services. Followers' personal behavior is likewise ordered, as in the case of set linguistic codes: No words with curses are spoken. Therefore, they do not say "hell-o" to one another; they say "peace." Proper etiquette is to be observed at Banquet Services: Food is abundant but is not to be wasted. Standards of dress are necessary. Women wear skirts, never pants, and men wear coats and ties. Knowledge of proper handling of food platters and dinner plates is also seen as an asset. But in spiritual matters, freedom is perceived as a value, so followers read such writers as macrobiotic thinker Michio Kushi and reincarnation exponent Edgar Cayce and allow the spirit to guide them "volitionally" when giving testimony or shouting praise during a Banquet Service. In Peace Mission aesthetics, a creative space is forged between structure and freedom, and this negotiation is represented in the performance of sacred song.

Indeed, in the actual performance of songs, musical precision is admired but is not required in congregational and choral activities. In the everyday musical life of the Peace Mission, the movement's dual emphasis on structure and freedom is represented in leaderless choruses; extensive, spontaneous congregational singing; singers who, in the majority of cases, cannot read music; and choral singing without a great deal of structured practice. Miss F reflected on the experience of being a member of the Rosebuds:

> We were never able to be together [to practice].... We learned what we had to learn in New York, ... the Rosebud Choir Members in New Jersey learned what they were supposed to learn, ... then those in Philadelphia, they learned what they were supposed to about the song. Then we would get together intermittently to see how it all goes. There would be three pianists, in New York, New Jersey, and Philadelphia. And we didn't have a conductor, instructor, or director. The only one we had was God, Father Divine's Holy Spirit that instructed us.... The miracle is when you have fifty or one hundred voices together that do not know music, and they only learn through reiteration and memory—that is a miracle. I have seen outstanding choirs and they have their books and no doubt know how to read the notes. But ours were purely inspirational from Father Divine's Holy Spirit.

Such inspiration, coupled with an intentional creativity and adaptability, carries across all the ways that Peace Mission members live their religion.

Father Divine and his followers drew from a diversity of musical styles, borrowing melodies from spirituals, gospel songs, jazz, Broadway show tunes, traditional church hymns, popular copyrighted compositions, and even classical music to create their song tradition. In this sense, their music has a kinship with that of Holiness churches in the 1920s and 1930s, where, according to the historian Lawrence Levine, "musically, they reached back to the traditions of the slave past and out to the rhythms of the secular black musical world around them. They brought into the church . . . the sounds of ragtime, blues, and jazz . . . [and] also the instruments."[22] At the same time that these Holiness churches incorporated popular tunes into their services, they imbued the words with a new, religious meaning. Similarly, the Peace Mission worked to renew lyrics from secular consciousness to "God-consciousness." Jazz was a problematic musical form and culture for many African American ministers and congregations in the 1920s and 1930s, but Father Divine, despite associating jazz with "the underworld and the world of debauchery, of vice, and of crime," worked to "transform" such music into acceptable church songs. On January 14, 1934, he preached about this process in a noon sermon at 20 West 115th Street in New York City:

> The beautiful songs and praises that are put forth into expression here through the many different compositions, most of them have come through and from the world of jazz. They are expressions of the individuals and of the world of jazzism as it has been converted unto God, and it will glorify God in the fullness. It is indeed wonderful. . . . Then when you see these beautiful songs coming forth in praises to God, but in the same melodies and tones as the jazz songs, you can see that it is the spirit of the jazz world being converted unto God.[23]

During the mid-1930s, when the Peace Mission sponsored radio broadcasts of its services, the songs of the Peace Mission sung congregationally with tunes borrowed from popular music of the era brought criticism and accusations of copyright law infringement, thereby forcing the members to stop singing certain compositions during services that were to be disseminated by radio. Father Divine addressed this issue of the "mortal version" of such songs by emphasizing the opportunity followers now had to compose their own original songs through his inspiration. In another sermon delivered at 115th Street in New York

City on February 25, 1936, and then immediately published in the movement's newspaper, the *Spoken Word*, he proclaimed,

> Everybody happy? It is indeed wonderful! While listening at that little Song, I thought of our Radio Broadcast. Many of your numbers have been cut off because of them being songs that have been copyrighted.... GOD is Spirit. God is all Gifts and GOD is all Talents. God is all WISDOM. GOD is also all UNDERSTANDING. Because of this, we do not have to depend on another. Why should you lurk in the ideas and opinions, the compositions, the ways and doctrines of others, when MY Spirit within you is the great Composer? My Spirit in you is the Great Inspirator. MY Spirit in you will inspire you, will give you all you need to say, will give you all you need to sing, will give you all of the understanding necessary to get the issue through, therefore, when you see these seeming oppositions arise, they are for this purpose, even if it were to the extent that we would refrain to go on the air, after the manner of men. I did not reach the Twenty odd Million by going on the mechanical radio. It is indeed wonderful![24]

Father's words were heeded and additional original songs were composed in the United States and in other countries, including Australia, Panama, and Switzerland, where non-American followers gathered for Banquet Services and "praise meetings" of their own creation modeled on the rituals they read about in movement publications, the *Spoken Word* (1934–1937) and the *New Day* (1937–1992), and in letters or material sent from Father Divine or other members in New York City or Philadelphia.[25] Of course, an understanding of Father's words, a sense that "the composer is within you," as one follower told me, did not preclude continued borrowing from other musical sources, both to bring the secular world into members' lives and to transform the compositions themselves.

That words can effect positive change in everyday life is a part of New Thought and Peace Mission belief. The Peace Mission's approach to all songs has been that they could potentially aid human beings and be turned into something powerful, spiritual, self-referential, and positive. For this reason, melodies from the secular world may be used to complement new spiritualized words. Dr. LaVere Belstrom, a composer of songs for the Crusaders, a fact he admitted to me with reluctance, noted that "quite a few of our songs have been presented by substituting Peace Mission words for the words of the world."²⁶ He saw no problem, therefore, with writing new words to the tune of Irving Berlin's "White Christmas" (1940) and renaming the composition "True Christmas":

> We're living in a true Christmas
> In FATHER's Spirit and His Mind.
> Where we feel His presence
> with Peace and gladness
> And love in our hearts and souls.
> His Spirit is now within us
> When we are conscious of His love.
> May we know HIM ever and live
> In the Holy Consciousness of GOD.²⁷

In another uncredited Crusaders Christmas song, "Santa Claus Is Coming to Town" (J. Fred Coots and Haven Gillespie, 1934) was re-created in "Divine style" as "Father Divine Is Everywhere":

> FATHER is here, FATHER is there.
> FATHER DIVINE is everywhere!
> I'm Talking About FATHER DIVINE!
>
> He makes us all so happy.
> He keeps us all so well.
> And every time you see us
> We have something new to tell. (*Spoken*) Well!²⁸

Finally, in a true representation of one American religious tradition negotiating the cultural traditions of another, the Crusaders adapted the "Notre Dame Victory March" (or "Fight Song"), retaining Michael J. Shea's tune from the first decade of the twentieth century but employing more relevant lyrics:

> Cheer, cheer, For FATHER DIVINE
> Wake up the echoes cheering His Name
> Send the volleyed cheers on high

> Shake down the thunder from the sky
> Whether the odds be great or small
> FATHER DIVINE will Reign over all.
> While His loyal Crusaders go marching
> Onward to Victory!
> (*Shouted*) Cheer! Cheer! Cheer![29]

Such new lyrical compositions gain their integrity through "evangelizing," which in the worldview of the membership enables them to be salvaged like jazz for God's work. The art of the Peace Mission sometimes registers despair through a gloss of happiness but always sees hope in the re-creation of the world—a practice observed even in their restoration and reuse of old buildings, part of what I have termed the followers' "vernacular architecture of intention." Such architectural adaptations and reversals can be seen, for example, in the way the followers did not destroy an inappropriate object of Victorian ornamentation in one of their residences on North Broad Street in Philadelphia—a hand-carved mahogany mermaid with exposed breasts—but instead reimagined it, with an appropriate cloth covering added.[30] The form's integrity was therefore preserved for appropriate reuse and display while being "converted" to the Peace Mission "standard."[31] This standard prevails, and continues to transform, fifty years after the context in which Fauset observed this group.

The followers of Father Divine are now a remnant of the previous community, numbering perhaps 150 members, but their faith remains strong as they sing at Banquet Services in church buildings, including the Peace Mission Evangelical Home in West Philadelphia, a residence for those who are now too infirm to work. Mother Divine and the followers have become friendly with the Shaker community in Sabbathday Lake, Maine, who have even included a few Peace Mission songs about Father and Mother in their own current repertoire. In Mother Divine's era, there has been a shift to include more songs on "Americanism" and toward less raucous, more genteel performances, but the sisters and brothers of the Peace Mission still sing about prejudice, racial injustice, the need for better government, and, always, about Father.

Miss G, living at the Circle Mission Church (situated on the same block on South Broad Street as Black gospel songwriter Charles Albert Tindley's United Methodist "Temple"), is still physically active. Recently, a well-meaning friend took some of the residents of the Circle Mission Church, including Miss G, to a concert featuring the white gospel music of Bill and Gloria Gaither, where they sang about going to heaven. Miss G appreciated the rhythms and said they sang well, but she noted how "they kept singing about 'we're going to be on the other shore.'" She said, "I don't want to be on the other shore. I want to be on this one. We don't sing just to sing, we . . . know what we're singing."

As the membership grows older, the frailty of age has affected their music. Miss K was recently unable to play the piano at the Holy Communion Banquet Services, where she has brilliantly searched for the proper key for hundreds of songs and guided the singing for years. Her absence meant that no one was available to provide piano accompaniment at services, but that did not stop the banquets, which run on their own spirited rhythm of over eighty years of song, accompanied or not; of spirit, quiet or enthusiastically expressed; and of food, always in abundance. In 2006, at the Holy Communion Banquet Service commemorating the sixtieth wedding anniversary of Father and Mother Divine, the Rosebuds, with their ranks severely depleted, used recordings of past singing to support their performance of the set of five sacred songs used to open the service. By April 2007, this innovation of supplementing the traditional anniversary songs was abandoned, due, I speculate, to the spirited effect that live performance by even a dozen of the sisters has on the service.

In September 2005, I brought a former student of mine who is a jazz trumpeter to the Holy Communion Banquet Service to play a song that, I had discovered, was written in 1938 by Duke Ellington to honor Father Divine. As the "Krum Elbow Blues" made its soulful way through the crowd, one could feel how the sound of this instrument and this music took them back to the movement's days of spirited prominence in Harlem and, at the same time, situated them calmly with the spirit in West Philadelphia.[32] After the banquet was over, followers told me how satisfying it was to know, in the words of Miss M, "that Father converted the blues!" In the Peace Mission, instruments such as the trumpet were never used for solo performances, which would exhibit too much of the self or personality to the detriment of the church as an impersonal body. Followers sometimes negotiated the use of instruments to enhance congregational singing, however, as Mr. Simon Peter and Johnny Porter did to exciting effect with such songs as "Do You Love That Body!" "You could feel the walls moving on the street, the vibration was so high," is how a childhood memory of those days was described by Mr. R, who was raised in the Peace Mission and now plays guitar at their services.[33] "You know, Dr. Primiano," recalled Mr. P about the music at those services, "we used to get down, way down."[34]

There is still much to learn about Father Divine's radio broadcasts of the 1930s and 1940s, the further role of breaking copyright in their musical creations and performances, and the influence of Father Divine on American popular music, as in the case of Johnny Mercer and Harold Arlen's song "Ac-Cent-Tchu-Ate the Positive," inspired by one of Father Divine's sermons.[35] This research is ongoing, as is the need for more general consideration of such historical pathways' impact on communications, popular music, and even copyright law.

Men and especially women who were present sixty years ago when Arthur Fauset did his field research can still be interviewed if one secures Mother Divine's permission and their trust. One such follower was Miss Mary Justice, who taught me a song that I would classify as an "antispiritual": "There's No Heaven in the Sky" does not look to the Christian heaven for a divine salve to earthly woes and oppression but rather invokes the sentiment earlier expressed by Miss G of this-worldly hopes for divine integration. The song may sound bitter, but it is sung with great emotion and triumph—what I have come to understand as this group's unique triumphal contestation of the Christian soteriological tradition combined with the joy of Father Divine's gospel of powerful mindfulness in the present that still guides the followers years after its first proclamation.

> There's no heaven in the sky
> Which has been some poor saint's cry.
> Longing for this happy day
> We now enjoy.
>
> We have heaven here on earth
> By our Father's transforming birth
> No more to die
> To meet our Savior in the sky.

> From the sky
> From the sky
> Thank you for taking
> Our minds and attentions from the sky.
> So for many, weary years
> We toiled in sorrow, pain, and tears
> Planning to die
> To meet our Savior in the sky.[36]

Understood from their emic or insiders' perspective, members of the Peace Mission rejected the promises of Christian denominations that failed to support their civil rights in favor of a sectarian religion that offered them security and specific, positive support of their human rights in their present lives. They followed Father Divine even if that meant separating from their families and working long hours at traditional jobs and then also for the church. Indeed, Father Divine's Peace Mission was a favorite example for Fauset in *Black Gods* of the economic, social, and spiritual power of indigenous African American religion: followers could create, change, and assume control over their own lives in a society that was otherwise difficult and abusive.

Over sixty years later, the followers are still exercising power over their own lives. While time has changed what they control and the amount of energy they have to control it, they maintain an enthusiasm for the mission and for Father Divine and a dominion over their own destiny that Fauset would admire. The Peace Mission followers may not have retained their economic power in American cities past the 1960s, but it is important to note that they maintained an economic presence, only closing their last hotel, the Divine Tracy, in July 2006.[37] This closing marked the end of their public enterprises. However, in the edifice of their cultural creations, their ritual foods, their restored buildings, their spiritual narratives, and, significantly, their songs and music, the followers retain something very personal and powerful.

Fauset's ethnography of the Peace Mission from the 1930s and 1940s has become a useful source of historical information about this uniquely American religious community. It points to an informative early method in the study and appreciation of urban intentional communities, large and small, and the expressive traditions and innovations that make them, and their contributions and cultures, particular. Fauset's reflexivity about the process of doing fieldwork within such a community—especially how to respect informants—was decades ahead of its time.

A Space of Possibility

Throughout his life, Fauset evidently continued to think well of the accomplishments and vision of the Peace Mission Movement. In the author's note to the 1971 paperback edition of *Black Gods*, he refers to the community directly when reiterating the point that "the American black church 'provided [the one] place where imaginative and dynamic blacks could experiment [without hindrance] in activities such as business, politics, social reform and social expression.'"[38] Barbara Savage, in her foreword to the 2001 paperback edition of *Black Gods*, comments that Fauset's original study "had focused on five small sects, none of which bore a direct role in the civil rights struggle as it came to be embodied by [Rosa] Parks and [Martin Luther] King. Fauset recognized this himself, as he spent the remainder of his author's note stretching to forge fragile links between Father Divine and the worldwide 'love not hate' movement of the 1960s and 1970s."[39] Savage's words echo remarks among scholars of the African American religious experience and other observers who have looked critically at Father Divine and his reputation. At stake is the question of how much Father Divine loved his race, for such assumptions underpin discussions of what constituted a leader in the movement for "civil rights" for African Americans. Yet much of this discussion might be seen to miss the point, as is noted, for example, in Jill Watts's 1992 study of Father Divine. Watts characterizes his position on race as rooted in his New Thought theological foundation:

> It becomes apparent that Father Divine was initially a reluctant social leader who based his secular programs on his version of New Thought ideology. For instance, he believed that poverty resulted from negative thinking, and he did not offer welfare to the poor. Instead, he focused on job training and offered his disciples a spiritual reorientation toward positive thinking. His attitude toward racism was similar. Like some postmodernists today, Father Divine insisted that race did not exist but was a product of the mind. Negative thinking had created race, an artificial

categorization that perpetuated oppression and inequality. Hence, Father Divine, who demanded that followers abandon negative language, extended that ban to racial labels. He also castigated those who identified themselves as black, contending that they were manifesting the derogatory qualities that society had assigned to African Americans.[40]

This deracialized perspective comes to light more fully in the fascinating example of photographic representations of Father and Mother Divine together, images that flooded movement premises after Father Divine's wedding to "Sweet Angel" in 1946 (and that remain on the walls today). All prints of these photographs of the couple were treated by specially trained followers to lighten the complexion of Father Divine and darken the complexion of his Canadian bride to unify their skin tones as much as possible. In earlier years, Father Divine had complained that newspapers, especially those owned by William Randolph Hearst, deliberately published the darkest photos of him available with the purpose of making him look criminal.

Fauset does not indicate whether he knew about these aspects of Father Divine's outlook on race after his many hours of participant observation at Banquet Services and living with members, or whether he was even conscious of this stance in the 1970s. If he knew about such an ideology or characterized it as Black self-hatred, he certainly did not hold it against Father Divine in his writing. What Fauset did recognize, and shares, for example, with contemporary analysts of African American expressive culture, such as hip-hop music, is the idea that the song culture of the Peace Mission "creates a space of possibility."[41] In the case of the Peace Mission, those possibilities have been spiritual, economic, musical, medical, and, yes, racial. When the congregation as a community, and as a community of individuals, sings a song such as "The Beautiful Body of God," they are praising the strength of the community of their church but also highlighting the conviction that Father Divine is God, personified in the body of a short, "dark-complected" man who loved to sing, eat, and speak in the spirit, like they do. For the members, the majority of whom were and are African American women, God is one of their own, with a special charisma that enabled him to also attract followers who were and were not dark-complected. The obvious appeal of the Peace Mission Movement was the space it created for a Black God.

No commemoration of Father Divine's passing on September 10, 1965, now known as the "Holy Days" within the movement's liturgical cycle, would be complete without singing the words "I Know You Are GOD" to the tune of the anthem of the civil rights movement, "We Shall Overcome." To this day, and throughout the year at services, followers sing with great enthusiasm a song about God in America:

> Here in America
> Is the Kingdom of Heaven
> Here in the land of the free
> We have the Body of GOD
> Here in America
> We have the new birth of freedom under God
> He brought us Peace
> He brought us Joy
> He brought us Hope, and Truth and Love
> Come on, Come on, join the Body of GOD!

The empowerment of Peace Mission members through their songs highlights one of Cornel West's points: that "the quest for black identity involves self-respect and self-regard, realms inseparable from, yet not identical to, political power and economic status."[42] Viewed through the lens of the followers' lyrics and songs, the frequent celebration of Father Divine's body continually conveys the message that the followers' bodies are of tremendous worth and, moreover, that political and economic power is in their hands, as well as in the hands of God. If, as West writes, "the fundamental crisis in black America is twofold: too much poverty and too little self-love," Father Divine's followers resolved those problems many years ago.[43]

Because of his agenda to challenge the Herskovits-Frazier debate about origins of African American culture, Fauset did not indicate or explicate Father Divine's erasure of racial identity but rather recognized his antidiscrimination activist stance. Put differently, Fauset did begin to formulate an emic interpretation of the community where he saw the empowerment that they gained from a life in the Peace Mission. It was not an easy life—followers worked hard and long—but there was joy in their decision to work together and to believe a dark-complected man to be God.

Even in the twenty-first century, if the Peace Mission followers read intricate theories of Black self-hatred and racial and body politics such as those included in the historical analyses offered by Beryl Satter and R. Marie Griffith, they do not see the relevance of that perspective to themselves or the fellow believers who came before them.[44] Nor would they share others' views of Father Divine's seemingly negative assessments of dark skin. In their worldview, an enunciated, intellectualized category of race has had nothing to do with their lives because, in actual, practical daily experience, they have achieved many years of empowerment, freedom, equality, respect, sustenance, and even love in a community that, while not for everyone or their families, has been positive for them. The members of the Peace Mission helped create and sustain a space where, for decades, they have had responsibility for or controlled their community's money, property, economic decisions, businesses, aesthetics, and ritual display.

The women in the Peace Mission have been especially influential. Their power has been real, not circumscribed, and felt both inside and outside their own religious community, whether they worked as domestics and contributed to the purchase of new Peace Mission properties, as cafeteria cashiers who made certain that the restaurant business ran professionally and honestly, or as one of Father Divine's secretaries, who ensured that accounts were accurate, bills were paid, correspondence was well prepared, and records were carefully kept.[45] Fauset, as a talented, innovative ethnographer—not afraid to study members of his own culture closely—recognized the power women acquired in the church headed by Father Divine. He saw it in their Banquet Services in New York City, their radical farming communities in western New York State, their hotels in Philadelphia. He undoubtedly heard it in their songs.

Whether Father Divine de-emphasized race or not, whether scholars today "colonialize" his movement with postmodern assessments about its adherents' lives and beliefs, members of the Peace Mission have for many years been empowered by both their faith and their own gentle negotiation and interpretation of that belief system.[46] I have had the privilege to see that this community—which most scholars think is now extinct, but which has actually existed longer without the physical presence of Father Divine than with him in their midst—is still alive, kicking, cooking, breathing, changing, and singing: "In the name of FATHER

DIVINE, In the name of MOTHER DIVINE, we have the Victory." Their energy, their control of their destinies, has continued to exist beyond the withdrawal of Father Divine, beyond the departure or death of followers they knew well, over the years of Mother Divine's personal jurisdiction. Mother Divine has introduced her own creative innovations, built on Father's ideas about appearance, health, eating, aging, spirituality, and the preservation of their heritage for the community's consideration, embrace, and negotiation. The Peace Mission followers have continued to interpret this belief system, whether they still work to sustain the community or now reside in the Peace Mission Evangelical Home.

Conclusion

Just when I think I understand the members of the Peace Mission, just when I feel that I fully appreciate their diversity of ideas and practices after many years of interacting with them, someone in the movement surprises me. On a summer Sunday afternoon in June 2007, I was kindly offered a ride by a Peace Mission member living at Woodmont—Father and Mother Divine's estate in Gladwyne, Pennsylvania—to a 2:00 p.m. Banquet Service. The follower arrived at my home on his Honda Gold Wing 1,500-cubic-centimeter, six-cylinder motorcycle. As I rode on the backseat of this vehicle—something I had never done before—and we drove through Philadelphia's Main Line suburbs, with Mr. R taking the turns slowly due to my fear of flying off the seat, I heard a familiar sound. Mr. R was playing a tape of his own guitar transcriptions of Peace Mission songs as we negotiated the winding roads. The unexpected richness of this occasion was something I thought Arthur Huff Fauset would have loved: the tradition of innovation evident in the everyday life of an African American religious community. In public and private, in ritual and the mundane, Peace Mission songs and music are everywhere, reminding followers of their lives in the church and Father Divine's admonition that the consciousness of God's presence will keep you well, healthy, happy, and singing.

The Peace Mission Movement expressed through an intentional use of architecture its own quest for a utopian perfection of consciousness in America. What is especially significant about this expression of perfection is that the movement members did not seek it by building environments of their own creation. Instead, the movement and its leader created a unique religious vernacular architecture not by architectural design but by a spiritualized appropriation of existing spaces. Through purchasing, restoring, reusing, and preserving structures and properties representing many different types of American architecture, Father Divine and his followers developed a theology of material culture and historic preservation that expressed a major theological perspective of their belief system—to spiritualize the material and to materialize the spiritual—all in the service of God and for the transformation of human nature.

10

"Bringing Perfection in These Different Places"

Father Divine's Vernacular Architecture of Intention

Introduction

If one were asked to cite notable examples of religious material culture in the United States, the list would no doubt include the built environments of the American utopian communities considered by Dolores Hayden in her classic 1976 study *Seven American Utopias: The Architecture of Communitarian Socialism, 1790–1975*. Hayden examines the quest for spiritual perfection as expressed in the distinct American religious communities of the Shakers of Hancock, Massachusetts; the Mormons of Nauvoo, Illinois; the Fourierists of Phalanx, New Jersey; the Perfectionists of Oneida, New York; the Inspirationists of Amana, Iowa; the Union Colonists of Greeley, Colorado; and the Cooperative Colonists of Llano del Rio, California. These sectarian groups developed models for what they believed to be perfect societies in America, a country understood as destined by God to be a new Eden.[1]

Comprehensive as Hayden's list is, there is an eighth perfectionist American intentional religious community that warrants such attention: the International Peace Mission Movement. The Peace Mission followers—inspired by their founder and leader, the Reverend M. J. Divine, also known as Father Divine—expressed through a vernacular architecture their own particular quest for a utopian perfection of consciousness in America.

The recognition, designation, and study of built environments as vernacular architecture by folklife scholars have centered on buildings, artifacts, and landscapes that reflect and share traditional conceptions,

---

Originally published in 2004.

skills, and aesthetics of a particular community.[2] Building typology and construction, however, which some readers may associate with the study of vernacular architecture, is not my focus here. This chapter will emphasize the very acts of everyday use that made and continue to make Peace Mission structures "vernacular"—that is, localized, negotiated, performed, re-created—spaces. Buildings are not only artifacts of expressive culture; they are also important sites for the continuous enactment of culture in everyday life. What is especially significant about the Peace Mission's expression of perfection is that members did not seek perfection by building environments of their own creation, but instead, in the words of Father Divine, they sought to "[bring] perfection" to structures already constructed. The movement created a unique religious vernacular architecture not through architectural design but through a spiritualized appropriation of existing spaces. Such religious vernacular architecture exemplifies the dynamic nature of all buildings as objects open to the expression of a religious belief system.

Through purchasing, restoring, reusing, and preserving structures and properties representing many different types of American architecture, Father Divine and his followers developed a theology of material culture and historic preservation that expressed a major theological perspective of their belief system—to spiritualize the material and to materialize the spiritual—all in the service of God and for the transformation of human nature. As Father Divine preached at a Sunday service in New York City on the evening of November 15, 1936, if a person kept positive ideas and spiritual thoughts in the mind and was present physically, this would naturally reproduce material results: "By inspiration, information will come. By concentration, the reproduction will be put forth into expression. The thing we vividly visualize, we tend to materialize, and that which we materialize, if we materialize it in consciousness by consciously living in the recognition of it, we will also Personify it."[3]

This chapter not only examines the historical record of the Peace Mission's materialized consciousness but also addresses the still-living religious community in Philadelphia as it continues to uphold, celebrate, and enhance Father Divine's architectural ministry. Examining this movement through the lens of vernacular architecture reveals the unique relationship between this religious tradition, the faith of its followers, its broader societal context, and the built and rebuilt environment.

Father Divine and the Peace Mission

Who was Father Divine, the charismatic African American leader believed by his followers to be God, and what was this movement he established that created a unique religious architecture by intention and preservation instead of by design and construction?[4] Peace Mission beliefs, as uniquely formulated by Father Divine, drew elements from several religious ideologies influential in late nineteenth- and early twentieth-century America—Adventist, Holiness, Roman Catholic, Black church, and storefront Christianity—and incorporated ideas from the New Thought movement especially, including Christian Science and the Unity School of Christianity. Father Divine "had become convinced of the presence of God within each person and at the same time continued to reflect on the connections between spiritual wholeness and a life with sufficient food and shelter and a modicum of human dignity."[5] Followers felt transformed by the presence of this mystical leader and the seemingly miraculous abundance of food served at a typical Peace Mission ritual occasion that Father Divine designated the "Holy Communion Banquet Service." This ritual feasting was central to his fame, as he and his followers dined, worshipped, sang, ecstatically danced, and praised God together.[6] These public display events of the bounty of God's spiritual and physical harvest included a great variety of foods, representative of the abundance received by followers who lived a life of faith and service to God—that is, Father Divine.[7] Many men and women became adherents as a result of such material displays in the face of their experience of urban poverty, particularly during the years of the Great Depression, when Father charged very little or only what one could afford for the food.[8]

The origins of this celibate American religious movement can be traced to Sayville, New York, on Long Island, where Father Divine came to public attention in the 1920s. He and his first wife, Peninnah, who was also African American, purchased in cash an eight-room house as a home and worship space in a predominantly white residential area.[9] A permanent group gathered around Father Divine in this house and in the surrounding neighborhood, and they lived a cooperative, communal lifestyle, first on Long Island and later in Harlem, where the Peace Mission became a major force within the African American community.

Father Divine's movement expanded beyond the United States to Canada, Australia, Panama, England, Germany, Austria, and Switzerland, and his models of community and the Banquet Service were extended there as well. His sermons were translated and read in French and German throughout the 1930s. In New York City, and especially in Harlem, he commanded enormous spiritual, economic, and political influence and respect. As a 1939 *New York Times Magazine* article on "this large Negro community" ("It's Not All Swing in Harlem") assessed,

> Harlem's intellectuals may deny the urge and decry the practice, but Harlem masses still believe in churches.... And ... Father Divine ... is the most significant and dynamic personality Harlem has known in the past two decades.... Father Divine has linked production, distribution, and consumption. And there is no magic or voodoo about his hold upon his followers. A big sign prominently displayed in the mission on 126th Street offers what many consider the best answer: "No true Divine follower on relief! Saved the City of New York $20,000,000 since 1932!"[10]

The Divine Cooperative Plan

Father Divine claimed that millions of dollars had been saved by the city because of his economic vision, called the "Divine Cooperative Plan." Father Divine's standards for followers were strict, as he insisted on "an honest day's work for an honest day's pay," and moral standards were equally strict: he banned smoking, drinking, gambling, swearing, and sexual relations among the followers, who were asked to live by this "International Modest Code." He provided, in return, economic security in the form of lodging, food, and employment. Among his programs was the opening of free employment bureaus where the Peace Mission worked at finding jobs at no charge for any individual. Economic ideas were a basic part of Father Divine's overall principles and could be commonly found in his sermons, lectures, letters, and even church bylaws.[11] His vision of God's economy stressed individual independence but also saw the cause of humanity served through a cooperative system of community sharing and spending of resources:

We usually have a-full and a-plenty to eat. That is the first thought, if you please. Plenty of comfort and convenience! Then the cost of living is cut from forty to seventy-five to eighty percent by MY Cooperative System and by unifying the people together, causing them to love one another.... There is a-plenty to do, a-plenty of labor, a-plenty of business and a-plenty of trade. All can be put into expression and be giving active service. If your business, profession, if your labor and your trade will become to be absolutely unselfish and work cooperatively, the very Spirit of MY Presence will lift up a standard so effectively that the spirit of progressiveness will be in evidence among you, even as I have it among ourselves and among MY immediate staff.[12]

The Peace Mission funded itself through a system of "profit-sharing—no Hoarding—no Graft or Greed."[13] Cash resources, as Father Divine preached in a sermon, were to be spread out across the movement through a profit-sharing plan:

But, by putting your means of exchange to work and putting it into circulation, causing it to go around according to the plan and purpose of God and man, then and there you are using your means of exchange for the purpose it was created. The means of exchange should be put into circulation, to cause you and others to be successful and prosperous. By so doing, you will be using your means of exchange according to the Gospel. Now isn't that Wonderful?[14]

As a part of this Cooperative Plan, "true followers" would not accept any type of government assistance from federal, state, or local sources and, in particular, were to refuse "relief" from national programs established during the 1930s to address poverty. As employees, church members were to take no tips, gratuities, bribes, or gifts for services. No type of insurance was to be obtained, whether for automobiles or homes, for theft, or for personal injury.[15] God, Father Divine, was the only source of compensation for property and personal possessions lost due to fire and, certainly, was the only power to rely on to prevent such hardship. All purchases of any kind or amount were to be made in cash. This "cash and carry system" prohibited use of personal checks, credit, or any type of installment plan. Father Divine set an example for his followers by always paying for properties in cash. Sometimes such payments were made with small bills, which were delivered to banks in several suitcases by followers on Father's behalf.

Materializing the Spiritual

As membership in the Peace Mission grew, so did the need for more space. The press chronicled Father Divine and his movement throughout the 1930s and 1940s (and until his death in 1965), drawing special attention to the movement's acquisition of real estate in New York City and elsewhere in the state, as well as in Philadelphia later.[16] A major part of the economic principles that Father Divine enacted and spoke about publicly to his followers and other listeners was the "private ownership of property honestly acquired." In 1943 Father Divine succinctly synthesized in a sermon his ideas on the importance of ownership and prosperity:

> I believe in private ownership of enterprise; I believe in the private ownership of personal and real property, but I believe in you acquiring the private ownership of enterprise, or personal and of real property honestly. I do not believe in you taking advantage of others to acquire your respective aim, but I do believe that a person who is qualified to advance and has the skill and the ability to increase his holdings and even his ability to acquire more skill and more understanding, more professions and more trades. I believe in mass production from every side! Aren't you glad![17]

After followers had satisfactorily paid all past debts and stabilized their personal finances, they were guided not to invest in stocks and bonds, as such investment was contrary to Peace Mission teachings, but to contribute any savings to property ownership. This component of the Cooperative Plan consisted of using the collective resources of members to purchase, at a reduced price, urban, suburban, and even rural properties in need of redevelopment "to be used for the advancement of FATHER DIVINE'S Work and Mission, thereby putting the money to exchange for the common good of humanity."[18] Father Divine would then direct those members, or "co-workers," who worked closely within the organization to renovate the properties for use as residences for members or as hotels, restaurants, grocery stores, barbershops, garages, income tax and secretarial services, or centers for domestic service. In the 1930s and 1940s, the Peace Mission also established cooperative farms in New York State, including a thirty-two-acre self-contained community in Kingston known as the Promised Land. These orchards and fields were soon supplying produce to the Peace Mission's urban businesses.[19]

This work of restoration and reuse had its roots in the monistic worldview of the Peace Mission, a perspective on the single governing principle of reality shared by such American metaphysical movements as Unity and Christian Science—all related to the nineteenth-century spiritual movement known as New Thought. This nondualistic view of what is "really real" can be observed in the words of one Peace Mission song, "There's No Heaven in the Sky": The present reality is heaven, and the development of perfect consciousness in this life is possible. Achieving such a consciousness would result in not only a source of spiritual supply but also an abundance that would meet all material needs. Father Divine's truth transcends the material world, but the material world still bears the reflection of that spiritual transcendence. Connecting with the "universal mind substance" enables individuals to re-create and rebuild their lives, whether they are direct followers of Father Divine or just touched by his message. To the Depression-era urban poor in Harlem and other communities of African Americans, referred to as "dark-complected people" due to Father Divine's avoidance of racial references, these were powerful ideas, as they were for many "light-complected" individuals in the United States, Canada, Europe, and Australia, as well.

Father Divine often amplified this theological perspective in messages concerning Peace Mission buildings. In a September 1938 statement to his followers gathered at Jamaica, Queens, he elaborated on how the restoration of buildings was connected to the restoration of the person:

> Then I say, you can see these old buildings in different communities that were run down, dilapidated, and absolutely good for nothing, as you may term them to be, as God is the Center of Attraction and a Standard of Perfection expressed, He demonstrates it by bringing perfection in these different places ... the perfection of competence ... the perfection of truth,

both in the minds and the hearts and lives of the children of men, and in the surroundings; renovating old material, natural buildings, remodeling and renovating them, causing them to be comfortable and convenient, causing them to have all improvements for the comfort and convenience of the inhabitants of such buildings a sample and an example for others.[20]

Father Divine had no reservations about reusing buildings acquired from other denominations, such as Roman Catholics or Baptists. No matter what a building's original purpose was, he held, once it is consecrated to the service of humanity, it resonates with "a positive vibration" that is experienced daily. He explained in 1947, in a private conversation in his office at the Circle Mission Church on Broad Street in Philadelphia, that

> the advantage of the sacredness of the edifices or the edifice there [is] because it has been under the jurisdiction of a religious organization that is highly admired by MYSELF and MY following.... We feel the atmosphere there as we do not feel or would not feel automatically in the beginning of a place until it is fully consecrated—if it has not been consecrated by others.[21]

Of course, any property could be converted to an "evangelical" purpose, and Father Divine would proudly announce recent acquisitions in his messages at Holy Communion Banquet Services:

> And making this an occasion of the season, through MY Condescension to present MYSELF and appear in Person, I have come to call your attention to the Blessings of those of the Followers who have recently purchased 22 E. Kinney Street [Newark, New Jersey]—having purchased it, renovated it and have now set it up for the Dedication and Consecration to the Service of God; for when you serve yourself and others ARIGHT you serve your fellowmen![22]

All Peace Mission properties and living quarters were "spiritualized" through their cleanliness and safety and their adornment with ubiquitous framed photographs of Father and Mother Divine and mottos of the mission in every room.[23] Such preparations marked a building's dedication and consecration to the service of God.[24] Properties with

Banquet Rooms would stand prepared for a Banquet Service, with clean plates, glasses, and silverware, always with the expectation of Father Divine's personal presence and reflecting the belief in his spiritual presence. Father Divine maintained offices in all major church properties, and he would unexpectedly arrive at these extensions to visit with staff. Large properties were important, but he acknowledged the spiritual significance of followers' domestic environments, as well. In the same November sermon, he proclaimed,

> I ABUNDANTLY and BOUNTIFULLY BLESS YOU ALL—causing your homes as selected and purchased and owned, to no longer be houses as they have been, of VICE and Crime and SIN, but DEDICATED as HOUSES of PRAYER, where you in your own Homes will be able to WORSHIP GOD under your own Vine and Fig Tree where no man can make you ashamed! ... I AM causing every Home, at least, I shall cause every home to be as a CHURCH! Aren't you glad! ... To be a CHURCH for PRAISE and WORSHIP, where you WORSHIP GOD by DAY and by NIGHT in all you SAY and in all you DO![25]

Father Divine in Philadelphia

In 1942 Father Divine left New York City due to legal difficulties involving a monetary judgment won in a lawsuit by a former member.[26] He settled permanently in Philadelphia, beyond the judicial reach of New York State authorities.[27] Several years after his first wife died, he took a second wife, a young, "light-complected" Canadian who had worked as one of his personal secretaries. She came to be known within the movement as Sweet Angel or Mother Divine.[28] Their marriage in 1946, although declared spiritual and celibate, provoked fear and anger within the racist climate of postwar America and surprise even within the movement itself.[29]

When Father Divine died in 1965—what Peace Mission members understand as the physical departure of God from this plane of existence to the spiritual plane—the second Mother Divine, or "Mother in the Second Body," as she was known to followers who believed in the possibility of soul transference and reincarnation, was left as the visible leader of the movement. In 1964, the year before Father Divine's death, the *New York Times* again highlighted the movement, noting how Father Divine had amassed a real estate portfolio worth an estimated $20 million.[30] The Peace Mission has continued living in community, mainly in the city of Philadelphia, for the decades since, although now reduced in membership, and still maintains a significant number of real estate holdings.

When Father Divine moved his congregation to Philadelphia from Harlem in the early 1940s, the Peace Mission began to sell off its New York City properties and purchase a series of commercial and residential buildings in the movement's new center of activity. The Peace Mission's physical presence in Philadelphia expanded over the next twenty years, through wise real estate investment and entrepreneurial innovation, to include three hotels in the city (as well as two hotels in northern New Jersey) and many other properties financed by the followers and classified by the Peace Mission as "Churches," "hotels catering to the general public," "hotels exclusively for followers," and "homes and businesses."[31] Several grand examples of Philadelphia Victorian architecture were acquired, and these buildings have been maintained and, in some cases, restored to pristine condition during the administration of Mother Divine. Mother Divine has worked to retain Father Divine's standards, and her interest in upholding Father Divine's economic policies involving the sacred importance of property and business ownership was reflected in her 1982 book *The Peace Mission Movement*:

> The Peace Mission has always served the community through its hotels, cafeterias, food markets, dress shops, barber shops, gas stations, shoe repairing and dry cleaning establishments and such services that provide the necessities of life at lower prices than can be found elsewhere. This is "preaching the gospel in dollars and cents" as Father Divine would say, by giving the best for the least. Therefore HE considered these businesses places to be more sacred than the churches.[32]

Many of the Philadelphia properties of the Peace Mission are in the Center City district and are presently used to house Peace Mission members, but there were once buildings in use throughout the city's neighborhoods. Father Divine saw something in these unappreciated buildings that other Philadelphians of the time did not. It should be noted that such restorations were conducted before the historic preservation of grand urban Victorian construction became an interest or priority. When the Peace Mission was making these purchases in the 1940s and 1950s, many citizens of Philadelphia considered such buildings to be architectural monstrosities that needed to be replaced.

Always interested in promoting the internationality of the Peace Mission, Father Divine dubbed one urban Victorian mansion at 1430 North Broad Street in North Philadelphia, which served as a sorority or residence for female community members visiting from other countries, the Divine International House. The house itself was designed by Will E. Decker and built around 1890 for lumberyard owner and real estate developer Charles E. Ellis. Among its features were a Romanesque Revival exterior, extensive hand-carved interior woodwork depicting mermaids and mythical animals, a staircase done in what architectural historian Robert M. Skaler has described as the Viking revival style, and eclectic Japanese, Italian Renaissance, Turkish, Romanesque, and Colonial details throughout. The response of the Peace Mission, which purchased the property in 1953, to the more immodest elements in the house's interior decoration is particularly illustrative of this sect's vernacular touch. Father Divine's modesty code held that male and female followers could not ride in the same automobiles (with the exception of Father Divine himself), that married guests were not permitted to reside in the same hotel rooms, and that Father and Mother Divine could not even share the same quarters in their residences. The mansion at 1430 North Broad Street contained a decorative feature provocative even for the Victorians, let alone the mid-twentieth-century followers of Father Divine: three hand-carved mermaids on the first floor were originally rendered with exposed breasts. Instead of destroying or removing these works of art that were inappropriate in a Peace Mission residence and at odds with its beliefs, the religious community negotiated a balance between the building's historical value and its own aesthetic of propriety. As one follower proudly explained, they "converted them to [the Peace Mission's] standard" by having followers sew proper cloth coverings for the mythical creatures. While removing the immodest architectural elements from their sight, they still preserved the architectural and historical integrity of the original domestic interior.

Approximately three blocks from this structure, on Sixteenth Street, lies another property maintained and preserved by the Peace Mission: what it has called Father Divine's Bible Institute of Philadelphia. This building is attributed to John McArthur Jr. and was erected between 1881 and 1883 for the owner of the Disston Saw Works. Among its many splendid rooms, the library has especially outstanding woodwork and a fireplace with tiles depicting Shakespearean characters. The various rooms of the house, in careful states of preservation, stand as impressive waiting rooms for guests who come to attend yearly Holy Communion Banquet Services there, particularly in honor of the wedding anniversary of Father and Mother Divine. A large room in the rear of the structure, which was added by a caterer who owned the building in the 1920s, was used by Father Divine for Banquet Services and later renovated, with new paint and light fixtures, in time for the fiftieth wedding anniversary celebration in 1996. In the 1950s this building was part of a complex of Peace Mission properties in the area that were used for Bible instruction and, significantly, for the production of the movement's newspaper, the *New Day*, which was published as a weekly until 1992.

Near the center of Philadelphia stands another intact Victorian, the Fraternity Peace Mission Evangelical Home at 507 South Broad Street. Designed in 1882 by George T. Pearson, this structure was originally owned by J. Dundas Lippincott, and the Peace Mission purchased the property in 1943. It is an eclectic design rooted in the Queen Anne style, the last remaining residential mansion in this vital part of the city. As elegant as this structure is as a residence for men, it also exemplifies the multipurpose nature of building use within the movement. In this case, the fraternity also houses church archives, including Father Divine's ministry of sermons, interviews, and letters, many of which were published and republished in the *New Day*. This building is located only blocks from John McArthur's elaborate Victorian City Hall, the very center of the city's financial and commercial core. The Peace Mission purchased buildings in many different neighborhoods and environments, including white residential, African American urban, city commercial, segregated suburban, and isolated rural areas.

Father Divine's use of church buildings for a variety of purposes complemented the practice found in American denominations in the years surrounding World War I of viewing such buildings as income-producing institutional and mission plants. Most denominations started promoting such endeavors as part of a church efficiency movement that stressed sound fiscal policy for congregations. Elbert Conover's 1928 text on church building, *Building the House of God*, suggests,

> Many existing buildings can be remodeled to enable the church to render a far more satisfactory program than has previously been possible.... In some sections, particularly in congested centers, there is need for church plants in which social service and educational activities require a large proportion of the space.... Sometimes, in order to maintain religious work in a city center where land values are exceedingly excessive, it seems necessary to devote a large part of the building space to income-producing purposes.[33]

Father Divine adopted a policy of church efficiency, but not one that concentrated on the construction of new church properties. He and his followers were solely interested in the restoration and reuse of older buildings for Peace Mission purposes, as their use of a former Pennsylvania Railroad YMCA building at Forty-First and Westminster Streets in West Philadelphia illustrates. Dubbed the Unity Mission Church, the building is the work of architect Thomas Lonsdale, with a construction cost of $100,000 in 1896. The followers purchased the abandoned and derelict property in 1943, as well as adjacent residential properties to house members in apartments, also establishing a Peace Mission Co-op Grocery Store to meet the needs of their own restaurant, their followers, and the neighborhood. The Peace Mission property included a cafeteria, public spaces and sitting rooms, a banquet room, and an auditorium for services. The building's original gymnasium space and kitchens were adapted for church use; children from the surrounding African American neighborhood, for example, would often play in the safety of the gymnasium.[34] This large building was sold in 2000, but nearby properties that were converted into the Peace Mission Evangelical Home in the late 1970s remain functional as a personal care facility open to Peace Mission members.

Hotels owned and managed by the Peace Mission not only contained guest rooms but also typically included a public restaurant or cafeteria, rooms for co-workers, an auditorium for daily religious meetings and songfests, and large halls for Holy Communion Banquet Services. The 246-room Divine Lorraine Hotel (sold in 2001) on North Broad Street functioned in such multiple ways, as did the 150-room Divine Tracy Hotel at 20 South Thirty-Sixth Street, adjacent to the University of Pennsylvania campus in West Philadelphia.[35] Built in 1901 and designed by architects Milligan and Webber, the former Tracy Apartment House was purchased in 1949 for $200,000 in cash. This hotel, which is still operational and open to the public at much lower than conventional rates, also contains the offices of Peace Mission Enterprises, which until recently included typing, notary, laundry, dry cleaning, and income-tax services. The Keyflower Dining Room served meals at the hotel until 2000, preparing specific macrobiotic dishes beginning in 1980, when Mother Divine reinvented the diets of followers to include more healthful foods. Although the public kitchen is now closed, the large Holy Communion Banquet Room in this building, fashioned out of its former bar and lounge areas, continues to see frequent use. In accordance with the Modest Code, married couples cannot reside in the same rooms, men and women remain segregated by gender, and guests must be met in the hotel's lobby. Peace Mission properties also never allowed racial segregation, making these institutions distinctive for their inclusion of members of all races, in addition to the quality of their services, in a period when African Americans were not permitted to stay at many urban hotels in the United States.[36]

One of the earliest Peace Mission building purchases in Philadelphia was the Circle Mission Church, Home and Training School of Pennsylvania on South Broad Street, formerly the Hotel Dale. This complex of buildings at Broad and Catherine Streets was developed in approximately 1905 into one property from twin Victorian homes built in 1889, with the Church Gospel Mission Home built as an adjacent structure in 1897.[37] All of these buildings were purchased in 1939 and were then transformed into Father Divine's headquarters and personal residence upon his 1942 arrival in Philadelphia. A spacious public dining room, dress shop, barbershop, library, classrooms, followers' rooms, multiple kitchens, and a Holy Communion Banquet room could be found at this site, which accommodated the residential and spiritual activities of many Peace Mission members. Father Divine used a large second-floor space as his personal office, where he would work with his many secretaries, dictating messages, answering correspondence, conducting business, and "interviewing" visitors who sought to speak to him. This front room had windows and a sizable balcony facing 764–772 South Broad Street, just ten blocks from the city's business, commercial, and governmental center. Father Divine employed the balcony as a public stage for appearances to his followers as well as the general public. He used this public space, for example, to present his new wife, Sweet Angel, as Mother Divine to gathered followers and passersby in August 1946.

Such holdings served a multitude of ambitious purposes, continually teaching the followers a framework of empowerment: spiritual, economic, and, of course, racial. With respect to the latter, Father Divine championed the integration of America and the application of the standards of the Bill of Rights to all its citizens. To pressure and remind Americans to "enact the Bill," as followers would say, Peace Mission members integrated everything: church cars (Father's automotive entourage often incorporated alternating black- and white-colored limousines, visibly "enacting the Bill" down a highway or through a city), church residences, and especially the Holy Communion Banquet Services, where members sat in an integrated pattern projecting out from Father and Mother Divine's places at the head of the table. In a book review of a work on Father Divine, historian Oscar Handlin recognized the relationship between Father Divine's plan for the distribution of goods and services and his policy of integration: "To the appeal of providential supply amid universal want, Father Divine joined absolute intransigence on the racial issue. To the residents of the Harlem slums the demand not for equal but identical treatment was indeed God-like."[38]

The Mount of the House of the Lord

Father Divine's vernacular architecture of intention, as well as what could be called his theology of historic preservation, is most prominently evident in the restoration, preservation, and reuse of Woodmont, a Victorian manor house found in the exclusive Main Line suburb of Gladwyne, not far outside Philadelphia (plate 10). Designed by the Quaker architect William L. Price and completed in 1894 for the industrialist Alan Wood Jr. at an estimated cost of $1,000,000, Woodmont is located at the highest point along the west bank of the

Schuylkill River. Architectural historian George E. Thomas, in his volume on Price, notes that

> the house was constructed of the local stone trimmed with limestone and finished on the interior by many of Philadelphia's principal decorative artists. The estate included its own power plant as well as stables, barns, and extensive gardens. . . . Woodmont . . . was an immediate triumph, imitated by other architects, and never eclipsed in the Philadelphia area in terms of ornateness and costliness. Especially astonishing was the five-story-high great hall rising to the peak of the immense tile-clad roof.[39]

The design of the estate's manor house was itself influenced by Biltmore, George W. Vanderbilt's sprawling house in Asheville, North Carolina. Father Divine received word about the Gladwyne property through a follower who worked as a domestic for the elderly owner, and he purchased the seventy-three-acre estate and house for $75,000 in cash in 1952. The *New York Times* indicated at the time of its dedication that "the followers of Father Divine . . . restored it to the grandeur of its early days themselves. The restoration work, real estate experts said, would have cost at least $250,000 had it been done by private contractors."[40]

Woodmont represents the pinnacle of Father Divine's perfectionist theology of transformation. He described this idea of change through religious intention in the early 1940s in a message at a Banquet Service at the Rockland Palace, at 155th Street and Eighth Avenue in New York City, and it is possible to apply his meaning to both the renewed lives of followers and the renewed lives of buildings touched by his movement:

> I am transforming the people by the renewing of their minds! I AM changing their minds! As well as I AM reforming them mentally, I AM actually TRANSFORMING them by the renewing of their minds! They have a different mind and different nature and different characteristics! They do not have the characteristics they had before they knew Me! They think, they act, they speak and they live and they even feel different, because they are NEW creatures, according to the Gospel! Aren't you glad![41]

He taught his followers that heaven can be found presently on earth and that the spiritual could transform the material anywhere. Also in New

York City, earlier, he preached, "Rest from doubts and fears! Rest from superstition! No longer imagining Heaven geographically, but the recognition of GOD'S ACTUAL HEAVEN in all places wheresoever you live Evangelically and are subject to true Evangelism, and angelism manifested in your system!"[42]

The Peace Mission purchased Woodmont, as it was literally about to be destroyed, for the cost to the owner of leveling the building. Dubbing the restored estate "the Mount of the House of the Lord," Father Divine saw the property as a fulfillment of his principle that "there is abundance in virtue"—that the accumulation of virtuous acts results in great, and often material, things for the community. Woodmont became one of Father Divine's grandest projects, one taken up and continued by his wife: to establish a place of beauty and spiritual perfection. As he had explained in 1942, "Then I say, VISUALIZE the PERFECT PICTURE and reproduce it, materialize it and multiply it, and live in the CONSCIOUSNESS of GOD'S Presence!"[43] Today, Woodmont has been maintained not only because the Peace Mission appreciates the heritage of American architecture but because it feels that within the beauty of architectural perfection, and perfection of landscape, followers and visitors may experience the abundance of God and further seek a unity with the consciousness of God. A 1999 description of the spiritual meaning of the property published by the movement presents it as a living "Garden of Eden," as the fusion of heaven and earth: "The mysterious, majestic beauties of Woodmont have been extolled to the highest—its picturesque Grounds and its intriguing Buildings. These are obvious to any eye. But there is a deep, Spiritual Magnitude of Woodmont also, which is apparent only to the Inner Eye."[44] Having reinvented the secular estate to fit into the Peace Mission theological perspective, Father Divine saw Woodmont as a new Temple of God; citing Isaiah 2:2–3 and Micah 4:1–2, he preached on June 24, 1953, that "as it was with the building of the Temple of the Lord in Jerusalem, in Mount Moriah, so it is in the rebuilding of the Temple of the Lord . . . at Philadelphia in Woodmont."[45]

The preservation and beautification of this property have had a notable influence on the expressive culture and general aesthetics of the movement. The hallmarks of the "Divine style" under Father Divine were bounty, community, integration, and a nationalist spiritual ethos called "Americanism." Influenced by Woodmont theology and under the leadership of Mother Divine, this aesthetic has been expanded to include safety, graciousness, orderliness, tradition, stasis, respectability, and propriety. A Victorian Quaker aesthetic may have inspired the creation of Woodmont, but the Peace Mission aesthetic has maintained it for fifty years. Woodmont stands as the embodiment of Father Divine's perfectionist utopian community vision, representing, with its workshops, garages, orchards, and fields, the synthesis of his communal lifestyle ideals. The property's pristine condition is an outgrowth of the marriage of Father Divine's emphasis on the principle of perfection and his understanding of an activist use of the material world to express that perfection.[46] This union encapsulates the theology of material culture he espoused, in which a sacramentalism of material usefulness is the primary objective of a world created by God and re-created, renewed, and restored by humans influenced by God.

In a celebratory meeting after midnight on September 13, 1953, in the auditorium of the Unity Mission Church on Forty-First Street in Philadelphia, Father Divine pronounced to his followers the meaning of the dedication and consecration of Woodmont from a theological and racial perspective:

> We know you all know a Standard of morality, of modesty, of Holiness, of Virtue and of Honesty, all of these attributes and qualities have been established and that is second to none! But as an abstract expression we are happy to say, the materialization of these things is taking place in our experience.... I have broken that line of demarcation and brought an end to localization! That's why you have the privilege and the pleasure to go up to the Mount of the House of GOD. And you may come in the front door! ... There was a gentleman called ME up or wrote ME whichever, and said he was once the chauffeur for one of the owners there. Even though being a chauffeur, he was not permitted to go in the front door! I AM not holding no grudge nor emphasizing anything that one should hold against the tide of that time, and the seasons of the time that brought about segregation and discrimination, inequality, oppression, and suppression because I had not brought an end to it as I have now! He testified the other day that he was happy to be there and

he could come in the front door! Even though it has been renovated and made new—some declare it's much better than it was before—you can come in and act and look like people—the kind of people God made![47]

That he was acquiring grand properties in which his followers might have worked as servants at one time was not lost on Father Divine. The use of such residences by his followers was a social and cultural irony that appealed to him throughout his ministry.

In September 1999, in a ceremony at Woodmont, the property was dedicated as a National Historic Landmark by the National Park Service. This occasion marked for Peace Mission members a zenith of public acceptance and respectability, not only of their property but of Father Divine's ideas of universal consciousness. This celebration of ownership, preservation, and transformation of the house's original purpose signaled the triumph of the principles of racial equality and integration that Father Divine championed.

As the movement's membership grows older and more reduced in number, Mother Divine is faced with the challenging task of seeing that these buildings are sold to owners and developers who are in harmonious enough alignment with Father Divine's ideals. In Peace Mission belief, if a person has not fully melded into the consciousness of God during his or her lifetime, that individual will most likely be reincarnated back into the world. Mother Divine, in keeping with this idea, seems content to let some of these buildings, which have been used for a time for God's purpose, "pass off and pass on" into another incarnation of service. The exception will be Woodmont, where Father Divine is buried and where his wife intends to establish a library and study center. Father Divine's tomb—with its granite walls imitating the shape of his Woodmont office, his red marble sarcophagus in the shape of the Ark of the Covenant, and its impressive bronze-figure-filled doors, called the *Portal of Life Eternal*—represents the most significant and original design statement the Peace Mission has made.[48] Yet, while the Shrine to Life, as the tomb is designated, is Mother Divine's feminized new creation and aesthetic statement, it is still built on Father's foundational notions of re-creation and reuse.

A Vernacular Architecture of Intention

The material culture of the Peace Mission invites both followers and non-followers into the perfectionist worldview of Father Divine. Followers produced a vernacular architecture of intention by transforming existing structures into unique religious environments best understood through a lens of usefulness. Henry Glassie, in his textbook on vernacular architecture, reminds readers that any sound consideration of vernacular architecture should involve constant reflection on buildings' usefulness and their interpretability as creative, artistic, expressive texts illuminating the lives of individuals and communities: "Architecture intrudes in the limitless expanses of space, dividing it into useful, comprehensible pieces.... We call buildings vernacular to highlight the cultural and contingent nature of all building."[49] Father Divine's approach to architecture was based on an idea of the potential of all buildings to aid human beings—the potential for their contingent nature to be turned into a source of power and a positive force that challenged the status quo. These structures aided Father Divine in the establishment and expansion of an economically viable religious organization; they also formed the foundation of his plan for improving and empowering his followers as free, self-sufficient human beings. The purchase of any particular building was based on its potential to be adapted and reconfigured as habitat, business, and church. Ownership and reuse also turned these buildings into symbols of economic viability and freedom of expression for Peace Mission community members within the religious, social, and financial constraints of contemporary American society. As Glassie argues, "Architecture gives physical form to claims and names, to memories and hopes. As a conceptual activity, architecture is a matter of forming ideas into plans, plans into things that other people can see. Architecture shapes relations between people. It is a kind of communication."[50]

Father Divine was a master of communication; as an orator operating in the traditional sermon style of the African American preacher, he would dazzle and mesmerize his audiences with the length of his unscripted homilies, the passion of their delivery, and the fluidity and liberating effect of their New Thought ideas. Father Divine also recognized the power of material culture as a tool for expression. He knew that actions sometimes spoke louder than words, especially to a general public who might not be exposed to his words but could certainly witness his works. In 1948, soon after the Peace Mission purchased the Lorraine Hotel at the notable intersection of Broad Street and Fairmount Avenue in North Philadelphia, Father Divine marked the new property with enormous signs high atop the eleven-story structure, replacing the previous rooftop "Hotel Lorraine," which faced north and south. He did not rename the building "Father Divine's Hotel" or the like, as one might expect; he spiritualized the former name by adding his own and consecrating it, so it became the Divine Lorraine Hotel. There his reinvention of this business stood as a beacon marking the northern sector of the city, announcing his presence in the two directions of this thoroughfare, as if the eyes of God were now literally observing the actions of all below and above. Father Divine understood the importance of such public display and intuited how, with the help of his followers, he might remake elements of even the most unyielding city to serve a positive purpose and serve his community, whether in Harlem, Newark, or Philadelphia. The potential of buildings in those cities related not only to the specific individuals who lived and worked in them; their potential, in his view, also radiated out to the wider community. Father Divine created urban networks reaching out from the inner city all the way to the suburbs in part to demonstrate, and insist upon, racial equality and justice.

Dell Upton's groundbreaking history of American architecture is especially noteworthy for the way it combines the canon of acknowledged American built environments with consideration of more modest structures. By integrating such diverse examples, he articulates the story of architecture as vernacular culture. Significantly, Upton makes a point to stress the importance of looking at how American architecture actually functions in everyday life: "Buildings are changed in construction and they are changed in use. They are used differently from the way they were intended and they are appreciated or experienced differently from the way architects or patrons might have imagined."[51] In an earlier article, Upton elaborates:

> Once introduced into the landscape, the identity of a building and the intentions of its makers are dissolved within confusing patterns of human perception, imagination, and use. Consequently, the meaning of a

building is determined primarily by its viewers and users. This process of creation goes on long after the crew leaves the site; it never stops. Every structure contains several different buildings as imagined by different segments of its public. None of these is necessarily consistent with the others, nor do any of them bear any necessary relationship to the intention of designer, builder, or client. Yet so much of architectural history is directed toward identifying the pure form, the original condition, the architect's intention. How relatively unimportant these are![52]

As architectural historian George E. Thomas has noted, there is little doubt that William Price wanted to attract attention to the house he designed for Alan Wood Jr. Over ninety years later, Woodmont retains its effect. A convert to the Peace Mission once remarked at a Holy Communion Banquet Service that the first time he saw Woodmont, Father Divine's "Mount of the House of the Lord," he said to himself, "I know if God had a house that had to be it." In preserving the Woodmont estate, Father Divine was not only interested in saving and restoring a significant piece of American architectural heritage. Restoring William Price's creation was secondary to the restoration of Father Divine's many African American followers to full and equal status in their own country. What better way to make his movement's essential points of contestation and re-creation than to purchase and reclaim one of the most illustrious examples of material culture in one of the wealthiest, whitest, and most segregated communities on the East Coast for the "dark-complected" God of the city and his followers to enjoy and transform into active symbols of their belief system? Such was the complexity of Father Divine's "process of creation," prompted by a building's purchase and restoration but moving outward to take on social and theological implications. Religious studies scholar Joseph Sciorra, discussing Puerto Rican vernacular architecture in New York City, recognizes how that community has created "local landscapes of empowerment" where "knowledge and skills developed amidst . . . destruction [and] are employed in transforming the rubble and ruin in a conscious rebuilding of urban communities." Citing the work of bell hooks, Sciorra explains, "It is within this imposed economic, political and social marginality that poor people of color struggle to change the existing conditions in which they live, by creating spaces of their own design that serve as locations of resistance to a system of inequality and domination."[53]

To fully consider Father Divine's vernacular architecture of intention, we must see the applications of his theological perspective to the built environment as texts, artifacts of material culture that warrant a political, cultural, and racial reading. Upton's architectural history survey is especially sensitive to the way buildings are fraught with issues of inclusion and exclusion in American society. Father Divine was keenly aware of this as he worked to transform an architecture of exclusion into one of inclusion by creating a "landscape of consumer citizenship" for his often poor and marginalized followers, many of whom experienced racial discrimination in their daily lives; his were efforts to not only complement but also actualize the "landscape of Republican citizenship" in the United States.[54] Father Divine understood the reality of racial discrimination in America, as well as the alienation of American cities, "where social atomization and the privatization of public space have been the rule." As Upton writes, "In the face of . . . enduring divisions in the American community, some designers have imagined new communities that might be inclusive but undisturbed by social divisions."[55]

Father Divine, as social designer, sought to create spaces for one such community to flourish. He sent clear messages about race and integration in his reuse of buildings for positive community purposes, marking them with signs proclaiming "Peace" or his role as "Pastor," working to create both religious space and publicly racialized space. Such efforts at transformation still endure in remaining Peace Mission Holy Communion Banquet Halls and are particularly well illustrated in the Chapel Dining Room at Woodmont, where discrimination is acknowledged spatially in the race-sensitive seating arrangements of Banquet Service guests. In this room, decorated with wood panels imported from one of the chapels of an Avignon pope (an addition to the house by its second owner, J. Hector McNeal), surrounded by plaster statues of Catholic saints, guests are carefully seated at the table to form an integrated grid of complexions, in fulfillment of the Peace Mission ideal of joining the peoples of the world.

Michael Owen Jones, in a classic article on redoing homes in Los Angeles, lists a variety of reasons for altering space. Among these are responding to changing physical needs; recognizing a good investment; maintaining a sense of authority and control over oneself, one's personal existence, and one's possessions; achieving intellectual and sensory goals involving control, construction, and learning of material culture and material space; actualizing self and self-worth through symbolic statements; and achieving social and community goals.[56] All of these reasons are relevant to the Peace Mission's history and ongoing practice of altering and maintaining space as an expression of sacred and social meaning. Father Divine used material culture and built environments to reconceptualize space in American cities. He engaged in this practice well before home remodeling and improvement and urban gentrification were common, let alone fashionable, and he involved individuals for whom such pursuits were otherwise personally unthinkable and unattainable. In the case of palatial Victorian urban residences, he chose properties that he undoubtedly appreciated as symbols of wealth, power, and fine living. The homes of the employer class therefore became African American domestic spaces, with the former servants of the wealthy assuming responsibility for the renewal, appreciation, and conversion of the ornate interiors to suit their own special needs. To borrow phrases from Akhil Gupta and James Ferguson concerning space in postmodernity, Father Divine, in a prior era and very early in the American struggle for racial justice, "reterritorialized" space, compelling his followers and other attentive Americans "to reconceptualize fundamentally the politics of community, solidarity, identity, and cultural difference."[57] Father Divine learned a lesson about power from the dominant Christian churches in the United States: namely, that a religious body needs to mark the city to be an effective change agent—religious real estate equals religious power. Through its sacralizing of former businesses, residences, and buildings purchased from other religious groups, the Peace Mission effectively created a unique landscape of the sacred in the secular urban context of twentieth-century America, even influencing similar efforts in communities abroad.[58]

Significantly, the Peace Mission continues to prize its vernacular architecture of intention up to the present day.[59] As Father Divine reconstructed buildings, he created a "new landscape of power" that worked to transform social identities and contest the political and symbolic economy of America.[60] These buildings helped to reinforce the positive trajectory of the lives of the movement's members, especially the women. These "sisters" of the Peace Mission, while retaining jobs in domestic service or as laborers, found empowerment in menial tasks done well and pride in their work, all achieved through praise and service to Father Divine and their own community.[61]

Into the twenty-first century, Father Divine's vernacular architecture continues to inspire and empower his community of followers, even in their reduced numbers and capacity. This unique and intentional use of material culture continues to guide the occupants of these religious structures to bring perfection to their lives and witness that goal to those who daily encounter them.

Mother Divine's innovations represent a far more potent harnessing of power based in the engagement of food to create order and sustain control. Mother Divine offers a portrait of a leader using a distinctive religious aesthetic of food—including the growing, selection, purchasing, cleaning, slicing, preparation, spicing, cooking, decoration, serving, and blessing of it, as well as a mode of dining blended with testifying—to maintain authority over her band of spiritual followers and order the world around her. This argument underscores the expressive significance of Mother Divine's innovations, foregrounding them as examples of the creative quality of religious belief—or what I have elsewhere termed "vernacular" belief and practice—that is so notably present within many indigenous American sectarian movements.

11

"And as We Dine, We Sing and Praise God"

Father and Mother Divine's Theologies of Food

The story of religion in America is more than a history of the conscious importation of established traditions to the United States from various parts of the globe—Roman Catholic, Eastern Orthodox Christian, many varieties of Protestant, Jewish, Muslim, Hindu, Buddhist. Equally significant to the narrative are indigenous American religions that evolved on the mainland both before and after its colonization by Europeans. Such resident systems of belief and practice include Native American religions as well as the multitude of hybridized movements that emerged over time out of the interpretation and adaptation of allochthonous religions in specific contexts within the country's physical-cultural landscape, from the Church of Jesus Christ of Latter-day Saints to Christian Science, from the Seventh-day Adventist Church to Scientology. This chapter discusses one such movement: an indigenous religion that was among the most visible urban traditions to emerge in the first half of the twentieth century. Identifying itself as the International Peace Mission Movement and founded by African American minister M. J. Divine, better known as Father Divine (1879–1965), this communal, intentional, celibate community has persisted, albeit with a greatly reduced membership, into the twenty-first century.

Father Divine's International Peace Mission Movement is one of the most colorful exemplars of the practice of faith through religious cookery in the United States. The movement's religious food culture began in the early twentieth century in Sayville, New York, on Long Island, when Father Divine first devised a ritualized Eucharistic celebration in the form of an actual dinner—in fact, a multicourse ban-

Originally published in 2014.

quet. Religion scholars Jualynne E. Dodson and Cheryl Townsend Gilkes describe Father Divine's movement as a tradition "where communion invokes a 'real meal' that includes all of the courses normally associated with a Thanksgiving or Christmas dinner."[1] This American religious love-feast linked the ritualistic eating of food with the spiritual nourishment of the movement's followers. Woven amid the abundance through the courses were homiletic texts—in the form of songs, testimonials, ecstatic dancing, and energetic preaching by God himself—that testified to the positive nature of Father Divine, extolled his formula for the practice of a "radical" religion, and proclaimed the sacred destiny of the United States. Indeed, followers revered and continue to revere Father Divine, "THE REVEREND M. J. DIVINE, MS. D., D. D., FOUNDER, BISHOP AND PASTOR OF THE PEACE MISSION MOVEMENT," as the incarnation of God in the body of a human being, a "Black God of the Metropolis," a significant figure in the history of American religion.[2]

Clearly illustrating how "food and religion are inevitably intertwined in American culture," the Father Divine story is a necessary foundation for the appreciation of another notable yet largely unstudied individual who made significant contributions at that same cultural intersection: Father's second wife, Mrs. Sweet Angel Divine.[3] Better known as Mother Divine (or, in keeping with the movement's understanding of reincarnation, "Mother Divine in the Second Body"), she assumed leadership of the Peace Mission after Father Divine died in 1965 and has shouldered the responsibilities of perpetuating his reputation and religious vision for nearly fifty years.

Beyond guarding the use of Father's spoken and written words, as well as his photographic image, Mother Divine has worked to sustain the movement's ritual traditions, spirituality, and sense of creativity and order. In the late 1970s, however, she went further, introducing her own distinctive and lasting contribution to the everyday lives of the followers who lived around her, as well as to the history and character of the Peace Mission. Impressed with what she had learned of the food philosophy known as macrobiotics, she radically changed members' eating habits. Moving the communitarian Peace Mission away from the rich starches, fried foods, and meat dishes reminiscent of the southern food traditions of its original adherents—including Father Divine himself—she adopted a macrobiotic-based vegetarian diet for her spiritual children. These dietary reformations, which included the use of organic ingredients, also transformed the types and preparation of foods served in the Keyflower, the movement's last public dining room in Philadelphia.

To understand the alteration of Peace Mission eating habits, we must appreciate that the study of food, while ostensibly mundane, is quite complex. In this case, it requires that considerable attention be paid to the personal feelings of followers and to the complex theological assumptions underpinning their religious community. The individuals who have inhabited the Peace Mission have consistently taken offense at what scholars and the popular press have written in the past concerning their founder and their own lives as members of a spiritual utopia. Therefore, they do not like to give interviews, disclose traceable background information, or reveal personal data about themselves, a preference compounded by their spiritual "impersonalism," a de-emphasis of self in favor of more appropriate concentration on the works of their God.

Using methods of historical and contemporary folkloristic ethnography, this analysis elaborates on the food innovations of Mother Divine—her own theology of food—examining how her dietary hierophany challenges general scholarly assumptions about homogeneity within sectarian communities, as well as previously drawn and inadequately informed conclusions about the foodways of the Peace Mission movement specifically. Such analysis speaks to the significance of this leader's use of dietary changes as a catalyst for transforming her followers' understanding of both the meaning of their bodies and the connection of food to religion, health, and longevity. Mother Divine's theology of food could, on the surface, be understood as a rather benign means of routinizing charisma—a second-generation sect leader's attempt to re-engage and energize her aging and declining flock with a fresh sensibility about the benefits of healthy food and balanced eating. I will argue, however, that Mother Divine's innovations represent a far more potent harnessing of power based in the engagement of food to create order and sustain control. Mother Divine offers a portrait of a leader using a distinctive religious aesthetic of food—including the growing, selection, purchasing, cleaning, slicing, preparation, spicing, cooking, decoration, serving, and blessing of it, as well as a mode of dining blended with testifying—to maintain authority over her band of spiritual followers and order the world around her.[4] This argument underscores the expressive significance of Mother Divine's innovations, foregrounding them as examples of the creative quality of religious belief—or what I have elsewhere termed "vernacular" belief and practice—that is so notably present within many indigenous American sectarian movements.[5]

"It's Good to Be around the Body of God": Father Divine and His Peace Mission

To appreciate the evolution of Mother Divine's ideas about food, one must review the history, beliefs, and practices of the Peace Mission.[6] Organized around the central figure of Father Divine in the early decades of the twentieth century, Peace Mission members, who were for the most part African Americans, particularly women, believed this charismatic, "dark-complected" minister (to use their term for racial differentiation) to be their deity of deliverance out of the "depressions, lacks, wants, and limitations" of everyday life.[7] Given the racism and discrimination faced by Black people in America during the Jim Crow era and beyond, these "lacks" were many and pervasive: limited civil rights, poor housing, undignified employment, racial segregation, lack of access to goods and services, nonexistent luxuries. Peace Mission beliefs—as uniquely formulated by Father Divine, drawing on aspects of several religious ideologies influential in late nineteenth- and early twentieth-century America, especially ideas from the New Thought movement—were in large part a response to these conditions.[8] Religious studies scholar Catherine Albanese summarizes what she understands as the roots of Father Divine's thinking and his early activities:

> Whatever his early years were like, Father Divine must have been a traveling preacher for some time when, according to reports, he appeared in Americus, Georgia, in 1912 and Valdosta, Georgia, in 1914. Here he taught a blend of mysticism and practicality in which,

if a person were truly identified with the Spirit of God, health and plenty would result. Most probably, he drew this idea partially from the perfectionism of holiness religion and partially from the mind-cure teachings that . . . were part of New Thought. Yet Father Divine made the idea his own and it became the basis of a lifetime of religious leadership.[9]

Beginning on Long Island in 1919, in Harlem from 1932 to the early 1940s, and in Philadelphia from 1942 to 1965, Father Divine created a "practical religion" of personal fulfillment through the merging of consciousness and resources, with himself as fiscal shepherd and God incarnate. Through his communal economic plan, Father advised followers to commit their individual savings to a larger accumulative purchasing force. With this support from his spiritual children, he assembled a portfolio of income-producing real estate and businesses in cities such as New York, Los Angeles, and Philadelphia, as well as in rural communities in the Hudson River Valley (known as the Promised Land).[10] These properties were acquired with no mortgages, with full payment strictly in cash, and often with white followers negotiating the purchases to nullify the racism that might otherwise have hindered the accrual of property in white communities. The Peace Mission also employed its members as "co-workers" in its own collectively administered and staffed hotels, shops, garages, farms, grocery stores, and cafeterias. These businesses served members of all races and religions without question, with the lodging offering African Americans, in particular, quality accommodations and services several decades before the changes brought about by the civil rights movement. Benjamin Kahan has referred to these entrepreneurial activities as Father Divine's system of self-sufficient "celibate economics"—not so much a Roosevelt-style New Deal in miniature as a uniquely imagined and structured new "Divine Deal."[11]

"The Abundance of the Fullness": Holy Communion Banquet Services

In addition to serving as rural centers of quiet repast for followers to counter the intensity of New York City, the Promised Land was designed to grow and supply food for the various cafeterias, grocery stores, and Holy Communion Banquet Services operating within the extended Peace Mission metropolis and feeding both followers and non-followers. This ministry of food distribution at affordable prices was a notable result of Divine economics and a key dimension of the Peace Mission's social justice program from the 1920s through the Depression era of the 1930s and well beyond, continuing up until the closing of the final public cafeteria, the Keyflower Dining Room in the Divine Tracy Hotel in Philadelphia, in the early 1990s. During interactions at Peace Mission restaurants and businesses, patrons were exposed to Father Divine's message through the staff, the portraits and religious mottos that were hung prominently throughout, and the stacks of the movement's newspaper, the *New Day* (published as a weekly until 1992), that were always available. It was the daily or weekly Holy Communion Banquet Services, however, that presented the greatest opportunity for the direct experience of Father's messages, whether they were read aloud, played as recordings, or offered by the magnetic pastor himself. Father Divine's followers felt transformed throughout his ministry by the presence of their mystical leader and energized by his preaching style. Father's sermons could be encountered as well in a variety of other contexts within Peace Mission life, such as prayer and praise services, "Righteous Government" meetings, and annual business meetings. The Banquet Services, however, were the central channel, tying his "words of spirit and life" to ritual feasting in an expression of spiritual and material abundance offered to all worthy communicants.[12]

The Banquet Service was not conceived or conducted as an elaborate church supper or an occasion for socializing and conversing with like-minded believers and visitors at a table while eating. Testifying and singing were to be robustly communicated to all who could hear, but mundane conversation among participants, even to comment about

Plate 1. Sister Ann Ameen, *Church with Red Door*, n.d., 38 × 35 inches. Leonard Norman Primiano Collection. Photograph by Don Dempsey.

Plate 2. Sister Ann Ameen, *Yellow Flowers on a Purple Background*, n.d., 26.5 × 38.5 inches. Leonard Norman Primiano Collection. Photograph by Don Dempsey.

Plate 3. Saint Joseph's Day altar, Fontana family, Gloucester, Massachusetts, March 2005. Photograph by Joseph Sciorra.

Plate 4. Saints' statues on Saint Joseph's Day, Scola family, Gloucester, Massachusetts, March 2005. Photograph by Joseph Sciorra.

Plate 5. Holy card depicting the Blessed Virgin Mary and the Girl Scouts. Italy, 1960s. Leonard Norman Primiano Collection.

Plate 6. Holy card depicting Our Mother of Perpetual Help. United States, 1930s. Leonard Norman Primiano Collection

Plate 7. Sacred Heart of Jesus, ex-voto in silver. Italy, nineteenth century. Leonard Norman Primiano Collection. Photograph by John Chew.

Plate 8. Man Seeking Help for His Cattle from Saint Chiaffredo. Italy, oil on metal. Leonard Norman Primiano Collection. Photograph by John Chew.

Plate 9. Portrait of Father Divine, Woodmont, Gladwyne, Pennsylvania. Photograph by Leonard Norman Primiano.

Plate 10. Woodmont, Gladwyne, Pennsylvania. Photograph by Leonard Norman Primiano.

Plate 11. Mother Divine seated at Holy Communion Banquet Service table, Chapel Dining Room, Woodmont, Gladwyne, Pennsylvania, July 24, 2011. Photograph by Leonard Norman Primiano.

Plate 12. Molded butter star topped with American flag, Holy Communion Banquet Service, Father Divine Day, Woodmont, Gladwyne, Pennsylvania, September 10, 2013. Photograph by Leonard Norman Primiano.

Plate 13. Mother Divine's place setting at the Holy Communion Banquet Service table, Circle Mission Church, Philadelphia, May 1, 2011. Photograph by Leonard Norman Primiano.

Plate 14. The Shrine to Life, Woodmont, Gladwyne, Pennsylvania. Photograph by Katie Reing.

Plate 15. Doors of the Shrine to Life, known as the *Portal of Life Eternal*, designed and sculpted by Donald De Lue, Woodmont, Gladwyne, Pennsylvania. Photograph by Katie Reing.

Plate 16. "The Builders," detail of the *Portal of Life Eternal* (sculptor Donald De Lue is on the right), Woodmont, Gladwyne, Pennsylvania. Photograph by Katie Reing.

the ritual to those in adjacent seats, was discouraged. This time was framed as an opportunity to commune with God, whether Father Divine was personally present or not. One communed with God through the choral and congregational singing; through the emotional testimonies of health renewed, lives restored, even objects recovered; and through the occasion's dramatic expression of "the abundance of the fullness," the actualization of plenty for those who had previously done without.[13]

A report from a nonmember provides useful details about early Banquet Services. Under pressure from the highly prejudiced Sayville community, the district attorney of Suffolk County in New York hired "the services of a good-looking and rather intelligent young colored woman" from Harlem in 1930 to infiltrate the community to inform him about the activities inside the movement's Sayville home base. The resulting report offered the following account of the food served during this era of the Peace Mission:

> They gave me a seat at the foot of the table, facing Father and Mother Divine. The meal served that night was hot tea, milk and postum, rice, macaroni, white potatoes, green peas, baked beans, mashed turnips, corn, baked tomatoes, turkey, ham chops, corn meal bread, biscuits, graham bread, cake, pie, peaches, and a salad and they served such meals every day. When they have company they serve a few other things to complete the meal, by adding veal stew and fried eggs. But they have the same every day. Turkey was served every day I was there, except Tuesday, they served fried chicken in the place of turkey.[14]

It is important to view such a description in context, as those in the predominantly white Sayville community would have read and understood it: in the midst of the world economic crisis known as the Great Depression, this bounty was being served in the household of an African American man who ostensibly did no work except for ministry. Already a full meal in an era of intense economic hardship, the Banquet Service escalated as the years progressed, going from full to sumptuous, particularly on special occasions. Assuring readers that "all of Father Divine's menus are lavish," the *New Day* presented in detail a "typical holiday menu" from September 13, 1962, the anniversary of the dedication of Woodmont, Father Divine's suburban Philadelphia estate:

MENU

Apricot Nectar

HORS D'OEUVRES

Hot:

Miniature Frankfurters

Gherkins Wrapped in Bacon

Miniature Fish Sticks

Crabettes

Cold:

Smoked Oysters

Cocktail Shrimps

Red Rose Caviar

Black Caviar

Norwegian Smoked Sild

Artichoke Hearts Antipasto

Smoked Fish Plate

VEGETABLES:

Creamery Whipped Potatoes

Wild Rice

Buttered Corn on the Cob

Sliced Fresh Buttered Carrots

Tiny Rosebud Beets

French String Beans with Mushrooms

Fresh Asparagus Spears with Hollandaise Pimento Sauce

SEA FOOD:

Ocean Fresh Fried Deep Sea Scallops

Imported Sauteed Frog Legs with Tartar Sauce

MEATS:

Small Baked Squabs with Tasty Fillings

Rare Roast Sirloin of Beef with Yorkshire Pudding

Baked Virginia Ham with Pineapple Garnish

Roast Capon with Chestnut Dressing and Cranberry Sauce

SALADS:
Lettuce Wedges and Sliced Tomatoes
Avocado Mandarin Plate
Waldorf Gelatin Mold
Pineapple Cottage Cheese Mold
Assorted Relish Plate with Olives and Celery
CHEESES:
Roquefort
Cheddar
Swiss
American Cheese
BREADS:
Crescent Butter Rolls
Fancy Danish Pastries
Ritz
Butter Baskets
Woodmont Blackberry Preserves
BEVERAGES:
Assorted Iced and Hot Beverages
FRUIT BOWL:
Fresh Assorted Fruit Bowl
DESSERT:
Fruit Medly [sic] Mold
Ice Cream Mold
Delectable Velvet Chocolate Pie
Blueberry Tarts
Fruit Cake[15]

The road from cornmeal biscuits and ham chops to Red Rose caviar and rare roast sirloin with Yorkshire pudding represents a fascinating thirty-year food transformation, an embodiment of his abundance-based beliefs blessed and distributed by Father Divine from the head of the long banquet table. Significantly, the evolution and diversification of dishes offered at these Banquet Services did not abate with Father's death. As explored below, Father's second wife would formulate and advance her own vision of how food relates spiritually to abundance, good health, old age, and happiness. Insight into the person of Mother Divine and her contributions to the Peace Mission's food culture allows for a richer appreciation of this community and the complexities of intentional religious communities in America more broadly.

"I Know You Are God": The Second Mother Divine

While an advocate of celibacy, Father Divine had two nonphysical "spiritual" marriages, the first to an African American woman named Peninnah, known as the first "Mother Divine."[16] In 1946, four years after Peninnah's unacknowledged death, he again legally wed. The marriage of the more than sixty-year-old Father Divine to a twenty-one-year-old white Canadian woman drew considerable public criticism to a religious group that was already a source of national conversation and controversy. As he had done many times in the past, Father Divine used this public commotion over his interracial marriage as a way to spread his messages. The marriage, he said, was the ultimate example of God's approval of racial integration, international peace, and the "life of Christ."[17]

The second Mother Divine was born Edna Rose Ritchings in Vancouver, British Columbia, in 1925.[18] In 1940 she encountered the teachings of Father Divine in Vancouver. She became convinced of his godhood and the belief that ultimate peace was attainable only by living a daily life inspired by Jesus Christ and Father Divine. In 1945 she moved to Philadelphia, took the name "Sweet Angel," and became one of Father's secretaries. In 1946 she declared to Father that she wanted to marry him for the sole reason that "I know you are God." They were legally wed on April 29 in Washington, DC, where interracial unions were permitted. Their marriage was proclaimed by Father Divine to be interracial, spiritual, and celibate, exemplifying his worldview and the true harmony of the nations of the world.

If the marriage was publicly controversial in postwar racist America, within the Peace Mission itself it was also a matter of concern for those members who did not understand Father's need for another marriage. While some individuals responded by leaving the movement, for those who remained, the wedding heralded an important event in the history of the Peace Mission, introducing a new, young, vigorous leader-in-waiting. In the minds of such followers, the Divine marriage marked a transition between two distinct eras, or "Dispensations," in the evolution of the Peace Mission movement. The earlier period was a time of struggle both within and outside the community of followers. Within the community, the struggle was to lift its many Black members out of poverty to economic independence. Outside the community, the struggle was primarily with racial prejudice. Father Divine fed and housed his "children," built businesses, acquired property, and fought political battles during this era. The second Dispensation, which began with the 1946 marriage, is seen by followers as "the realization of heaven on earth."[19] With greater economic stability and racial equality secured, the Peace Mission, under its second Mother, has focused increasingly on educating the public about Father's teachings and on the pursuit of mental and physical "purity" in support of its followers' spiritual health.

Since Father Divine's physical passing in 1965, Mother Divine has presided over the Peace Mission, and the movement has developed a matriarchal quality. Mother has maintained her husband's moral and religious standards while looking after the spiritual and temporal needs of their "children," or followers. With a current membership of about fifty elderly men and women, Mother Divine leads the Peace Mission from her Woodmont estate in Gladwyne, Pennsylvania (plate 11).[20] What primarily keeps followers spiritually, mentally, and materially connected to God and his "Spotless Virgin Bride" are their three "Holy Communions," the formal and informal meals that they share together in faith each day.

"Real, Real, Real": The Banquet Service as Eucharist

Father Divine often referred to the formal Holy Communion Banquet Service as a ritual: "Our Private Banquet is the place where we take our Daily Communion. That is our system of our [sic] religious ritual."[21] For scholarly purposes, the Banquet Service certainly qualifies as a ritual, for it is "a repeated socio-religious behavior: a chain of actions, rites, or ritual movements following a standard protocol."[22] The second Mother Divine's book describes this Holy Communion as "the only sacrament observed by the followers and [one that] is performed daily as a ritual in the Churches and private homes."[23]

The Banquet Service is an intense demonstration of reverence and devotion. For visitors who come to dine without proper initiation, such an unabashed expression of belief can prompt surprise or even embarrassment. Indeed, the Peace Mission has maintained one of the most sensual Eucharists of all such rituals to emerge out of the Christian tradition. Andrew McGowan acknowledges that "it takes some effort to perceive the Eucharist of later Christian tradition as food, let alone as a meal. Yet Christian liturgical tradition has eating and drinking at its origin, not merely as incidental actions in religious ritual, but as actual food."[24] The Peace Mission Eucharist effectively involves all the human senses, as one touches the plates, vocalizes a testimony, hears the songs and sermon, tastes the foods, smells the aromas, and sees a dazzling assortment of sights—from women known as Father's "Rosebuds" dressed in red, white, and blue uniforms to thoughtfully designed flower arrangements and even sculpted foods, such as butter lilies and lamb-shaped ice cream (plate 12).

The members, even as twenty-first-century octogenarians, still proclaim that their God is "real, real, real," and that the Banquet Service is the generator of this nexus of the material and the spiritual.[25] Transitional and transformative in nature, the banquet literally fills the individual physically while making everyone at the table, from adherents to harmonizers to visiting strangers, into participant observers in what followers believe is the celebration and generation of positive consciousness and "atONEment" with the spirit of God, Father Divine.[26] Simply being present forces one to engage in regulated behaviors guided by Father's enacted tradition. Peace Mission rituals are powerful public display events centered on food, but they are also religious performances built on an artistic outpouring and amalgamation of timing, precision, personal behavior, manner, etiquette, appearance, posture, and expressions of speech and song.

"It Was Time for Them to Learn How to Eat": From Traditional to Nutritional

In the 1984 edition of his well-regarded study of Father Divine, historian Robert Weisbrot discusses, in his concluding chapter, the final years and achievements of Father Divine's ministry. In the 1960s, he writes, Mother Divine had taken on "the daily administration of the Peace Mission" and was "working closely with Father Divine's able secretarial staff." He goes on to offer this assessment of her leadership:

> Although not an innovator or social crusader as Father Divine had been in his prime, Mother Divine had proven herself well suited to lead the Peace Mission in its search for spiritual purity and organizational stability. She made an impressive, intelligent, demure presence at Peace Mission banquets, and a graciously effective diplomat to guests from all walks of life. It was clear that Father Divine's earlier social radicalism was to be merely revered, not revived, but within the Peace Mission's own centers the Father's vision of a chaste, integrated communal society would go on as before.[27]

While Mother Divine may have appeared as a "demure presence" at the banquets of this period, she was actually evaluating these rituals and planning a series of changes to her followers' foodways—transformations that she would also offer up, in the spirit of her husband, to the public at large. At the same time that Weisbrot was preparing his epilogue, Mother Divine was setting into motion a personal plan to invigorate her community both spiritually and physically through a renewed notion of purity.

Emulating Father's economic and spiritual entrepreneurism, Mother Divine conceptualized in the early 1980s a new business enterprise, a reorientation of the last Peace Mission restaurant controlled by her followers. The restaurant would serve a new type of healthy food that she and her followers could also eat for their own well-being and "purity." At the Keyflower Dining Room, Mother Divine combined the business of retail food preparation with the necessities of sustaining her followers by synthesizing the ideas of Father Divine and the philosophy of macrobiotics, an approach to food and eating that originated in Japan and gained popularity in some American circles in the later twentieth century. Mother Divine's influence over her followers thus became more literal and bodily as she took control of what they ate. What Mother carried out was the radical transformation of her followers into macrobiotic vegetarians, employing a unique and distinctive approach to food selection, preparation, presentation, and consumption based on whole cereal grains, beans, and fresh, locally grown produce consumed in season, with no meat, dairy products, nightshade vegetables, white sugar, or white flour permitted.

In Philadelphia, informational lectures and cooking courses on the macrobiotic system were already available by the late 1970s. The transformation of the foods served at Mother Divine's hotel cafeteria and banquet tables took hold in the early 1980s, when she began attending such lectures in Center City. Mother was especially drawn to the lectures of Stanley Walker, an African American macrobiotic counselor and follower of Michio Kushi, a well-known advocate of macrobiotics. Walker could not help but notice a well-dressed middle-aged woman often seated in the back row of the room where he lectured. When she finally approached him to introduce herself, he was amazed to learn that this woman was none other than Mrs. Sweet Angel Divine. Mother Divine expressed to Walker her interest in macrobiotics and her desire to spread the practice to the followers of her husband's religious movement. Walker was well aware of Father Divine and his work from eating meals at Peace Mission cafeterias in the 1960s for very reasonable prices or for free. Mother Divine sought to hire Walker to teach the principles of macrobiotics to the followers responsible for food preparation at the Keyflower, as well as in her own household. He enthusiastically agreed, bringing his wife, Geraldine, into the process. So began Mother's unique experiment—her bold reordering of the ways her followers would eat and think about food. Geraldine Walker recounts her early experiences working with Peace Mission followers in these terms:

> [Mother] invited us to come to the Keyflower and there were nine cooks and they were all observing and we did a level one cooking class.

It was Spring 1985. . . . It did not catch on right away. [It was a] hard time [for] them. . . . [Mother Divine] wanted me to do whatever I knew. She was the one [who put her foot down] doing that behind the scenes. Mother took the leadership and said this lady and her husband are coming to show you a healthier way of eating. And that was it. All she wanted me to do was teach them what I knew and they took notes, and they were standing and observing. And next week, I went and started cutting [in a macrobiotic manner] and prepping. First, they watched and then they started to participate and that's how it went like that. . . . At one point, they went completely macrobiotic, and they really didn't like it. They really rebelled. . . . So because of that she brought back the meat and slowly some more things have come, and she justifies it as a vast improvement to their meals.[28]

Mother Divine may well have been attracted to the holistic macrobiotic philosophy simply because it was "alternative." Coming herself from a belief system that held unconventional views of the relationship of spirit and body and their connection to eating and health, she likely felt comfortable with the personal and societal challenges that macrobiotics presented and the language and concepts its educators used. That macrobiotics emerged from Japan and not America posed a bit of a problem, as it went against the grain of the Peace Mission's nationalistic propensities, but any such misgivings would have been outweighed by its "holistic approach to life, the integration of spirituality with physical health and wellness."[29]

A larger obstacle Mother Divine would have had to navigate, in reconciling this new orientation and the Peace Mission's, was Father Divine himself. Her husband had in the past directly castigated diners who admired the physical benefits of the Banquet Services alone ("The Kingdom of God is not meat and drink") as well as those who asked to abstain from certain foods at his table.[30] Father Divine consistently portrayed such requests as an excessive reliance or focus on the material over the spiritual, an ambiguity he could not abide. Responding in 1933 to the complaint of a California visitor who expected that "there would be no taking of life in Heaven" but saw meat being served at the banquet table, he preached,

GOD through the mouth of Paul, by the inspiration of the Spirit . . . said, "Eat what is set before you and ask no questions." . . . The next point of view for your consideration, to those that are of the dietarians and metaphysicians, I would like to say I AM not taking thought of what I will eat today for tomorrow, and neither AM I taking consideration what I shall wear. . . . I would not be free indeed if I were bound as to what I should eat, drink or wear. I do not take thought! . . . I AM not bound not to eat it, I AM not bound to eat it.[31]

As Father's congregants grew older, he did become more conciliatory. Twenty years later, at the Circle Mission Church, he honored the request of some diners for unsalted food, but he maintained that such dietary precautions were unnecessary: "I would like to say that I have requested and asked the cooks and others who are preparing the food to prepare food suitable for the dietetians [sic] and for all those who do not care for seasoned food; although, if you have been awakened in the Light of Truth, you may be able to eat anything and it will not hurt nor harm you."[32]

Early in his ministry and years before Mother encountered his teachings in British Columbia, Father Divine preached to his followers a very specific gospel of eternal health and physical resilience: "Father Divine has come to save the body. The mind and the spirit are already saved. But the body has been dying. I have come in order that your bodies might live forever."[33] In Father's view, across the decades, there was nothing wrong with the meals served from Peace Mission kitchens; they energized his followers' physical forms and revitalized their spiritual relations with him. As Jill Watts notes, "He linked health to appetite and encouraged his followers to eat large well-balanced meals."[34] R. Marie Griffith goes further, observing, "Emphatically targeted on health, nonplussed by illness, Divine refused even to speak of those who died in his midst—asserting only in the abstract that those who allowed themselves to expire had not believed fully in him."[35]

While Father Divine preached about the human body being physically sustained by spiritual connectivity to him, Mother Divine, representing the second generation of believers, was forced to deal with troubling evidence to the contrary. She associated the traditional Peace Mission diet of heavy, fatty, salty, sugary foods with the fact that loyal followers were becoming ill and dying, even if they were living to advanced ages. Even more jolting, Mother witnessed Father's declining health, including complications from diabetes, throughout the late 1950s and into the 1960s.[36] Father Divine's physical death—or, to his followers, the "voluntary passing" of his body—in 1965 was no doubt an incredible blow. She and the members attempted to blunt the incongruity of God dying of illness brought on by age and other health factors by creatively reinterpreting his departure from the scene as totally voluntary, a supreme sacrifice. Mother Divine erected an art-filled tomb at their Woodmont estate that she paradoxically called the Shrine to Life, borrowing a theme from the Christian theology of the Resurrection.

Though some followers reverted to eating meat as Mother Divine implemented her transformation of the community's diet, macrobiotic food choices remained part of the daily dishes offered at the Keyflower until its closing. This fare reflected a vernacular macrobiotics—a hybrid of macrobiotic ideals and Peace Mission needs. Such offerings included miso soup; brown rice and other grains; nondairy vegetable entrees; meat alternatives such as tofu, tempeh, and seitan; organic fruit and produce; and bancha, or green, tea. The same menu could be found upstairs at the Holy Communion Banquet Services in the Divine Tracy Hotel dining room and, of course, in the Chapel Dining Room at Woodmont.

Banquets prepared by the hotel and Woodmont staff included such entrees as soy-sage balls with shitake mushrooms in a ginger-miso sauce, tofu with mustard topping, tempeh sautéed with root vegetables, dairy-free mushroom stroganoff, sautéed tofu over whole-wheat fettuccini, and seitan sautéed with red and green peppers. Salads were accompanied by freshly picked watercress, basil, mint, or edible flowers. Grains such as short-grain brown rice accompanied by the sesame-seed-and-salt condiment called *gomashio* were a matter of course, as were organic juices and desserts sweetened with brown rice syrup.[37] Such banquets stood in stark contrast to those served in the past in Brooklyn, Sayville, Harlem, Newark, Jersey City, or wherever Father Divine's community established an outpost. These feasts were marked by collard greens cooked with fatback, macaroni and cheese, corn pudding, white rice with brown gravy, mashed and baked sweet potatoes topped with marshmallows, fried pork chops, roasted chicken with cornbread dressing, and roasted duck with baked apples.

In the context of a religious community mindful of its traditions, Mother Divine enacted further changes that were, in their way, quite dramatic. Father Divine, for example, made it a point always to punctuate the table with starched linen napkins rolled and positioned in a glass at each place. Mother Divine changed this practice at Woodmont, having the nonlinen napkins folded and placed on the table itself (plate 13). Also, at Father's banquets the salads were always served after the entrees; Mother decided that they should be served first. These adjustments were tantamount to changing the order of a Eucharistic service, or the formal ordinance concerning the decoration of an altar or Communion table in a church.

In a rare 1996 interview, Mother Divine explained her original rationale for making the changes in what food was served. Noting that in the late 1960s the Peace Mission was asked by the Philadelphia Redevelopment Authority to renovate the Divine Tracy Hotel or sell it, Mother Divine decided to upgrade it because of its location in the section of Philadelphia known as University City, home to the University of Pennsylvania and Drexel University.

> We felt that there [in that area], that we could contact a different type of person, so they could learn to know Father Divine and what he advocated more than just thinking of him as a minister of the Gospel that was interested in feeding the people material food because they were in want. And I felt too that the Peace Mission had been feeding families for three generations and that it was time for them to learn how to eat. So we decided to change the menu at the Divine Tracy from the traditional type of food—which was a lot of meat, potatoes, gravy, and vegetables—to a more nutritional diet advocating what Father advocated [which] was prevention. He really believed in preventative health. We decided to do away with white sugar and white flour and all additives and preservatives and serve chicken and turkey and tofu and tempeh and that sort of thing. And we served desserts, and when we first started, there were not so many healthy desserts on the market, but we made our own and we made them with rice syrup, different types of sweeteners that were more healthy and people were very happy to change.... Also, people who lived in the Peace

Mission had special diets and Father wanted to accommodate them. Father was trying to accommodate them so they could stick to their diet and live in the Peace Mission.[38]

This valuable reflection shows Mother Divine drawing statements from her husband's sermons that support her position while dismissing others. Here Mother is theologizing certain ideas of Father Divine's and, like the second generation of believers in the early Christian Church, picking those that promote her agenda. Her decisions exemplify how she, as a religious leader, used her own vernacular theological logic to develop a unique understanding of what was consistent with Peace Mission ideology and what was advantageous to the survival of a declining community.

There is no direct evidence that Mother Divine was familiar with the New Thought ideas of Charles and Myrtle Fillmore's Unity Society of Christianity, as Father was, but her actions evoked that metaphysical movement's similarly contradictory advocacy of vegetarianism in the face of their foundational belief that "the mind could correct all."[39] Her statement also reflects a decision to depart from Father's purpose of working to assist the poor directly, especially Black Americans, in cities by supplying a cuisine that they recognized as familiar. She was instead reaching out to a larger, more diverse audience—reminiscent of the era of Peace Mission communities in Australia, Panama, Switzerland, Germany, and England—especially the multiracial and multiethnic international community surrounding the universities. She wanted to feed them affordably but also educate them about natural whole foods—an approach that would, ideally, awaken in them an interest in Father Divine and a receptivity to higher spiritual transformation. From the comfort of her Main Line estate and its seventy-three acres, she could commune with nature and engage the city and its population indirectly through these initiatives, heeding the macrobiotic call "to abandon self-destructive habits and bring [one's] way of eating and living into greater harmony with nature."[40] Living a life infused with "Woodmont consciousness," as the special atmosphere of the estate was known, Mother could meld Father Divine's principles of higher spiritual consciousness with the wholehearted resolve to honor nature through the cleansing of body and mind.

Mother Divine's Theology of Food

What, then, is Mother Divine's theology of food and of the body? It centers on the idea that whole food—healthfully prepared, very reasonably priced, and eaten in a spotlessly clean environment—has a spiritual impact. For her, that is a religious principle. If for Father Divine nourishment was a necessary physical means of a spiritual renewal, for Mother, nutrition plays a different role, one more directly and more avowedly theological. Father "rejoiced" in abundance, as the Bible says; it was a sign of one's spirituality that one had abundance. Mother Divine envisioned a different form of abundance as the reward of righteous eating, directly connected to longevity—even the notion of immortality. Indeed, in this view, the way people achieve eternal life in the physical heaven Father identifies as the United States is by being inwardly clean and whole, a state of purity achieved partly through healthful eating. Proper food not only feeds one but cleanses one internally, in the same manner as one should keep the body externally clean. Goodness is therefore a matter not only of behavior but of one's actual physical makeup. In Mother Divine's theology of food, righteousness equals longevity, and internal righteousness has to do with what is consumed. Mother Divine's theology of the body emphasizes health, exercise, and the path to Divine consciousness through eating well. Fascinatingly, these changes seem to have had an impact on the membership: their longevity since the 1980s has been striking, with some members living beyond one hundred years.

The ninth edition (2011) of the anthology *Extraordinary Groups: An Examination of Unconventional Lifestyles*, a text used in a variety of undergraduate courses on American religious movements, concludes in its updated report on the Peace Mission that Father Divine's utopia "is in trouble. . . . But the movement has not changed."[41] Whether it is the place of scholars to declare a particular religion "in trouble" is a matter for debate within the discipline or, perhaps, the classroom. The present exploration of Mother Divine's Peace Mission, however, specifically challenges any perceptions that readers might have about the static nature of sectarian movements, or for that matter any system of religious belief and practice. This chapter hinges on the observation and argument that the lived expressions of everyday religious life are in creative and constant flux.[42] The expressive culture of food is one of the keys to unlocking the intricacies and nuances of the vernacular religion of both everyday believers and religious leaders. In the case of Mother Divine, the banquets, as transformative and sustaining ritual public display events, served as markers of her contributions to the movement and her evolution from transitional figure to leader, from concerned leader to innovator, and from vernacular theologian of food to sustaining force for a tradition in decline.

The intention of this chapter is to chronicle the development of a sacred sense of place by an American sectarian religion and the complementary creation of a provocative twentieth-century religious "shrine" within that space. Particular attention will be given to the intersection of vernacular religious creativity and professional expertise in the design and adornment of the building. This essay, therefore, is centered on a shrine, a monument, a piece of architecture, a decorative statement, a memorial building, an office, a tomb, a tabernacle, and a holy place, a center of creativity, power, and, ultimately, control, all in one. I argue that the shrine concretizes not the expectation of homogeneity within sectarian religious belief but the necessary flexibility of its standards, in this case as an embodiment of Peace Mission vernacular religiosity, even for the leader of the movement.

12

"As a Living Shrine I Came"

Remembrance, Creativity, and Paradox in God's American Tomb

"I AM THE SHRINE"
The Shrine of the mind is the real Shrine,
A Shrine that you can carry with you all the time,
A Shrine that cannot be burned by fire,
A Shrine that can never die,
A Shrine that cannot pass away—
A Shrine that stands throughout all eternity,
That is the kind of Shrine to have once and forever;
Being conscious of GOD's Presence, live it and express it,
You will carry your Shrine with you!
I AM THE SHRINE! Now keep ME in your mind!
Throughout all eternity!
Throughout all eternity!
—Peace Mission song, no composer or lyricist credited, no known date of composition

The intention of this chapter is to chronicle the development of a sacred sense of place by an American sectarian religion and the complementary creation of a provocative twentieth-century religious "shrine" within that space. Particular attention will be given to the intersection of vernacular religious creativity and professional expertise in the design and adornment of the latter building. This chapter, therefore, is centered on a shrine, a monument, a piece of architecture, a decorative statement, a memorial building, an office, a tomb, a tabernacle, and a holy place, a center of creativity, power, and, ultimately, control, all in one.

Originally published in 2018.

This "shrine" can be found near the city of Philadelphia, Pennsylvania. It honors an individual whose followers believe that he is God. The unique creation of a North American indigenous religion, it represents a meaningful union of devotionalism and creativity, of tradition and innovation. The edifice is the tomb holding the body of an African American minister and religious innovator, the Reverend Major Jealous Divine, better known as Father Divine, founder of the International Peace Mission Movement (plate 14). In a religious tradition that made a practice of buying and reusing existing architecture and American built environments for its community's own spiritual, social, and communal purposes instead of constructing new buildings, the Shrine to Life, as it is called within the movement, is one of only three original or new buildings designed and paid for by Father Divine's followers—the other two being a library/museum and a visitor center. The shrine, however, is the only Peace Mission building specifically constructed for a religious purpose. The occasion of its design—the physical death of the human embodiment of God, Father Divine—ushered in a period of powerful theological reflection for Father Divine's spiritual wife, Mother Divine, and their followers, who were taught not to believe in an afterlife, heaven, or even the reality of illness and death. Where, then, would God's holy physical body be buried? In a structure of what style and shape? Representing an outpouring of reflection, creativity, and remembrance and ultimately reinforcing the unique expressive culture of this American religious community, the Shrine to Life was the paradoxical result of such deliberations. An embodiment of Peace Mission vernacular religiosity, it also demonstrates more broadly the potential for flexibility and resilience in such indigenous sectarian systems of belief.[1]

    I end this introduction with a request that my readers bear with me as I present, first, an extended contextualization of the Peace Mission as a distinct religious movement. The "sensuous life of a religion" such as that of the Peace Mission, to quote religious studies scholar David Morgan, is complex and changeable, as it shapes, colors, and organizes the relationship of believers to the divine.[2] Indeed, an understanding of this shrine as a sacred structure connects its preservation of the material presence of the sacred to other shrines that one may encounter throughout the world within the framework of a highly specific belief system. What could this structure's design, a granite-columned tent topped by a pyramid and marked by great bronze-figured doors, be communicating to someone who encounters it in the garden of a fine Victorian-era estate that has been repurposed as the home base of a sectarian religious community? How do followers within that community understand the shrine's purpose and significance—and how, through the lens of its larger historical and cultural context, might we? The individual design of this American shrine instantiates its purpose, for it holds none other than the body of God.

Father Divine and the International Peace Mission Movement

The Reverend M. J. Divine was the Peace Mission's prime mover, its founder, bishop, and pastor, according to his followers. By the second decade of the twentieth century, he had proclaimed that he was an incarnation of the Christian God and had developed around him, in New York City and surrounding areas, a celibate, perfectionist, communitarian, racially integrated, and economically self-sufficient religious movement. Father Divine, whose actual date of birth is not recognized by the Peace Mission (some historians cite 1879) but who died, or "physically gave up his bodily form," in 1965, is an enigmatic figure—yet, at the same time, remains one of the most photographed and journalistically scrutinized national religious innovators of the twentieth century. Constantly under reevaluation by American religious historians, social critics, and other public observers of his work, he has been both appreciated as an early crusader in the fight for African American civil rights and social justice and criticized as a self-promoter and the leader of a cult.[3]

In Peace Mission theology, Father Divine is not only the religious founder but also God the Creator, the Redeemer, and the Sanctifier, reincarnated in the United States. To Peace Mission followers, God did not visit the Americas thousands of years ago, as is taught by another American indigenous religion, the Church of Jesus Christ of Latter-day Saints (or the Mormons); God was, instead, present throughout much of the twentieth century, where one could find him building a popular movement and business empire in New York or Philadelphia.

During the Great Depression of the 1930s and the upheaval of the Second World War, many felt transformed in the presence of this commanding mystical leader, drawn by his spirit-filled preaching style as well as his good works—most notably, his championing of full rights for African Americans in every dimension of American society, including housing, employment, and public access to facilities. Of particular interest was the seemingly miraculous abundance of food served at a regular Peace Mission ritual occasion known as the Holy Communion Banquet Service. This ritual feasting was central to Father Divine's theology and his fame, as he and his followers dined, worshipped, sang, danced, and praised God together. Under Father Divine's charismatic and enterprising leadership, the Peace Mission grew nationally and internationally, emerging from its origins in Brooklyn in 1914 and its early years on Long Island to establish headquarters in Harlem in 1932 as it gained momentum and resources. The movement soon spread to Switzerland, Germany, Australia, England, Panama, and throughout the United States, from Brooklyn to Seattle, from Chicago to Los Angeles. The Peace Mission was particularly attractive to many African Americans and people of Caribbean descent, and especially to women, though it also had white members, particularly former Christian Scientists who joined in the 1930s and 1940s.

Through a communal economic plan built on collective real estate purchases and community business ventures, Father Divine and his followers amassed great wealth in New York City during the Depression era and into the 1940s. Across a variety of locations, the Peace Mission employed "co-workers," or its most devoted followers, in collectively owned residences, grocery stores, barbershops, garages, domestic services, and cafeterias. These businesses served members of all races and religions without question at extremely reasonable prices, offering African Americans, especially, quality accommodations and integrated services at a time when they were often denied such things due to racial discrimination. These establishments, distinguished by the proclamations of "Peace" or "Peace Mission" or "Thank You, Father" hanging in their windows or painted on their doors, along with their requisite displays of photographs of Father Divine, could be found throughout Harlem in the 1930s and 1940s. The presence of the Peace Mission made the community safer and served its population, turning Father Divine and his followers into both an urban spiritual force and a political force in

New York that even candidates for mayor or state governor, for example, needed to consider and court.

A Practical Religion

Father Divine called his faith a "practical religion" and "practical Christianity."[4] A contemporary Peace Mission website offers a clear explanation of his concept:

> People today need something more than a theoretical religion; they need a living, pulsing working force in their lives that is going to solve problems now; not some time in a future imaginary heaven. . . . The Peace Mission Movement is such a practical religion and its churches give to the people a spiritual sustenance for their daily spiritual and material needs on earth.[5]

Father Divine taught that there was no afterlife in the traditional Christian sense, and that it was foolish to look to "the sky" for future happiness and contentment when one could work toward and attain it in the present plane of existence. Money, therefore, was never to be spent frivolously. Father Divine followed one economic principle unfailingly: that there was social power—especially for the marginalized population of urban Blacks—in accumulated community wealth. There was freedom for the individual when one could depend on the collective resources and skills of the Peace Mission family.

Wherever the Peace Mission established itself, the municipality would feel an economic benefit. Father Divine's "Divine Cooperative Plan" called on his followers to be honest, to never accept government money or welfare, to never make purchases on credit, and to pool personal finances together for group investment projects. He found employment for his out-of-work female followers by establishing agencies for domestic service. In the Philadelphia area throughout the 1970s, such workers were widely appreciated for their industry, reliability, and honesty. Peace Mission members also opened other local businesses, such as garages, grocery stores, barbershops, and typing services. Father Divine then guided his followers to pool their financial resources to obtain, preserve, beautify, restore, and secure land and properties around and beyond the city. They learned how to repair, construct, or restore these buildings and their infrastructure, such as plumbing and heating, and also maintain the community's fleet of automobiles and other required machinery. All bills were to be paid in cash, precluding the need to ever carry checks or a credit card or take out a mortgage for real estate. Followers' homes, businesses, automobiles, and lives were never insured for fire, casualty, or accident because, according to Peace Mission teachings, the only insurance needed was the assurance of being blessed by God, Father Divine. All these measures allowed for individual resources to be saved and pooled for group investment.

A Vernacular Architecture of Intention

In New York City, Father Divine sought for his movement's use not older church buildings constructed by other religious groups but secular buildings, such as former catering halls, hotel banquet rooms, and even casinos, which were then transformed by his followers for reuse according to their religious and community purposes. These secular properties were sanctified through the positive nature of their new intended use and were transformed in an emergent process I have called a "vernacular architecture of intention."[6] Through an intentional use of secular spaces and a spiritualized appropriation of existing spaces, Father Divine and the Peace Mission expressed their own ideals, furthering their quest for a utopian perfection of consciousness in America. Beyond restoring these buildings to maximize their cleanliness, comfort, and use, Father Divine deployed these spaces as public representations of his community's "victory" over material "lacks, wants, and limitations," which they achieved through commitment to his belief in a present earthly heaven and the attainability of "the abundance of the fullness" through positive consciousness and adherence to his moral code, which forbade drinking, smoking, swearing, lying, discriminating, and engaging in sexual relations.

In 1942, after refusing to pay a former follower $6,000 that she won in a settlement against him in a New York court, Father Divine left the city and moved his headquarters to Philadelphia. Father's "spiritual children" soon sold their properties in New York and joined him in the City of Brotherly Love. The movement then began to purchase old hotels in Philadelphia and New Jersey to house followers and to offer inexpensive, nondiscriminatory, high-quality accommodations to the public. Each establishment's secular name and original signage were kept, but with "Divine" added, as in the case of Philadelphia's Divine Lorraine and Divine Tracy Hotels. In an American city like Philadelphia in the 1940s and 1950s, it undoubtedly brought Father Divine great satisfaction to accentuate his presence in the urban landscape through such public announcements. It was clear that these spaces had been reclaimed and repurposed to meet new religious aims and standards—what he called his "International Modest Code"—and were being presented as beacons of hope and empowerment so that anyone, of any "race, creed, or color," might be inspired by this "radical and fanatical," as Father described it, communitarian religion with a "dark-complected" leader—a particularly bold and significant gesture in 1940s and 1950s America.[7]

As was the case in New York in the 1930s and 1940s, in Philadelphia from the 1950s through the 1970s there was ample evidence of Father Divine's influence. You saw his hotels throughout the city; followers employed by his domestic service might work for you; maybe you ate breakfast, lunch, or dinner at one of his Peace Mission cafeterias. When Philadelphia made several impassioned attempts in the 1940s to have the United Nations headquartered in the city near Independence Hall, Father Divine, to the delight of his congregation, urged UN representatives and President Harry Truman to make this blessed proposal a reality. Though it failed to materialize following a Rockefeller gift to purchase land in Manhattan for the site, Father Divine characterized Philadelphia in 1949 as "the Country Seat of the World" and "the Country Seat of Democracy," proclaiming the city to be "the only place where Democracy is truly at work. It is the nucleus from which MY Work of Righteousness is spreading to all nations of the world. . . . As Philadelphia is the Cradle of Democracy, the birthplace of the Constitution and of the Declaration of Independence, it is similarly the Country Seat of Human Rights."[8]

Though the Peace Mission had access to many buildings, Father Divine, enacting his teaching of practical religion, neither built nor purchased distinctive church structures for his congregation's use as worship spaces. Older buildings in Philadelphia, such as former YMCAs, Catholic schools, or Masonic halls from the Victorian era, were highly desirable to the Peace Mission because of their size and their available auditorium spaces with stages for oratory, prayer, and scripture meetings, as well as their reasonable acquisition prices throughout the 1940s and 1950s. Of course, the exigencies of the Peace Mission's daily Holy Communion Banquet Services—the three-hour Eucharistic meals consisting of forty courses each that served to exemplify "the practicality of our spiritual devotion and service to GOD and unto man"—necessitated not traditional ecclesiastical amenities such as sanctuaries, sacristies, or fellowship halls but, rather, large meeting spaces with multiple conjoined tables and extensive adjacent kitchen, food preparation, and supply areas.[9] In Philadelphia, the Divine Lorraine Hotel on North Broad Street, the Circle Mission Church at Broad and Catherine Streets, the "Bible Institute" near the campus of Temple University, and the Unity Mission Church, a former Pennsylvania Railroad YMCA building in West Philadelphia, were four such sites able to accommodate the movement's large Holy Communion Banquet Services.[10]

Woodmont: "The Mount of the House of the Lord"

Of all of the Philadelphia-area Peace Mission properties, none could match the splendor of the movement's last major real estate acquisition, in 1952: a seventy-three-acre Victorian estate in the Philadelphia suburb of Gladwyne called Woodmont, which was purchased for $75,000, the projected cost to the current owner of the manor house's demolition.[11] While it appears that the primary purpose of this purchase was for it to serve as Father and Mother Divine's "country estate," as well as a rest center for followers, by the late 1950s, it had become the place where Father Divine, in his later years of infirmity and illness, could retreat from public view. The acquisition of this property provided the occasion for one of Father Divine's final bursts of theological creativity, in helping to explain its sacred purpose. Woodmont, an estate built for the family of one wealthy white industrialist, would now serve the extended, integrated family of the Peace Mission, and all would be welcome to enter "through the front door." Father Divine proclaimed that, through his church's ownership of the property, he had "broken that line of demarcation and brought an end to localization," referring to the separation of the races and to racial discrimination.[12] He saw himself as fulfilling the founder of Philadelphia's dream of true brotherly love, declaring at the September 10, 1953, dedication of Woodmont, "I come to you carrying out God's plan in the name of William Penn."[13]

As early as 1949, Father Divine, citing his 1936 "Righteous Government Platform" for ending racial discrimination, referred to America itself as "predestined to be The Mount Of The House Of GOD where the children of men shall live in peaceful and quiet resting places, where no man can make them afraid!"[14] He would end up bestowing that honor more specifically upon Woodmont, which was christened "the Mount of the House of the Lord." Just as he had drawn on various belief systems (such as evangelical Christianity, Pentecostalism, Roman Catholicism, Methodism, and the New Thought movement) in the formulation of Peace Mission ideology in the 1920s, in his characterization of Woodmont at its dedication, Father Divine combined his familiarity with Judeo-Christian scripture (citing Isaiah 2:2–3 and Micah 4:1–2) and his own interpretation of American and religious history. In this Divine-style rendering of religious space, Woodmont was not Jesus's or Puritan John Winthrop's "city upon a hill" but a more particular vision of such a beacon—a "dark-complected" God's "house upon the hill," with the backdrop of the local Philadelphia region standing in for Jerusalem.

> (FATHER speaks as follows:)
> Then Solomon began to build the House of the LORD at Jerusalem in Mount Moriah. Then the LORD began to build the house of the LORD in Philadelphia in Woodmont; where the LORD appeared at the signing of the Declaration of Independence and at the drafting of the Constitution and its Amendments; where the people proclaimed Liberty throughout all the land and the Pilgrim Fathers came in the name of the Quakers and made Philadelphia, through the signing of the Declaration of Independence and the drafting of the Constitution and its Amendments—the city of "BROTHERLY LOVE." . . .
> And the LORD came and made it in the latter days—confirming the City of "BROTHERLY LOVE" . . . and the *Cradle of Democracy*, making it the COUNTRY SEAT of the WORLD! And thence HE starts to build the Temple of GOD. Not at Jerusalem in [M]ount Moriah, but at the NEW JERUSALEM, better known as Philadelphia, at Woodmont!

STAFF: That is so wonderful, FATHER Dear.

ONE OF THE STAFF: It's no wonder I always look down on the village of Conshohocken and[,] seeing the houses and churches with their spires, think it looks just like Jerusalem.

ANOTHER OF THE STAFF: That is wonderful, FATHER Dear.

MOTHER DIVINE: It has a spiritual significance.

SECRETARY: Then we have the River Jordan, known as the Schuylkill [R]iver.[15]

Such statements were more than grand, provocative instances of creative association at a ceremony. Father Divine's followers absorbed and were persuaded by these themes, like his other teachings, in a continuous way, reading them as articles in the *New Day*, the movement's newspaper, over and over again or hearing them repeated, in the mode of monastic recitation of scripture, at community meals, which amplified their impact.

There to reinforce such teachings and help to develop the movement's sense of sacred space was his "light-complected" second wife, "Sweet Angel" Divine, known as Mother Divine, the Canadian follower whom he married in 1946—a controversial interracial celibate or "spiritual" marriage—when he was sixty-eight and she was twenty-one years old.[16] Since the community was celibate, Father Divine's spiritual marriages were a matter of great interest and curiosity to both movement insiders and the public. Father Divine offered that his second marriage was theologically significant because it marked the unification of the races with God, was a celebration of purity and virginity, and served as a reminder of the reality of reincarnation—as Sweet Angel Divine was, Father explained, the reincarnation of the Virgin Mary herself, as well as of his first wife, the "dark-complected" Peninnah or "Sister Penny," who died in the early 1940s. The second Mrs. Divine would go on to reside at the estate for nearly forty years after Father Divine's passing, until her own death, or "transcendence," in 2017, and she continued to work to consecrate Woodmont as a space of sacred significance both for the followers and to the outside world. The design and construction of a suitable tomb for her husband was a major creative expression of these years, as she both augmented Father's teachings and put her own imprint on the movement.

Father's Passing

Father Divine's physical passing on September 10, 1965, was a shock to his followers, even if he had been mostly out of view due to ill health during his final years. He had openly preached that those who established perfect consciousness with the "Divine Mind Substance," as mediated through him and his teachings, would avoid illness and even death. While his followers were not given funerals and their deaths were not publicly recognized, the death of Father Divine—who had long been a well-known and controversial figure in the United States, frequently featured in newspapers—was a significant event for followers and nonfollowers alike. After a large public viewing of his body at Woodmont, Father Divine was temporarily buried in the ground at the publicly accessible area of West Laurel Hill Cemetery in suburban Bala Cynwyd, not far from the estate. In the wake of his passing, his followers would frequent his grave, alone and in group processionals on Sundays; they would gather around his grave and sing Peace Mission songs to him. At the same time, it was acknowledged that Father's passing had been his own decision, and that his spirit remained in communication with those who wished to contact him. To mark his ever-presence, a custom was established of serving food from each course at Holy Communion Banquet Services to Father's accustomed place at the table, where Mother Divine physically presided as church exemplar—a practice that continues even in the present day for both Father and Mother Divine, since her own death.

Creating this tradition was only the start of Mother Divine's efforts to honor her deity husband; she would soon begin work on a tomb/shrine and, with it, solidify the transfer of his power as leader to herself. She surely wanted to retain proximity to, if not outright control over, his physical remains—but why locate a material memorial for one of the "Black Gods of the Metropolis" (as anthropologist/folklorist Arthur Huff Fauset called him in 1944), a figure whose work was essentially centered in urban areas where his following lived, in an exclusive, leafy suburb well outside the center of his ministry on the streets of Philadelphia?[17] And what sort of memorial could she construct within a tradition and aesthetic that did not include new architecture, that did not make use of statuary, and that had even avoided memorializing the first Mother

Divine with so much as a notable grave site? Furthermore, Father Divine himself appeared to discourage the creation of physical sacred shrines when one could, instead, commune with his consciousness, as God, personally and mentally. As far back as 1933, he preached,

> But I AM speaking of the average person thinking of coming to eat even at this Table—to shake hands with ME—to go out to Sayville, or any material place that has been "shrinefied" by the mortal versions of the human mind. Shrines are created, I say, through and by the mortal version of the human mind that is devout and sincere—believing vividly in the sacredness of something, someone, or some place, and through their zealousness they create for them all sorts of shrines throughout the land and they will be shrines expressed to others as unto them that are on the mortal plane in that same state of consciousness that they are in. . . . The same like manner in reference to Sayville, Long Island [where Father Divine lived and established his Peace Mission's foundational outpost]. It has been, or has proved to be, an international, interracial and interdenominational shrine. But why was it? It was through and by the mortal version of the human mind, not by the true spiritual interpretation of things. That place there, could not, or would not be any more than any other ground in MY Version, but in the mortal versions of the human mind they observe things of that kind, so they create for themselves and make shrines, and if I had not come, there would have been a continuation of shrines throughout the land even as they began once again with ME and around ME where I AM, and therefore they began making to themselves idle gods of material expressions of things, and not the true and the Living One.[18]

Father taught his followers that he himself, ever representing a connection with divine truth, was the shrine, as opposed to "shrinefied" material places:

> As a Living Shrine I Came, throwing aside all of the inanimate shrines of the land, presenting myself as a living sacrifice before the children of men that they might gaze upon the PERFECT PICTURE, mentally and spiritually; their prayers will be heard and answered speedily the same

as others have been answered through and by the spirit of sincerity. That is the mystery![19]

As a Living Shrine I Came ... as a Shrine I Stand, as a Shrine I Move, I Live and I have My Being, and when you think of ME with the spirit of sincerity, and think harmoniously in this direction, your prayers will be heard and answered.[20]

This point was accentuated in a Peace Mission liturgical song, "I Am the Shrine," in which it was observed that "The Shrine of the mind is the real Shrine ... I AM THE SHRINE! Now keep ME in your mind!"

In addition to all these considerations, given Peace Mission standards of monetary practicality, would it be possible to ask the unified yet separately administered churches of the mission for funding, since, in an effort to protect against future lawsuits, neither Father Divine nor Mother Divine had any personal savings or property under their own names?

The Shrine to Life

Even in the face of these rather daunting obstacles and theological paradoxes, Mother still wanted to honor her husband—his life, work, and mission—materially, architecturally, and concretely at Woodmont with a structure to serve as his resting place. Her personal creative response was to advocate for a costly Shrine to Life.[21] Transforming a garden space into a tomb, the Shrine to Life marked the first time a professionally designed and newly constructed building was introduced on any Peace Mission property. Architect William Heyl Thompson and his associate Richard Murphy were hired to design and supervise construction, and, with the agreement of Mother Divine, they erected a structure that incorporated Jewish, Egyptian, and American themes: a granite tent of uncarved blocks with a pyramidal roof. Inside, Father Divine's body would be laid in an evocation of the Ark of the Covenant.

A commemorative booklet issued by the Peace Mission, first on the occasion of the structure's dedication in September 1968 and then again at the dedication of its great bronze doors in 1970, offers both descriptive details and invaluable insights into how this tomb of God was understood by Mother Divine and the movement's membership. In one solution to the problem of designing a visual statement to honor the very human form of a deity, the building was awash in biblical references and allusions, offering a word-based connection to the Judeo-Christian tradition, as opposed to a more representational, material-centered aesthetic. "The Shrine at Woodmont" is described in the booklet as follows:

> The Shrine to Life at Woodmont, powerful in its simplicity, denotes the Personal Life of FATHER DIVINE. Its peaceful atmosphere conveys HIS Serenity and Humility. Its strength and purity of line, HIS staunch stand for the high moral and spiritual values of life made clear by HIS Own Example which are the foundation stones of the Peace Mission Movement as it stands today, a bulwark of faith in a troubled world.
>
> Its purpose is twofold. It is the Holy Sanctuary enshrining the Body of God FATHER DIVINE and it is a reminder of the consistency and continuity of GOD's covenant fulfilled from the beginning of Biblical history to the present time. . . .
>
> The Shrine places on record in granite the advent of the dispensation on earth in Bodily Form in fulfillment of His covenant to "establish a holy people unto himself. . . ."
>
> Framed by the trees of the garden, the simple mass of Sierra White granite walls of the Shrine stands out in bold relief against a green background. Twenty-six feet in diameter, it rises out of the center of a circular court surrounded by a low parapet wall. At the four corners, four free standing columns support the large pyramid, the apex of which is twenty-five feet above the main floor level. This is reminiscent of the Tabernacle and four supporting pillars of the Tent containing the Ark of the Covenant as described in Exodus XXV.
>
> At the base of the pyramid, a large transitional octagonal canopy has been placed to shed water. From this, between the four columns, are the convex-concave curved walls or curtains hung from the roof, again reminiscent of the walls of the Tent, which are floating and completely surrounded by glass to give the illusion of lightness. As one enters the Shrine, you behold the beautiful Ark of the Covenant upon which two golden bronze Cherubim kneel calm and serene. The radiant red granite Ark rests upon a circular dais of the granite. There are three matching

benches, one in front of each of the convex-concave walls. The floor is a green and black Opalescent granite.

Beyond the Ark, the golden dove ascends in free flight under the bronze letters PEACE.

Above the walls of the pyramid are lined with gold mosaic tile, the crown of the apex of which is glass through which one can view the clouds and sky.

The *Portal of Life Eternal*

During the design process, Mother Divine agreed that the building's unadorned exterior walls needed some type of complementary flourish to enhance the architectural statement. The best such complement, it was decided, would be large carved bronze doors. But what sort of carving or design, and in what style, would be appropriate for the doors of a shrine that already featured such a mix of genres? Abstract modernism was the inclination of the sculptor who had initially been commissioned, Bruce Moore of Washington, DC. That design was rejected in 1967 by Thompson and Murphy.[22] The architects then asked another well-known sculptor, Donald H. De Lue, to consider a design for the doors. De Lue, a representational sculptor, visited Woodmont, the shrine site, and, of course, the woman commissioning this work, Mother Divine. As De Lue scholar D. Roger Howlett writes, "While sitting with Mother Divine, De Lue remarked of [his] drawing [of the doors] that 'the sun was always at high noon.' Mother Divine turned to De Lue and said, 'That's right out of Father Divine's mouth—you must be listening to him.' De Lue had the commission."[23]

De Lue first modeled the two cherubim to sit above the ark and the bronze ascending dove. These pieces were dedicated, along with the shrine building, on September 10, 1968. He then worked on the doors—collectively titled the *Portal of Life Eternal*—for the next two years (plate 15). Mother Divine would make the final decisions about the doors, but their imagery appears to have been the result of a lengthy negotiation between De Lue's ideas and style and Mother Divine's thoughts on what would be suitable and appropriate to honor Father Divine. Mother Divine's secretary's notebook, from the archive of Father Divine's Library and Museum at Woodmont, indicates at least four visits by Mother to

De Lue's studio in Red Bank/Leonardo, New Jersey. Howlett observes, "The many drawings show that revisions were made in iconography and arrangement again and again. The doors were dedicated and unveiled September 10, 1970. The complicated composition and extensive iconography executed in extremely high relief worked well for both Mother Divine and Donald De Lue."[24] Howlett also notes that De Lue was given a great deal of independence in his depiction of the figures:

> The *Portal of Life Eternal* allowed De Lue not only to build an iconography for the Peace Mission Movement, but to expand iconographically on his own themes of spirituality and patriotism.... He said, "I am especially interested in this project because they are allowing me to do the figures as I want. Most times your design has to conform to the ideas of those who are granting the commission. But this one I can design as I want." De Lue's own deeply held belief in the American Republic and the striving of spiritual man coincided with the major tenets of the Peace Mission Movement. De Lue believed firmly in great men and heroes, but he believed more firmly in the beauty of the individual and collective spirit. The *Portal of Life Eternal* is his essay in bronze on the subject.[25]

De Lue designed five hundred pounds of sculpture: twenty-four reliefs to be hung on the doors, which were themselves ten feet, six inches high, six feet, six inches wide, and three inches thick.[26] The works could all be removed from behind for periodic cleaning and polishing. Though the Peace Mission did not prohibit visual representations of Father Divine—photographic images of him graced every room of their properties—his visage was nowhere to be found in this bronze assemblage. Instead, there were metaphorical reminders of the dawning of a "new day" and the dispensation of a transformed, integrated society and culture that began for all humanity when Father Divine's human presence appeared on earth. The figures included images of interracial brotherhood, with two men warmly embracing; unmasked Justice weighing the extremes of good and evil; an angel with a flaming sword triumphing over a fallen spirit, representative of evil and fallen consciousness; and "The Builders," a section celebrating interracial togetherness through harmonious work. Indeed, De Lue was so taken with this theme that he sculpted a likeness of himself as one of the builders (plate 16). Whatever meaning De Lue may have intended for certain figures as he designed them, the Peace Mission's interpretation of particular reliefs clearly cast them as symbols of what Father Divine called "Americanism," a universal American manifest destiny coupled with a religious devotion to American secular principles and symbols as God-given.[27] The dedicatory shrine booklet published by the Peace Mission explains that two floating angelic figures to the left and right of the sun are intended as a celebration of America:

> Beneath the sun, leaping upward in glad rejoicing for the Reign of God on earth, Liberty, with bells ringing, rejoices over her country that has given GOD the privilege and the place to wed HIS creation and establish HIS kingdom on earth, and The Constitution, with the torch and the law in her hands and the American flag behind her, gives legal authority for the magnification of the established law into the Law of the Spirit of Life.

Below the sun is a small earth that marks the city of Father Divine, Philadelphia:

> As man reaches for GOD's Hand, his feet extend downward into the smaller circle of the earth. Thus Heaven and earth are brought together as material man becomes spiritualized in oneness with his GOD. Philadelphia, Cradle of Democracy, further proclaimed the Country Seat of the World by FATHER DIVINE, is indicated on the North American continent by a small star.

One element of De Lue's reliefs that undoubtedly called for the creative interpretation of Peace Mission moral standards by Mother Divine and her church advisors was a visual hallmark of the sculptor's style: the depiction of mythological and human figures as nude or near nude. Indeed, De Lue's shrine doors are filled with nudity. For this celibate movement, one that separated men from women in mixed-race living accommodations and that did not even permit men to wear short pants that exposed their legs in the community restaurants and hotels, while doing yard work, or on the grounds of the Woodmont estate as visitors, the acceptance of such immodest representations would seem incongruous, at minimum.[28] The movement had already gone so far as to make cloth coverings for immodest architectural elements found in Victorian properties they acquired—specifically, female mermaids with exposed breasts carved into the banisters in a house on Broad Street in Philadelphia.[29] In the garden at Woodmont, very close to where the shrine was placed, a reproduction of a statue of Hermes (the *Seated Hermes* of Herculaneum) that had been left by the previous owner was "evangelized," or adorned with a metal loincloth, to hide his exposed offending body parts. One would think that allowing several of the reliefs on the *Portal*, the doors of Father Divine's resting place, to depict figures in a state of dishabille would have been at odds with the Peace Mission Modest Code—but in this case, it was permitted and/or overlooked, presumably for artistic reasons. Mother Divine approved the designs, and her will prevailed.[30]

Living with the Shrine

Mother Divine and the band of followers residing at Woodmont have lived with this shrine for almost half a century. Increasingly aware that the movement was not growing and that material, visual markers would be needed for future generations to remember Father Divine, Mother Divine kept developing Woodmont as a destination for potential religious tourism and pilgrimage. Peace Mission publications presented Woodmont as "A World Set Apart," a place possessing "an aura of Divine Grandeur." One such description, from 1999, of the suburban property's spiritual meaning characterizes Woodmont as a living "Garden of Eden," the fusion of heaven and earth: "The mysterious, majestic beauties of Woodmont have been extoled to the highest—its picturesque Grounds and its intriguing Buildings. They are obvious to any eye. But there is a deep Spiritual Magnitude of Woodmont also, which is apparent only to the Inner Eye."[31]

Unable to sustain the membership base of the Peace Mission through a magnetic larger-than-life presence or dynamic preaching style of her own, Mother Divine assumed the role of caretaker and sustainer of Father Divine's reputation and religious vision. In particular, she guided the use of artistic expression and communication to generate a "sense of religious place" about Woodmont. This was evident in the creation of songs about "the Woodmont consciousness," in the distinctive selection, preparation, and presentation of foods at the elaborate Banquet Services hosted at the house, and through traditions of upkeep that included ordered perfection, ornamentation, and decoration, especially with flowers.[32] "Here . . . peace, brotherhood, independence, and virtue depict Father Divine's America," the mansion's printed visitor's brochure announces. On Sunday afternoons, when it is open to visitors, "Rosebuds" from the movement's band of unmarried, virginal female followers, patriotically dressed in red blazers, white blouses, and blue skirts, offer tours of the mansion, also explicating the shrine and the imagery on its doors. The shrine's garden setting puts it in direct vertical alignment with the room that Father Divine used as an office at Woodmont. As both rooms have the same general shape, the followers began referring to Father's tomb as his "office in the garden," adding a utilitarian or domestic dimension to the structure.[33] In addition to the bouquets of fresh flowers left consistently at the shrine's base and a single rosebud often placed on the ark, an American flag was added to the space, along with a spray of seven silver bells down the center of the pyramid above the ark, a remnant from one of Father and Mother Divine's wedding anniversary celebrations.

The estate was declared a National Historic Landmark in 1999. Mother Divine oversaw the erection of a tourist center in the 2000s, and a combined library and museum opened in 2017, with walls erected by Amish stonemasons from Lancaster. These additions complemented the main house, the grounds, and the shrine, offering visitors a more robust spiritual experience, but such developments also drained the movement's reserves at a time when it needed financial resources to pay, for example, for the health expenses of the aging membership, who had no health insurance other than Medicare. This expansion was perhaps undertaken in part as a deterrent to future real estate speculation, given Woodmont's seventy-three acres of prime land in an extremely desirable residential suburb. The library did not open to the public until 2017, so Mother Divine had plenty of time to consider basing it in a more urban location at a lower cost: the Peace Mission still held properties in Philadelphia that were directly associated with Father Divine's ministry, such as the Circle Mission Church, and repurposing such a site would have been in keeping with Father Divine's practicality and past practices. "The Circle," as this building is known in the community, had originally been built and operated as the public Hotel Dale and had functioned as Father's residence and church headquarters through most of the 1940s and 1950s before his move to Woodmont; by the time the library was being planned, it housed only a few followers and was an ideal candidate for rehabilitation. But Mother Divine insisted that Woodmont was holy ground. "The Mount of the House of the Lord" had to be the central focus, the home base for potential visitors, the long-term location of the movement's visible history. It was here that she made permanent the ideals of Father Divine, celebrating the material presence of the holy within the framework and context of the particular indigenous American sectarian belief system she represented through the creation of a uniquely representative sacred space—the Shrine to Life.

Conclusion

The Peace Mission's Shrine to Life celebrates the paradox of marking the end of Father Divine's ministry and his human passing while also, for his community of followers, still pulsating with the living sacred presence of his eternal consciousness, offering a oneness they have long sought to attain. After her husband's death, it took Mother Divine time to consolidate her power over the movement, and she used a keen sense of religious place to strengthen that hold by sacralizing her residence, making it the inevitable resting place for her husband's earthly remains. This can be seen against a backdrop of the history of Christian martyrs and relics: as the bones of Saint Peter are venerated below the high altar of the Vatican, bolstering the claim to authentic apostolic succession for the Roman pontiff, so the sacred remains of Father Divine secure Woodmont's position on a higher plane, as a space of elevated consciousness, and Mother Divine's place within that consecrated landscape. Such was the appeal of this consolidation of sacred space that none of the contradictions inherent to the shrine or obstacles to its design and execution—its cost as new construction rather than a repurposing of existing assets, its suburban location, its recasting of the mission's internal theological teaching, its contradiction of the movement's emphasis on modesty—stopped the structure from being built or sacralized.

In her 2016 study of racial identity during the Great Migration of African Americans out of the South and into the cities of the North, Midwest, and West, American religious historian Judith Weisenfeld identifies the Peace Mission as one of several early twentieth-century Black sectarian movements "whose members believed that understanding black people's true racial history and identity revealed their correct and divinely ordained religious orientation."[34] Such a "religio-racial" belief system was especially compelling to African Americans and Caribbean immigrants in America at the time. In the case of the Peace Mission, all racial references were avoided in everyday speech, as were specific uses of the terms "black" and "white" to differentiate on the basis of race; the descriptive substitutes, as noted, were "dark-complected" and "light-complected." Reviewing census, voting, and even draft records, Weisenfeld shows how these followers put into everyday practice what they believed about race, as they would categorize themselves not as "Negro" but as "human."[35]

In the aesthetic/artistic form it finally took, the Shrine to Life amounted to a creative nexus between professional artists and a particular religious personality—the representation of Mother Divine's own vernacular religious creativity.[36] For Mother Divine, this material expression was symbolic of the movement and the leader whose legacy she strove to preserve, celebrate, and venerate. While not devaluing Father Divine's consistent championing of equal treatment for individuals of color, Mother Divine chose to emphasize—or perhaps was more comfortable with—Father Divine's deity and its connection to an American manifest destiny rather than the social justice causes he had championed while alive. Whether she was aware of the paradoxical qualities inherent in the shrine, she no doubt also saw the tomb as a conduit for sustaining her own power as leader of the Peace Mission movement.

Rooms at Woodmont—like those of other Peace Mission properties and residences—are consistently equipped with altar-like displays of photographs of both Father and Mother Divine, small shrines that remind followers and visitors of the "ever-presence" of their God and his "spotless virgin bride." Mother Divine, innovative and astute, made Father's tomb into a formal but also a domestic space, one available to her and her followers in the estate garden of their grand home. Folklorist Kay Turner, in her work on the art and meaning of women's altars, notes that such special sites are both connected to and "a place apart" from the domestic environment. Turner writes,

> A woman's personal altar evokes her particular—her intimate—relationship to the divine, human, and natural realms. There she assembles a highly condensed symbolic model of connection by bringing together sacred images and ritual objects, pictures, mementos, natural materials, and decorative effects which represent different realms of meaning and experience—heaven and earth, family and deities, nature and culture, Self and Other. By actively engaging the Divine at this self-created sacred place, she makes her altar a living instrument of communication, a channeling device for integration, reconciliation and creative transformation.[37]

The Shrine to Life is Mother Divine's intriguing vernacular religious embodiment of the women's altar ideal and tradition: a shrine to memory, a shrine to devotion, a shrine to creativity, and a shrine to power, in this case her power as God's wife. Turner adds, "The altar is a woman's access to her kind of power, power shared with and through [others], both human and divine."[38]

The Shrine to Life represents Mother Divine's understanding of the personal and emotional attachment that followers would have to the body of her husband, as well as her need to consolidate her leadership position and power over the membership by creating a new and special sense of place related to his embodied divinity. After Father Divine's death, Mother Divine consciously promoted the sacrality of Woodmont, solidifying the estate's position as the movement's home base and spiritual center through the earthly remains of her husband. The scholarly study of place, which looks to Michel de Certeau, Edward Soja, and Henri Lefebvre for a theoretical foundation, "envisions places as events or performances that make available the human practices and processes involved in their construction, as a way to understand that places are never 'finished' or complete, but are always becoming," as folklorist Rosina S. Miller explains.³⁹ Though Woodmont communicates a sacred permanence through its natural and built environments, the present study has shown how the Shrine to Life offered Mother Divine the opportunity to convey her own vernacular religious ideas and attend to emergent necessities of representation and leadership within the movement. In a continuation of that practical sacred expression by her followers, after Mother Divine's own "transcendence" in 2017, it was announced that her body, too, would be interred in the tomb that she had built for God under the dove of peace. Her completed granite sarcophagus was adorned in 2018 with a bronze rose—a motif of life, beauty, and perfection that she often used to describe her spiritual husband and God.

My underlying argument in these chapters has been consistent: to study American religious communities, one needs to be attentive to the dynamic quality of what I call "vernacular religion"—that is, religion as it is lived and negotiated, interpreted and created in human institutions and everyday life. One of the most effective ways to appreciate the sometimes dramatic, sometimes subtle, affectively public or powerfully private nature of vernacular religion is first and foremost through a determined and sensitive consideration of the expressive culture found in a community of individuals, certainly including traditions and uses of belief, foodways, speech and song, dress, architecture, art and craft, and notions of healing. I want to reiterate how important it is to state and restate this basic folklife-studies theoretical and methodological orientation to the study of religion.

CODA

Encountering the Female Divine . . . Literally

Ethnographic Writing about Mother and Father Divine's Peace Mission Movement

In many ways, this entire book has been about the relationship of ethnographers to the religious individuals whom we study. I have tried to address the relations among "informants," "consultants," and "contributors" in this kind of fieldwork. What is agency, and how are issues of agency specifically related to ethnographic writing? Trained in folkloristic ethnography and religious studies, I see folkloristics making an important contribution to the work of ethnographers of religion.

Building on recent debates in the anthropology of religion, I return to these issues of fieldwork methodology in my study of the expressive culture of the American sectarian religion known as Father Divine's International Peace Mission Movement. My underlying argument in all of this work is consistent: to study American religious communities, one needs to be attentive to the dynamic quality of what I call "vernacular religion"—that is, religion as it is lived and negotiated, interpreted and created in human institutions and everyday life.[1] One of the most effective ways to appreciate the sometimes dramatic, sometimes subtle, affectively public or powerfully private nature of vernacular religion is first and foremost through a determined and sensitive consideration of the expressive culture found in a community of individuals, certainly including traditions and uses of belief, foodways, speech and song, dress, architecture, art and craft, and notions of healing. I want to conclude this collection by reiterating how important this basic folklife-studies-based theoretical and methodological orientation is to the study of religion.

Originally published in 2017.

Contemporary studies of American religious folklife place an emphasis on describing, analyzing, and comparing the culture of communities defined by their religious belief systems. Such communities can also be defined by shared geography, age, gender, economy, occupation, leisure, and medical, political, or other beliefs. Religious folklife stresses the significance of aesthetic or artistic creativity and creation; historical process; the construction of mental, verbal, or material forms; and the enduring relationship and subtle balance between utility and creativity in such forms within cultures. The methodology of religious folklife studies includes exhaustive historical research that makes use of all available sources, as well as fieldwork that includes ethnographic observation, thick description, and interviewing. Often taking a reciprocal or collaborative ethnographic approach, this method and subsequent analysis allow people to speak for themselves, using their own aesthetic and classificatory systems—at times influenced by, but often outside, reified institutional or intellectual structures—to explain their religious beliefs and practices to those scholars who have been given the privilege to know, understand, appreciate, and learn from their religious lives.

These principles of the folklore and folklife approach to ethnographic method and analysis have been very influential for me as I formed my own approach to studying a challenging and remarkable American religion, one that could be described as "alternative" to conventional American social and religious structures. For over twenty-five years, I have done ethnographic work with the remaining members of the indigenous American intentional religious community known as the Peace Mission, belonging to a tradition of innovative, radical, positive religious communitarianism that includes the Oneida Community, the Harmonists, and the Shakers. The Peace Mission movement, as this book describes, was organized in the first two decades of the twentieth century around the charismatic African American minister known as Father Divine. A few dozen remaining members currently live in or outside Philadelphia, where the movement relocated in the 1940s from New York City. It is the conviction of Peace Mission followers that Father Divine is God. Peace Mission beliefs are a unique formulation based on Father Divine's personal spiritual insights and his synthesis of several religious traditions that were influential in late nineteenth- and early twentieth-century America: Adventist, Holiness, Roman Catholic, Black church, storefront Christianity, and New Thought. Father Divine came to public attention in 1920 in Sayville, New York, when he began to gather a multiracial group of followers. He soon transformed this following into an expansive religious cooperative that emphasized moral living, hard work, social justice, racial equality, and peaceful coexistence with the world. He banned smoking, drinking, gambling, swearing, and sexual relations, compelling followers to live by what he deemed the "International Modest Code." By working to "harmonize with Father's spirit," followers were taught, they would achieve lasting health, increasing prosperity, and ultimate salvation in his oneness. His ideology of positive thinking promised economic success and personal empowerment. He gained tens of thousands of followers by midcentury, not only in the continental United States but also in Canada, Australia, Switzerland, Germany, France, England, and Panama.

My work with the contemporary congregation, who are reduced in number, mostly elderly, and largely female, has been filled with elation, complexity, and calories, as anyone who has attended a three-hour, multicourse Peace Mission Holy Communion Banquet Service can attest. Chief among those remaining movement members that I have had the honor to consult with over the years is Mother Divine herself—Father Divine's second wife, his "spotless virgin bride," according to Peace Mission theology, and the movement's leader since his death in the mid-1960s. Since their marriage in 1946, much theological reflection, expression, and enumeration within the movement have been directed toward the celibate, spiritual marriage of Father Divine to this much younger, white Canadian woman and her role within the mission.

Mother Divine died in March 2017 at the age of ninety-one after leading the community for more than forty years.[2] She continues to be observed by her followers, or spiritual children, as both the reincarnation of Father's first wife, Peninnah, and the incarnation of the Virgin Mary, and she is understood as the unifier of the international, universal, and interracial aspects of the religion, as well as the exemplar of the feminine ideal as the celibate bride of God, or Father Divine. Mother Divine was a living divine maternal figure for the membership, who believe she will continue to be available for harmonious contact by all believers and friends of the movement, as is Father Divine. Mother Divine's role as a religious leader and innovator is complex and worthy of serious scholarly attention in itself,[3] but here I would like to explore the complications that her role as a living divinity presented to me as an ethnographer studying this aging but still vibrant and expressive religious community.

As a part of my scholarship on the Peace Mission over the last two decades, I was presented in 1998 with the intriguing prospect of preparing a short entry on Mother Divine for Serinity Young's *Encyclopedia of Women and World Religion* (Macmillan, 1998). Well aware of the movement's disdain for past scholarship and coverage in the popular press, and its members' particular distaste for articles treating Father and Mother Divine personally, I knew that this assignment would pose a challenge. My solution was to employ the method known as "reciprocal ethnography" in the preparation, writing, and editing of the article.[4]

The Peace Mission's history and contemporary presence have fascinated scholars of American religion since its inception. Sociologists of American "sectarian" religion have studied Father Divine as a figure representing Max Weber's notion of the "charismatic" religious leader. Historians have chronicled his work, analyzing the success of his overall political and social agenda as well as investigating the historical roots of George Baker, the man who is believed to have become Father Divine. The most prominent histories have been authored by Robert Weisbrot (*Father Divine and the Struggle for Racial Equality*, published in 1983) and Jill Watts (*God, Harlem U.S.A.*, published in 1992). These scholarly texts are but two of many volumes written about Father Divine, including what could be described as examples of descriptive sociology,[5] evangelical Christian tracts against this American "cult," such as Velmer Gardner's 1952 *I Spent the Night in the Devil's House*, and exposés from major publishers on the abuses and deceptions of the movement, such as John Hoshor's 1936 *God in a Rolls Royce: The Rise of Father Divine, Madman, Menace, or Messiah?* and Sarah Harris's 1953 *Father Divine: Holy Husband*. Father Divine's role in "influencing" Jim Jones and the formation of his Peoples Temple, infamous for the 1978 mass suicide, is recounted in David Chidester's insightful *Salvation and Suicide: Jim Jones, the Peoples Temple, and Jonestown* (Indiana University Press, 2003, revised 2009).

After more than half a century of such publications, the response of Peace Mission members to the suggestion of further research into Father Divine or the movement is not particularly positive. Mother Divine, for example, told me how much she disliked the books by Weisbrot and, especially, Watts, whose work she felt took tremendous liberties in presenting the history of George Baker and identifying him as the man who became Father Divine. The Peace Mission has denied this identity for Father as far back as a famous two-part 1936 *New Yorker* magazine report on him from when he was a major political and economic force in Harlem, "Who Is This King of Glory?"[6] Members, in fact, will not even say the name George Baker, instead uttering the initials "G. B." only when they must, and Mother Divine once informed me that she hired a lawyer in 1979 to make the Library of Congress delete the name George Baker from the card catalog heading for Father Divine. This deletion was successfully accomplished in 1982.[7]

Furthermore, it is not surprising that the contemporary Peace Mission community dislikes and distrusts scholars and the process of scholarly research when one realizes that, though this religion has in fact existed almost as long without Father Divine being alive as with him being physically present, scholars of American religion essentially disregarded them as a viable American religious community after Father Divine's death. I have often asked myself, Could this lack of attention to the religious leadership of a woman and the lives of her mainly female followers be an indication of scholarly chauvinism? I should add that there has been, relatively recently, an additional historical study of the Peace Mission's western New York State agrarian utopian communities, written by Pulitzer Prize–winning historian Carleton Mabee, *Promised Land: Father Divine's Interracial Communities in Ulster County, New York* (Purple Mountain Press, 2008). The followers see this book as a more positive contribution, but one still filled with inappropriate references to Father Divine as a human being and not an incarnational figure.

A particularly vivid example of the Peace Mission's distrust of those who wish to "study" them can be seen in the experience of my fellow folklorist Deborah Bailey, who worked intrepidly with the community in the late 1980s while at the University of Pennsylvania, writing a paper for Professor Dell Hymes's graduate course on the ethnography of speaking. Bailey was given permission to do ethnographic work on the religious speech acts of members, but only if she promised the follower assigned to her, Miss Heart, never to publish her research. Bailey, ever the ethical folklorist, in a very early example of a feminist and morally responsible ethnographic approach to issues defined by the people being studied, went on to produce a paper of over a hundred pages that she never published, in fulfillment of her vow during the ethnographic work. This story, of course, stands in stark contrast to the approach of another researcher of the Peace Mission whom I encountered, ostensibly a graduate student at New York City's New School for Social Research, who showed me the hidden recorder she was employing at Banquet Services to tape members' testimonials to use for her master's thesis. (I am pleased to report that, after this woman proudly revealed to me her hidden microphone at a second banquet, I informed a follower of her unethical practices and never saw her again at their services.)

Drafting an article, then, from my own research for a publication that would be including it as a biographical entry on Mother Divine herself certainly posed a challenge. I instinctively felt that the only way to proceed was to employ a dialogical method, writing about this figure by using her own knowledge and her own sense of how she wanted to be represented, along with material that I had researched, to flesh out an article that would both have scholarly integrity and not be insulting to its subject. Influenced by the work of folklorists Elaine Lawless and Glenn Hinson and anthropologist Luke Eric Lassiter, I came to the awareness that the method I needed to use in the preparation, writing, and editing of the article, what I had to apply by necessity, was the ethnographic method known as "collaborative" or "reciprocal" ethnography. A direct outgrowth of the sensitivities of folklorist David Hufford's "experience-centered approach" to belief studies, this has been beautifully described by Luke Lassiter as "a model that explicitly seeks to resituate control and authority within the ongoing dialogue about the evolving ethnographic text itself rather than with the single-voiced author," a format in which "dialogue is not just represented but sought at every point in the development of the ethnographic text."[8]

My efforts to find the right approach came to fruition one fall afternoon in 1997 at Father and Mother Divine's office on the seventh floor of the now-closed Divine Tracy Hotel near the University of Pennsylvania campus, one of a series of integrated hotels of high quality and safety that the mission ran according to Father Divine's strict moral codes for many years in Philadelphia, Newark, and Jersey City, New Jersey.[9] I had mailed Mother Divine a copy of the rather short encyclopedia entry (it was no more than two and a half single-spaced pages). I arranged this meeting to conduct what I hoped would be a review of the piece and a discussion of what changes needed to be made to improve it, to correct it, and to "bring it up to Father's standards." This was, after all, God's wife I was going to interview, according to her followers, and I appreciated that this occasion presented me with the opportunity to speak directly with a major personality in the rich tapestry of important figures in the history of American religion. There is a wonderful song that is sung in the Peace Mission community, "There Ain't No Heaven in the Sky": God is right here on earth, in their belief, and Mother Divine is the human embodiment of that divine principle.

Mother met me with her secretary, Miss Edna Mae Claybrook, and one of her trusted advisors, Miss Anita, was also seated in the room. To say that I was very curious to hear her opinion of the article is a bit of an understatement. Instead of critiquing it, however, Mother Divine began by simply announcing, "Very good, Dr. Primiano, would you read the article to us." So there, in front of God's wife, with the sunlight streaming through the curtains, I slowly read an encyclopedia article that I had written about her and waited for her response. It was as ethnographically surreal a context as one can imagine. As I read the article, Mother would sometimes nod, sometimes shake her head "no," and sometimes exchange glances with the others; once she chuckled, and once she grunted. I finished my recitation, and Mother responded, "Okay, Dr. Primiano, now please reread the article, sentence by sentence, and we will comment." I could not tell whether Mother was using the royal "we," speaking for all the ladies assembled in the office, or actually referring to Father Divine and herself. But that is what I did, as an ethnographic writer taking his cues and instructions from the living folk.

Thus began an approximately two-hour review of the article in which we addressed words, phrases, facts, and ideas. We had a dialogue, for example, about such minor details as the way the occupation of Mother Divine's father was cited and, more significantly, how I described Father Divine. In this piece, I had written that Father Divine was a charismatic African American religious leader. Miss Edna Mae was troubled by this statement, asking me why I could not simply refer to Father as an "American religious leader." Conscious as Peace Mission members are to avoid references to race, she asked whether I really needed to bring this element into consideration in such a central way. That issue has been a major point of contention, and this was a real moment when compromise would be necessary to embody my conception of a socially just ethnographic method. "Well, Miss Edna Mae," I explained, "wasn't the fact that Father appeared as a man of dark complexion [the terminology employed in the movement to refer to African Americans] important to the basic message of Father Divine—that God had come in the body of a humble, dark man?" "Well, yes," Miss Edna Mae agreed. In this way, we came to a point of understanding, and she respected the decision I made to describe Father Divine that way, satisfied that I had taken the time to understand their community's theology well enough that I could discuss it with her in an informed manner.

So we went through the article line by line, discussing its content, and I made changes and carefully argued for its integrity until all were satisfied. I felt pleased and relieved that the entry could appear, and that I could show it to the subjects, without any reservations. In regard to reciprocal research relations and the study of religion, Mel Prideaux has noted, "Without reciprocity—without receiving something in return—we risk alienating and abusing the communities we seek to understand."[10] What I hope that I gave in return to Mother Divine and the Peace Mission followers in the process of reciprocal ethnography, as an informed non-member, was an expression of recognition, respect, and deference to this woman revered as a female divine, in a demeanor that this community of believers found appropriate.

I asked for a photograph of Father and Mother Divine to accompany the piece, and at a later date, we examined over fifty photos to choose just the right one. As with the text, we literally worked together on the project, and I not only felt satisfied that this piece maintained the integrity that I would hope to achieve with any piece of scholarship; I felt happy that Mother would continue speaking to me after the encyclopedia was available to the public.

After the article was published, I went on to write three other pieces using a similar methodology of collaboration: an article on what I call Father Divine's "vernacular architecture of intention" (chapter 10), one on the creativity of their voluminous tradition of religious music and song (chapter 9), and one on their foodways and related traditions (chapter 11). At the time of this writing, I have been working on articles examining the Peace Mission's use of photography and treatment of flowers, extending my general study of the movement's expressive culture. The complexities of a collaborative approach are many and need to be further outlined in future publications, but I feel that this approach of representation, translation, and analysis of their religious beliefs and practices has helped me work toward a socially just longitudinal study of this unique religious culture. I have been able to maintain solidarity with this community over the length of my study, offering a critical voice, one to which they can respond. Such work is in no way easy; it consistently presents questions and challenges. I am especially indebted to the anthropological approaches of Luke Eric Lassiter as elucidated in many articles and books, including his *Chicago Guide to Collaborative Ethnography* (University of Chicago Press, 2005), which helped me formulate a more explicit and deliberate practice of collaborative ethnography while continuing to explore the folkloristic contributions and parameters of such ethnographic methods.

My visits to the Peace Mission usually include attendance at their Holy Communion Banquet Services, where I sit with followers in their sacred space and essentially do my ethnographic work alongside them. On such occasions, I openly take ethnographic notes, and I "testify" about my upcoming professional talks about the community. This approach of being consistently mindful of who has control of the story grows organically out of a folklife-studies sensibility and sensitivity to the complexities of representing the lives of others. Such a reciprocal ethnography embodies social justice and advocacy for our contributors, vivifying contemporary concerns in folkloristic ethnography as well as the moral concerns of the Roman Catholic liberal arts university where I am presently employed. This approach has allowed me to sustain a positive, honest, and respectful insider/outsider relationship with this community and with their leader. It was an honor to know Mother Divine and to have her act as a "contributor," not merely as an "informant" or "consultant," to my scholarly work on her life and ministry.

Kim Knott, in her evocative essay on insider/outsider perspectives in the study of religious communities, has observed that "the problem of the insider and outsider is as vital now for understanding the theory and method of religious studies as it was when the latter first emerged as a discipline separate from theology more than a century ago."[11] My extensive fieldwork experience with the Peace Mission has allowed me to maintain both an insider and an outsider relationship, which has enabled me to be accepted by the community as part of a group of nonmembers whom they designate as "harmonizers." My own appreciation for the complexities of such an insider/outsider bond has assisted my analysis of how this movement and other communities that occupy a similar position in the sociocultural landscape understand religion—and, most valuably, enhanced my practice of what I consider the art of doing folkloristic ethnography about religion. I have been open about the fact that I am not a follower of the Peace Mission and that I actually belong to a different religion. Still, the consensus among them is that only someone who is the reincarnation of a former member could appreciate the theological outlook of Father Divine as much as I do. Rather than feel uncomfortable about their interpretation of me, I have been honored to receive their trust, and it is this trust that has allowed me to engage in fruitful long-term reciprocal ethnography and better document, analyze, and understand this unique community's vernacular religion and its expression.

ACKNOWLEDGMENTS

INTRODUCTION

I would like to thank Robert Atkinson, David Azzolina, Camille Bacon-Smith, Deborah Ann Bailey, Ruth Anna Cary, Michael J. Chiarappa, Sharon Cochrane, Karen Hudson, David J. Hufford, Deanna Kemler, E. Ann Matter, Robert Blair St. George, Stephen Stuempfle, H. William Westerman, and Don Yoder for their contributions and bibliographic assistance in the preparation of this chapter. I am especially grateful to Becky Vorpagel for her critical comments and folkloristic expertise, and to Kathleen Malone O'Connor for her indispensable insights into the study of religion. A version of the introduction, "Vernacular Religion and the Search for Method in Religious Folklife," appeared in *Western Folklore* 54, no. 1 (January 1995): 37–56, and is published by permission of the Western States Folklore Society.

CHAPTER 1: TEXTURES OF A RELIGIOUS LIFE

I would particularly like to thank the following individuals who assisted me in the preparation of this article: Deborah Ann Bailey, Lourdes Barretto, Sharon Cochrane, Justin Fakiani, Delf Hohmann, Diane E. Goldstein, Paul Smith, Philip Hiscock, Barbara Rieti, Douglas Thompson, Mary Thompson, Don Dempsey, Seth Freebie, Anne Schwelm, Abel Rodríguez, Anne Jenner, and Lars Jenner. Peter Narváez introduced me to Sister Ann Ameen and has been incredibly generous with his time and knowledge. Anne Budgell, who also introduced me to Sister Ann, has warmly shared her own insights about this special woman, and kindly read a draft. Stephen George helped me with valuable bibliographic sources and other information on Newfoundland. Barbara Mercer and John Mercer aided my research with their voluminous knowledge of Newfoundland culture. Arthur Petten and Joyce Petten graciously welcomed me into their home. The careful reading of Charlie McCormick, my colleague at Cabrini College, was an enormous asset. Kathleen

Malone O'Connor's perceptive comments on drafts of this piece were also invaluable. A version of chapter 1, "Textures of a Religious Life: The Vernacular Religious Art of Sister Ann Ameen," appeared in "Art and the Religious Impulse," ed. Eric Michael Mazur, special issue, *Bucknell Review* 46, no. 1 (2002): 62–83, and is published by permission of the author's estate.

CHAPTER 2: THE VOW AS VISUAL FEAST

This chapter was first presented as a paper as part of a panel at the 2003 meeting of the American Folklore Society. The research was supported by a faculty development grant from Cabrini College. I wish to thank Deborah Ann Bailey, Lourdes Barretto, John DiMucci, Margaret Kruesi, Charlie McCormick, Kathy McCrea, Kathleen Malone O'Connor, and Joan Saverino, as well as Anne Schwelm and Corey Salazar of Cabrini College's Holy Spirit Library, for their assistance. I am especially grateful to Katie Reing for her technical assistance, and to Nicholas Rademacher, Joseph Sciorra, and Nancy Watterson, who read final drafts. A version of chapter 2, "The Vow as Visual Feast: Honoring St. Joseph in Sicilian American Homes," appeared in *Traditiones* 36, no. 1 (2007): 113–25, and is published by permission of Ingrid Slavec Gradišnik, chief co-editor of *Traditiones*.

CHAPTER 3: POSTMODERN SITES OF CATHOLIC
SACRED MATERIALITY

A version of chapter 3, "Postmodern Sites of Catholic Sacred Materiality," appeared in *Perspectives on American Religion and Culture*, ed. Peter W. Williams (Blackwell, 1999), 187–202, and is published by permission of John Wiley & Sons.

CHAPTER 4: ARTIFACTS OF BELIEF

This research was supported by a faculty development grant from Cabrini College. I wish to thank Deborah Ann Bailey, Father Eugene Carrella, Nick Dominijanni, Tracey Greenwood, Robert Glenn Howard, the late Yvonne Lange, Andrew Madonia, E. Ann Matter, J. Melvin, Lisa Ratmansky, Chantal Rich, Mariolina Salvatori, Joseph Sciorra, Sister Mary Louise Sullivan, Don Yoder, and Kathleen Malone O'Connor, as well as Anne Schwelm, Michael LaMagna, and the late Corey Salazar of Cabrini

College's Holy Spirit Library, for their assistance. I am grateful to Katie Reing, Kathy McCrea, Patti Stocker, Don Dempsey, and Ben Danner for their technical assistance; Jonnie Guerra and Anne Skleder for their support; Jonathan McLelland for his translation skills; and John DiMucci, J. Gregory Garrity, Matthew Serfass, Matthew Slutz, and Nancy Watterson, who read drafts. A version of chapter 4, "Artifacts of Belief: Holy Cards in Roman Catholic Culture," appeared in *Experiencing Religion: New Approaches to Personal Religiosity*, ed. Clara Saraiva, Peter Jan Margry, Lionel Obadia, Kinga Povedák, and José Mapril (LIT Verlag, 2016), 119–42, and is published by permission of Veit D. Hopf, editor of LIT Verlag.

CHAPTER 5: CATHOLICIANA UNMOORED

I wish to thank Joelle Collins, Ben Danner, Kathy McCrea, John DiMucci, Laura Sauer Palmer, Nicholas Rademacher, Lisa Ratmansky, Patti Stocker, and William Westerman, as well as Sara Drew of Cabrini College's Holy Spirit Library, for their assistance. I am especially grateful to Rosangela Briscese and Joseph Sciorra for their unfailing support, and to my colleague Nancy Watterson, who read drafts of this piece. Thanks also to my friend, former Cabrini College campus minister John DiMucci, who taught me how to query and use eBay for objects. My interest had been naturally piqued by gifts to me that John had won in the site's auctions. A version of chapter 5, "Catholiciana Unmoored: Ex-Votos in Catholic Tradition and Their Commercialization as Religious Commodities," appeared in *Graces Received: Painted and Metal Ex-Votos from Italy*, ed. Rosangela Briscese and Joseph Sciorra (Calandra Institute, 2012), 8–37, and is published by permission of the author's estate.

CHAPTER 6: THE GAY GOD OF THE CITY

I would like to thank the members of Dignity/Philadelphia for their time, assistance, and candor; the staff of the Cabrini College Library for aiding my research; and John DiMucci, Kathleen M. Joyce, Nancy L. Watterson, and my Cabrini College colleague Charlie McCormick for their careful readings of drafts of this essay. Sherry Becht, Rosemarie DeMaio, Alan Silverman, Anne Schwelm, Kathleen Malone O'Connor, Deborah Ann Bailey, Justin Falciani, Ron Karstetter, Michael L. Murray, Steven F. Reynolds, Lourdes Barretto, and Leo A. Murray, SJ, were all enormously helpful. A version of chapter 6, "The Gay God of the City:

The Emergence of the Gay and Lesbian Ethnic Parish," is reproduced from *Gay Religion*, ed. Scott Thumma and Edward R. Gray (AltaMira Press, 2005). © AltaMira Press, 2005, reproduced by arrangement with AltaMira Press.

CHAPTER 7: WHAT IS VERNACULAR CATHOLICISM?
I wish to thank the members of Dignity/Philadelphia who spoke with me. Many thanks to Deborah Ann Bailey, Justin Falciani, Lars Jenner, Anne Jenner, and Kathleen Malone O'Connor for editorial assistance and support. A version of chapter 7, "What Is Vernacular Catholicism? The 'Dignity' Example," appeared in *Acta Ethnographica Hungarica* 46, nos. 1–2 (2001): 51–58, and is published by permission of the author's estate.

CHAPTER 8: "I WOULD RATHER BE FIXATED ON THE LORD"
Shorter versions of this chapter were presented at the 1992 meeting of the American Folklore Society in Jacksonville, Florida, and the meeting of the American Academy of Religion in San Francisco. I also presented a form of this chapter as a lecture in November 1992 sponsored by the University of Oregon's Folklore and Ethnic Studies Program. I thank Daniel Wojcik for arranging that occasion. I could not have completed this research without the cooperation of Dignity/Philadelphia. I especially thank my informants for allowing me to speak with them and to record our conversations and interviews. E. Ann Matter of the University of Pennsylvania has been an invaluable resource and critic throughout my study of the Dignity community. I am also grateful to Kathleen Malone O'Connor for her comments and editorial assistance. A version of chapter 8 is reprinted with permission from "'I Would Rather Be Fixated on the Lord': Women's Religion, Men's Power, and the 'Dignity' Problem," *New York Folklore* 19, nos. 1–2 (1993): 89–103. © 1993 by New York Folklore Society.

CHAPTER 9: "THE CONSCIOUSNESS OF GOD'S PRESENCE WILL KEEP YOU WELL, HEALTHY, HAPPY, AND SINGING"
This chapter was first presented at panels at the 2004 meeting of the American Academy of Religion and the 2005 meeting of the American Folklore Society. I am especially thankful for the assistance of Mother

Divine and various members of the Palace Mission and Circle Mission churches in Philadelphia; without their generous time and consideration, this research would not have been possible. This work was supported by a faculty development grant from Cabrini College. I also wish to thank Deborah Ann Bailey, Lourdes Barretto, John DiMucci, Shirley Dixon, Margaret Kruesi, Kathy McCrea, Kathleen Malone O'Connor, and Katie Reing, as well as Anne Schwelm and Corey Salazar of Cabrini College's Holy Spirit Library. My student Andrew M. Madonia was an invaluable research assistant. I am most grateful to Jeffrey Gingerich, Darryl Mace, Lisa Ratmansky, and my religious studies colleague Nicholas Rademacher, all from the Cabrini College writing group, for their comments and assistance during the draft stage. Fellow folklorists and Cabrini colleagues Charlie McCormick and Nancy L. Watterson, also members of the Cabrini writing group, kindly and diligently read drafts of this chapter. A version of chapter 9, "'The Consciousness of God's Presence Will Keep You Well, Healthy, Happy, and Singing': The Tradition of Innovation in the Music of Father Divine's Peace Mission Movement," appeared in *The New Black Gods: Arthur Huff Fauset and the Study of African American Religions*, eds. Edward E. Curtis IV and Danielle Brune Sigler (Indiana University Press, 2009), 91–115, and is published by permission of the author's estate.

CHAPTER 10: "BRINGING PERFECTION IN THESE DIFFERENT PLACES"
This chapter was first presented at a panel on "Reappraising North American Religious Architecture" at the 2001 meeting of the Society of Architectural Historians. I am grateful to Brian C. R. Zugay for organizing that panel and for his assistance and expertise in American religion and architecture. A version of this chapter was also presented as a paper at the 2001 meeting of the American Folklore Society in Anchorage, Alaska. Most importantly, this piece was presented to the members of the Peace Mission Movement, with Mrs. S. A. Divine, better known as Mother Divine, in attendance, in June 2001. I have made every effort in the production of this work to consult members of the Peace Mission Movement and apply a reciprocal ethnographic method, treating Father Divine's followers not as informants but as consultants about their own lives, traditions, and movement. I especially thank Mother Divine for her assistance, as well as several "co-workers," including Miss

Roma Gravure, Mr. Philip Life, Miss June Peace, Miss Dorothy Darling, and many other members of the Palace Mission and Circle Mission churches. I also wish to thank Deborah Ann Bailey, Lourdes Barretto, Katie A. T. Beauchesne, Teilhard Beauchesne, Sherry Becht, Rosemarie DeMaio, Shirley Dixon, Brian Gregory, Kathleen Malone O'Connor, Katie Reing, Ted Salmon, Anne Schwelm, Matthew Serfass, Joseph Sciorra, Alan Silverman, Robert Morris Skaler, George E. Thomas, Dell Upton, and Nancy Waterson. Charlie McCormick and Michael L. Murray kindly read drafts of the piece. A version of chapter 10, "'Bringing Perfection in These Different Places': Father Divine's Vernacular Architecture of Intention," appeared in *Folklore* 115 (2004): 3–26. Published by the Folklore Society and reprinted by permission of Taylor & Francis Ltd., www.tandfonline.com.

CHAPTER 11: "AND AS WE DINE, WE SING AND PRAISE GOD"
I wish to thank Deborah Ann Bailey, Ben Danner, John DiMucci, Will Luers, Kathleen Malone O'Connor, Kathy McCrea, Nicholas Rademacher, Lisa Ratmansky, and Geraldine Walker, as well as Anne Schwelm of Cabrini College's Holy Spirit Library, for their assistance. I am especially grateful to Rudy V. Busto and Ben Zeller for their unfailing support, and to my colleagues Laura Sauer Palmer, Matt Slutz, and Nancy L. Watterson, who read multiple drafts of this piece. Of course, this research would not have been possible without the assistance of Mother Divine and the brothers and sisters of Father Divine's International Peace Mission Movement in Philadelphia. Their kindness and cooperation have been extraordinary. The title of this chapter is taken from the words of Mother Divine (field notes, Holy Communion Banquet Service, Woodmont, January 10, 2010). A version of chapter 11, "'And as We Dine, We Sing and Praise God': Father and Mother Divine's Theologies of Food," was originally published in *Religion, Food, and Eating in North America*, ed. Benjamin E. Zeller, Marie W. Dallam, Reid L. Neilson, and Nora L. Rubel (Columbia University Press, 2014). Copyright © 2014 Columbia University Press. Reprinted with permission of Columbia University Press.

CHAPTER 12: "AS A LIVING SHRINE I CAME"
My thanks to the late Mother Divine and the members of the Peace Mission for their ever-present hospitality and assistance, especially Miss

Yvette Calm and Christopher Stewart, Woodmont's archivist. I am also grateful to Raquel Romberg for inspiring me to write this piece, and to my two anonymous manuscript reviewers, as well as to Peter Carswell, Laura and David Palmer, Patti Stocker, and Anne Schwelm of Cabrini University's Holy Spirit Library. J. Gregory Garrity, Abel Rodríguez, and Matt Slutz graciously read drafts of the manuscript. Katie Reing photographed the shrine. A version of chapter 12, "'As a Living Shrine I Came': Remembrance, Creativity, and Paradox in God's American Tomb," appeared in *Magic, Ritual, and Witchcraft* 13, no. 2 (Summer 2018): 164–89. Copyright © 2018 University of Pennsylvania Press. All rights reserved.

CODA

I wish to thank Deborah Ann Bailey, Nicolas Le Bigre, J. Gregory Garrity, Laura Sauer Palmer, Anne Schwelm, Matt Slutz, and Nancy L. Watterson for their assistance with this piece. A version of the coda, "Encountering the Female Divine . . . Literally: Ethnographic Writing about Mother and Father Divine's Peace Mission Movement," appeared in "Forum 34-35: Religion, Anthropology, and the 'Anthropology of Religion,'" *Antropologicheskij forum/Forum for Anthropology and Culture* 13 (2017): 84–94, and is published by permission of Catriona Kelly, editor of the English-language version of *Forum for Anthropology and Culture*.

NOTES

FOREWORD
1 "The Divine Hotel's Policy—Rules and Regulations," n.d.
2 See chapter 5.
3 See chapter 9.
4 See chapter 9.
5 See the introduction to this volume.
6 See introduction.

INTRODUCTION
1 This methodological reflexivity must apply to reflections about the methods of *doing* ethnography (e.g., participant observation, fieldwork interviewing) as well as theorizing based on ethnographic contents and even more complex reflections on ethnographic reflexivity (e.g., fieldworker-informant relations).
2 Two good assessments of the historical usage in scholarship of the terms "folk religion" and "popular religion" can be found in Don Yoder, "Toward a Definition of Folk Religion," *Western Folklore* 33, no. 1 (1974): 2–15, reprinted in *Discovering American Folklife: Studies in Ethnic, Religious, and Regional Culture* (Ann Arbor: UMI Research Press, 1990), 67–76; and Francois-Andre Isambert, *Le sens du sacre: Fete et religion populaire* (Paris: Les Editions de Minuit, 1982), 8–16.
3 Yoder, "Toward a Definition of Folk Religion," 67–84, esp. 2–3 and 67–68.
4 Jeff Todd Titon, *Powerhouse for God: Speech, Chant, and Song in an Appalachian Baptist Church* (Austin: University of Texas Press, 1988), 144.
5 Other folklorists have added little insight on this matter, usually reinforcing a residualized view of the religion of the "folk." See the works of John Messenger, "Folk Religion," in *Folklore and Folklife: An Introduction*, ed. Richard M. Dorson (Chicago: University of Chicago Press, 1972), reprinted in *Religion and the People, 800–1700*, ed. James Obelkevich (Chapel Hill: University of North Carolina Press, 1979); William M. Clements, "The American Folk Church in Northeast Arkansas," *Journal of the Folklore Institute* 15 (1978): 161–80; William M. Clements, "The Folk Church: Institution, Event, Performance," in *Handbook of American Folklore*, ed. Richard M. Dorson (Bloomington: Indiana University Press, 1983), 136–44; David J. Hufford, "Ste. Anne de Beaupre: Roman Catholic Pilgrimage and Healing," *Western Folklore* 44 (1985): 194–207; David J. Hufford, "Contemporary Folk Medicine," in *Other Healers: Unorthodox Medicine in America*, ed. Norman Gevitz

(Baltimore: Johns Hopkins University Press, 1988), 228–64; Elaine J. Lawless, *Handmaidens of the Lord: Pentecostal Women Preachers and Traditional Religion* (Philadelphia: University of Pennsylvania Press, 1988); and Titon, *Powerhouse for God*. A recent folkloristic effort that avoids the pitfalls of official/folk religious dichotomizations is the volume edited by Ruel W. Tyson Jr., James L. Peacock, and Daniel W. Patterson, *Diversities of Gifts: Field Studies in Southern Religion* (Urbana: University of Illinois Press, 1988), which concentrates on "local religion" in the American South. There has been some engagement with the issue of the two-tiered model in the last two decades, arising from various quarters within history, anthropology, sociology, and religious studies, providing fresh assessments not previously in evidence. In particular, the following scholars have shed new light on the problematic influence of the two-tiered model on the study of religion: Peter Brown, *The Cult of the Saints: Its Rise and Function in Latin Christianity* (Chicago: University of Chicago Press, 1981); Peter Burke, "Popular Culture between History and Ethnology," *Ethnologia Europaea* 14 (1984): 5–13; Natalie Zemon Davis, "Some Tasks and Themes in the Study of Popular Religion," in *The Pursuit of Holiness in Late Medieval and Renaissance Religion*, ed. Charles Trinkaus and Heiko A. Oberman (Leiden: Brill, 1974), 307–36; Natalie Zemon Davis, "From 'Popular Religion' to Religious Cultures," in *Reformation Europe: A Guide to Research*, ed. Steven Ozment (St. Louis: Center for Reformation Research, 1982), 321–43; William A. Christian Jr., *Local Religion in Sixteenth-Century Spain* (Princeton: Princeton University Press, 1981); William A. Christian Jr., "Folk Religion: An Overview," in *The Encyclopedia of Religion*, vol. 5, ed. Mircea Eliade (New York: Macmillan, 1987), 370–74; Robert Towler, *Homo Religiosus: Sociological Problems in the Study of Religion* (London: Constable, 1974); Peter Hendrik Vrijhof and Jacques Waardenburg, eds., *Official and Popular Religion: Analysis of a Theme for Religious Studies* (The Hague: Mouton, 1979). Unfortunately, none of them have provided a viable alternative concerning the study of religion as it is lived. There are also works that raise many important questions concerning the study of "popular religion" in historical and contemporary perspective: Thomas A. Kselman, "Ambivalence and Assumption in the Concept of Popular Religion," in *Religion and Political Conflict in Latin America*, ed. Daniel H. Levine (Chapel Hill: University of North Carolina Press, 1986), 24–41; Thomas A. Kselman, *Belief in History: Innovative Approaches to European and American Religion* (Notre Dame: University of Notre Dame Press, 1991); Mary R. O'Neil, "From 'Popular' to 'Local' Religion: Issues in Early Modern European Religious History," *Religious Studies Review* 12, nos. 3–4 (1986): 222–26; and Michael R. Candelaria, *Popular Religion and Liberation: The Dilemma of Liberation Theology* (Albany: State University of New York Press, 1990), chap. 1. Ellen Badone, in her introduction to *Religious Orthodoxy and Popular Faith in European Society*, ed. Ellen Badone (Princeton: Princeton University Press, 1990), recognizes the pitfalls of the two-tiered model but nevertheless retains it as a point of reference.

6 Vrijhof and Waardenburg, *Official and Popular Religion*, 235.

7 See the work of David J. Hufford, *The Terror That Comes in the Night: An Experience-Centered Study of Supernatural Assault Traditions* (Philadelphia: University of Pennsylvania Press, 1982), for an explanation of his experience-centered approach and his application of it to occasions of supernatural encounter. See also Hufford, "Ste. Anne de Beaupre," for a consideration of religious healing within the Roman Catholic tradition. Another scholar who addresses supernatural experience without sociocultural or psychological reduction is anthropologist Felicitas D. Goodman, in *How about Demons? Possession and Exorcism in the Modern World* (Bloomington: Indiana University Press, 1988), 123-26. A less satisfying attempt to deal with supernatural experiences that reduces them to the cultural source hypothesis is Carol Zaleski, *Otherworld Journeys: Accounts of Near-Death Experience in Medieval and Modern Times* (New York: Oxford University Press, 1987). A recent notable example of a scholar who psychologizes religious belief and "folk Catholicism" is Michael P. Carroll, in *The Cult of the Virgin Mary: Psychological Origins* (Princeton: Princeton University Press, 1986), *Catholic Cults and Devotions: A Psychological Inquiry* (Montreal: McGill-Queen's University Press, 1989), and *Madonnas That Maim: Popular Catholicism in Italy since the Fifteenth Century* (Baltimore: Johns Hopkins University Press, 1992), whose psychoanalytic work is purely reductionistic, though he must be given credit for his serious consideration of such religious phenomena as the stigmata, the liquefaction of blood relics, the rosary, and Marian apparitions. See the review of Carroll's 1986 book on Marian devotions, *The Cult of the Virgin Mary: Psychological Origins*, by Jeffrey Burton Russell in *Journal of the American Academy of Religion* 55 (1987): 593-97, and my own review of his 1989 work analyzing Catholic devotionalism in *Journal of American Folklore* 105 (1992): 250-52.

8 Since 1984, I have been using the term "vernacular religion" in both publications and public presentations, first as a cautionary alternative to "folk" and "popular religion" and then as a term representing my own understanding of lived religion. For an early attempt at discussing the importance of individual religious creativity in contemporary America, see my article "Feminist Christian Songs: Occasions of Vernacular Religious Belief," *New Jersey Folklore* 10 (1985): 38-43. My critique of recent scholarship from the perspective of this developing theory of vernacular religion can be found in several of my book reviews: review of *The Household of Faith: Roman Catholic Devotions in Mid-Nineteenth Century America* by Ann Taves, in *Records of the American Catholic Historical Society of Philadelphia* 98 (1987): 120-22; review of *The Christian Home in Victorian America, 1840-1900* by Colleen McDannell, in *Journal of American Folklore* 102 (1989): 371-73; review of *Living Stones: The History and Structure of Catholic Spiritual Life in the United States* by Joseph P. Chinnici, OFM, in *Records of the American Catholic Historical Society of Philadelphia* 101 (1990): 64-66.

9 Other scholars have used the term "vernacular religion" in specific ways. In a review of David Hall's recent book on popular religion in early New England, Philip F. Gura makes no other mention of the term except in his title, and that

use may have simply been an editorial choice. Philip F. Gura, "Wonders of the Puritan World: Vernacular Religion in Seventeenth-Century New England," review of *Worlds of Wonder, Days of Judgment: Popular Religious Belief in Early New England* by David D. Hall, *American Quarterly* 41 (1989): 543–48. David D. Hall, in *Worlds of Wonder, Days of Judgment: Popular Religious Belief in Early New England* (New York: Knopf, 1989), 8, does use the term within the text of his book, saying that the Reformation "affirmed a vernacular religion, as in a Book of Common Prayer." "Vernacular" here is a linguistically based cultural designation in which a religious institution used the same language as its faithful, as well as the religion of people who shared the same language. The word "vernacular" reflects a variety of linguistic and cultural situations in which there is one or more high written languages belonging to the elite and educated, with one or more spoken or vernacular languages or dialects used in common speech. "Vernacular" thus signifies a linguistically coded social hierarchy.

10   David Chrystal, *A Dictionary of Linguistics and Phonetics* (Oxford: Basil Blackwell, 1989), 236.

11   Margaret Lantis, "Vernacular Culture," *American Anthropologist* 62 (1960): 202–16, quote on 203–4. One additional use of "vernacular" can be observed in Michael Pickering and Tony Green, "Toward a Cartography of the Vernacular Milieu," in *Everyday Culture: Popular Song and the Vernacular Milieu*, ed. Michael Pickering and Tony Green (Philadelphia: Open University Press, 1987), 2. Pickering and Green employ a materialist understanding of culture to bracket their definition of "vernacular" context, which they limit solely to the local environment and specific immediate situations. Unfortunately, they circumscribe the usefulness of the vernacular milieu by assimilating it into the "national culture" on the one hand and undercutting its autonomy by marginalizing it as "non-official" on the other. See also their ideas on "vernacular song" (173–78).

12   Quotes from Jan Harold Brunvand, *The Study of American Folklore* (New York: Norton, 1986), 413, and Amos Rapoport, *House Form and Culture* (Englewood Cliffs: Prentice Hall, 1969), 3.

13   Alan Gowans, "The Mansions of Alloways Creek," in *Common Places: Readings in American Vernacular Architecture*, ed. Dell Upton and John Michael Vlach (Athens: University of Georgia Press, 1986), 392.

14   See Dell Upton, "The Power of Things: Recent Studies in American Vernacular Architecture," in *Material Culture: A Resource Guide*, ed. Thomas J. Schlereth (Lawrence: University Press of Kansas, 1985), 57. An additional discussion of the meaning of vernacular architecture can be found in Camille Wells, introduction to *Perspectives in Vernacular Architecture*, vol. 2, ed. Camille Wells (Columbia: University of Missouri Press, 1986).

15   Suggested in remarks by Henry Glassie from the opening lecture of his course on vernacular architecture, September 9, 1986. See the chapter "Home" in Henry Glassie, *Passing the Time in Ballymenone: Culture and History of an Ulster Community* (Philadelphia: University of Pennsylvania Press, 1982),

327–424, for a fuller realization of his ideas on the making and culture of built environments.
16   Yoder, "Toward a Definition of Folk Religion," 80.
17   Thomas A. Kselman, in *Miracles and Prophecies in Nineteenth-Century France* (New Brunswick: Rutgers University Press, 1983), 7, has adroitly noted in reference to the historical study of "popular belief and behavior" that these "occur within a political and institutional context; in fact they helped to shape that context and were in turn affected by it."
18   Tyson, Peacock, and Patterson employ "the metaphor of 'gesture'" in their anthology *Diversities of Gifts*, explaining it as "living forms through which the various religious traditions express themselves" (xii). Much of what seems to be embraced by this term is also present in my understanding of the verbal and material expressions of religious belief.
19   See the excellent introductory essay by Wendy James and Douglas H. Johnson, eds., in *Vernacular Christianity: Essays in the Social Anthropology of Religion Presented to Godfrey Lienhardt* (New York: Lilian Barber Press, 1988), 12, an anthropological consideration of the way Christianity has been conceived and misconceived by Western Christians. In this essay, James and Johnson examine "native" Christianity in a way suggestive of my development of the term "vernacular religion." As I propose that all religion is inherently vernacular religion, so, for them, "every Christian is a native."
20   Wilfred Cantwell Smith, *The Meaning and End of Religion* (1962; New York: Harper and Row, 1978), 51. See 160–61 for comments on how cumulative traditions change due to the actions of "outstanding individuals" and "quite ordinary folk." Though he tends to cast religious leaders as innovative and creative and the receptive nature of the religious community members as preservative, Smith is quite clear about the individual nature of living a religious tradition. For his explanation that belief is not identical with but rather an expression of faith, see his *Faith and Belief* (Princeton: Princeton University Press, 1979).
21   Lawless, *Handmaidens of the Lord*, 14.
22   Yoder has made mention of "the components of the individual mind" in various articles. In his definitional essays on folk medicine ("Folk Medicine," in *Discovering American Folklife*, 86) and folk religion ("Toward a Definition of Folk Religion," 82), he speaks of the individual in relation to the work of the Swiss folklife scholar Richard Weiss. In his 1976 article "Folklife Studies in American Scholarship," Yoder refers several times to the individual life within the context of the past and "in the midst of social conflict, the present, and the future." See Don Yoder, "Folklife Studies in American Scholarship," 43–61, quote on 51.
23   For example, Jack Santino, in "On the Nature of Healing as a Folk Event," *Western Folklore* 44 (1985): 153–67, assumes in his treatment of healing as a folk event that medical beliefs of interest to a folklorist are those reflecting a community foundation. He states in the first sentence of his article, "Folk medicine is effective,

among other reasons, because it derives from and draws on a community's shared values, beliefs, and symbols, and involves performance, custom, and behavior."

24 See Wayland D. Hand, introduction to *Popular Beliefs and Superstitions from North Carolina*, vol. 6 of *The Frank C. Brown Collection of North Carolina Folklore*, ed. Newman Ivey White (Durham: Duke University Press, 1961), xix–xlvii; Larry Danielson, "Religious Folklore," in *Folk Groups and Folklore Genres: An Introduction*, ed. Elliott Oring (Logan: Utah State University Press, 1986), 45–69; Donald E. Byrne Jr., "Folklore and the Study of American Religion," in *Encyclopedia of the American Religious Experience*, vol. 1, ed. Charles H. Lippy and Peter W. Williams (New York: Scribner's, 1988), 88–100; and Lawless, *Handmaidens of the Lord*, for examples of genre classification of religious folklife. See Leonard Norman Primiano, "Intrinsically Catholic: Vernacular Religion and Philadelphia's 'Dignity'" (PhD diss., University of Pennsylvania, 1993), for a further discussion of this issue.

25 It is worth noting the difficulties of scholarly transmission of these terms and ideas. While the term "idiolect" seems to refer to the linguistic system of a single individual, the term "idioculture," in the hands of folklorists Regina Bendix, in "Marmot, Memet, and Marmoset: Further Research on the Folklore of Dyads," *Western Folklore* 46 (1987): 171–91 (quote on Fine and the term "idioculture" at 173), and Gary Alan Fine, does not refer to the culture of single individuals but rather emphasizes the small group. From Fine's perspective, the relationship of the prefix "idio-" to the noun "culture" is adjectival, preserving emphasis on the group. See Gary Alan Fine, "Popular Culture and Social Interaction: Production, Consumption, and Usage," *Journal of Popular Culture* 11 (1977): 453–54, 463; Gary Alan Fine, "Small Groups and Culture Creation: The Idioculture of Little League Baseball Teams," *American Sociological Review* 44 (1979): 733–45; Gary Alan Fine, "The Manson Family: The Folklore Traditions of a Small Group," *Journal of the Folklore Institute* 19 (1982): 47; and Gary Alan Fine, "Community and Boundary: Personal Experience Stories of Mushroom Collectors," *Journal of Folklore Research* 24 (1987): 223–40. Culture, for Fine, refers only to group phenomena, and idioculture refers to individual examples of the interacting group (that is, the small group). Another way to understand idioculture is in the possessive sense of the culture of the individual, as in my term "uniculture." Both Fine and Bendix display a folkloristic predisposition for group analysis that overshadows the significant role the individual plays in culture creation. Fine does briefly refer to the importance of the individual in "Community and Boundary." For an emphasis on the individual within the context of the creation of material culture, see the work of Michael Owen Jones, *The Hand Made Object and Its Maker* (Berkeley: University of California Press, 1975), revised in 1989.

26 Bendix, "Marmot, Memet, and Marmoset," 190–91.

27 The term "uniculture" has also been used in the popular press to mean the growing homogenization of world cultures into a global culture. See "Uniculture Shock," *Chicago Tribune Magazine*, March 16, 1986.

28 Jay Mechling, "'Banana Cannon' and Other Folk Traditions between Human and Nonhuman Animals," *Western Folklore* 48 (1989): 321.
29 Ibid.
30 Folkloristically, uniculture can be seen as the all-embracing concept within which vernacular religion is a subset. Religiously, however, vernacular religion can be seen as the foundation that spiritually determines every human value, within which uniculture is a subset.
31 See Quentin Donoghue and Linda Shapiro, *Bless Me Father for I Have Sinned: Catholics Speak Out about Confession* (New York: Primus, 1984).
32 See Margot Adler, *Drawing Down the Moon: Witches, Druids, Goddess-Worshippers, and Other Pagans in America Today* (Boston: Beacon, 1986), and T. M. Luhrmann, *Persuasions of the Witch's Craft: Ritual Magic in Contemporary England* (Cambridge, MA: Harvard University Press, 1989).
33 My brief comments here stem from field research that I was allowed to do within the Philadelphia chapter of Dignity (1986–1987) and the subsequent amplification and application of my theory of vernacular religion to the individuals in this group. See Primiano, "Intrinsically Catholic."

CHAPTER 1. TEXTURES OF A RELIGIOUS LIFE

1 The first of this chapter's epigraphs is from Sister Ann Ameen, *Leadings of the Holy Spirit*, vol. 2, 11. (This is a set of three pamphlets that Sister Ann had privately published, which she sent out to various individuals. The volumes contain no stated date or publisher.) The second epigraph is from Ecclesiasticus, or the Wisdom of Jesus the Son of Sirach, 38:34. The third is from Henry Glassie, in *The Spirit of Folk Art: The Girard Collection at the Museum of International Folk Art* (New York: Abrams, 1989), 42.
2 For a definitional discussion of vernacular religion, see the introduction to this volume. See also Leonard Norman Primiano, "Folk Religion," in *Folklore: An Encyclopedia of Beliefs, Customs, Tales, Music, and Art*, ed. Thomas A. Green (Santa Barbara: ABC-CLIO, 1997), 710–17.
3 Christine Moeller and J. M. Sullivan wrote thoughtful appreciations of Sister Ann and her work at the time of her death. See Christine Moeller, "Newfoundland Treasure Lost," *Rug Hooking Guild of Newfoundland and Labrador Newsletter* 4, no. 1 (Spring 1998): 5, 7, plus unnumbered two-page insert; J. M. Sullivan, "Ann Sharpe Ameen Brown," *Globe and Mail*, April 23, 1998, A24.
4 In Newfoundland, rugs are often referred to as "mats." A hooked or poked rug is a textile in which ripped or torn strips of cloth or yarn are forced through the meshing of a piece of burlap. A design drawn on the surface usually serves as the model for the desired image. For discussions of this tradition in Newfoundland, see Colleen Lynch, "The Fabric of Their Lives," in *The Fabric of Their Lives: Hooked and Poked Mats of Newfoundland and Labrador* (St. John's: Art Gallery, Memorial University of Newfoundland, 1980); Gerald L. Pocius, "Hooked Rugs

in Newfoundland: The Representation of Social Structure in Design," *Journal of American Folklore* 92 (1979): 273–84.
5 Ameen, *Leadings of the Holy Spirit*, 2, 15.
6 Newfoundland joined the Canadian Confederation in 1949. The province of Newfoundland and Labrador is the most easterly of the Atlantic provinces. It includes the island of Newfoundland, several smaller islands that surround it, and the enormous northern territory of Labrador, which is connected to the Canadian mainland. When Newfoundlanders refer to "Newfoundland," they usually mean the island itself, as opposed to the province, which includes Labrador.
7 The *Bay Roberts Guardian* had taken this article from a report in the *Montreal Gazette*.
8 Art historians David Morgan and Sally M. Promey have preferred to call such American artistic expressions the "visual culture of American religions." See David Morgan and Sally M. Promey, *Exhibiting the Visual Culture of American Religions* (Valparaiso, IN: Brauer Museum of Art, Valparaiso University, 2000). American religious historian Colleen McDannell has referred to such material culture as "material Christianity." See Colleen McDannell, *Material Christianity: Religion and Popular Culture in America* (New Haven: Yale University Press, 1995).
9 See chapter 2 in this volume.
10 For a discussion of such terminology, see Roger Cardinal, "Toward an Outsider Aesthetic," in *The Artist Outsider: Creativity and the Boundaries of Culture*, ed. Michael D. Hall and Eugene W. Metcalf Jr. (Washington, DC: Smithsonian Institution Press, 1994), 20–43. For a definition of "art brut," see Roger Cardinal, "Art Brut," in *Dictionary of Art*, vol. 2, ed. Jane Turner (New York: Macmillan, 1996), 515–16. For a definition of "naive art," see Roger Cardinal, "Naive Art," ibid., vol. 4, 39–42. The periodical *Raw Vision* offers a constellation of such terms in each issue. See also folklorist Henry Glassie's reflections on art and folk art: "Folk Art," in *Folklore and Folklife: An Introduction*, ed. Richard M. Dorson (Chicago: University of Chicago Press, 1972), 253–80; Glassie, *Spirit of Folk Art*; and Henry Glassie, *Material Culture* (Bloomington: Indiana University Press, 1999).
11 Charles G. Zug III, "Folk Art and Outsider Art: A Folklorist's Perspective," in Hall and Metcalf, *Artist Outsider*, 151–52.
12 Joel Kopp and Kate Kopp, *American Hooked and Sewn Rugs: Folk Art Underfoot* (Albuquerque: University of New Mexico Press, 1995), 109.
13 Some Newfoundlanders recalled to me that Ameen did at times have young women who lived with her in St. John's assist with the hooking.
14 Lynch, "The Fabric of Their Lives," 12; see also Kopp and Kopp, *American Hooked and Sewn Rugs*, 132–33.
15 So described by folklorist Jenny Michael in a personal communication.
16 A consideration of Squires and his work can be found in James Wade, "Gerald Leopold Squires," in *Dictionary of Newfoundland and Labrador Biography* (St. John's: Cuff, 1990), 323; see also Des Walsh and Susan Jamieson, *Gerald Squires, Newfoundland Artist* (St. John's: Breakwater Books, 1995).

17 Peter Gard, "Sister Act," *Canadian Art*, Spring 1994, 46–48.
18 Barbara Kirshenblatt-Gimblett, "Objects of Memory: Material Culture as Life Review," in *Folk Groups and Folklore Genres: A Reader*, ed. Elliott Oring (Logan: Utah State University Press, 1989), 329–37.
19 Oring, *Folk Groups and Folklore Genres*, 329.
20 For an examination of the ways the elderly shape memory projects and perform them before witnesses in the task of self-definition and life review, see Mary Hufford, Marjorie Hunt, and Steven J. Zeitlin, *The Grand Generation: Memory, Mastery, Legacy* (Washington, DC: Smithsonian Institution Traveling Exhibition Service; Seattle: University of Washington Press, 1987); Patrick Mullen, *Listening to Old Voices: Folklore, Life Stories, and the Elderly* (Bloomington: Indiana University Press, 1992); Barbara Myerhoff, *Number Our Days* (New York: Simon and Schuster, 1978).
21 Bruce Johnson, personal communication, September 1995.
22 Kirshenblatt-Gimblett, "Objects of Memory," 336.
23 Pocius, "Hooked Rugs in Newfoundland," 278. Pocius makes the point that rugs with geometric designs would be placed on the kitchen floor of Newfoundland homes for everyday family use, while those with more innovative patterns would be positioned on the floor of the front room, where guests of a higher social status, such as clergy or merchants, were received (274, 284).
24 Gerald L. Pocius, "Holy Pictures in Newfoundland Houses: Visual Codes for Secular and Supernatural Relationships," in *Media Sense: The Folklore-Popular Culture Continuum*, ed. Peter Narváez and Martin Laba (Bowling Green, OH: Bowling Green State University Press, 1986), 124–48; Gerald L. Pocius, *A Place to Belong: Community Order and Everyday Space in Calvert, Newfoundland* (Athens: University of Georgia Press, 1991).
25 Pocius explains the Newfoundland rug-hooking tradition as presenting "the extremes of stability and innovation, but instead of an individual making a choice between conformity (expressed in the use of geometric antecedents) and individuality (in the use of a unique antecedent), most women used both styles." See "Hooked Rugs in Newfoundland," 280–81.
26 See Philip Scharper and Sally Scharper, eds., *The Gospel in Art by the Peasants of Solentiname* (Maryknoll: Orbis, 1984).
27 Catherine L. Albanese, "Exchanging Selves, Exchanging Souls: Contact, Combination, and American Religious History," in *Retelling US Religious History*, ed. Thomas A. Tweed (Berkeley: University of California Press, 1997), 203, 224.
28 When Albanese speaks of contact between religions, she is not limiting her discussion to contact between, for example, Christian denominations. She sees religious contact and exchange touching all religious communities within the American environment.
29 See Genevieve Lehr, "Anglican Church," in *Encyclopedia of Newfoundland and Labrador*, vol. 1, ed. Joseph R. Smallwood (St. John's: Cuff, 1981), 48–51; David G. Pitt, "Methodism," ibid., vol. 3 (1991), 519–27; Burton K. James, "Pentecostal

Assemblies of Newfoundland," ibid., vol. 4 (1993), 251–55; and Raymond J. Lahey, "Roman Catholic Church," ibid., 622–31.

30 Bruce Johnson suggests that these landscapes, "although probably loosely based on actual places, are constructed scenes, places reinvented and improved upon by Sister Ann's imagination. Other than frequent references to rolling green hills, sea-birds, and the odd fishing trawler, these spaces are not necessarily indicative of Newfoundland. . . . Sister Ann's landscapes are more aligned with the ideals of Arcadia or, more aptly, Eden—her imaginings ordered more by ideal and design than by reality." See Bruce Johnson, introduction to *Faith and Work: The Hooked Mats of Sister Ann Ameen* (St. John's: Memorial University of Newfoundland, 1995).

31 See also Albanese's study of her poet grandfather's rich artistic and religious life and his process of coming to religious belief: Catherine L. Albanese, *A Cobbler's Universe: Religion, Poetry, and Performance in the Life of a South Italian Immigrant* (New York: Continuum, 1997).

CHAPTER 2. THE VOW AS VISUAL FEAST

1 Folklorist Joseph Sciorra has done outstanding work on Italian American Catholic yard shrines, vernacular chapels, religious processions, and nativity crèches. See, for example, Joseph Sciorra, "Yard Shrines and Sidewalk Altars of New York's Italian-Americans," in *Perspectives in Vernacular Architecture*, vol. 3, ed. Thomas Carter and Bernard L. Herman (Columbia: University of Missouri Press, 1989), 185–98; Joseph Sciorra, "'We Go Where the Italians Live': Religious Processions as Ethnic and Territorial Markers in a Multi-Ethnic Brooklyn Neighborhood," in *Gods of the City: Religion and the Contemporary American Urban Landscape*, ed. Robert Orsi (Bloomington: Indiana University Press, 1999), 310–40; and Joseph Sciorra, "Imagined Places, Fragile Landscapes: Italian American *Presepi* (Nativity Crèches) in New York City," *Italian American Review* 8, no. 2 (Autumn–Winter 2001): 141–73.

2 Gábor Barna, "Objects of Devotion or Decoration? The Role of Religious Objects in Everyday Life in the Nineteenth and Twentieth Centuries," in *Religion in Everyday Life: Papers Given at a Symposium in Stockholm, 13–15 September 1993*, ed. Nils-Arvid Bringéus (London: Coronet Books, 1994), 105–20. The article is particularly useful for its integration of historically informed work with contemporary ethnography.

3 Studies of religious objects in American Roman Catholic and Protestant homes have used religious magazines and guidebooks as research sources. See, for example, Ann Taves, *The Household of Faith: Roman Catholic Devotions in Mid-Nineteenth-Century America* (Notre Dame: Notre Dame University Press, 1986), and Colleen McDannell, *The Christian Home in Victorian America, 1840–1900* (Bloomington: Indiana University Press, 1986).

4 For one example, a study of the sale and distribution of contemporary Catholic religious articles in Philadelphia, see Leonard Norman Primiano, "Post-Modern Sites

of Catholic Sacred Materiality," in *Perspectives on American Religion and Culture*, ed. Peter W. Williams (Malden, MA: Basil Blackwell, 1999), 187–202, chapter 3 in this volume. While not ethnographic, the following studies have explored religious iconography in American homes: David Halle, *Inside Culture: Art and Class in the American Home* (Chicago: University of Chicago Press, 1993); David Morgan, *Visual Piety: A History and Theory of Popular Religious Images* (Berkeley: University of California Press, 1998); and David Morgan, *The Sacred Gaze: Religious Visual Culture in Theory and Practice* (Berkeley: University of California Press, 2005).

5 Barna, "Objects of Devotion or Decoration?," 109.
6 Ibid., 116. See also Leonard Norman Primiano, "What Is Vernacular Catholicism? The 'Dignity' Example," *Acta Ethnographica Hungarica* 46, nos. 1–2 (2001): 51–58, chapter 7 in this volume.
7 Barna, "Objects of Devotion or Decoration?," 105.
8 Kay Frances Turner, *Beautiful Necessity: The Art and Meaning of Women's Altars* (New York: Thames and Hudson, 1999).
9 Robert Thomas Teske, *Votive Offerings among Greek-Philadelphians: A Ritual Perspective* (New York: Arno Press, 1980); and Robert Thomas Teske, "Votive Offerings and the Belief System of Greek-Philadelphians," *Western Folklore* 44 (1985): 208–24. See also Sciorra, "Yard Shrines and Sidewalk Altars."
10 Elmar Klinger, "Vows and Oaths," in *The Encyclopedia of Religion*, vol. 15, ed. Mircea Eliade (New York: Macmillan, 1987), 301.
11 Ibid., 303.
12 This synthesis also owes a debt to the ideas of those pillars of religious folklife scholarship, Richard Weiss and Don Yoder, as well as the American Catholic theologian Richard P. McBrien. See Weiss, *Volkskunde der Schweiz* (Erlenbach-Zurich: Eugen Rentsch Verlag, 1946); Yoder, "Toward a Definition of Folk Religion," *Western Folklore* 33, no. 1 (1974): 1–15; McBrien, *Catholicism* (San Francisco: HarperSanFrancisco, 1994); and McBrien, ed., *The HarperCollins Encyclopedia of Catholicism* (San Francisco: HarperSanFrancisco, 1995), 256–58, 1148.
13 "Sacred Relics," in *The Catholic Encyclopedia*, ed. Robert C. Broderick (Nashville: Thomas Nelson, 1976), 518–19.

CHAPTER 3. POSTMODERN SITES OF CATHOLIC SACRED MATERIALITY

1 See also Robin Clark, "Another Sale! by St. Joseph," *Philadelphia Inquirer*, September 23, 1990 (city edition), 1; Mitchell Pacelle, "Some People Will Try Anything Except Lowering the Asking Price," *Wall Street Journal*, September 17, 1990.
2 Peter Brown, *The Cult of the Saints: Its Rise and Function in Latin Christianity* (Chicago: University of Chicago Press, 1981).
3 Helena Waddy Lepovicz, *Images of Faith: Expressionism, Catholic Folk Art, and the Industrial Revolution* (Athens: University of Georgia Press, 1991); Adolf Spamer, *Das Kleine Andachtsbild vom XIV. bis zum XX. Jahrhundert* (Munich: Bruckmann, 1930).

4   Christine A. Cartwright, "Indian Sikh Homes Out of North American Houses: Mental Culture in Material Translation," *New York Folklore* 7 (1981): 97–111; Martha Cooper and Joseph Sciorra, *R.I.P. Memorial Wall Art* (New York: Henry Holt, 1994); Donald J. Cosentino, ed., *Sacred Arts of Haitian Vodou* (Los Angeles: UCLA Fowler Museum of Cultural History, 1995); Kurt C. Dewhurst, Betty MacDowell, and Marsha MacDowell, *Religious Folk Art in America: Reflections of Faith* (New York: Dutton, 1983); Ysamur Flores-Peña and Roberta J. Evanchuk, *Santería Garments and Altars: Speaking without a Voice* (Jackson: University of Mississippi Press, 1994); Gregory Gizelis, "The Use of Amulets among Greek Philadelphians," *Pennsylvania Folklife* 20, no. 3 (1971): 30–37; David Halle, *Inside Culture: Art and Class in the American Home* (Chicago: University of Chicago Press, 1993); Yvonne Lange, "Lithography, An Agent of Technological Change in Religious Folk Art: A Thesis," *Western Folklore* 33, no. 1 (1974): 51–64; Pierre Lessard, *Les petites images dévotes* (Quebec: Presses de l'Université Laval, 1981); Yvonne J. Milspaw, "Protestant Home Shrines: Icon and Image," *New York Folklore* 12, nos. 3–4 (1986): 119–36; David Morgan, "Imaging Protestant Piety: The Icons of Warner Sallman," *Religion and American Culture* 3 (1993): 29–47; Robert Anthony Orsi, *The Madonna of 115th Street: Faith and Community in Italian Harlem, 1880–1950* (New Haven: Yale University Press, 1985); Robert Anthony Orsi, "The Center Out There, in Here, and Everywhere Else: The Nature of Pilgrimage to the Shrine of St. Jude, 1929–1965," *Journal of Social History* 25 (1991): 213–32; Gerald L. Pocius, "Holy Pictures in Newfoundland Houses: Visual Codes for Secular and Supernatural Relationships," in *Media Sense: The Folklore-Popular Culture Continuum*, ed. Peter Narváez and Martin Laba (Bowling Green, OH: Bowling Green University Popular Press, 1986), 124–48; Joseph Sciorra, "Yard Shrines and Sidewalk Altars of New York's Italian-Americans," in *Perspectives in Vernacular Architecture*, vol. 3, ed. Thomas Carter and Bernard L. Herman (Columbia: University of Missouri Press, 1989), 185–98; Joseph Sciorra, "Multivocality and Vernacular Architecture: The Our Lady of Mount Carmel Grotto in Rosebank, Staten Island," in *Studies in Italian American Folklore*, ed. Luisa Del Giudice (Logan: Utah State University Press, 1993), 203–43; Richard H. Shaner, "Living Occult Practices in Dutch Pennsylvania," *Pennsylvania Folklife* 12, no. 3 (1961): 62–63; Richard H. Shaner, "Recollections of Witchcraft in the Oley Hills," *Pennsylvania Folklife* 21 (Folk Festival Supplement, 1972): 39–43; Robert Thomas Teske, "The Eikonostasi among Greek-Philadelphians," *Pennsylvania Folklife* 23, no. 1 (1973): 20–30; Robert Thomas Teske, *Votive Offerings among Greek-Philadelphians: A Ritual Perspective* (New York: Arno Press, 1980); Robert Thomas Teske, "Votive Offerings and the Belief System of Greek-Philadelphians," *Western Folklore* 44 (1985): 208–24; Kay Frances Turner, "Mexican American Home Altars: Towards Their Interpretation," *Aztlan: International Journal of Chicano Studies Research* 13, nos. 1–2 (1982): 309–26; Kay Frances Turner, "The Cultural Semiotics of Religious Icons: La Virgen de San Juan de los Lagos," *Semiotica* 47 (1983): 317–61; Kay Frances Turner, "Mexican-American Women's Home Altars: The Art of Relationship" (PhD diss., University

of Texas, Austin, 1990); Kay Turner and Suzanne Seriff, "Giving an Altar: The Ideology of Reproduction in a St. Joseph's Day Feast," *Journal of American Folklore* 100 (1987): 446–60; John Michael Vlach, "Morality as Folk Aesthetic," in *The Old Traditional Way of Life: Essays in Honor of Warren E. Roberts*, ed. Robert E. Walls and George H. Schoemaker (Bloomington, IN: Trickster Press, 1989), 28–39; Don Yoder, "Fraktur: An Introduction," in *Pennsylvania German Fraktur and Printed Broadsides: A Guide to the Collections in the Library of Congress* (Washington, DC: Library of Congress, 1988), 9–19, reprinted in Don Yoder, *Discovering American Folklife: Studies in Ethnic, Religious, and Regional Culture* (Ann Arbor: UMI Research Press, 1990), 271–81; Dan Yoder, *The Picture-Bible of Ludwig Denig: A Pennsylvania German Emblem Book* (New York: Hudson Hills Press, 1990); Don Yoder and Thomas E. Graves, *Hex Signs: Pennsylvania Dutch Barn Symbols and Their Meaning* (New York: Dutton, 1989).

5 Leonard Norman Primiano, "Folklife," in *Folklore: An Encyclopedia of Beliefs, Customs, Tales, Music and Art*, ed. Thomas A. Green (Santa Barbara: ABC-CLIO, 1997), 322–31.

6 John Dillenberger, *The Visual Arts and Christianity in America: The Colonial Period through the Nineteenth Century* (Chico, CA: Scholars Press, 1984); Peter W. Williams, "Religious Architecture and Landscape," in *Encyclopedia of the American Religious Experience*, vol. 3, ed. Charles H. Lippy and Peter W. Williams (New York: Scribner's, 1988), 1325–39; Peter W. Williams, *Houses of God: Region, Religion, and Architecture in the United States* (Urbana: University of Illinois Press, 1997).

7 Colleen McDannell, *Material Christianity: Religion and Popular Culture in America* (New Haven: Yale University Press, 1995); David Morgan, ed., *Icons of American Protestantism: The Art of Warner Sallman* (New Haven: Yale University Press, 1996); David Morgan, *Visual Piety: A History and Theory of Popular Religious Images* (Berkeley: University of California Press, 1998).

8 Charles L. Briggs, *The Woodcarvers of Cordova, New Mexico: Social Dimensions of an Artistic "Revival"* (Albuquerque: University of New Mexico Press, 1989); Jorge Durand and Douglas S. Massey, *Miracles on the Border: Retablos of Mexican Migrants to the United States* (Tucson: University of Arizona Press, 1995); Gloria Fraser Giffords, *Mexican Folk Retablos*, rev. ed. (Albuquerque: University of New Mexico Press, 1992); Laurie Beth Kalb, *Crafting Devotions: Tradition in Contemporary New Mexico Santos* (Albuquerque: University of New Mexico Press, 1994).

9 Mary Ann Borrello and Elizabeth Mathias, "Botánicas: Puerto Rican Folk Pharmacies," *Natural History* 86, no. 7 (1977): 64–73; Joseph M. Murphy, *Santería: An African Religion in America* (Boston: Beacon, 1988).

10 See Margo Adler, *Drawing Down the Moon: Witches, Druids, Goddess-Worshippers, and Other Pagans in America Today* (Boston: Beacon, 1986), for a representative discussion of Wiccan and pagan periodical literature found in these stores, as well as for a discussion of the communal diversity and overlap that these stores serve.

11 Kathleen Malone O'Connor, "The Alchemical Creation of Life (Takwin) and Other Concepts of Genesis in Medieval Islam" (PhD diss., University of Pennsylvania, 1994).
12 David J. Hufford, "The Love of God's Mysterious Will: Suffering and the Popular Theology of Healing," *Listening* 22 (1987): 225-39.
13 Richard P. McBrien, *Catholicism* (San Francisco: HarperSanFrancisco, 1994), 1250.
14 Richard P. McBrien, "Roman Catholicism," in *The Encyclopedia of Religion*, vol. 12, ed. Mircea Eliade (New York: Macmillan, 1987), 441. See also Andrew M. Greeley, *God in Popular Culture* (Chicago: Thomas More Press, 1988); Andrew M. Greeley, "Protestant and Catholic: Is the Analogical Imagination Extinct?," *American Sociological Review* 54 (1989): 485-502; Andrew M. Greeley, *The Catholic Myth: The Behavior and Beliefs of American Catholics* (New York: Scribner's, 1990); and David Tracy, *The Analogical Imagination* (New York: Crossroad, 1981).
15 Ann Taves, *The Household of Faith: Roman Catholic Devotions in Mid-Nineteenth-Century America* (Notre Dame: Notre Dame University Press, 1986), 10.
16 McDannell, *Material Christianity*, 167-73; Taves, *Household of Faith*, 21-45.
17 McDannell, *Material Christianity*, 66; Colleen McDannell, *The Christian Home in Victorian America, 1840-1900* (Bloomington: Indiana University Press, 1986); Colleen McDannell, "Catholic Domesticity, 1860-1960," in *American Catholic Women: A Historical Exploration*, ed. Karen Kennelly (New York: Macmillan, 1989), 48-80; Colleen McDannell, "Parlor Piety: The Home as Sacred Space in Protestant America," in *American Home Life, 1880-1930: A Social History of Spaces and Services*, ed. Jessica H. Foy and Thomas J. Schlereth (Knoxville: University of Tennessee Press, 1992), 162-89.
18 Milspaw, "Protestant Home Shrines."
19 Margaret Kruesi, "Symptoms, Signs and Miracles: Narratives of Illness and Healing at the St. John Neumann Shrine, Philadelphia, Pennsylvania" (PhD diss., University of Pennsylvania, 1995).
20 McDannell, *Material Christianity*, 170.
21 For a Freudian analysis of the cults and devotions of Catholics, see the work of Michael P. Carroll: *The Cult of the Virgin Mary: Psychological Origins* (Princeton: Princeton University Press, 1986); *Catholic Cults and Devotions: A Psychological Inquiry* (Montreal: McGill-Queen's University Press, 1989); *Madonnas That Maim: Popular Catholicism in Italy since the Fifteenth Century* (Baltimore: Johns Hopkins University Press, 1992); and *Veiled Threats: The Logic of Popular Catholicism in Italy* (Baltimore: Johns Hopkins University Press, 1996).
22 Virgilio Elizondo, "Our Lady of Guadalupe," in *The HarperCollins Encyclopedia of Catholicism*, ed. Richard P. McBrien (San Francisco: HarperSanFrancisco, 1995), 594-96.
23 Michael W. Cuneo, "The Vengeful Virgin: Case Studies in Contemporary American Catholic Apocalypticism," in *Millennium, Messiahs, and Mayhem: Contemporary Apocalyptic Movements*, ed. Thomas Robbins and Susan J. Palmer (New York: Routledge, 1997), 175-94; Daniel Wojcik, *The End of the World as We Know*

It: Faith, Fatalism, and Apocalypse in America* (New York: New York University Press, 1997), 60–96.
24. Lydia Fish, "Ethnicity and Catholicism," *New York Folklore* 8 (1982): 83–92; Jack Santino, "Catholic Folklore and Folk Catholicism," *New York Folklore* 8 (1982): 93–106.
25. Charles Lippy, *Being Religious, American Style: A History of Popular Religiosity in the United States* (Westport, CT: Greenwood, 1994), 185; Peter W. Williams, *Popular Religion in America: Symbolic Change and the Modernization Process in Historical Perspective* (Urbana: University of Illinois Press, 1989), 141–42.
26. Morgan, "Imaging Protestant Piety"; Morgan, *Visual Piety*; Morgan, *Icons of American Protestantism*.
27. Morgan, "Imaging Protestant Piety," 43.
28. Ibid.
29. Elizabeth McAlister, "A Sorcerer's Bottle: The Visual Art of Magic in Haiti," in Cosentino, *Sacred Arts of Haitian Vodou*, 306.
30. See the introduction to this volume. See also Leonard Norman Primiano, "Folk Religion," in Green, *Folklore*, 710–17.
31. Robert Anthony Orsi, "What Did Women Really Think When They Prayed to Saint Jude?," *US Catholic Historian* 8 (1989): 78.
32. Robert Anthony Orsi, "'Mildred, Is It Fun to Be a Cripple?': The Culture of Suffering in Mid-Twentieth Century American Catholicism," *South Atlantic Quarterly* 93 (1994): 582. See also Robert Anthony Orsi, *Thank You, St. Jude: Women's Devotion to the Patron Saint of Hopeless Causes* (New Haven: Yale University Press, 1996), 14–18.
33. Orsi, "Center Out There," 219.
34. Mark Searle, "Liturgical Movement," in McBrien, *HarperCollins Encyclopedia of Catholicism*, 783–85; James F. White, *Roman Catholic Worship: Trent to Today* (New York: Paulist Press, 1995), 71–114.
35. "Constitution on the Sacred Liturgy," *Documents of Vatican II* (New York: Guild Press, 1966).
36. White, *Roman Catholic Worship*, 115–40.
37. See *Catechism of the Catholic Church* (New York: Paulist Press, 1994), 1667–79.
38. See the introduction to this volume.
39. Matei Calinescu, *Five Faces of Modernity* (Durham: Duke University Press, 1987), 262. See also McDannell, *Material Christianity*, 163–67.

CHAPTER 4. ARTIFACTS OF BELIEF

1. David Morgan, "Thing," *Material Religion* 7, no. 1 (2011): 140–46.
2. Identifying sources for the creation of holy cards is challenging because an individual card may carry an image created in one country, be designed or printed in another, and be found/used/collected elsewhere.
3. Birgit Meyer, David Morgan, Crispin Paine, and S. Brent Plate, "Special Issue: Key Words in Material Religion," *Material Religion* 7, no. 1 (2011).

4   Leonard Norman Primiano, "Catholiciana Unmoored: Ex-Votos in Catholic Tradition and Their Commercialization as Religious Commodities," in *Graces Received: Painted and Metal Ex-Votos from Italy*, ed. Joseph Sciorra and Rosangela Briscese (New York: Calandra Institute Press, 2011), 8–37, chapter 5 in this volume.
5   Maurice Rickards, *Encyclopedia of Ephemera* (New York: Routledge, 2000).
6   Richard P. McBrien, *Inside Catholicism: Rituals and Symbols Revealed* (San Francisco: HarperCollins, 1995), 31, 39, 61.
7   Don Yoder, *The Pennsylvania German Broadside: A History and Guide* (University Park: Pennsylvania State University Press, 2005).
8   Robert Wildhaber, introduction to *Swiss Folk Art* (Washington, DC: Smithsonian Institution, 1968), 9.
9   Graziano Toni, *The First International Catalog of Holy Cards* (Milan: Unificato, 2009); and Graziano Toni, *International Catalog of the Holy Cards of the 20th Century* (Milan: Unificato, 2010). An examination of these volumes, which feature examples from Toni's collection of Italian holy cards, reveals an incredible representation of time, ingenuity, devotion, and artfulness, highlighting five hundred years of holy card creation in Europe.
10 Father Eugene Carrella, an avid collector of holy cards in the United States, has an extensive collection of European-produced holy cards of saints and has identified nearly two dozen holy card publishers from their printed trademarks. Examples from his collection can be found in Barbara Calamari and Sandra DiPasqua, *Holy Cards* (New York: Abrams, 2004); Barbara Calamari and Sandra DiPasqua, *Saints* (New York: Penguin, 2007); and Thomas Craughwell, *This Saint's for You! 300 Heavenly Allies for Architects, Athletes, Brides, Bachelors, Babies, Librarians, Murderers, Whales, Widows, and You* (Philadelphia: Quirk Books, 2007).
11 Toni's catalog is invaluable for determining actual dates of printing and manufacture through close attention to stylistic motifs.
12 Richard P. McBrien, ed., *The HarperCollins Encyclopedia of Catholicism* (San Francisco: HarperSanFrancisco, 1995).
13 David Morgan, *Visual Piety: A History and Theory of Popular Religious Images* (Berkeley: University of California Press, 1998).
14 David Morgan, ed., *Icons of American Protestantism: The Art of Warner Sallman* (New Haven: Yale University Press, 1996).
15 Beth Williamson, *Christian Art: A Very Short Introduction* (New York: Oxford University Press, 2004), 14.
16 Adolf Spamer, *Das Kleine Andachtsbild vom XIV. bis zum XX. Jahrhundert* (Munich: Bruckmann, 1930), 9.
17 For further details on the history of the printing process, see Peter C. Marzio, *The Democratic Art: Pictures for a 19th-Century America: Chromolithography, 1840–1900* (Boston: Godine, 1979).
18 See Kelly Donahue-Wallace, "Hide Paintings, Print Sources, and the Early Expression of a New Mexican Colonial Identity," in *Transforming Images: New Mexican Santos in-between Worlds*, ed. Claire Farago and Donna Pierce (University Park:

Pennsylvania State University Press, 2006), 145–58; Claire Farago, "Competing Religious Discourses in Postcolonial New Mexico," ibid., 194–212; and Toni, *First International Catalog*.
19 Marzio, *Democratic Art*, 8.
20 See Saul Zalesch, "The Religious Art of Benziger Brothers," *American Art* 13, no. 2 (1999): 74–77, for a brief discussion of the artists who made inexpensive paintings that were exported and sold by such publishers/distributors of religious goods in the United States as the Benziger Brothers.
21 Ann Taves, *The Household of Faith: Roman Catholic Devotions in Mid-Nineteenth-Century America* (Notre Dame: University of Notre Dame Press, 1986), 13.
22 Leonard Norman Primiano, "Post-Modern Sites of Catholic Sacred Materiality," in *Perspectives on American Religion and Culture*, ed. Peter W. Williams (Malden, MA: Basil Blackwell, 1999), 191–92, chapter 3 in this volume.
23 David Morgan, *The Sacred Heart of Jesus: The Visual Evolution of a Devotion* (Amsterdam: Amsterdam University Press, 2008), 22.
24 See Suzanne K. Kaufman, *Consuming Visions: Mass Culture and the Lourdes Shrine* (Ithaca: Cornell University Press, 2005).
25 Robert A. Orsi, *Thank You, St. Jude: Women's Devotion to the Patron Saint of Hopeless Causes* (New Haven: Yale University Press, 1996).
26 See Yvonne Lange, "Lithography, An Agent of Technological Change in Religious Folk Art: A Thesis," *Western Folklore* 33, no. 1 (1974): 51–64; Yvonne Lange, "In Search of San Acacio: The Impact of Industrialization on Santos Worldwide," *El Palacio* 94, no. 1 (1988): 18–24; and *Santos de Palo: The Household Saints of Puerto Rico* (New York: Museum of American Folk Art, 1991).
27 Farago, "Competing Religious Discourses," 209.
28 See Patrick A. Polk, *Haitian Vodou Flags* (Jackson: University Press of Mississippi, 1997); and Nancy Josephson, *Spirits in Sequins: Vodou Flags of Haiti* (Atglen, PA: Schiffer, 2007).
29 Martha Cooper and Joseph Sciorra, *R.I.P. Memorial Wall Art* (New York: Henry Holt, 1994).
30 The archiving of holy cards in university libraries and the collecting of cards by various fascinated individuals suggest the need for a more ethnographically based study and analysis of the imagery and handwritten texts associated with holy cards and the individuals who used—and in some cases continue to use—such cards in Europe and the United States.
31 The discussion that follows is based on Pierre Lessard, *Les petites images dévotes: Leur utilisation traditionalle au Quebec* (Quebec: Presses de l'Université Laval, 1981), quotes from 2–3.
32 For Newfoundland examples, see Gerald L. Pocius, "Holy Pictures in Newfoundland Houses: Visual Codes for Secular and Supernatural Relationships," in *Media Sense: The Folklore-Popular Culture Continuum*, ed. Peter Narváez and Martin Laba (Bowling Green, OH: Bowling Green State University Press, 1986), 124–48.

33 Thomas Allan Brady, "Amulets," in *New Catholic Encyclopedia*, vol. 1 (New York: McGraw-Hill, 1967), 457–58.
34 *Catechism of the Catholic Church* (New York: Catholic Book Publishing Co., 1994), 417.
35 Diana George and Mariolina Rizzi Salvatori, "Holy Cards/*Immaginette*: The Extraordinary Literacy of Vernacular Religion," *College Composition and Communication* 60, no. 2 (2008): 250–84.
36 Lessard, *Les petites images dévotes*, 45.
37 Toni, *International Catalog*, 11.
38 Ibid.
39 Morgan, "Thing," 143.
40 Robert Glenn Howard, "A Theory of Vernacular Rhetoric: The Case of the 'Sinner's Prayer' Online," *Folklore* 116, no. 2 (2005): 178–82; Robert Glenn Howard, *Digital Jesus: The Making of a New Christian Fundamentalist Community on the Internet* (New York: New York University Press, 2011), 73.
41 See Joseph Sciorra, *Built with Faith: The Italian American Imagination and Catholic Material Culture in New York City* (Knoxville: University of Tennessee Press, 2015).
42 David Chidester and Edward T. Linenthal, eds., *American Sacred Space* (Bloomington: Indiana University Press, 1995), 15.
43 Robert Maniura, "Icon/Image," *Material Religion* 7, no. 1 (2011): 53.

CHAPTER 5. CATHOLICIANA UNMOORED

1 See Doris Francis, ed., *Faith and Transformation: Votive Offerings and Amulets from the Alexander Girard Collection* (Santa Fe: Museum of New Mexico Press, 2007), and Mary Lee Nolan and Sidney Nolan, *Christian Pilgrimage in Modern Western Europe* (Chapel Hill: University of North Carolina Press, 1989).
2 See Michael P. Carroll, *Madonnas That Maim: Popular Catholicism in Italy since the Fifteenth Century* (Baltimore: Johns Hopkins University Press, 1992), 83; David Morgan, *The Sacred Heart of Jesus: The Visual Evolution of a Devotion* (Amsterdam: Amsterdam University Press, 2008).
3 See José Cláudio Alves de Oliveira, "From Shape to Content: The Variety and Expression of Ex-Votos in Brazil," in *Requesting Miracles: Votive Offerings from Diverse Cultures*, exhibition catalog (Winter Park, FL: Alice and William Jenkins Gallery at Crealdé School of Art, 2010), 20–25, for a presentation of vivid examples in Brazilian sanctuaries; and Federica Ugolini Lettieri, "Historical and Artistic Considerations on the Collection of Mariners' Votive Offerings in the Montenero Sanctuary," in *Mariners' Votive Offerings in the Montenero Sanctuary/ Ex voto marinari de Santuario di Montenero*, exhibition catalog (Philadelphia: Port of History Museum at Penn's Landing, 1984), 47–55, for a discussion of an Italian context.
4 Francesco Faeta, "The Ritual Contexts of Italian Ex-Votos," in Francis, *Faith and Transformation*, 60.

5   See David Freedberg, *The Power of Images: Studies in the History and Theory of Response* (Chicago: University of Chicago Press, 1989), 136–37. The University of Pennsylvania Museum of Archaeology and Anthropology, for example, has several Etruscan terracotta votives in the form of heads and feet on display. See Jean MacIntosh Turfa, *Catalogue of the Etruscan Gallery of the University of Pennsylvania Museum of Archaeology and Anthropology* (Philadelphia: University of Pennsylvania Museum of Archaeology and Anthropology, 2005), 45, 48–49. See also Jean MacIntosh Turfa, "Anatomical Votives and Italian Medical Traditions," in *Murlo and the Etruscans: Art and Society in Ancient Etruria*, ed. R. D. De Puma and J. P. Small (Madison: University of Wisconsin Press, 1994), 224–40, for a discussion of these objects and their role in Etruscan religious practice. Greek traditions in Paestum, a Greek colony in southern Italy, are referenced in Rebecca Miller Ammerman, *The Sanctuary of Santa Venera at Paestum II: The Votive Terracottas* (Ann Arbor: University of Michigan Press, 2002); see also Bjorn Forsen, *Griechische Gliederweihungen: Eine Untersuchung zu ihrer Typologie und ihrer religions-und sozialgeschichtlichen Bedeutung*, vol. 4 (Helsinki: Papers and Monographs of the Finnish Institute at Athens, 1996).

6   Quote from Bradley P. Nystrom and David P. Nystrom, *The History of Christianity: An Introduction* (New York: McGraw-Hill, 2004), 109. See also Peter Brown, *The Cult of the Saints: Its Rise and Function in Latin Christianity* (Chicago: University of Chicago Press, 1981).

7   Nystrom and Nystrom, *History of Christianity*, 109. See, for example, *The Ecclesiastical History* of Christian bishop and historian Eusebius of Caesarea (ca. 260–ca. 339). Eusebius, in *The History of the Church: From Christ to Constantine*, trans. G. A. Williamson (New York: Dorset Press, 1984), relates the story (book 6, chapter 5) of the Alexandrian martyr Potamiana, who promised the soldier Basilides after his respectful treatment of her on the way to her martyrdom that she would pray for him when she was with the Lord.

8   Arnold Angenendt, "Relics and Their Veneration," in *Treasures of Heaven: Saints, Relics, and Devotion in Medieval Europe*, ed. Martina Bagnoli, Holger A. Klein, C. Griffith Mann, and James Robinson (New Haven: Yale University Press, 2010), 24.

9   See Freedberg, *Power of Images*, 136–60.

10 Mariolina Rizzi Salvatori, "Understanding Ex-Votos," in *Requesting Miracles* exhibition catalog, 26.

11 Carroll, *Madonnas That Maim*, 82, refers to these paintings as *tavolette dipinti*. The website of the Museo del Paesaggio in Verbania, Italy, notes,
    Ex-votos can be classified as follows:
    Nonmaterial: legacies of goods or money, novenas, pilgrimages, fasts, etc.
    Material:
    Representational: three-dimensional reproductions of parts of the body, tools,
        buildings, etc.; paintings, oleographs, photographs, etc.
    Symbolic: hearts, plaits, candles, etc.

Circumstantial: objects having physical relevance to the event (crutches, weapons, etc.)
Gifts: jewels, cloth, animals, etc.
Buildings: churches, chapels, altars, etc.
"The Collection of Ex-Voto Paintings," www.museodelpaesaggio.it (accessed September 26, 2011).

12. Salvatori, "Understanding Ex-Votos," 26; see also Carroll, *Madonnas That Maim*, 84.
13. Gloria Fraser Giffords, "Promises and Answers: Retablos and Ex-Votos," in *Saints and Sinners: Mexican Devotional Art* (Atglen, PA: Schiffer, 2006), 197; see also Gloria Fraser Giffords, *Mexican Folk Retablos*, rev. ed. (Albuquerque: University of New Mexico Press, 1992).
14. Salvatori, "Understanding Ex-Votos," 29; see also Carroll, *Madonnas That Maim*, 84.
15. See Freedberg's discussion of the main figurative formulas of the votive genre, as well as the popularity and effectiveness of the votive image, in *Power of Images*, 153–60.
16. Rosa Giorgi, *The History of the Church in Art*, trans. Brian Phillips (Los Angeles: J. Paul Getty Museum, 2004), 6.
17. Linda Degh and Andrew Vazsonyi, "The Memorate and the Protomemorate," *Journal of American Folklore* 87 (1974): 225–39.
18. Caecilia Davis-Weyer, *Early Medieval Art, 300–1150* (Toronto: University of Toronto Press, 1986), 47–49.
19. Diana Webb, "Domestic Religion," in *Medieval Christianity: A People's History of Christianity*, vol. 4, ed. Daniel E. Bornstein (Minneapolis: Fortress, 2007), 305.
20. See the introduction to this volume.
21. Don Yoder, "Toward a Definition of Folk Religion," in *Discovering American Folklife: Essays on Folk Culture and the Pennsylvania Dutch* (Mechanicsburg, PA: Stackpole Books, 2001), 80.
22. Richard McBrien, ed., *The HarperCollins Encyclopedia of Catholicism* (San Francisco: HarperSanFrancisco, 1995), 1320.
23. John Dillenberger, ed., *Martin Luther: Selections from His Writings* (New York: Anchor, 1962), xiv.
24. Michel Mollat du Jourdin, preface to *Mariners' Votive Offerings* exhibition catalog, 11–12.
25. Margaret Dorgan, "Prayer," in McBrien, *HarperCollins Encyclopedia of Catholicism*, 1037.
26. Leon Anderson, "Analytic Autoethnography," *Journal of Contemporary Ethnography* 35 (2006): 373–95.
27. For another collector's statement about an assemblage of vernacular religious art, see Janis Lyon and Dennis Lyon's brief remarks in Charles M. Carrillo and Thomas J. Steele, *A Century of Retablos: The Janis and Dennis Lyon Collection of New Mexican Santos, 1780–1880* (Phoenix: Phoenix Art Museum, 2007), 8.

28 Clara Bargellini, "Ex-Voto to the Virgin of the Rosary," in *Painting a New World: Mexican Art and Life, 1521–1821*, ed. Donna Pierce, Rogelio Ruiz Gomar, and Clara Bargellini (Austin: University of Texas Press, 2004), 43.

29 Werfel's "personal preface" to what became a popular novel in 1941, and subsequently a 1943 film, states that he wrote the book in fulfillment of a vow—a sort of literary ex-voto for escaping the encroaching Nazi occupation of France: "In the last days of June 1940, in flight from our mortal enemies after the collapse of France, we reached the city of Lourdes.... It was, I repeat, a time of great dread. But it was also a time of great significance for me, for I became acquainted with the wondrous history of the girl Bernadette Soubirous and also with the wondrous facts concerning the healing of Lourdes. One day in my great distress I made a vow. I vowed that if I escaped from this desperate situation and reached the saving shores of America, I would put off all other tasks and sing, as best I could, the song of Bernadette. This book is the fulfillment of my vow." Franz Werfel, *The Song of Bernadette*, trans. Ludwig Lewisohn (New York: Viking, 1942), 6. As noted, ex-votos can also take the form of buildings, and it was this manifestation that I encountered first in the United States. In Philadelphia, German American parishioners of the Church of St. Peter the Apostle built a shrine to Our Lady of Perpetual Help over one hundred years ago as part of a vow made to safeguard the congregation from an influenza outbreak. Whether this narrative is factually true or not, this is the story that I was told as a child, to great effect. It is said that Thomas, in periods of career desperation, made a vow to Saint Jude Thaddeus that if he achieved success, he would build a shrine to the saint in the United States. As one of the great American Catholic public votive actions of the late twentieth century, Thomas organized, helped construct, and contributed consistently to the hospital that opened in 1962 to treat "catastrophic" children's diseases. See "All about Danny Thomas," St. Jude Children's Research Hospital website, www.stjude.org (accessed September 26, 2011), and also the preface of Robert A. Orsi's *Thank You, St. Jude: Women's Devotion to the Patron Saint of Hopeless Causes* (New Haven: Yale University Press, 1996).

30 See, for example, illustrations in Yoder, "Toward a Definition of Folk Religion," and in Don Yoder, *The Pennsylvania German Broadside: A History and Guide* (University Park: Pennsylvania State University Press, 2005), and throughout the journal he edited, *Pennsylvania Folklife*.

31 See chapter 3 in this volume.

32 See chapter 4 in this volume.

33 Louis Inturrisi, "Votive Figures for Collectors," *New York Times*, February 19, 1989, 12, www.nytimes.com.

34 An examination of eBay's website reveals some remarkable numbers touted by the company: "With more than 94 million active users globally, eBay is the world's largest online marketplace, where practically anyone can buy and sell practically anything.... eBay connects a diverse and passionate community of individual buyers and sellers, as well as small businesses. Their collective impact on e-

commerce is staggering: In 2010, the total worth of goods sold on eBay was $62 billion—more than $2,000 *every second*." See eBay website, "Who We Are," www.ebayinc.com (accessed September 2, 2011).

35 Bill Brown, "The Collecting Mania," *University of Chicago Magazine* 94, no. 1 (2001), http://magazine.uchicago.edu.

36 Jay P. Dolan, *The American Catholic Experience: A History from Colonial Times to the Present* (Notre Dame: University of Notre Dame Press, 1992), 429–30.

37 See Tom Roberts, "Parish Closing Traumas Spread," *National Catholic Reporter*, January 23, 2009, http://ncronline.org; Richard McBrien, "Parish Mergers: So Tough to Balance Resources and Personnel," *National Catholic Reporter*, March 21, 2011, http://ncronline.org.

38 John Thavis, "Vatican Prepares Document on Clergy-Laity Relationship," *National Catholic Reporter*, June 28, 2011, http://ncronline.org.

39 See Dwayne Campbell, "Colorful Keepsakes from Closed Churches: A Sale Offers Pieces of Catholic History," *Philadelphia Inquirer*, June 20, 2004, http://articles.philly.com.

40 Email message to author, September 2, 2011.

41 Spelling, punctuation, and style here reflect the passage on the access date: eBay website, "Catholic," http://popular.ebay.com (accessed September 2, 2011).

42 Listing for "Italian Painted Ex-voto 'A Farmer Prays for His Cattle'" (item number 190259653408), October 16, 2008, eBay (webpage no longer available; URL unrecorded, accessed October 26, 2008).

43 See Alfredo Vilchis Roque and Pierre Schwartz, *Infinitas Gracias: Contemporary Mexican Votive Painting* (San Francisco: Seuil Chronicle, 2004), for a discussion of contemporary Mexican *retablos*.

44 For example, see Colleen McDannell, *Material Christianity: Religion and Popular Culture in America* (New Haven: Yale University Press, 1995); Colleen McDannell, *Picturing Faith: Photography and the Great Depression* (New Haven: Yale University Press, 2004); David Morgan, *Visual Piety: A History and Theory of Popular Religious Images* (Berkeley: University of California Press, 1998); David Morgan, *The Sacred Gaze: Religious Visual Culture in Theory and Practice* (Berkeley: University of California Press, 2005); David Morgan, *The Lure of Images: A History of Religion and Visual Media in America* (London: Routledge, 2007); David Morgan, ed., *Religion and Material Culture: The Matter of Belief* (New York: Routledge, 2010).

45 See Leonard Norman Primiano, "Material Culture," in *Encyclopedia of Global Religion*, ed. W. C. Roof and M. Juergensmeyer (Thousand Oaks, CA: Sage, 2012), for an extensive bibliography of folklorists studying religious material culture.

46 Morgan, *Religion and Material Culture*, 12.

47 Morgan, *Lure of Images*, 246–48.

48 See chapter 3 in this volume.

49 See Peter Brown's *praesentia* of the sacred, *Cult of the Saints*, 86–105, and McDannell's Catholic kitsch in *Material Christianity*, 163–97.

50. Susan Brinkmann, "Sacred Relics Sold on eBay: Boycott Urged," *Catholic Standard and Times*, November 20, 2006, www.catholic.org.
51. Catholic News Agency, "Sale of Relics 'Unacceptable Business,' Says Vatican Cardinal," February 12, 2008, www.catholicnewsagency.com.
52. eBay website, "Human Remains and Body Parts Policy," http://pages.ebay.com (accessed September 2, 2011). All spelling, punctuation, and style reflect the passage on the access date.
53. Patrick J. Geary, *Furta Sacra: Thefts of Relics in the Central Middle Ages* (Princeton: Princeton University Press, 1991).
54. Carroll, *Madonnas That Maim*, 84–85.
55. Allen F. Roberts, "Tempering 'the Tyranny of Already': Re-Signification and the Migration of Images," in Morgan, *Religion and Material Culture*, quotes on 115, 132, 122.
56. Nicholas Barnard, *Living with Folk Art* (New York: Thames and Hudson, 1998), quotes on 14, 124, and illustration.
57. "Embodied Placemaking in Urban Public Spaces," part 1, *Center for 21st Century Studies: A Newsletter from the University of Wisconsin-Milwaukee* 1 (Winter 2011): 4. See also David Gonzalez, "Still Taking to the Streets to Honor Their Saints," *New York Times*, June 6, 2010, www.nytimes.com.
58. See Brown, *Cult of the Saints*; Geary, *Furta Sacra*.
59. Jean Baudrillard, *The System of Objects* (1968; New York: Verso, 2006), quotes on 97, 55. See also Stewart's discussion of collectors: "The ultimate term in the series that marks the collection is the 'self,' the articulation of the collector's own 'identity.'" Susan Stewart, *On Longing: Narratives of the Miniature, the Gigantic, the Souvenir, the Collection* (Durham: Duke University Press, 1993), 162–63. A useful edited "collection" on the phenomenon of collecting for novice readers is John Elsner and Roger Cardinal, eds., *The Cultures of Collecting* (London: Reaktion Books, 1994).
60. See, for example, Fiona Candlin and Raiford Guins, eds., *The Object Reader* (London: Routledge, 2009).
61. Bill Brown, "Thing Theory," *Critical Inquiry* 28, no. 1 (2001): 1–22.
62. Brown, "Collecting Mania"; Bill Brown, *A Sense of Things: The Object Matter of American Literature* (Chicago: University of Chicago Press, 2002).
63. Brown, "Collecting Mania."
64. See comments on the fate of New York City's American Folk Art Museum in Robin Pogrebin, "Options Dim for Museum of Folk Art," *New York Times*, August 24, 2011, www.nytimes.com.
65. Folklorist Henry Glassie, writing about the importance of understanding "context" when approaching exhibitions of folk art, cautions, "The danger is to think we are encountering folk art directly or interpreting it correctly when all we have done is to build a false context around it out of the culture we know best, our own." Henry Glassie, "Folk Art in the Girard Collection," in *The Spirit of Folk Art: The Girard Collection at the Museum of International Folk Art* (New York: Abrams,

1989), 17. Glassie writes about experiencing a collection of folk art through the perspective of its collector in his essay "Folk Art in the Girard Collection" (16–24). The controversies over the dislocation of native, regional, vernacular, and folk art and artifacts in new contexts, especially in museum exhibitions, as well as the recontextualization of utilitarian objects for museum display, are discussed in Sally Price, *Primitive Art in Civilized Places*, 2nd ed. (Chicago: University of Chicago Press, 2001), and Ivan Karp and Steven D. Lavine, eds., *Exhibiting Cultures: The Poetics and Politics of Museum Display* (Washington, DC: Smithsonian Institution Press, 1991).

66 Stewart, *On Longing*, 165.
67 Georges Didi-Huberman, "Ex-Voto: Image, Organ, Time," *L'Esprit Créateur* 47, no. 3 (2007): 7, 14.

CHAPTER 6. THE GAY GOD OF THE CITY

1 Daniel A. Helminiak, *Catholicism, Homosexuality, and Dignity: Questions and Answers* (Washington, DC: Dignity USA, 1996).
2 Pat Roche, ed., *Dignity/USA 25: A Chronology, 1969–1994* (Washington, DC: Dignity USA, 1995). When I write "Dignity/Philadelphia," I am referring to the local chapter. My use of "Dignity" usually refers to the Philadelphia chapter, but the context indicates whether I am using the name to refer to Dignity in a more general sense as a national organization.
3 Richard P. McBrien, ed., *The HarperCollins Encyclopedia of Catholicism* (San Francisco: HarperSanFrancisco, 1995), 963.
4 See Joseph Harris, "The Church and Its Choices If the Priest Shortage Continues," *National Catholic Reporter*, September 3, 1999, 18.
5 Don Brophy, "The Parish of Choice," *America*, November 19, 2001, 13.
6 McBrien, *HarperCollins Encyclopedia of Catholicism*, 958.
7 McGreevy makes the point that "from the Council of Trent [1545–1563] . . . onward, canon law stressed that the parish served all of the souls living within its boundaries," and that occasionally there was a need for national parishes to serve the people of a distinct national or racial character. John T. McGreevy, *Parish Boundaries: The Catholic Encounter with Race in the Twentieth-Century Urban North* (Chicago: University of Chicago Press, 1996), 11.
8 Jay P. Dolan, *The American Catholic Experience: A History from Colonial Times to the Present* (Garden City, NY: Doubleday, 1985), 195–218; Charles R. Morris, *American Catholic: The Saints and Sinners Who Built America's Most Powerful Church* (New York: Times Books, 1997).
9 Brophy, "Parish of Choice," 13.
10 See, for example, Robert Orsi's account of Italian Harlem in *The Madonna of 115th Street: Faith and Community in Italian Harlem, 1880–1950* (New Haven: Yale University Press, 1985), 69–74. McGreevy also writes of the debates about retaining national parishes over "territorial" parishes in the postwar period (*Parish Boundaries*, 82–84).

11 For example, in the case of five remaining Polish ethnic parishes, membership in the congregation, as well as a place in the parish school, is permitted as long as one parent is of direct Polish heritage, no matter the distance the parish is from the individual's home.
12 John Boswell, *Christianity, Social Tolerance and Homosexuality: Gay People in Western Europe from the Beginning of the Christian Era to the 14th Century* (Chicago: University of Chicago Press, 1980), 91–117; John F. Harvey, *The Homosexual Person: New Thinking in Pastoral Care* (San Francisco: Ignatius Press, 1987), 95–117; Mark D. Jordan, *The Silence of Sodom: Homosexuality in Modern Catholicism* (Chicago: University of Chicago Press, 2000), 26–37.
13 See Jordan, *Silence of Sodom*, for a critical commentary on homosexuality in modern Catholicism.
14 Don Yoder, "Toward a Definition of Folk Religion," in *Discovering American Folklife: Studies in Ethnic, Religious, and Regional Culture* (Ann Arbor: UMI Research Press, 1990), 280.
15 The specific occasion for Dignity chapters being asked to leave Catholic parishes was the passing of a resolution in the House of Delegates at the Dignity/USA 1987 national convention in Bal Harbour, Florida. The resolution stated (emphasis mine),
   We believe that gay men and lesbian women can express their sexuality in a manner that is consonant with Christ's teaching. *We believe that we can express our sexuality physically in a unitive manner that is loving, life giving and life affirming.* We believe that all sexuality should be exercised in an ethically responsible and unselfish way.
16 *National Catholic Reporter*, August 16, 1991.
17 Congregation for the Doctrine of the Faith, "Letter to the Bishops of the Catholic Church on the Pastoral Care of Homosexual Persons," 1988, 2 (emphasis mine).
18 This quotation is from a March 30, 1986, Easter Sunday interview on the University of Pennsylvania's FM radio program *Gay Dreams* with the current chapter president and a female member of Dignity.
19 Shortly before this interview, the archdiocese had, in fact, closed St. Peter Claver Church as a fully functioning parish, still allowing masses to be said on Sunday for the small number who wished to attend. "Of course," said my interlocutor, the archdiocese "would never send their people to Dignity for Mass. They are sent to St. John the Evangelist." He noted that "St. Peter Claver has as many people at their Sunday Masses as Dignity on Thirteenth Street." Had the gay congregation of Dignity been allowed to operate out of St. Peter Claver, that parish perhaps would have remained open and been more robust and financially sound in the eyes of the archdiocese. See Vincent F. A. Golphin, "Black Catholics Angry about Closing of Parish," *National Catholic Reporter*, May 9, 1986, 24, for specific details concerning the closing of St. Peter Claver.
20 Begun as a Home Liturgy Group meeting in a member's apartment, the chapter held liturgies for six months in St. Rita of Cascia Church on South Broad Street in 1974. This was its only time meeting in an archdiocesan property.

21 In the 1990s, heterosexual men who left the priesthood to marry, especially members of an organization called CORPUS (the Association for an Inclusive Priesthood), also presided at Dignity liturgies.
22 I would estimate that 20 percent of the individuals in attendance at Dignity Masses during the late 1980s and early 1990s were not Roman Catholic.
23 A Catholic friend of this man saw his participation in this way: "Buddy is saying the Agnus Dei and the Our Father; he's Jewish, it's hilarious. . . . But there's a commonality of us all; he was a part of the community and worshipping the same God that we all believe in but at our service. Right now he's living with an ex-Catholic who doesn't go to Dignity." I sat next to this man at one of the Masses. He told me that, while he was not considering converting to Roman Catholicism, he liked the atmosphere and solidarity of these liturgical occasions.
24 Not all gay visitors cared for their experience at Dignity. One young man characterized the social hour after Sunday Mass as nothing but a "meat market." This man approached me after a public lecture I had given on Dignity and stated his opinions. He told me of the less than favorable impression of Dignity that he formed in the half-dozen times he had gone to Mass there.
25 See Fish's differentiation between "ethnic Catholic" and "ethnically Catholic" in Lydia Fish, "Ethnicity and Catholicism," *New York Folklore* 8 (1982): 83–92.
26 Joseph J. Casino, "From Sanctuary to Involvement: A History of the Catholic Parish in the Northeast," in *The American Catholic Parish: A History from 1850 to the Present*, vol. 1, ed. Jay P. Dolan (New York: Paulist Press, 1987), 101.
27 Casino also notes that "there never was anything that could be called the 'typical' parish" ("From Sanctuary to Involvement," 101). Each congregation was unique because of the ethnic community, the leadership, the local concerns, and the individual personalities of the Catholics who constituted it.
28 Several members of the liturgical committee had no problem with the practice of having non-Catholic Eucharistic ministers. Stephen explained to me,
   To me personally, it's not such a big issue. . . . I believe it's the Liturgy Committee policy that as long as you believe that it's the body and blood, it's okay, you can be a Eucharistic minister. That's the general consensus of the community after tons of arguments. At one time, they didn't want non-Catholic readers for the same reason. As long as you have the reverence for the body and blood of Christ, and in my mind even if you thought it was just symbolic, but you still had the reverence or symbolism of what was going on, I don't have a problem with that.
29 *Independence* 13, no. 5 (1986): 1–2.
30 *Independence* 13, no. 4 (1986): 1.
31 McGreevy, *Parish Boundaries*, 5.
32 Robert A. Orsi, "The Religious Boundaries of an In-Between People: Street *Feste* and the Problem of the Dark-Skinned Other in Italian Harlem, 1920–1990," in *Gods of the City*, ed. Robert A. Orsi (Bloomington: Indiana University Press, 1999), 281.

33   See, e.g., "Landmark Catholic Churches Closing," *Washington Post*, December 27, 1987; "Detroit Prelate Backs Plan to Close 43 Churches," *Los Angeles Times*, October 15, 1988; James Risen, "Day Bittersweet for Detroit's Aging Parishes," *Los Angeles Times*, December 25, 1988; Bob Secter, "Chicago Archdiocese to Shut 31 Parishes, Many Schools in Sweeping Cost-Cutting," *Los Angeles Times*, January 22, 1990; "Talk of More Church Closings Provokes Ire in Philadelphia," *National Catholic Reporter*, July 3, 1998; Teresa Malcolm, "Parish Closings Predicted," *National Catholic Reporter*, April 3, 1998.
34   Morris, *American Catholic*, 299–300; Brophy, "Parish of Choice."
35   Brophy, "Parish of Choice," 12.

CHAPTER 7. WHAT IS VERNACULAR CATHOLICISM?

1   Daniel A. Helminiak, *Catholicism, Homosexuality, and Dignity: Questions and Answers* (Washington, DC: Dignity USA, 1996).
2   Dignity/Philadelphia Information Sheet, 1987.
3   See chapter 6 in this volume.
4   Dignity/USA, "Sexual Ethics: Experience, Growth, Challenge," in *Dignity/USA* 21 (December 1989): 2.

CHAPTER 8. "I WOULD RATHER BE FIXATED ON THE LORD"

1   For succinct statements on the position of the Roman Catholic Church, see John F. Harvey, "Homosexuality," in *The New Catholic Encyclopedia*, vol. 7 (New York: McGraw-Hill, 1967), 116–19, and the updated entry in *The New Catholic Encyclopedia*, vol. 17 (Supplement) (New York: McGraw-Hill, 1979), 271–73. On homosexuality and the Roman Catholic tradition, see also Harvey's *The Homosexual Person: New Thinking in Pastoral Care* (San Francisco: Ignatius Press, 1987); Herbert F. Smith and Joseph A. Dilenno, *Sexual Inversion: The Questions with Catholic Answers* (Boston: St. Paul Editions, 1979); Jeannine Gramick and Pat Furey, eds., *The Vatican and Homosexuality: Reactions to the "Letter to the Bishops of the Catholic Church on the Pastoral Care of Homosexual Persons"* (New York: Crossroad, 1989); Robert Nugent, ed., *A Challenge to Love: Gay and Lesbian Catholics in the Church* (New York: Crossroad, 1983); Robert Nugent and Jeannine Gramick, eds., *A Time to Speak: A Collection of Contemporary Statements from US Catholic Sources on Homosexuality, Gay Ministry and Social Justice* (Mt. Rainier, MD: New Ways Ministry, 1982); Jeannine Gramick, *Homosexuality in the Priesthood and the Religious Life* (New York: Crossroad, 1989); John Gallagher, ed., *Homosexuality and the Magisterium* (Mt. Rainier, MD: New Ways Ministry, 1983); Task Force on Gay/Lesbian Issues, *Homosexuality and Social Justice* (San Francisco: Consultation on Homosexuality, Social Justice, and Roman Catholic Theology, 1986); James G. Wolf, ed., *Gay Priests: Research and Comment* (New York: Harper and Row, 1989); Barbara Zanotti, ed., *A Faith of One's Own: Explorations by Catholic Lesbians* (Trumansburg, NY: Crossing, 1986).

2 Vernacular religion is, by definition, religion as it is lived: as human beings encounter, understand, interpret, and practice it. Since religion inherently involves interpretation, it is impossible for the religion of an individual not to be vernacular. Vernacular religious theory involves an interdisciplinary approach to the study of the religious lives of individuals, with special attention to the process of religious belief, the verbal and material expressions of religious belief, and the ultimate object of religious belief. (See the introduction to this volume.)

3 Some lesbian and feminist authors contend that lesbianism is experienced as a given for some women and is a political or personal choice for others. Dolores Maggiore writes, "For some, lesbianism remains a state of awareness of self experienced at an early age: one realizes a difference, an attraction to women. Proponents of this view say that they always knew that they were lesbians. For them, there was no choice: they were lesbians and they had to follow their inclination. For others, lesbianism is a political choice, a conscious rejection of the patriarchy, of traditional roles for women, of limitations placed on women's control of their own lives. It is a conscious embrace by women of women as their primary emotional, erotic, and spiritual attachments." Dolores J. Maggiore, "Lesbianism," in *Encyclopedia of Homosexuality*, vol. 1, ed. Wayne R. Dynes (New York: Garland, 1990), 709. All three of the lesbian members or former members of Dignity whom I interviewed told me that they did feel that they were born homosexual.

4 See, for example, John J. McNeill, *Taking a Chance on God: Liberating Theology for Gays, Lesbians, and Their Lovers, Families, and Friends* (Boston: Beacon, 1988).

5 I use the terms "homosexual," "gay," and "lesbian" in this chapter. Their distinctive meanings can cause confusion. Wayne R. Dynes and Warren Johansson explain that the term "homosexual" has long been "the most generally accepted designation for same-sex orientation" (*Encyclopedia of Homosexuality*, 555) and that the word "gay" is "often taken as the contemporary or colloquial equivalent of homosexual without further distinction," despite its different history and political shading. They note further that "many lesbian organizations now reject the term gay, restricting it to men, hence the spread of such binary phrases as 'gay and lesbian' and 'lesbian and gay people.' Such ukases notwithstanding, expressions such as 'Is she gay?' are still common among lesbians" (see "Gay" and "Homosexual" entries in *Encyclopedia of Homosexuality*, 455–56 and 555–56). For the most part, Dignity members to whom I spoke were careful to differentiate between gay men and lesbian women when referring to and addressing the men and women of the chapter. The Roman Catholic hierarchy, in its documents, usually does not acknowledge any differentiation between a "homosexual" person and a "gay" person, possibly because the Church neither admits the existence of a gay culture nor acknowledges that gayness can be a category of self-identification. In the 1986 Vatican "Letter to the Bishops of the Catholic Church on the Pastoral Care of Homosexual Persons," for example, the word "gay" is never used. Nor is the word "lesbian." I seek at once to remain attentive to the complexities of the historical and contemporary usage of these terms and to fulfill the methodologi-

cal imperative of a folkloristic emic analysis, which must give highest priority to the self-identification of individuals.
6   All names of individuals have been changed to protect their privacy.
7   Joseph P. Goodwin defines "camp" as "an attitude, a style of humor, an approach to situations, people, and things. The camp point of view is assertively expressed through exaggeration and inversion, stressing form over content, deflating pomposity, mocking pretension, and subverting values. . . . Sometimes (but certainly not always) camp behavior is effeminate. Like much gay humor, camp plays with stereotypes, carrying them to extremes, flouting heterosexual values. Camp shows the world 'as it could be,' while saying, 'My God, what if it were that way?' Camp is a metacultural statement, an aspect of culture commenting on culture. Camp can be solely playful, but often it is a serious medium, providing a weapon against oppression." Joseph P. Goodwin, *More Man Than You'll Ever Be: Gay Folklore and Acculturation in Middle America* (Bloomington: Indiana University Press, 1989), 38–39.

CHAPTER 9. "THE CONSCIOUSNESS OF GOD'S PRESENCE WILL KEEP YOU WELL, HEALTHY, HAPPY, AND SINGING"

1   By contrast, see, for example, John Hoshor, *God in a Rolls-Royce: The Rise of Father Divine, Madman, Menace, or Messiah* (New York: Hillman-Curl, 1936); Jan Karel Van Baalen, *The Chaos of Cults*, 3rd ed. (Grand Rapids, MI: Eerdmans, 1942); and Sara Harris, *Father Divine: Holy Husband* (Garden City, NY: Doubleday, 1953).
2   For a discussion of folklife studies, see Leonard Norman Primiano, "Folklife," in *Folklore: An Encyclopedia of Beliefs, Customs, Tales, Music, and Art*, vol. 1, ed. Thomas A. Green (Santa Barbara: ABC-CLIO, 1997), 322–31.
3   Compare Robert Weisbrot, *Father Divine and the Struggle for Racial Equality* (Urbana: University of Illinois Press, 1983), and Jill Watts, *God, Harlem U.S.A.: The Father Divine Story* (Berkeley: University of California Press, 1992).
4   For example, Arthur Huff Fauset, *Black Gods of the Metropolis: Negro Religious Cults of the Urban North* (1944; reprint 1971; Philadelphia: University of Pennsylvania Press, 2002), 64–65, 83–85, 104–6, 118–19; "Life is a happy song," Fauset, *Black Gods*, 118.
5   Fauset, *Black Gods*, 117–19.
6   This approach to the leadership and structural elements of the Peace Mission is still taken in sociological, historical, and religious studies anthologies that examine the movement. See, for example, Joseph R. Washington, *Black Sects and Cults* (1972; Lanham, MD: University Press of America, 1984); J. Gordon Melton, ed., *Encyclopedic Handbook of Cults in America* (New York: Garland, 1992); Robert Weisbrot, "Father Divine's Peace Mission Movement," in *America's Alternative Religions*, ed. Timothy Miller (Albany: State University of New York Press, 1995), 285–90; and Richard T. Schaefer and William W. Zellner, *Extraordinary Groups: An Examination of Unconventional Lifestyles*, 8th ed. (New York: Worth, 2008).

For pedagogical purposes, the top-down approach to organized religions continues to take precedence among scholars.

7   "Divinites" is a designation employed in Fauset, *Black Gods*, 58, that I have never heard used within the conversation of members of the contemporary Peace Mission Movement; the members refer to themselves as "sister" or "brother," Father and Mother Divine's "children," or "followers of Father Divine."

8   Fauset, *Black Gods*, 117. There was tremendous public curiosity about the movement starting in the 1930s with such articles as St. Clair McKelway and A. J. Liebling, "Who Is This King of Glory?," *New Yorker*, June 13, 1936, 21–34; June 20, 1936, 22–32; June 27, 1936, 22–36; and Edwin T. Buehrer, "Harlem's God," *Christian Century* 52 (December 11, 1935): 1590–93. The mission was also prominently on display in a 1936 report by the *March of Time*, a weekly newsreel series shown in movie theaters from 1935 to 1951, produced by the editors of *Time* magazine.

9   Fauset, *Black Gods*, 117–19. I have sought out other ethnographic notes from Fauset's work with the Peace Mission, but there is very little relevant material about his dissertation research included in the Arthur Huff Fauset Collection, Special Collections Department, Van Pelt Library, University of Pennsylvania. I also asked Mother Divine in April 2007, during the preparation of this piece, about any available and relevant correspondence between Father Divine, the movement, and Fauset. While Mother Divine remembers Fauset, she could not recall any specific correspondence or locate any at the time.

10 Fauset, *Black Gods*, 117. When the ethnographic study is of the Peace Mission, an additional consideration is that throughout its history, Father Divine and the movement have received considerable negative coverage from the print media and have been offended by writers denigrating what they believe to be the deity of Father Divine. Most biographies of the Reverend M. J. Divine by scholars consider his past history as a man born in the United States, and the ahistorical consciousness of the movement sees such scholarship as inappropriate and as "lowrating" Father. The movement also disapproves of being designated an African American religious "cult." They feel that the Peace Mission is neither a "cult" nor exclusively African American. While there is a large African American (and female) membership contingent, members believe that the movement has appealed to both sexes and all races and is international in scope. There remain scholars who engage in simple public denigration of Father Divine, apparently not concerned that there are individuals who still consider him their God. Henry Louis Gates Jr., for example, in a response to a letter to the editor of the *New York Times* about Father Divine, finished his point with this: "Father Divine convinced thousands (he claimed millions) of his followers that he was God—and if that's not a con, then I'm sweet Daddy Grace" (reply to letter to the editor, *New York Times Book Review*, May 7, 1989, 41).

11 James V. Spickard, J. Shaun Landres, and Meredith McGuire, eds., *Personal Knowledge and Beyond: Reshaping the Ethnography of Religion* (New York: New York University Press, 2002), 5.

12 I used my time over the years to develop questions that I could ask Mother Divine and the followers, based not on what popular writers or other scholars said about them but on what they said about themselves. Those questions formed the basis of filmed interviews in 1996–1997, which are the foundation of "The Father Divine Project," produced by videographer Will Luers and myself. These videos can be found at https://vimeo.com/channels/326983. We have received Mother Divine's permission to post this material. I have continued asking questions and taking notes since 1997, and my current research on the music of the Peace Mission is based on much of that fieldwork. As I began writing and contemplated publishing about the movement, I engaged in a reciprocal form of ethnographic experience in which I have presented material to the community or had Mother Divine or individual members read and then engage me about the material I had composed about them. A discussion of my reciprocal approach can be found in the coda of this volume. For other useful discussions of ethnography, religion, and reciprocal method, see Spickard, Landres, and McGuire, *Personal Knowledge*; for reflexive ethnography, see Charlotte Aull Davies, *Reflexive Ethnography: A Guide to Researching Selves and Others* (London: Routledge, 1999); and for reciprocal ethnography, see Luke Eric Lassiter, *The Chicago Guide to Collaborative Ethnography* (Chicago: University of Chicago Press, 2005).

13 See chapter 10 in this volume.

14 Many followers of Father Divine receive spiritual names at some point during their time in the Peace Mission. Those names, such as Miss Holy Grace, Miss Sunshine Bright, Miss Stark Happiness, Mr. Loving Jeremiah, Mr. Equality Smart, or Mr. Radical Love, could come into their consciousness in a dream or a vision or through some other metaphysical contact with Father, or they could simply illustrate some characteristic of the follower's personality. Followers, as previously noted, resist revealing any facts about their personal identities and lives before entering the Peace Mission. I have not revealed the name of any follower currently living, with the exception of Mother Divine, and have used an initial instead. I also will not reveal the approximate ages of any individual member. For the sake of reader clarity, however, I feel it is necessary to state that the sisters and brothers in the first decade of the twenty-first century are generally between seventy and one hundred years old. I have retained the names of deceased members previously interviewed.

15 Miss G, interview with the author, 2004. Two excellent recent introductions to the subject of sacred and religious song in America are Stephen A. Marini, *Sacred Song in America: Religion, Music, and Public Culture* (Urbana: University of Illinois Press, 2003), and Philip V. Bohlman, Edith L. Blumhofer, and Maria M. Chow, eds., *Music in American Religious Experience* (New York: Oxford University Press, 2006). The music and songs of the Peace Mission were noted even in the earliest articles written about the movement. See, for example, Buehrer, "Harlem's God," 1590–93, and the three-part report by McKelway and Liebling, "Who Is This King of Glory?" In the 1950s, Harris's *Father Divine*, a text reviled by the

movement, gave considerable attention to songs, even noting the following in a discussion of the Rosebuds choral group: "Whether songs of praise to Father Divine or whether songs inspired by anger against the injustices Negroes have suffered in America, the Buds' songs are no orthodox hymns. They are original, colorful, completely alive outpourings. Often they attain the very heights of folk art" (298). Beryl Satter, "Marcus Garvey, Father Divine and the Gender Politics of Race Difference and Race Neutrality," *American Quarterly* 48 (1996): 43–76, in her historical study of race and gender, states that it was Peace Mission women who "created a distinctive Divinite culture" (58), and this creativity included a culture of music and song (59).

16 Father Divine often mentioned how he was once offered a large sum of money for one composition, presumably from a popular song publisher or the Victor Talking Machine Company, which he turned down because, as he put it, "If I would sell an inspiration I would be worse than Judas who sold the Body of the Inspiration" (July 24–25, 1945, message; printed in *New Day*, February 28, 1959, 3).

17 Printed in *New Day*, July 11, 1970, 5.

18 *New Day*, August 27, 1942, 75.

19 See Leonard Norman Primiano, "Mother Divine," in *Encyclopedia of Women and World Religion*, vol. 2, ed. Serinity Young (New York: Macmillan, 1998).

20 Miss F, interview with the author, 2004.

21 Miss K, interview with the author, 2004.

22 Lawrence W. Levine, *Black Culture and Black Consciousness: Afro-American Folk Thought from Slavery to Freedom* (New York: Oxford University Press, 1977), 180.

23 Printed in *New Day*, April 20, 1957, 4–5.

24 *Spoken Word*, February 29, 1936, 4.

25 Weisbrot, *Father Divine and the Struggle for Racial Equality*, 75–76, explains the development of each publication.

26 LaVere Belstrom, interview with the author, 2004.

27 *I Come to Light Your Candles* (n.d.), 17.

28 Ibid., 5.

29 *Crusader Song Book* (n.d.), 5. Crusaders' Day, which is celebrated on Father's Day in June, recalls the 1960 occasion when Father Divine donned a Crusaders powder-blue jacket for the festivities at Woodmont. See Mother Divine, *The Peace Mission Movement* (Philadelphia: Imperial Press, 1982), 32, for a further explanation of this male group within the movement. Today, many Crusaders songs are sung on this occasion, and a small booklet of their lyrics has been created to promote congregational singing, since the ranks of the Crusaders are so depleted. The two Christmas songs, which are quoted here, are taken from another small booklet, also printed to assist congregational singing of songs by followers and visitors, particularly during a celebration developed by Mother Divine known as the American Christmas.

30 See chapter 10 in this volume.

31 Mr. L, interview with the author, 2004.

32 See Fauset, *Black Gods*, 93, on "Krum Elbow."
33 Mr. R, interview with the author, 2005.
34 Mr. P, interview with the author, 2005.
35 See Gene Lees, *Portrait of Johnny: The Life of John Herndon Mercer* (New York: Pantheon, 2004), 145.
36 See "Heaven," Father Divine Project, https://vimeo.com/channels/326983/41590692.
37 See chapter 10 in this volume.
38 Fauset, *Black Gods*, xxiii.
39 Ibid., xv.
40 Watts, *God, Harlem U.S.A.*, xi–xii, and Satter, "Marcus Garvey, Father Divine," 43–76, problematize the race issue in relation to Father Divine and the followers even further. To read of Father Divine's place within American metaphysical religion, see Catherine L. Albanese, *A Republic of Mind and Spirit: A Cultural History of American Metaphysical Religion* (New Haven: Yale University Press, 2007), 476–78.
41 Imani Perry, *Prophets of the Hood: Politics and Poetics in Hip Hop* (Durham: Duke University Press, 2005), 25.
42 Cornel West, *Race Matters* (New York: Vintage, 2001), 97.
43 Ibid., 93.
44 Satter, "Marcus Garvey, Father Divine"; R. Marie Griffith, "Body Salvation: New Thought, Father Divine, and the Feast of Material Pleasures," *Religion and American Culture* 11 (2001): 119–53; and R. Marie Griffith, *Born Again Bodies: Flesh and Spirit in American Christianity* (Berkeley: University of California Press, 2004).
45 For a discussion of the female body within the Peace Mission, see Griffith, "Body Salvation." Marla F. Frederick, *Between Sundays: Black Women and Everyday Struggles of Faith* (Berkeley: University of California Press, 2003), makes a strong argument about how social scientists have misunderstood the experience and practice of faith in the lives of African American women. Spirituality, she argues, should be observed not only in religious "signs, symbols, rituals, and structures" (ix) but also in relation to the cultures of work, tithing, education, personal behavior, sexuality, and activism that fill their lives. Although Frederick's analysis is based on a study of the African American women of Halifax County, North Carolina, the conclusion of this ethnography of spirituality is equally valid for the women of the Peace Mission Movement and the way they view the multitude of connections between their religious and so-called secular lives. Followers of Father Divine would see work of even the most menial or physical quality, for example, as an enactment of their faith in Father Divine, their belief in his divinity, and their dedication to promoting the unity and strength of their community.
46 I have endeavored to study, deeply rather than superficially, the vernacular religion of the Peace Mission members—that is, the religion of their everyday lives and the subtle and dramatic ways practitioners of this belief system creatively re-create their religion—with the conviction that individual members of so-called

sects can be understood to have a vernacular religion to the same extent that Catholics, Buddhists, and Jews do. For my definition of vernacular religion, see the introduction to this volume.

CHAPTER 10. "BRINGING PERFECTION IN THESE DIFFERENT PLACES"

1. See Conrad Cherry, ed., *God's New Israel: Religious Interpretations of American Destiny*, rev. ed. (Chapel Hill: University of North Carolina Press, 1998), for a collection of readings tracing the national mythology of America's destiny as a providentially chosen land.
2. See Warren E. Roberts, "Folk Architecture," in *Folklore and Folklife: An Introduction*, ed. Richard M. Dorson (Chicago: University of Chicago Press, 1972), 281–93; Dell Upton and John Michael Vlach, eds., *Common Places: Readings in American Vernacular Architecture* (Athens: University of Georgia Press, 1986); and Henry Glassie, *Vernacular Architecture* (Bloomington: Indiana University Press, 2000).
3. *New Day*, November 16, 1991, 11.
4. Three noteworthy book-length studies of Father Divine and the Peace Mission are Kenneth E. Burnham, *God Comes to America: Father Divine and the Peace Mission Movement* (Boston: Lambeth, 1979); Robert Weisbrot, *Father Divine and the Struggle for Racial Equality* (Urbana: University of Illinois Press, 1983); and Jill Watts, *God, Harlem U.S.A.: The Father Divine Story* (Berkeley: University of California Press, 1992). These texts cover the activities of Father Divine during his ministry, and Watts speculates on the historical beginnings of George Baker, the man who would later be identified as Father Divine. Mother Divine and the followers, of course, disagree with such personal assessments of Father Divine, whose nature they understand as purely spiritual, and they see such historical theorizing as disrespectful and unnecessary.
5. Catherine L. Albanese, *America: Religions and Religion*, 2nd ed. (Belmont, CA: Wadsworth, 1992), 209.
6. These Banquet Services continued with the remnant of the community into the twenty-first century.
7. See the description in William M. Kephart, *Extraordinary Groups: The Sociology of Unconventional Life-Styles* (New York: St. Martin's, 1987), 94–99.
8. It is significant to note that the majority of the Peace Mission's membership has been female.
9. This original residence of Father Divine and Peninnah, or the first Mother Divine, at 72 Macon Street has been preserved by the Peace Mission as a holy site and is referred to within the movement as the "Home of the Soul." The present Mother Divine occasionally held Holy Communion Banquet Services there and used the property as a place for rest and meditation.
10. Ollie Stewart, "It's Not All Swing in Harlem," *New York Times Magazine*, October 1, 1939, 7, 20.

11 See, for example, *Church Discipline, Constitution, and By-Laws of Unity Mission Inc.* (n.d.).
12 Father Divine, July 24, 1940, in Father Divine, *The Peace Mission Movement as Explained by Father Divine* (Philadelphia: New Day Publishing, n.d.), 34.
13 Father Divine, February 7, 1937, in Father Divine, *Peace Mission Movement*, 42.
14 Ibid., 12.
15 The payment of taxes was allowed because it "is constitutional; in short evangelical." Father Divine, January 11, 1944, in Father Divine, *Peace Mission Movement*, 36.
16 See, for example, *New York Times*, August 4, 1938, 3; August 7, 1938, 62; August 10, 1938, 3; May 2, 1939, 25; June 16, 1939; July 2, 1939, E10; August 20, 1939, E2, 26; July 9, 1945, 18; February 18, 1947, 27; December 2, 1948, 33; May 19, 1949, 31; September 11, 1953, 98; November 18, 1962, 124; May 19, 1964, 65. This coverage continued even when Father moved the Peace Mission from New York City to Philadelphia in 1942. Legal complications involving other members and their request for a return of donations were the immediate cause of this move, but Father Divine announced that it was because of "the antagonistic and malicious" attitude that the people, public officials, and press of the city had shown toward him and "because of the disrecognition of those who are in authority of my work and mission." *New York Times*, July 20, 1942, 15.
17 Father Divine, February 28, 1943, in Father Divine, *Peace Mission Movement*, 40–41.
18 Mother Divine, *The Peace Mission Movement* (Philadelphia: Imperial, 1982).
19 *New York Times*, August 7, 1938, 62.
20 *New Day*, September 12, 1938, 13.
21 *New Day*, August 16, 1947, 13.
22 November 22–23, 1945, message, reprinted in *New Day*, November 30, 1991, 3.
23 February 16–17, 1950, message, reprinted in *New Day*, April 16, 1983, 5.
24 See Paul E. Ivey, "Christian Science Architecture in the American City: The Triumph of the Classical Style," in *Faith in the Market: Religion and the Rise of Urban Commercial Culture*, ed. John M. Giggie and Diane Winston (New Brunswick: Rutgers University Press, 2002), 108–32, for a useful article on the religious architecture designed for American cities by Christian Scientists, another New Thought religious movement.
25 November 22–23, 1945, message, reprinted in *New Day*, November 30, 1991, 3.
26 See *New York Times*, January 4, 1940, 44; December 11, 1947, 27.
27 *New York Times*, July 20, 1942, 15.
28 See Leonard Norman Primiano, "Mother Divine," in *Encyclopedia of Women and World Religion*, vol. 2, ed. Serinity Young (New York: Macmillan, 1998), 678–79.
29 *New York Times*, August 8, 1946, 20.
30 *New York Times*, September 13, 1964, 53.
31 Properties listed in Mother Divine, "The Peace Mission Movement in Philadelphia," *New Day Digest* 1 (1995, reprint 1999): 22.

32 Mother Divine, *Peace Mission Movement*, 29.
33 Elbert M. Conover, *Building the House of God* (New York: Methodist Book Concern, 1928), 193–95.
34 See Robert Morris Sklarer, *West Philadelphia: University City to 52nd Street* (Charleston, SC: Arcadia, 2002), 115.
35 *New York Times*, May 19, 1949, 31.
36 Sklarer, *West Philadelphia*, 29.
37 See Robert Morris Sklarer, *Philadelphia's Broad Street: South and North* (Charleston, SC: Arcadia, 2003), 19.
38 Oscar Handlin, "The Magnet of a Cult," *New York Times Book Review*, October 25, 1953, 14.
39 George E. Thomas, *William L. Price: Arts and Crafts to Modern Design* (New York: Princeton Architectural Press, 2000), 66, 265.
40 *New York Times*, September 11, 1953, 98.
41 *New Day*, January 1, 1942, 15.
42 November 15, 1936, reprinted in *New Day*, November 16, 1991, 1.
43 *New Day*, January 1, 1942, 15.
44 *New Day Digest* 1 (September 1999): 13.
45 *New Day*, September 15, 1979, 45, reprinted in Mother Divine, *Peace Mission Movement*, 59.
46 *New Day*, May 21, 1942, 50.
47 Reprinted in *New Day*, September 5, 1992, 3-4.
48 The doors were created by the sculptor Donald De Lue. See D. Roger Howlett, *The Sculpture of Donald De Lue: Gods, Prophets, and Heroes* (Boston: Godine, 1990), 1159–65. See also the description of the shrine in Mother Divine, *Peace Mission Movement*, 60–64.
49 Architecture can be comprehensible to sensitive scholars of both humble and grand built environments, but, even more significantly, it is comprehensible to the designers, builders, and inhabitants of that created space. "Buildings, like poems and rituals, realize culture," Henry Glassie writes in the opening of his textbook on vernacular architecture. "Architecture intrudes in the limitless expanses of space, dividing it into useful, comprehensible pieces." See Glassie, *Vernacular Architecture*, 12, 17, 21. See also 46–47 on the relationship between building designers, builders, and users.
50 Glassie, *Vernacular Architecture*, 22.
51 Dell Upton, *Architecture in the United States* (Oxford: Oxford University Press, 1998), 12.
52 Dell Upton, "Architectural History or Landscape History?," *Journal of Architectural Education* 44 (1991): 197.
53 Joseph Sciorra, "Return to the Future: Puerto Rican Vernacular Architecture in New York City," in *Re-Presenting the City: Ethnicity, Capital and Culture in the Twenty-First Century Metropolis*, ed. Anthony D. King (London: Macmillan, 1996), 61.

54 Upton, *Architecture in the United States*, 13.
55 Ibid., 101–2.
56 Michael Owen Jones, "L.A. Add-Ons and Re-Dos: Renovation in Folk Art and Architectural Design," in *Perspectives on American Folk Art*, ed. Ian M. G. Quimby and Scott T. Swank (New York: Norton, 1980), 325–63.
57 Akhil Gupta and James Ferguson, "Beyond 'Culture': Space, Identity, and the Politics of Difference," *Cultural Anthropology* 7 (1992): 9.
58 See *New Day Supplement*, April 29, 1956, S2, S103.
59 Mother Divine has been recognized by preservation organizations for her commitment to maintain a number of properties in Philadelphia. In May 2003, for example, she was awarded the Henry Jonas Magaziner Award by the Historic Preservation Committee of the Philadelphia chapter of the American Institute of Architects. See Susan Glassman, "Mrs. M. J. Divine Wins 'Magaziner' Award," *Philadelphia Architect*, June 2003, 10.
60 The phrase is from Sharon Zukin, "Space and Symbols in an Age of Decline," in King, *Re-Presenting the City*, 49.
61 See Beryl Satter, "Marcus Garvey, Father Divine and the Gender Politics of Race Difference and Race Neutrality," *American Quarterly* 48 (1996): 43–76, for her analysis of Father Divine's understanding of "race neutrality" and its effects on his largely African American and female followers. However, Satter's comments on "the latter history of the Peace Mission" (66) do not reflect the movement's ideas on race and gender in the almost forty years since Father Divine no longer personally led the movement. In this period, the role of nationalism and consciousness of racism and sexism have been companion themes in the lived reality of Peace Mission members' lives and in their understanding of the teachings of Father Divine.

CHAPTER 11. "AND AS WE DINE, WE SING AND PRAISE GOD"

1 Jualynne E. Dodson and Cheryl Townsend Gilkes, "'There's Nothing Like Church Food': Food and the US Afro-Christian Tradition: Re-Membering Community and Feeding the Embodied S/spirit(s)," *Journal of the American Academy of Religion* 63, no. 3 (1995): 529.
2 The phrase is from Arthur Huff Fauset, *Black Gods of the Metropolis: Negro Religious Cults of the Urban North* (1944; reprint 1971; Philadelphia: University of Pennsylvania Press, 2002). See also Leonard Norman Primiano, "'The Consciousness of God's Presence Will Keep You Well, Healthy, Happy, and Singing': The Tradition of Innovation in the Music of Father Divine's Peace Mission Movement," in *The New Black Gods: Arthur Huff Fauset and the Study of African American Religions*, ed. Edward E. Curtis IV and Danielle Brune Sigler (Bloomington: Indiana University Press, 2009), chapter 9 in this volume.
3 Daniel Sack, "Food and Eating in American Religious Cultures," in *Perspectives on American Religion and Culture*, ed. Peter W. Williams (Malden, MA: Blackwell, 1999), 203.

4 It is beyond the scope of this chapter to consider fully the gendered aspects of this argument, but future research will address that dimension, as well as the politics of race in a sectarian movement that has ostensibly erased race. See Beryl Satter, "Marcus Garvey, Father Divine and the Gender Politics of Race Difference and Race Neutrality," *American Quarterly* 48 (1996): 43–76; and Leonard Norman Primiano, "'Bringing Perfection in These Different Places': Father Divine's Vernacular Architecture of Intention," *Folklore* 115 (2004): 24, n. 14, chapter 10 in this volume.

5 Leonard Norman Primiano, "Manifestations of the Religious Vernacular: Ambiguity, Power, and Creativity," in *Vernacular Religion in Everyday Life: Expressions of Belief*, ed. Marion Bowman and Olo Valk (Sheffield, UK: Equinox, 2012), 382–94, and introduction to this volume.

6 "It's Good to Be around the Body of God" is a Peace Mission song frequently offered during Holy Communion Banquet Services.

7 "If We Divide against Ourselves How Can We Expect to Have Victory over Depressions, Lacks, Wants and Limitations?," http://peacemission.info (accessed August 22, 2021).

8 Jill Watts, *God, Harlem U.S.A.: The Father Divine Story* (Berkeley: University of California Press, 1992), 1–71; Catherine Albanese, *A Republic of Mind and Spirit: A Cultural History of American Metaphysical Religion* (New Haven: Yale University Press, 2007), 476–78; and Catherine Albanese, *America: Religions and Religion*, 5th ed. (Boston: Wadsworth, 2013), 149–50.

9 Catherine Albanese, *America: Religions and Religion*, 2nd ed. (Belmont, CA: Wadsworth, 1992), 209.

10 Carleton Mabee, *Promised Land: Father Divine's Interracial Communities in Ulster County, New York* (Fleischmanns, NY: Purple Mountain Press, 2008).

11 Benjamin Kahan, "The Other Harlem Renaissance: Father Divine, Celibate Economics, and the Making of Black Sexuality," *Arizona Quarterly* 65, no. 4 (2009): 48–49.

12 "The Ground Breaking Ceremony for Father Divine's Library," http://peacemission.info (accessed August 22, 2021).

13 "The Deliverer Has Truly Come," *Liberty Net*, www.libertynet.org.

14 "Sayville's Colored Messiah Investigated by Dist. Atty.," *Suffolk County News*, April 25, 1930, 7.

15 *New Day*, February 14, 1976, 7, 17.

16 Watts, *God, Harlem U.S.A.*, 45–47.

17 "Since the First Use of Atomic Energy in 1945," http://peacemission.info (accessed August 22, 2021).

18 Leonard Norman Primiano, "Mother Divine," in *Encyclopedia of Women and World Religion*, vol. 2, ed. Serinity Young (New York: Macmillan, 1998), 678–79.

19 Quote from field notes, Holy Communion Banquet Service, Woodmont, May 8, 2011.

20 Primiano, "'Bringing Perfection,'" 14–18.

21 May 28, 1941, message, reprinted in *New Day*, February 4, 1978, 11.
22 Juha Pentikainen, "Ritual," in *Folklore: An Encyclopedia of Beliefs, Customs, Tales, Music, and Art*, 2nd ed., ed. Charlie T. McCormick and Kim Kennedy White (Santa Barbara: ABC-CLIO, 2011), 1110.
23 Mother Divine, *The Peace Mission Movement* (Philadelphia: Imperial Press, 1982), 27–28.
24 Andrew McGowan, "Food, Ritual, and Power," in *Late Ancient Christianity: A People's History of Christianity*, ed. Virginia Burrus (Minneapolis: Fortress, 2010), 145.
25 Father Divine frequently punctuated his sermons with reminders to his followers of the presence and reality of God in the midst of his Church, a point often referenced and reiterated at contemporary Holy Communion Banquet Services.
26 Quote from field notes, Holy Communion Banquet Service, Unity Mission Bible Institute, February 6, 2011.
27 Robert Weisbrot, *Father Divine and the Struggle for Racial Equality* (Urbana: University of Illinois Press, 1983), 220. See also Robert Weisbrot, "Father Divine's Peace Mission Movement," in *America's Alternative Religions*, ed. Timothy Miller (Albany: State University of New York Press, 1995), 289.
28 Geraldine Walker, interview with the author, June 20, 2011.
29 Kimberly J. Lau, *New Age Capitalism: Making Money East of Eden* (Philadelphia: University of Pennsylvania Press, 2000), 62. See also Albanese, *Republic of Mind and Spirit*, 484–88.
30 November 13–14, 1951, message, reprinted in *New Day*, February 7, 1976, 6.
31 November 17, 1933, message, reprinted in *New Day*, February 26, 1977, 11.
32 March 10, 1950, message, reprinted in *New Day*, March 13, 1976, 19.
33 From an unpublished edition of Fauset's *Black Gods of the Metropolis* in Fauset Collection, box 5, folder 98, p. 87, cited in Clarence E. Hardy III, "'No Mystery God': Black Religions of the Flesh in Pre-War Urban America," *Church History* 77, no. 1 (2008): 144.
34 Watts, *God, Harlem U.S.A.*, 67. R. Marie Griffith, using Watts as a source, notes the influence on Father Divine of New Thought, most especially the Unity School ideas of Charles Fillmore. Particularly important for Griffith is Father Divine's arrival at the conviction that the human body is an important materialized reflection of a developed, spiritualized consciousness. My own work on the expressive culture of the Peace Mission seen through use of space, the built environment, photography, song, and foodways bears out this sacralization of the material, as well as its framing as a means of powerful spiritual advancement and social liberation for followers. Griffith's analysis is a valuable reading of the history of the Peace Mission; however, according to my ethnographic research on the contemporary movement, her perspective does not speak to the diverse ways that Father Divine addressed issues of the body or the way that the mission has developed since 1965. R. Marie Griffith, "Body Salvation: New Thought, Father Divine, and the Feast of Material Pleasures," *Religion and American Culture* 11 (2001): 119–53;

R. Marie Griffith, *Born Again Bodies: Flesh and Spirit in American Christianity* (Berkeley: University of California Press, 2004).
35 Griffith, *Born Again Bodies*, 153.
36 Weisbrot, *Father Divine and the Struggle for Racial Equality*, 219–20.
37 See D. Wood, "Divine Liturgy," *Gastronomica* 4, no. 1 (2004): 19–24, for a description of a Divine Tracy Hotel Banquet Service circa 2001–2002.
38 Mother Divine, interviews with the author, filmed by Will Luers, May 25 and June 18, 1996.
39 Trudy Eden, "Metaphysics and Meatless Meals: Why Food Mattered When the Mind Was Everything," in *Food and Faith in Christian Culture*, ed. Ken Albala and Trudy Eden (New York: Columbia University Press, 2011), 172; see also Beryl Satter, *Each Mind a Kingdom: American Women, Sexual Purity, and the New Thought Movement, 1875–1920* (Berkeley: University of California Press, 1999), 105–10, 251.
40 Lau, *New Age Capitalism*, 65.
41 Richard T. Schaefer and William W. Zellner, *Extraordinary Groups: An Examination of Unconventional Lifestyles*, 9th ed. (New York: Worth, 2011), 275–76.
42 Leonard Norman Primiano, "Vernacular Religion and the Search for Method in Religious Folklife," *Western Folklore* 54, no. 1 (1995): 37–56, introduction to this volume; Primiano, "Manifestations of the Religious Vernacular."

CHAPTER 12. "AS A LIVING SHRINE I CAME"

1 I have been engaged in ethnographic participant observation with Father Divine's Peace Mission for over twenty-five years. The followers, who are now elderly and greatly reduced in number, have grown quite conscious of and sensitive to past scholarly description and analysis and journalistic accounts of their leader, his teachings, and their religious practices and alternative lifestyle. They are therefore highly resistant to ethnographic interviews. I have been fortunate to remain close to the community as a non-member through respectful interaction and consultation, which has permitted me to be present at both mundane and significant activities, ask questions whenever possible, and gather primary source materials. Such data have allowed me to reconstruct the narrative of the creation of the Shrine to Life that is at the center of this chapter and to evaluate the building's meaning and function. This work is part of a larger study of the unique expressive culture of this indigenous American religion.
2 David Morgan, "The Look of the Sacred," in *The Cambridge Companion to Religious Studies*, ed. Robert A. Orsi (New York: Cambridge University Press, 2012), 317.
3 See Robert Weisbrot, *Father Divine and the Struggle for Racial Equality* (Urbana: University of Illinois Press, 1983); Jill Watts, *God, Harlem U.S.A.: The Father Divine Story* (Berkeley: University of California Press, 1992); Carleton Mabee, *Promised Land: Father Divine's Interracial Communities in Ulster County, New York* (Fleischmanns, NY: Purple Mountain Press, 2008); Judith Weisenfeld, *New*

World A-Coming: Black Religion and Racial Identity during the Great Migration (New York: New York University Press, 2016). For texts authored by the Peace Mission, see Mother Divine, *The Peace Mission Movement* (Philadelphia: Imperial Press, 1982), and LaVere Belstrom, *Rediscovering God: Our International Treasure* (2005), http://peacemission.info (accessed June 14, 2018).

4 "Practical religion," in reference to discussion of a faith of practice, was coined by the Anglican evangelical preacher, writer, and bishop J. C. Ryle (1816–1900). It is not known whether Father Divine ever read Ryle's works, but the Peace Mission would undoubtedly claim that Father's inspirations were original.

5 "The Circle Mission and Its Network of Churches," http://peacemission.info (accessed August 28, 2021).

6 Leonard Norman Primiano, "'Bringing Perfection in These Different Places': Father Divine's Vernacular Architecture of Intention," *Folklore* 115, no. 1 (2004): 3–26, chapter 10 in this volume.

7 Standard terms of the time for racial differentiation were never employed by members under Father Divine's teaching; they instead used "dark-complected" or "light-complected" when such descriptions were necessary.

8 "This (Philadelphia) Is the Country Seat of Democracy," www.libertynet.org (accessed June 14, 2018).

9 *Church Discipline Constitution and By-Laws of Circle Mission Incorporated, New York City* (n.p., 1941), 21.

10 Primiano, "Bringing Perfection," and chapter 10 in this volume.

11 Woodmont was actually one of three estates purchased by the Peace Mission, including Crum Elbow (1938), directly across from President Franklin D. Roosevelt's Hyde Park property, and the Tarrytown Estate (1941) in West Chester County, New York.

12 *New Day*, September 5, 1992, 3–4; September 12–13, 1953.

13 *New Day*, September 19, 1953, 3–4.

14 Given September 13–14, 1949; *New Day Digest*, September 1999, 11.

15 June 24, 1953, reprinted in *New Day Supplement*, September 11, 1954, S28.

16 Leonard Norman Primiano, "Mother Divine," in *Encyclopedia of Women and World Religion*, vol. 2, ed. Serinity Young (New York: Macmillan, 1998), 678–79.

17 Arthur Huff Fauset, *Black Gods of the Metropolis: Negro Religious Cults of the Urban North* (1944; reprint 1971; Philadelphia: University of Pennsylvania Press, 2002).

18 Message given at 67 West 130th Street in New York City on June 1, 1933, http://peacemission.info (accessed June 14, 2018). D. Roger Howlett notes, "The shrine was rumored at the time to have cost a half-million dollars." See D. Roger Howlett, *The Sculpture of Donald De Lue: Gods, Prophets, and Heroes* (Boston: Godine, 1990), 165. See also Howlett's source, *Main Line Chronicle* (Ardmore, PA), September 5, 1968, 12.

19 *New Day*, March 31, 1962, 28.

20 "The Shrine to Life," http://peacemission.info (accessed August 28, 2021).

21 Father Divine did use the term "Shrine-ship degree of expression" in reference to individuals who journeyed to Sayville in the 1920s for healing, noting that "hundreds were healed by merely walking on the ground!" See "The Shrine to Life."
22 *New Day*, September 5, 1992, 11, quoting Howlett, *Sculpture of Donald De Lue*.
23 *New Day*, September 5, 1992, 11–12; Howlett, *Sculpture of Donald De Lue*, 162.
24 *New Day*, September 5, 1992, 12; Howlett, *Sculpture of Donald De Lue*, 165.
25 *New Day*, September 5, 1992, 12–13; Howlett, *Sculpture of Donald De Lue*, 165.
26 Howlett, *Sculpture of Donald De Lue*, 162.
27 Mother Divine, *Peace Mission Movement*, 35–38.
28 A Peace Mission website makes clear to visitors of Woodmont: "Adherence to the International Modest Code established by Father Divine is required: no smoking, drinking, obscenity, vulgarity, profanity, undue mixing of sexes, receiving of gifts, presents, tips or bribes. *Dress Code* requires modesty—*no shorts or sleeveless tops, ladies should wear a dress or skirt*" (emphasis in original), http://peacemission.info/ (accessed June 14, 2018).
29 Primiano, "'Bringing Perfection,'" 10–11, and chapter 10 in this volume.
30 Christopher Stewart, Woodmont archivist and a follower of Father Divine, in personal communication, offered a sensitive emic interpretation of events leading to the design of the doors' adornment. Concerning the presence of the unclothed statue of Hermes, he explained, "I believe that the tolerance for the bare-chested figures and the child in the formal garden has to do with the fact that they are not intrinsically erotic; in the fall and redemption narrative, especially as read by the Peace Mission, the doors' context in fact makes this particular nakedness an affirmation of innocence and an active negation of the erotic by narrative and by elision." About the figures on the shrine door, as approved by Mother Divine, he clarified:

> No figure on the door represents genitalia, and only "Spiritualized Man" is turned to face the viewer—a mere scrap of sculpted cloth that appears windswept rather than tied on covers the genitalia. So the signifiers of eros are markedly absent even though De Lue exults in the human form throughout.... So it appears there is a matter of degree and explicitness that was taken into consideration when deciding what among existing features and on those constructed for the Shrine could and could not be tolerated.... We know that Mother saw preliminary drawings and full scale clay mock-ups, and from photographs we know that some initial designs were altered before completion. This undoubtedly reflects Mother's engagement with the process.... [With regard to the] nude figures on the doors, I do not recall seeing clear commentary or record, but the naked ones are the ones most central to the narrative of fall and redemption and almost certainly reflect the imposition and recension of the Adamic curse, shame in nakedness being one component of the curse (along with exile from Eden and the immediate Presence of God, necessity of labor, pain in childbirth, enmity with serpents, and death). Presumably when the curse is truly abolished, so are its stipulations,

and the glorified figures represent the full restoration of innocence. Both falling and ascending "man" are naked, but hieratic proportion makes falling man the smallest of all the figures, quite small relative to all others. It is also likely that some thought was given to the body as the Image of God, and to the symbolism of nothing being hidden from God, the state of the soul being an open book. Certainly Mother would not have accepted the designs if She'd found them offensive.... Mr. De Lue's other work demonstrates a deep and abiding fascination with religion and mythology, and that taken with the narrative nature of the door figures and with a sculptor's veneration of the human form makes it highly probable that he had such valuations in mind. (personal email communication, April 14, 2018)

31 *New Day Digest*, September 1999, 1, 13.
32 See Leonard Norman Primiano, "'And as We Dine, We Sing and Praise God': Father and Mother Divine's Theologies of Food," in *Religion, Food, and Eating in North America*, ed. Ben Zeller, Marie Dallam, Reid L. Neilson, and Nora Rubel (New York: Columbia University Press, 2014), 42–67, chapter 11 in this volume.
33 Followers had previously referred to the site of his "temporary enshrinement," or grave, at West Laurel Hill Cemetery in Bala Cynwyd, Pennsylvania, from 1965 to 1968 as Father Divine's "apartment."
34 Weisenfeld, *New World A-Coming*, 5.
35 Ibid., 4.
36 Leonard Norman Primiano, "Vernacular Religion and the Search for Method in Religious Folklife," *Western Folklore* 54, no. 1 (1995): 37–56, introduction to this volume.
37 Kay Turner, *Beautiful Necessity: The Art and Meaning of Women's Altars* (New York: Thames and Hudson, 1999), 27.
38 Ibid., 165.
39 Rosina S. Miller, "Place," in *Folklore: An Encyclopedia of Beliefs, Customs, Tales, Music, and Art*, vol. 3, ed. Charlie T. McCormick and Kim Kennedy White (Santa Barbara: ABC-CLIO, 2011), 999.

CODA

1 See Leonard Norman Primiano, "Vernacular Religion and the Search for Method in Religious Folklife," *Western Folklore* 54, no. 1 (1995): 37–56, introduction to this volume, and Leonard Norman Primiano, "Manifestations of the Religious Vernacular: Ambiguity, Power, and Creativity," in *Vernacular Religion in Everyday Life: Expressions of Belief*, ed. Marion Bowman and Ulo Valk (New York: Routledge, 2014), 382–94.
2 See two relevant obituaries: William Grimes, "Mother Divine, Who Took Over Her Husband's Cult, Dies at 91," *New York Times*, March 14, 2017, and Aubrey Whelan, "Mother Divine, Leader of the International Peace Mission, Dies at 92," *Philadelphia Inquirer*, March 6, 2017.
3 See chapter 11 in this volume.

4 This approach is used to great effect by Elaine J. Lawless in *Handmaidens of the Lord: Pentecostal Women Preachers and Traditional Religion* (Philadelphia: University of Pennsylvania Press, 1988) and *Holy Women, Wholly Women: Sharing Ministries of Wholeness through Life Stories and Reciprocal Ethnography* (Philadelphia: University of Pennsylvania Press, 1993); Glenn Hinson, *Fire in My Bones: Transcendence and the Holy Spirit in African American Gospel* (Philadelphia: University of Pennsylvania Press, 1999); Luke Eric Lassiter, *The Power of Kiowa Song: A Collaborative Ethnography* (Tucson: University of Arizona Press, 1998); Elizabeth Campbell and Luke Eric Lassiter, *Doing Ethnography Today: Theories, Methods, Exercises* (Malden, MA: Wiley-Blackwell, 2014).

5 See, for example, William Kephart's article in his collection *Extraordinary Groups: The Sociology of Unconventional Life-Styles*, currently refreshed by Richard T. Schaefer and William W. Zellner in a 2011 edition of the text.

6 S. C. McKelway and A. J. Liebling, "Who Is This King of Glory?," *New Yorker*, June 1936, reprinted in St. Clair McKelway, *Reporting at Wit's End: Tales from the* New Yorker (New York: Bloomsbury, 2010), 80–122.

7 See "Copy of the Letter from the Library of Congress on Catalog Heading for Father Divine," http://peacemission.info.

8 David Hufford, *The Terror That Comes in the Night: An Experience-Centered Study of Supernatural Assault Traditions*, rev. ed. (Philadelphia: University of Pennsylvania Press, 1989); Luke Eric Lassiter, "Authoritative Texts, Collaborative Ethnography, and Native American Studies," *American Indian Quarterly* 24, no. 4 (Fall 2000): 605.

9 See chapter 10 in this volume.

10 Mel Prideaux, "Ethics and Undergraduate Research in the Study of Religion: Place-Based Pedagogy and Reciprocal Research Relations," *Teaching Theology & Religion* 19, no. 4 (2016): 337, https://doi.org/10.1111/teth.12346.

11 Kim Knott, "Insider/Outsider Perspectives," in *The Routledge Companion to the Study of Religion*, ed. J. Hinnells (New York: Routledge, 2010), 271.

FURTHER READING

QUEER STUDIES AND RELIGION

Boyarin, Daniel, Daniel Itzkovitz, and Ann Pellegrini, eds. *Queer Theory and the Jewish Question*. Columbia University Press, 2003.

Coviello, Peter. *Make Yourselves Gods: Mormons and the Unfinished Business of American Secularism*. University of Chicago Press, 2019.

Frank, Gillian A., Bethany Moreton, and Heather R. White, eds. *Devotions and Desires: Histories of Sexuality and Religion in the Twentieth-Century United States*. University of North Carolina Press, 2018.

Godbeer, Richard. *Sexual Revolution in Early America*. Johns Hopkins University Press, 2002.

Jakobsen, Janet R., and Ann Pellegrini. *Love the Sin: Sexual Regulation and the Limits of Religious Tolerance*. Beacon Press, 2004.

Jordan, Mark. *The Invention of Sodomy in Christian Theology*. University of Chicago Press, 1998.

———. *The Silence of Sodom: Homosexuality in Modern Catholicism*. University of Chicago Press, 2000.

Krutzsch, Brett. *Dying to Be Normal: Gay Martyrs and the Transformation of American Sexual Politics*. Oxford University Press, 2019.

Martin, James, SJ. *Building a Bridge: How the Catholic Church and the LGBT Community Can Enter into a Relationship of Respect, Compassion, and Sensitivity*. Harper One, 2017.

McNeil, John J. *The Church and the Homosexual*. Revised and expanded ed. Beacon Press, 1988.

Petro, Anthony M. *After the Wrath of God: AIDS, Sexuality, and American Religion*. Reprint, Oxford University Press, 2019.

Stuart, Elizabeth. *Gay and Lesbian Theologies*. Ashgate, 2003.

Talvacchia, Kathleen T., Michael F. Pettinger, and Mark Larrimore, eds. *Queer Christianities: Lived Religion in Transgressive Forms*. New York University Press, 2014.

Wilcox, Melissa M. *Queer Religiosities: An Introduction to Queer and Transgender Studies in Religion*. Rowman and Littlefield, 2021.

CONTEMPORARY CATHOLICISM

Byrne, Julie. *The Other Catholics: Remaking America's Largest Religion*. Columbia University Press, 2016.

Cressler, Matthew J. *Authentically Black and Truly Catholic: The Rise of Black Catholicism in the Great Migration*. New York University Press, 2017.
Ferraro, Thomas J., ed. *Catholic Lives, Contemporary America*. Duke University Press, 1997.
Kane, Paula M. *Sister Thorn and Catholic Mysticism in Modern America*. University of North Carolina Press, 2013.
Maldonado-Estrada, Alyssa. *Lifeblood of the Parish: Men and Catholic Devotion in Williamsburg, Brooklyn*. New York University Press, 2020.
Moore, Brenna. *Kindred Spirits: Friendship and Resistance at the Edges of Modern Catholicism*. University of Chicago Press, 2021.
Orsi, Robert A. *History and Presence*. Harvard University Press, 2016.
Ronan, Marian. *Tracing the Sign of the Cross: Sexuality, Mourning, and the Future of American Catholicism*. Columbia University Press, 2009.

THE PEACE MISSION MOVEMENT

Griffith, R. Marie. *Born Again Bodies: Flesh and Spirit in American Christianity*. University of California Press, 2004.
Johnson, Sylvester A. *African American Religions, 1599–2000: Colonialism, Democracy, and Freedom*. Cambridge University Press, 2015.
Kahan, Benjamin. *Celibacies: American Modernism and Sexual Life*. Duke University Press, 2013.
Watts, Jill. *God, Harlem U.S.A.: The Father Divine Story*. University of California Press, 1992.
Weisenfeld, Judith. *New World A-Coming: Black Religion and Racial Identity during the Great Migration*. New York University Press, 2017.

RELIGION AND MATERIALITY

Bielo, James S. *Materializing the Bible: Scripture, Sensation, Place*. Bloomsbury Publishing, 2021.
Chamberlain, Ava. *The Notorious Elizabeth Tuttle: Marriage, Murder, and Madness in the Family of Jonathan Edwards*. New York University Press, 2012.
Eichler-Levine, Jodi. *Painted Pomegranates and Needlepoint Rabbis: How Jews Craft Resilience and Create Community*. University of North Carolina Press, 2020.
Finch, Martha L. *Dissenting Bodies: Corporealities in Early New England*. Columbia University Press, 2010.
Glassie, Henry H., and Pravina Shukla. *Sacred Art: Catholic Saints and Candomblé Gods in Modern Brazil*. Indiana University Press, 2017.
Gross, Rachel B. *Beyond the Synagogue: Jewish Nostalgia as Religious Practice*. New York University Press, 2021.
Hendrickson, Brett. *The Healing Power of the Santuario de Chimayó: America's Miraculous Church*. New York University Press, 2017.
Houtman, Dick, and Birgit Meyer, eds. *Things: Religion and the Question of Materiality*. Fordham University Press, 2012.

Hughes, Jennifer Scheper. *Biography of a Mexican Crucifix: Lived Religion and Local Faith from the Conquest to the Present*. Oxford University Press, 2010.

Levitt, Laura. *The Objects That Remain*. Pennsylvania State University Press, 2020.

Lindman, Janet Moore, and Michele Lise Tarter, eds. *A Centre of Wonders: The Body in Early America*. Cornell University Press, 2001.

Lindsey, Rachel McBride. *A Communion of Shadows: Religion and Photography in Nineteenth-Century America*. University of North Carolina Press, 2017.

Pérez, Elizabeth. *Religion in the Kitchen: Cooking, Talking, and the Making of Black Atlantic Traditions*. New York University Press, 2016.

Plate, S. Brent. *Key Terms in Material Religion*. Bloomsbury Academic, 2015.

Polk, Patrick A. *Sinful Saints and Saintly Sinners at the Margins of the Americas*. Exhibition catalog. Fowler Museum, UCLA, 2015.

Promey, Sally M., ed. *Sensational Religion: Sensory Cultures in Material Practice*. 2014; reprint, Yale University Press, 2017.

Sciorra, Joseph. *Built with Faith: Italian American Imagination and Catholic Material Culture in New York City*. University of Tennessee Press, 2015.

Turner, Kay. *Beautiful Necessity: The Art and Meaning of Women's Altars*. Thames and Hudson, 1999.

Whitehead, Amy. *Religious Statues and Personhood: Testing the Role of Materiality*. Bloomsbury Publishing, 2013.

RELIGION AND FOLKLORE

Brady, Erika. *Healing Logics: Culture and Medicine in Modern Health Belief Systems*. Utah State University Press, 2001.

Foster, Michael Dylan. *The Book of Yōkai: Mysterious Creatures of Japanese Folklore*. University of California Press, 2015.

Howard, Robert Glenn. *Digital Jesus: The Making of a New Christian Fundamentalist Community on the Internet*. New York University Press, 2011.

Kitta, Andrea. *The Kiss of Death: Contagion, Contamination, and Folklore*. University Press of Colorado, 2020.

Magliocco, Sabina. *Witching Culture: Folklore and Neopaganism in America*. University of Pennsylvania Press, 2004.

Mould, Tom. *Still, the Small Voice: Narrative, Personal Revelation, and the Mormon Folk Tradition*. Columbia University Press, 2011.

Otero, Solimar. *Archives of Conjure: Stories of the Dead in Afrolatinx Cultures*. Columbia University Press, 2020.

Wojcik, Daniel. *The End of the World as We Know It: Faith, Fatalism, and Apocalypse in America*. New York University Press, 1997.

INDEX

Note: Photo plates are indicated by *p1, p2, etc.*

aesthetics, 32–33; of Peace Mission, 150, 155, 170, 185–86, 238; of vernacular Catholicism, 38

African American Christians: art tradition, 27–28; Fauset on, 147, 165

African Americans: Father Divine "dark-complected people" reference to, 175, 198; Father Divine on derogatory qualities assigned to, 163–64; Father Divine on full rights of, 220; International Peace Mission Movement majority of, 198, 220; Peace Mission properties quality service to, 182, 199, 220; Weisenfeld racial identity study of, 237

Afro-Caribbean botánicas sale items examples, 43

agency, 73, 241

AIDS, Dignity and, 112, 115–16, 118, 127, 134, 139. *See also* Dignity

Albanese, Catherine L., 27, 198–99, 267n28

altars: of Sicilian Americans, 30, 32–34; Turner on women, 238; as vows of gratitude, 35–36. *See also* Joseph (Saint) home altars

Ameen, Ann "Sister Ann," xii; Ameen, K., marriage to, 19, 23–24, 28; Bethany House of, 23; on bold colors in hooked rugs, 22–23, 26; British royalty deception by, 18–19; conversion of, 19; hooked rug art, 16, 18–22, 29; hooked rugs as paintings in wool, 19–21, 26, 28; on hooked rug vision, 17; material expression of religious belief, 20, 21, 25; mission activities, 19, 23–25, 29; multiple marriages of, 18; Newfoundland home of, 17–18, 26, 29; Protestant Evangelical Christianity of, 18, 20, 24, 28–29; public profile of, 25; religious narratives of, 24–25; solitary life of, 23–24; spiritual autobiography of, 18, 23–25; suicide attempt, 19; in United States, 18–19, 24, 27–28. *See also* religious hooked rugs

Ameen, Kattar (Reverend): infidelity of, 24; Sister Ann Ameen marriage to, 19, 23–24, 28

American Black Church, 163

American Catholics: Easter table holiday foods, 31–32; ex-votos and, 93–98; liturgical movement of, 53; McGreevy on, 119; postmodern devotional items, 53; post-Vatican II practice differences, 52–54; on religious objects, 53–54; religious traditions among, 31; Sciorra on Italian, 268n1; seven fishes Christmas Eve meal, 31; St. Jude Shop material culture of, 51

American ecclesiastical architecture and art, 42

American Folklore Society, 10, 149, 252, 254, 255

American Protestant *memorates*, 51–52

amulet, sacramentals compared to, 69–70

Angenendt, Arnold, 78

Anthony (Saint) altars, 32

Anthony of Padua (Saint) relic in Kilner's Church Goods store, 46

307

Appadurai, Arjun, 93
Arlen, Harold, 161
artifacts of belief, holy cards as, 57–59
art tradition, of African American Christians, 28
auto-ethnography, of ex-votos, 84

Bailey, Deborah, 245–46
Baker, George, 244, 245
Banquet Service. *See* Holy Communion Banquet Service
Barclay Street art, 47
Bargellini, Clara, 84
Barna, Gábor, 32, 33
Bateson, Gregory, 10
Baudrillard, Jean, 98
beliefs: experiential factors for systems of, 4; holy cards as artifacts of, 57–59; lived religion practice negotiations and, 6; vernacular religion emphasis on study of, 12; Yoder on unified system of, 7. *See also* religious beliefs
Belstrom, LaVere, 157–58
Bendix, Regina, 10, 264n25
Benedict XVI (pope), 107
Benziger, Joseph Charles, 64
Benziger Brothers publishing business, holy cards production by, 45, 64–65
Bethany House, 23
Bible Institute of Philadelphia, 180
biological and sacred family representations, at Saint Joseph home altars, 37
Black Madonna, of Sicilian Americans, 37
British royalty deception, by Sister Ann Ameen, 18–19
Brophy, Don, 106, 120
Brown, Bill, 88, 99
"The Builders" detail, of *Portal of Life Eternal* door design, 233, *p16*

candle lighting, of votive, 83
Carrella, Eugene (priest), 274n10
Carroll, Michael P., 96, 261n7
Casino, Joseph, 114–15, 284n27
Catholic Church: Code of Canon Law of Roman, 61; homosexuality exclusionary position of, 107–8, 110, 128, 283n15; post-Vatican II closings of, 89–90. *See also* American Catholics; European Catholics; French Canadian Catholicism; post-Vatican II Catholicism; Roman Catholics; Vatican II; vernacular Catholicism
Catholic collectibles (Catholiciana): availability of, 88–89; Baudrillard on, 98; from church closings, 89–90; eBay sale of, 89–96, 100, 279n34; from Europe, 45; holy cards as, 58; Taves and McDannell on peddler sale of, 45; Victorian interest in, 46
Catholic kitsch, in St. Jude Shop, 54–55
Catholic material culture: retail stores sale of, 42, 43; of sacramentals, 45; St. Jude Shop and American, 51
Catholic publishing companies, for parochial school system, 45–46
Catholic sacred items, xi; postmodern sites of, 41–55; St. Jude Shop and, 54–55
Cayce, Edgar, 155
celibacy: of Father Divine and Mother Divine marriage, 177, 204, 226, 243; in Father Divine hotel, x; Peace Mission tradition of, 154, 171, 195, 219, 226; *Portal of Life Eternal* door design considerations, 233–34
de Certeau, Michel, 238
de Champaigne, Philippe, 85
de Chardin, Pierre Teilhard, 51
Chidester, David, 73, 244
choral groups in music tradition, of International Peace Mission Movement: Crusaders, 154, 157–58, 159, 290n29; Lilybuds, 154; Rosebuds, xiii, 154, 155, 160, 206, 235, 289n15
Christian iconography, 27; imagery disallowed during controversy of, 62; of

Sister Ann Ameen hooked rug art, 16, 18–22, 29
Christianity: ex-voto offerings and, 77; institutional, 32–33; James and Johnson on native, 263n19; material culture imagery and symbols of, 40, 41, 42; official religion and, 7; sacramentality in, 38; saint cult, 77, 81; Sister Ann Ameen Protestant Evangelical, 18, 20, 28
chromolithography of holy cards, by Sharp, 63
church decorations, sacramentals of, 45
Church Gospel Mission Home, 182
Church with Red Door scripture rug, of Sister Ann Ameen, *p1*
Circle Mission Church, 159–60, 176, 182, 210, 224, 235–36
Clare of Assisi (Saint), 50
Claybrook, Edna Mae, 247
Code of Canon Law, on sacramentals, 61
commercialization, of ex-votos, 98–101
Committee for Women's Concerns, in Dignity/Philadelphia, 134
commodification of religion, 94, 97
communion, in vernacular Catholicism, 39
congregational singing, in Peace Mission, 150, 154–55, 160, 201, 290n29
Conover, Elbert, 181
conversion, of Sister Ann Ameen, 19, 20
creative spirituality, of Wicca, 11–12
Creator God, Father Divine as incarnation of, 146, 151, 155, 164–65, 171, 173, 177, 196, 199, 201, 204, 206, 210–11, 218, 219, 238–39, 242
cult: International Peace Mission Movement as, 219, 244; saint, 77, 81
culture: Dignity gender-conservative, 132–33; Dignity male, 132–34; expressive, 7, 241; idioculture, 10, 264n25; religious understanding from ethnography, xi; sacred materiality and tradition of, 44; uniculture, 10, 11, 264n27, 265n30. *See also* material culture

Davies, Kevin, 118
dead relatives, Sicilian Americans communication with, 30, 37
death. *See* physical passing
Decker, Will E., 179
De Lue, Donald H., 231–34, *p15*, *p16*
devotionalism: of Dignity, 126; of European Catholic homes, 46; ex-votos and, 84; holy cards and, 71; Orsi on, 52–53; post-Vatican II Catholicism change in, 72, 88; of Roman Catholics, 32, 37; sacred materiality and, 53; of Shrine to Life, 218; of Sicilian Americans, 30, 37; in vernacular religious displays, 33, 37
DiCocco, Louis, 47, 48
DiCocco, Mark G., 44
DiCocco, Norma, 47
Didi-Huberman, Georges, 100–101
Dignity (organization of LGBTQ Catholics), 104–5; AIDS and, 115, 116, 118, 127, 139; asked to leave parishes, 107, 128, 283n15; church status of, 108, 109; diverse ethnic backgrounds in, 110, 112–13; as ethnic parish church, 107, 109, 114, 116, 118–19, 132; gender-conservative culture of, 132–33; lesbian Catholics in, 130–41; male culture of, 132–35; material culture connection of, 113, 126; membership in, xii, 107; sexual ethics statement of, 128–29; spirituality sexual nature at, 138–40; vernacular Catholicism example, 123–29
Dignity/Philadelphia, 12, 104, 105–7, 119–21; Committee for Women's Concerns in, 134; Father Jake and, 108, 124–25; lesbian Catholics and male eroticism expression, 133–37; lesbian Catholics lack of presence in, 132–33, 135, 137, 141; male eroticism in, 133–37; member statements, 108; non-Catholic Eucharistic ministers at, 116, 284n28; origins of, 123–24; participation in, xii, 116–18, 284n24; priest presiders at, 110–11, 116,

Dignity/Philadelphia (*cont.*) 284n21; service description, 115; service location of, 109, 124; St. Peter Claver Catholic Church and, 109, 283n19

diocesan bishop, parish organization by, 106

diverse ethnic backgrounds, in Dignity, 112–13

Divine Cooperative Plan, of Father Divine, 172–74, 199, 221–22

Divine International House, Skaler on, 179

Divine Lorraine Hotel, 182, 189, 223, 224

Divine Tracy Hotel, 145, 162, 246; food preparation at, 154, 211; Keyflower Dining Room in, 149, 182, 197, 200, 207–9, 211; Mother Divine upgrade to, 212–13

Dodson, Jualynne E., 196

Dorgan, Margaret, 83–84

Drews, Paul, 3

dyadic folklore, Mechling on, 10, 11

dyadic idioculture, of heterosexual couples, 10, 264n25

Easter, American Catholics holiday foods, 31–32

eBay sale of Catholic collectibles, 58, 59, 89–96, 100, 279n34

Ellington, Duke, 160

Ellis, Charles E., 179

entrepreneurial activities, of Father Divine, 172–76, 178, 199

ethnic parishes, 66, 106, 283n11; Dignity as, 105, 107, 109, 113, 118–19, 121, 132

ethnographic reflexivity, 1, 5, 12, 13, 259n1

ethnographic writing, on International Peace Mission Movement, 241–50

ethnography: ex-votos auto-, 84; International Peace Mission Movement writing, 241–50; Peace Mission ethnographic work, xii, 144–67, 288n10; religious culture understanding from, xi. *See also* reciprocal ethnography

Eucharistic celebration, of Father Divine, 195–96, 205, 224, *p12*; McGowan on, 206. *See also* Holy Communion Banquet Service

Europe, Catholic collectibles from, 45

European Catholics, devotionalism of homes, 46

evil eye talisman, 31

experiential factors, for belief systems, 4

expressive culture, 26, 98, 241; Peace Mission and, 150, 185, 214–15, 218, 249, 297n34; religious beliefs and, 7, 146, 147

Ex-Voto de 1662, of de Champaigne, 85

ex-votos: American Catholics and, 93–98; auctions, 91–92; auto-ethnography of, 84; Christianity and offerings of, 77; classifications of, 277n11; commercialization of, 98–101; described, 75; Didi-Huberman on, 100–101; forms of, 75–76; Giorgi on, 79–80; historical developments of, 77–79; of Man Seeking Help for His Cattle, 91, *p8*; Mollat du Jourdin on, 83; painted, 78, 82, 84–85, 87, 91, 94, 96, 99, 101, *p8*; for personal piety, 76; in postmodern world, 84–93; Primiano collection of, x–xi, 84–87; as private vow, 82–83; Sacred Heart of Jesus, 76, 88, *p7*; as supernatural narrative visualized art, 79–81; vernacular religion and, 81–82; as vow and prayer, 81–84

Ex-Voto to the Virgin of the Rosary, Bargellini on, 84

Farago, Claire, 67–68

Father Divine, 144, 292n4; African Americans referenced as "dark-complected people" by, 164–65, 175, 190, 198, 223, 225–26, 237, 299n9; Baker as, 244, 245, 292n4; celibate marriage to Mother Divine, 154, 177, 204, 226, 243; as Creator God incarnation, 146, 151, 155, 164–65, 171, 173, 177, 196, 218, 219,

238–39, 242; on derogatory qualities assigned to African Americans, 164–66; Divine Cooperative Plan of, 172–74, 199, 221–22; Ellington song to honor, 160, 178; entrepreneurial activities of, 172–76, 199; on eternal health and physical resilience, 210; Eucharistic celebration of, 195–96, 205, 224, *p12*; Fauset on, 145–48, 163–67, 227; on full rights of African Americans, 220; in Harlem, 160, 171–72, 175, 199, 220–21; hotel rules and regulations, x, 154–55; International Modest Code of, 172, 179, 182, 219–21, 243, 300n28; interracial marriage of, 204, 226; material culture use by, 188–89, 192; move from New York, 178, 199, 293n16; on music tradition creative meaning, 152–53; on ownership and prosperity, 174–75; Peace preferred greeting, x, 154, 191; Peninnah as first wife of, 171, 204, 226, 243, 292n9; perfectionist worldview of, 169, 184, 186, 188; physical passing of, 165, 205, 211, 227–29, 236; portrait of, *150*, *p9*; on practical religion, 221–22; publications on, 163–64, 244–45; race neutrality and, 163–64, 175, 198, 237, 295n61, 299n7; racial identity and, 165; radio broadcasts, 156–57, 161; sermons motivated by songs, 152; transformation theology of, 184–85; Watts study of, 163–64. *See also* Philadelphia architecture

Fauset, Arthur Huff, 161; on African American Christians, 147, 165; *Black Gods of the Metropolis* of, 145, 147, 148, 162, 163, 227; on Father Divine, 145–48, 163–67, 227; on Peace Mission, 147–48, 163–67; on Sing Happy, 146

fieldwork methodology, 241

Fillmore, Charles, 213, 297n34

Fillmore, Myrtle, 213

Fine, Gary Alan, 10, 264n25

first-class relic, 46

fishing industry, in Gloucester, Massachusetts, 35

folk artist, Zug on, 21

folklife: Catholic, 56; individual believer unexamined element of, 9; scholars of, 59, 86, 145, 242; vernacular religion incorporation in study, x, 1, 2, 6, 13, 42, 87, 93, 131, 148, 241, 249

folklore: dyadic, 10, 11; human interaction context, 10; of intimacy, of Bendix, 10; religious, 1–13; studies approach, xi, 1, 2, 3, 6, 9, 80, 93, 242; vernacular religion incorporation in study, 5, 13, 69

folkloric methodologies, 1–2

folklorist: on belief system experiential factors, 4; on religion in everyday life, 3; religion problematic terminology for, 3; religious beliefs in fieldwork of, 2; Sciorra on Italian American Catholics, 268n1; vernacular Catholicism understanding by, 33

folk medicine, Santino on, 263n23

folk religion, 2; Drews on unofficial religion of, 3; Yoder residualistic conception of, 3, 259n2

Fontana, Katie, 35, 39; in Mother of Grace Club, 36; Saint Joseph's Day altar, *p3*

food distribution, through Holy Communion Banquet Service, 200–201

foodways. *See* religious foodways

Forster, Art, 99

Fraternity Peace Mission Evangelical Home, 180

French Canadian Catholicism, 68–69

Gard, Peter, 23

Gardner, Velmer, 244

gay and lesbian sexuality, 134–35, 138–40; Dignity Catholic faith retention, 105, 120

gender, religion and, 132–33, 141, 182, 242, 289n15

gender-conservative culture, of Dignity, 132–33
Giacalone, Margaret, 37
Giffords, Gloria Fraser, 79
Gilkes, Cheryl Townsend, 196
Giorgi, Rosa, 80
Gladwyne, Pennsylvania: songs of dedication at, 154; Woodmont at, xiii, 154, 167, 183–87, 224, 299n11, *p10*
Glassie, Henry, 6, 17, 188, 281n65
Gloucester, Massachusetts: car caravans Saint Joseph feast day, 34; hazardous fishing industry in, 35; Mother of Grace Club in, 36–37; Saint Joseph sacred relationship in, 37–38; Sicilian American home altars in, 32, 33, 34; Sicilian fishing families in, 34–35; women's faith response adversity in, 34–35
Goodwin, Joseph P., 287n7
Gowans, Alan, 5
Green, Tony, 262n11
Gregory the Great (pope), 80
Griffith, R. Marie, 166, 210, 297n34
Gura, Philip F., 261n9

Hall, David D., 261n9
Handlin, Oscar, 183
Harlem, Father Divine in, 145, 171–72, 175, 199, 220–21
Harris, Sarah, 244
Hayden, Dolores, 169
Hermes statue, *Portal of Life Eternal* door design and, 234, 300n30
heterosexual couples, dyadic idioculture of, 10, 264n25
Hinson, Glenn, 246
historical developments, of ex-votos, 77–81
historicization, in vernacular Catholicism, 39
holy cards, 49, 86–87; in America, 58, 64–68; American chromolithograph of Sharp, 64; as artifact of belief, 57–59; Benziger on, 64; of Blessed Virgin Mary and Girl Scouts, 57, *p5*; of Carrella, 274n10; Christian imagery production and distribution, 61–64; decay of, 71–73; de-emphasis of, 53; devotionalism and, 71; Farago on, 67–68; history of, 62–63; for immigrant retention of faith, 66; Lange on, 67–68; Maniura on, 73; McBrien on, 58; Morgan on, 61, 72; of Neumann to North American, 45; of Our Mother of Perpetual Health, 65, *p6*; for personal piety, 66; production and efficacy, 59–61; for protection, 69–70; publishing companies for, 64–65; Quebecois example, 68–71; religious material culture and, 59; as sacramentals, 56, 57, 60–61; for Saint Jude devotion, 66; Toni on, 71–72; vernacular Catholicism and, 71; on Virgin May Lourdes of Fatima, 66; Wildhaber on, 59
Holy Communion Banquet Service, of Peace Mission, 149, 150, 160, 243; abundance representation in, 171; Father Divine custom after physical passing, 227; food distribution through, 200–201; menu for, 201–3; molded butter lilies at, 206, *p12*; Mother Divine at, 205, *p11*; Mother Divine place setting, 212, *p13*; property acquisitions announced at, 176; as religious ritual, 195, 205–6; religious service of, 150
home placement, of religious material culture, 37, 40, 42, 46
homosexuality: Catholic Church exclusionary position on, 107, 110, 128, 283n15; Dignity on God creation of, 12, 132; lack of choice in, 132, 140; spirituality and, 138, 139, 141
homosexual organizations, xii. *See also* Dignity

homosexuals, 286n5; Ratzinger on negativity toward, 107, 108, 128
hooked rugs: Newfoundland craft of, 16, 21, 26, 265n4, 267n23; Pocius on, 26; religious themes of, 21, 26; Sister Ann Ameen art of, 16, 18–22, 29; Sister Ann Ameen on vision of, 17; Sister Ann Ameen paintings in wool, 19–21, 26, 28; Sister Ann Ameen use of bold colors in, 22, 23, 26. *See also* religious hooked rugs, of Sister Ann Ameen
hooks, bell, 190–91
Hoshor, John, 244
hotels, of Father Divine, 178, 181; celibacy and sex-segregation in, x; modesty commitment, x, 179, 182; racial segregation refusal, x, 182, 237; rules and regulations of, x. *See also specific hotels*
Howlett, D. Roger, 231, 232, 299n18
Hufford, David J., 246, 261n7
human interaction, folklore and context of, 10
hymns, 36, 111, 133, 156, 289n15

idioculture, heterosexual couples dyadic, 10, 264n25
imagery, Christian iconography controversy and, 62
imitation, in vernacular Catholicism, 39
immigrants: Catholic, 65; ethnic or national parishes for, 66, 106, 283n11; holy cards for retention of faith of, 66; piety, 53
incarnation: Father Divine as Creator God, 146, 151, 171, 196, 218, 219, 238–39, 242; Mother Divine as Virgin Mary, 243
individual believer: Catholic confession and, 11; ex-votos and, 81; factors influencing, 7; folklife unexamined element of, 9; official religion and, 8; religious beliefs of, 4, 8, 12, 20, 51, 52; vernacular religion and, 126, 128

individual spirituality, negotiations of, xii
inductive process, for lived religion, 4
infidelity, of Ameen, K., 24
institution, religion as, 7, 8
institutional Christianity, 32, 128
intention, vernacular architecture of, 188–93, 222–24
intercession, 34, 38, 55, 62, 74, 76, 79, 81, 82, 83, 84
International Modest Code, of Father Divine, 172, 179, 182, 219–21, 223, 243; Woodmont visitors and, 300n28
International Peace Mission Movement: African Americans majority in, 198, 220; critical publications on, 244; as cult, 145, 219, 244; Dodson and Gilkes on, 196; ethnographic writing on, 241–50; music tradition in, 144–67; *New Day* publication of, 157, 180; *Spoken Word* publication of, 157; vernacular architecture and, 168–93
interracial marriage, of Father Divine and Mother Divine, 204, 226
Inturrisi, Louis, 87

Jake (priest), Dignity/Philadelphia and, 108, 124–25
James, Wendy, 263n19
Johnson, Douglas H., 263n19
John XXIII (pope), 88
Jones, Jim, 244
Jones, Michael Owen, 191–92
Joseph (Saint): Fontana on relationship to, 35–36; Gloucester car caravans on feast day of, 34; sacred relationship with, 37–38; statue for house sale, 41, 42, 44, 50, 55
Joseph (Saint) home altars: biological and sacred family representations at, 37; of Giacalone, 37; Gloucester large displays of, 32, 33, 34; Mother of Grace Club tradition of, 36; petitionary letters at, 37; religious vow to holy figures and, 34–35; as votive offerings, 34

Jude (Saint), holy cards for devotion of, 66
Justice, Mary, 161

Kahan, Benjamin, 199
Keyflower Dining Room, 149, 200; macrobiotic food at, 182, 197, 207–9, 211
Kilner, Isaac, 46
Kilner's Church Goods: Barclay Street art sold at, 47; parochial school system sales by, 65; Saint Anthony of Padua relic in, 46; Sisters Lounge at back of, 46–47, 65–66
Kirshenblatt-Gimblett, Barbara, 23, 26
Knott, Kim, 249
Krum Elbow Blues, 160
Kushi, Michio, 155, 208

landscapes, in Sister Ann Ameen scripture rugs, 28, 268n30
Lange, Yvonne, 67–68
Lantis, Margaret, 5
Larouche-Villeneuve Collection of holy cards: Lessard on, 68–71; Simard as overseer of, 68
Lassiter, Luke Eric, 246, 249
Lawless, Elaine J., 8, 246
Leadings of the Holy Spirit (Ameen, A.), 265n1
Lefebvre, Henri, 238
Leo V (emperor), 62
lesbian Catholics: Dignity gender-conservative culture, 132–33; Dignity male culture, 132–34; Dignity/Philadelphia lack of presence by, 132–33, 135, 137, 141; Dignity/Philadelphia male eroticism expression, 134–37
lesbianism, 286n3
Lessard, Pierre, 68–71
"Letter to the Bishops of the Catholic Church on the Pastoral Care of Homosexual Persons," Ratzinger and, 107, 108, 128

LGBTQ Catholics, xi, 105; Catholic hierarchy and, 108; on God's creation of, 114; public claim of, 120. *See also* gay and lesbian sexuality; homosexuality; lesbian Catholics
liberation theology, of Latin and South America, 27
Linenthal, Edward, 73
Lippincott, J. Dundas, 180
liturgical art objects, sacramentals of, 45
liturgical calendar, for Peace Mission songs, 153–54, 165
liturgical movement, of American Catholics, 53
liturgical space, 48, 115, 124, 137
liturgical transformations, in post-Vatican II, 88–89
lived religion, 1, 3, 6, 261n8; belief and practice negotiations, 6; of Dignity, 131; scholar inductive process for, 4, 42, 241; of Sister Ann Ameen, 20, 29
Lonsdale, Thomas, 181
Lourdes of Fatima, Virgin Mary apparitions, 32, 43, 51, 66, 85
Luther, Martin, 82–83

Mabee, Carleton, 245
macrobiotic diet, 196, 213; at Keyflower Dining Room, 182, 197, 207–9, 211; lectures and cooking courses on, 208
Maggiore, Dolores, 286n3
male culture, of Dignity, 132–34
Maniura, Robert, 73
Man Seeking Help for His Cattle painted ex-voto, 91, *p8*
marriages: of Ameen, K., to Sister Ann Ameen, 19, 23–24, 28; Father Divine and Mother Divine celibate, 177, 204, 226, 243; interracial of Father Divine and Mother Divine, 204, 226; marriage songs, 154; new definition of, 139; Sister Ann Ameen multiple, 18

material culture: American ecclesiastical architecture and art, 42; Barna on study challenges, 32; Catholic, 42, 43, 44, 45, 51; of Christian imagery and symbols, 40, 41; Dignity members connection to, 113, 126; examples of, 20; Father Divine use of, 168, 188–89, 190, 192; Morgan on, 93–94; Pickering and Green on, 262n11; postmodernism on, 33; Protestantism, 51–52; Sister Ann Ameen religious belief expression, 20, 21, 25. *See also* Catholic material culture

material religion, of Father Divine, 170, 174–77

McArthur, John Jr., 180

McBrien, Richard P.: on holy card, 58; on sacramentality, 60

McDannell, Colleen, 42, 45

McGowan, Andrew, 206

McGreevy, John, 119, 282n7

Mechling, Jay: on dyadic folklore, 10, 11; uniculture and, 11

mediation: in Catholicism, 82; in vernacular Catholicism, 39

memorates: American Protestant, 51–52; votives and, 80

memory objects, 72, 267n20; of Sister Ann Ameen scripture rugs, 23–24

Mercer, Johnny, 161

Merton, Thomas, 51

methodological reflexivity, 1, 5, 13, 259n1

methodological tool, vernacular religion as, xi

Miller, Rosina S., 239

mission activities, of Sister Ann Ameen, 19, 23–24

modesty: Father Divine hotel commitment to, x, 179, 182. *See also* International Modest Code

molded butter star, at Holy Communion Banquet Service, *p12*

Mollat du Jourdin, Michel, 83

monumental scripture rugs, of Sister Ann Ameen, 21, 29

Morgan, David, 218; on *Head of Christ*, 51–52, 61; on holy cards, 61, 72; on material culture, 93–94

Mother Divine, 144, 153; birth of, 204; celibate marriage to Father Divine, 154, 177, 204, 226, 243; Divine Tracy Hotel upgrade, 212–13; at Holy Communion Banquet Service, 205, *p11*; as leader after Father Divine death, 144, 177–78; meeting with, xiii, 148; Peace Mission perpetuation, 177–78, 196, 205, 207, 234–35; Philadelphia architecture properties and, 187, 295n59; physical passing of, 204, 226, 243; place setting at Holy Communion Banquet Service, 212, *p13*; reciprocal ethnography with, xii–xiii, 244, 289n12; theology of food, 214–15; tomb of, 239; as Virgin Mary incarnation, 226, 243; Weisbrot on leadership of, 207; at Woodmont, 205, 226, *p11*

Mother of Grace Club: Gloucester fishermen wives in, 36; Gloucester religious and ethnic organization of, 36; religious activities of, 36, 37; Saint Joseph home altars tradition and, 36

Murphy, Richard, 229, 231

music tradition, of International Peace Mission Movement, 144–67; Belstrom composer of, 157–58; choral groups of, xii, 154, 155, 157–58, 159, 160, 206, 235, 289n15; Father Divine on creative meaning of, 152–53; Father Divine sermons motivated by songs, 152; members empowerment through, 165; musical styles diversity, 155–56; Sing Happy and, 146; song as sacred inspirations, 152, 153; song creation theology, 152; world music lyrical compositions, 157–59. *See also* songs, of Peace Mission

National Historic Landmark, Woodmont as, 187, 235
national parishes, 105, 106, 283n11
National Shrine of Saint Jude Thaddeus, 52–53
native Christianity, 263n19
negotiation, xii; lived religion belief and practice, 6, 7, 27, 29, 71, 81; in Peace Mission, 156, 166, 167; in vernacular Catholicism, 38, 39, 42, 112, 123, 128, 129
Neumann, John (Bishop): holy cards of, 45; relic of, 46; shrine of, 85
New Age/pagan/Wiccan retail stores, 43
New Day publication, of International Peace Mission Movement, 157, 180, 202, 226
Newfoundland: geographic location of, 266n6; hooked rug craft of, 16, 21, 28, 265n4, 267n23; religion in, 19, 24, 26, 27–28, 41, 55; Sister Ann Ameen home in, 17–18, 29; Sister Ann Ameen hooked rugs depiction of, 22; Squires art on, 22
New Thought movement, 171, 175, 198, 213, 225, 243, 297n34
New York, Father Divine move from, 178, 199, 293n16
non-Catholic Eucharistic ministers, at Dignity/Philadelphia, 116, 284n28
non-clerical parish administrators, 106

objectification, in vernacular Catholicism, 39
official religion, xi–xii, 2–3, 259n5; Catholic Church and, 125; Christianity and, 7; Lawless on, 8; Troeltsch on, 3; vernacular practice in, 8; vernacular religious ideas compared to, 8–9, 262n11
Orsi, Robert A., 52–53, 120
Our Lady of Guadalupe, 43, 50
Our Mother of Perpetual Health holy card, 65, *p6*

Padre Prio (Saint), 37
painted ex-votos, 76, 78, 80, 84, 85, 91, 94; Carroll on, 96; Forster and, 99; of Man Seeking Help for His Cattle, 91, 92, *p8*; *Pietà*, 84–85; Yoder on, 85
painted holy cards, 60, 63, 67
paintings in wool, Sister Ann Ameen hooked rugs as, 19–21, 25, 26, 28
parishes: Brophy on, 106, 120; Casino on, 114–15; closing of, 120; description of, 105–6; Dignity as, 115–19; Dignity asked to leave, 107, 128, 283n15; diocesan bishop organization of, 106; national, 106, 283n11; non-clerical parish administrators in, 106; priest shortages in, 89, 106; traditional, 12, 54, 109, 110, 114, 127. *See also* ethnic parishes
parochialization, in vernacular Catholicism, 39
parochial school system: Catholic publishing companies for, 45–46; holy card and, 61–62; Kilner's Church Goods sales to, 65; legalism on, 113; suburban, 59
Paul VI (pope), 88
Peace, Father Divine preferred greeting of, x, xii, 154, 191
Peace Mission, xi; aesthetic of, 155, 179, 185–86, 238; African Americans quality service in properties of, 182, 199, 220; celibacy tradition in, 154, 171, 195, 219, 226, 233; congregational singing in, 150, 154–55, 160, 201, 290n29; ethnographic work of, xii, 144–67, 288n10; expressive culture of, 150; Father Divine and, 171–72; Fauset fieldwork approach to, 147–48; Fauset on, 163–67; followers everyday lives of, 154–55, 291n46; interview and observation reticence in, 147, 197, 298n11; Mother Divine perpetuation of, 177–78, 196, 205, 207, 234–35; only one race commitment, x, 237; Promised Land of, 199–200; racial

identity and, 237; women influence in, 166, 291n45. *See also* Holy Communion Banquet Service; International Peace Mission Movement

The Peace Mission Movement (Mother Divine), 178

Pearson, George T., 180

Peninnah, as Father Divine first wife, 171, 204, 226, 243, 292n9

perfectionist worldview, of Father Divine, 184, 186, 188

petitionary letters, at Saint Joseph home altars, 37

petitionary prayer, Dorgan on, 83–84

Philadelphia architecture: Bible Institute of Philadelphia, 180, 224; Church Gospel Mission Home, 182; Circle Mission Church, 159–60, 176, 182, 210, 224, 235; Divine International House, 179; Father Divine holdings of, 177–78, 223, 224; Fraternity Peace Mission Evangelical Home, 180; hotels, 178, 181–82; Mother Divine properties and, 187, 295n59; restoration and reuse of, 178–83, 199; Unity Mission Church, 181, 186, 224

physical passing (death): of Father Divine, 165, 205, 211, 219, 227–29, 236; of Mother Divine, 204, 226, 243

Pickering, Michael, 262n11

Pietà painted ex-voto, 84–85

piety: Dignity members for, 127; ex-votos for person, 76, 79; holy cards for personal, 60, 65, 66; personal, 45, 48, 53, 70, 126; Toni on changes in, 71; visual, 61

pilgrimage sites, 32, 37, 234

Pocius, Gerald L., 26, 267n23, 267n25

popular religion, xii, 2, 3, 4, 5; vernacular religion compared to, 9; Yoder on, 259n2

Portal of Life Eternal, 187; "The Builders" detail of, 233, *p16*; celibacy considerations in, 233–34; door design of De Lue, 231–32, 294n48, *p15*; Hermes statue and, 234, 300n30; Stewart on, 300n30

postmodernism, 1, 33; American Catholic devotional items, 53; ex-votos and, 84–93; on material culture, 33; sacred materiality of Catholic sites, 41–55

post-Vatican II Catholicism: American Catholics practice differences, 54, 113, 120; church closings, 89–90; on devotionalism, 71, 88; Dignity and, 105, 113; holy card decline, 58, 59, 71; liturgical transformations in, 88–89; sanctuary, 48; traditions, quality, style practice, 54, 55

practical religion, Father Divine on, 221–23

prayer: books, 64, 65, 72, 125–26; cards, 58; Dignity group, 127; ex-votos as vow and, 74, 75, 76, 81–84; Father Divine and, 177, 200, 227–29; holy cards and, 71, 88; petitionary, 83–84, 91, 152–53; service for AIDS, 112

Price, William L., 183, 190

Prideaux, Mel, 248

priests: parish shortages of, 89, 106; presiders at Dignity/Philadelphia, 110–11, 115, 116, 133, 284n21

Primiano, Leonard Norman, x–xi, 19, 124–25, 137, 161, 247

production and efficacy, of holy cards, 59–61

pro-life movement objects, in St. Jude shop, 50

Promised Land: for Peace Mission food supply, 175, 199–200; Peace Mission song, 151

protection: ex-votos for, 76; holy cards for, 69–70, 73

Protestant Evangelical Christianity, of Sister Ann Ameen, 18, 20, 28, 29

Protestantism material culture: Sallman art, 51–52; St. Jude Shop and images of, 51

publications: on Father Divine, 148, 244–45; International Peace Mission Movement critical, 244–45; *New Day*, 157, 180; Peace Mission Movement, 234; *Spoken Word*, 157

public profile, of Sister Ann Ameen, 25

public vows, 82

publishing companies: Catholic for parochial school system, 45–46; for holy cards, 64–65

Quebec City, Canada: Larouche-Villeneuve Collection holy cards at, 68–71; Lessard study of French-speaking Catholics in, 68–69

queer theology, 123

race neutrality, Father Divine and, 164, 175, 198, 237, 280n15, 295n61, 296n4, 299n7

racial discrimination: experience of, 186, 191, 198, 220, 224; Father Divine Righteous Government Platform on, 225

racial identity, xii; Father Divine and, 165; Weisenfeld on Peace Mission and, 237

racial segregation, Father Divine hotel refusal of, x, 182, 198, 237

radio broadcasts: of Dignity president, 109, 283n19; of Father Divine, 156–57, 161; of Sister Ann Ameen, 25

The Rapture scripture rug, of Sister Ann Ameen, 21

Ratkus, Mark, 117

Ratzinger, Joseph (cardinal), 107, 108, 128

reciprocal ethnography, 246; with Mother Divine, xii–xiii, 244, 248, 249, 250, 289n12; Prideaux on, 248; in religious folklife studies, 242

reflexivity: ethnographic, 12, 13, 259n1; methodological, 1, 5, 259n1; religious folklore study relationship with, 1

relics: Angenendt on, 78; concern for sale of, 95; discarding of, 88, 89; for everyday life sacramentality, 41; history of, 63, 98, 236; holy cards as, 72; miraculous nature of, 77, 96; of Neumann, 46; of Saint Anthony of Padua, 46

religion: Father Divine on practical, 198–99, 221–23; folk, 2–3, 259n2; folkloric scholarship on, 9; as institution, 7; lived, 1, 3, 4, 6, 20, 29, 42, 131, 241, 261n8; in Newfoundland, 27–28; Smith on reification of, 7–8; two-tiered model of, 3–4, 259n5

religion and gender, 132–33, 141, 182, 242, 289n15

religion and race, 289n15; Father Divine and, 163–67, 175, 220, 225

religious beliefs: expressive culture and, 7; folklorist fieldwork and, 2, 9, 242; holy cards and, 59; of individual believers, 11, 12, 114, 126; of Peace Mission, 171, 179, 198, 249; processes of, 6–7; psychology of, 4; of Sicilian Americans on healing, 30, 37; Sister Ann Ameen material expression of, 18, 20; Sister Ann Ameen narratives of, 25; social contexts for, xii; systems of, 44, 90; traditional, 31

religious culture, ethnography understanding of, xi

religious folk art, xii, 43, 55, 59, 67–68, 85. *See also* religious hooked rugs

religious folklife studies, reciprocal ethnography in, 242

religious folklore, 1–13

religious foodways, xi, 31–32; through Holy Communion Banquet Service, 200–206; Mother Divine changes to Peace Mission, 194–215; Mother Divine theology of food, 214–15; order and control in, 197–98; Woodmont nonlinen napkins, 212, *p12*. *See also* macrobiotic diet

religious healing: Sicilian Americans belief in, 30, 32, 37; Sister Ann Ameen and, 24

religious hooked rugs, of Sister Ann Ameen, 21, 22, 26, 28; *Church with Red Door*, *p1*; Gard colors criticism of, 23; Kirshenblatt-Gimblett on, 23, 26; landscapes in, 28, 268n30; linear process for, 22; as memory objects, 23–24; monumental, 21, 29; number and size of, 21; pictural, 28; prayer while hooking, 22; *The Rapture*, 18, 21; scriptural, 18, 28–29; wall hanging intended for, 22, 26; *Yellow Flowers on a Purple Background*, *p2*. *See also* hooked rugs

religious identity of American religion, Albanese on, 27, 198–99, 267n28

religious material culture: Barna research on, 32, 33; Catholic, 41–55; examples of, 20; holy card and, 59; for home placement, 40, 42

religious narratives: of ex-votos, 80; of Peace Mission, 162; of Sister Ann Ameen, 24–25

religious objects: American Catholics on, 31, 32, 33, 53–55; to purchase, 50, 51, 52; studies of, 268n3

religious service, of Peace Mission Holy Communion Banquet Service, xiii, 149, 150, 154, 160, 176, 180, 182, 183, 190, 200, 220, 243, 249; as Eucharist, 205, 224; menu of, 211

religious themes, of hooked rugs, 21. *See also* religious hooked rugs

religious tradition: among contemporary American Catholics, 31; about sacred materiality, 44, 48; of Sicilian American home altars, 32–37; Smith on, 263n20; of vernacular Catholicism, 32

religious utopianism, 168, 169, 186, 222, 245

religious vernacular architecture, 168, 170, 188, 193

religious vows: of gratitude in altars, 35; of Luther, 82–83; obligations and tasks support by, 35; as part of plea, 76, 85; of poverty, 82; Saint Joseph altars from holy figure, 34

restoration: in Philadelphia architecture, 150, 178–83, 199; in vernacular architecture, 170, 171, 174–77; at Woodmont, 184, 190

retablos, Mexican, 34, 43, 79, 87, 91, 92, 97

retail stores: Catholic material culture sales by, 42, 43; Christian imagery and symbols sold in, 40; examples of sale items, 43, 55–56; Kilner's Church Goods, 46–47, 65–66; New Age/page/Wiccan, 43; Our Lady of Guadalupe images in, 43

Righteous Government Platform, on racial discrimination, 225

Ritchings, Edna Rose. *See* Mother Divine

Roberts, Allen F., 96

Roman Catholics: Code of Canon Law on sacramentals, 61; devotionalism, 32, 37; individual believers and confession in, 11; interaction with Protestants, 27; sacramentality term of, 44–45

rosary, 34, 36, 45, 49–50, 66, 88, 127; de-emphasis of, 53

Rosebuds choral group, of International Peace Mission Movement, xiii, 154, 155, 160, 206, 235, 289n15

rules and regulations, of Father Divine hotels, x

sacrament, sacramental compared to, 61

sacramentality: Catholic term of, 44–45, 53–55; McBrien on, 60; misrepresentation of, 90; relics for everyday life, 41; in vernacular Catholicism, 38 sacramentals: amulets compared to, 70; *Catechism of the Catholic Church* on, 70; of Catholic material culture, 44–45; of church decorations, 45; definition of, 61, 70; holy cards as, 57, 60–61; of liturgical objects, 45; Roman Catholic Code of Canon Law on, 61; sacrament compared to, 61; of Sicilian Americans secular family items, 30; St. Jude Shop Catholic, 48–50, 52. *See also* holy card

Sacred Heart of Jesus, 32, 45, 49, 66, 76, 90, 97, 126–27; ex-voto, 88, *p7*

sacred inspirations, of Peace Mission songs, 153

sacred materiality, xii; culture and religious tradition about, 44, 73; devotionalism and, 53; postmodern sites of Catholic, 41–55; study of, 93

sacred relationship, with Saint Joseph, 37–38

sacred space: Chidester and Linenthal on, 73; shrine as sense of, 216–39

saint cult, Christianity and, 77, 81

Saint Joseph's Day altar: of Fontana family, 34, *p3*; statues, 37, *p4*

Sallman, Warner, 51–52, 61

Salvatori, Mariolina, 78–79

Santeria, 43, 54

Santino, Jack, 263n23

Satter, Beryl, 166, 289n15

Savage, Barbara, 163

Sciorra, Joseph, xiv, 34, 92, 97–98, 190

Scott, George Gilbert, 5

scriptural word images: of African Americans, 27; of Sister Ann Ameen, 28; at St. Jude Shop, 51–52

Second Vatican Council. *See* Vatican II

secularization, 31, 33

Serenus of Marseille (bishop), 80–81

sex-segregation, in Peace Mission properties, x, 179, 182

sexual ethics, 108; Dignity statement on, 128–29, 283n15

Sharp, William, 64

Sharpe, Martin, 18

shrine: of Neumann, 46, 85; Peace Mission song on, 217, 229; sacred sense of place, 216–39

Shrine to Life, 187, 211, 229–39; De Lue *Portal of Life Eternal* doors design, 231–34, 294n48, 300n30, *p15*, *p16*; description of, 218, 230–31, *p14*; Thompson and Murphy design of, 229, 231

Sicilian Americans: altar locations of, 30, 32–34; Black Madonna of, 37; dead relative communication, 30, 37; devotionalism of, 30, 36, 37; Gloucester fishing families, 34–35; Padre Pio saint of, 37; religious healing belief, 30, 37; Turner on altars of St. Joseph, 33; women's sensibility, 37. *See also* Joseph (Saint) home altars

Simard, Jean, 68

Sing Happy follower, of International Peace Mission Movement, 146

Sister Ann. *See* Ameen, Ann

Sisters Lounge, in Kilner's Church Goods store, 46, 65–66

Smith, Wilfred Cantwell, 7–8, 263n20

Snow, Elizabeth, 18

social contexts: for religious beliefs, xii; of vernacular religion, xii

Soja, Edward, 238

solitary life: of American Catholics, 11; of Sister Ann Ameen, 23–24

song creation theology, of Peace Mission, 152; on shrine, 217, 229

The Song of Bernadette (Werfel), 50, 85, 279n29

songs, of Peace Mission, 146, 151, 156, 158, 159, 165, 289n15; creation theology of, 152; Father Divine sermons motivated by, 152; Gladwyne, Pennsylvania dedication, 154; liturgical calendar for, 153–54; performance of, 155, 160, 161,

167, 227; sacred inspirations of, 153, 157, 196; of shrine, 217, 229
spiritual autobiography, of Sister Ann Ameen, 18, 23–25
spirituality: African American women, 291n45; Christian, 76, 80, 82; Dignity sexual nature of, 114, 138–40; of Father Divine, 214; holistic, 209; negotiations of individual, xii; Vatican II, 72; vernacular, 136; vernacular architecture materializing, 174–77; Wicca creative, 11–12
Spoken Word publication, of International Peace Mission Movement, 157
Squires, Gerald, 22
statues: religious, 32, 34, 45, 70, 86, 98, 191; retail stores sale of, 43, 97; of Saint Joseph for house sale, 41, 42, 44, 50, 55; Saint Joseph's Day altar and, 37, *p4*; St. Jude Shop saints, 48–49
stigmata, Carroll on, 261n7
St. Jude Shop, xi; American Catholic material culture and, 44, 51; books in, 51; Catholic kitsch in, 50, 54–55; Catholic sacramentals in, 48–50, 52; description of, 47–49; examples of religious folklife, 55; images as foundation of, 52; Internet marketing and sales of, 47; as large Philadelphia retail store, 44; personal use objects in front of, 49; post-Vatican II practices and, 54; pro-life movement objects in, 50; Protestantism material culture images at, 51; retail catalogs of, 47; Saint Joseph house sale statue at, 50, 55; scriptural word images at, 51–52; statues of saints in, 49
St. Peter Claver Catholic Church, Dignity/Philadelphia and, 109, 283n19
suicide attempt: of Jim Jones, 244; of Sister Ann Ameen, 19
supernatural encounters: Carroll on stigmata, 261n7; ex-votos as narrative of, 79–81; Hufford on, 261n7
Sweet Angel Divine. *See* Mother Divine

talisman, 69–70; of evil eye, 31
Taves, Ann, 45; on Catholic publishers, 65
Teske, Robert, 34
Theodora (empress), 62
Thomas, George E., 184, 190
Thompson, William Heyl, 229, 231
Toni, Graziano, 71–72
transformation theology, of Father Divine, 184–85
Troeltsch. Ernst, 3
Turner, Kay: on Sicilian American altars, 33; on women's altars, 238
two-tiered model, of religion, 2–4, 259n5

uniculture, 10, 11, 264n25, 265n30
United States, Sister Ann Ameen in, 18–19, 23, 24, 27, 28
Unity Mission Church, 181, 186, 224
Unity Society of Christianity, 151, 171, 213, 297n34
universalization, in vernacular Catholicism, 39
Upton, Dell, 6, 189–91

Vatican II: documents of, 51, 123, 125, 128; reforms of, 53, 88; St. Jude Shop images of Jesus, 49. *See also* post-Vatican II Catholicism
vernacular: arts and, 6; Lantis on, 5; term defined, 5
vernacular architecture: Glassie on, 6, 188; Gowans on, 5; of intention, 150, 188–93, 222–24, 248; International Peace Mission Movement and, 169–93; materializing spirituality in, 174–77; restoration in, 170, 171, 174–77; Scott on, 5; Upton on, 6, 189–91; of Woodmont, xiii, 154, 167, 183–87, 224–27, 299n11, *p10*. *See also* Philadelphia architecture
vernacular Catholicism: Barna on, 32; characteristics of, 33, 38–39; communion in, 39; description of, 126;

vernacular Catholicism (*cont.*)
Dignity example of, 123–29; folklorists understanding of, 33; of French Canadians, 68–71; historicization in, 39; holy cards and, 58, 67, 71; imitation in, 39; mediation in, 39; negotiation in, 39; objectification in, 39; parochialization in, 39; sacramentality in, 38; of Sicilian American women, 37; St. Jude Shop and, 52; universalization in, 39

vernacular religion, 11, 241, 261n8; belief systems study emphasis in, 12; of Book of Common Prayer, 261n9; described, 286n2; devotionalism in, 33, 37; ex-votos and, 81–82; folklore or folklife study of individual, 13; food and, 211, 214–15; Hall and Gura on, 261n9; as methodological tool, xi, 12; official religion ideas compared to, 8–9; popular religion compared to, 9; Sister Ann Ameen's art as, 16–17, 21, 29; social contexts of, xii

vernacular religious displays, as decorative and devotional, 33

vernacular religious ideas, official religion compared to, 8–9

vernacular term defined, 5

Victorian interest in Catholic collectibles, 46

Virgin Mary: devotions, 36, 71, 127; holy card of Blessed Virgin Mary and Girl Scouts, 57, *p5*; images, 49, 50, 52, 64; Lourdes or Fatima apparitions, 32, 43, 51, 66, 85; Mother Divine as incarnation of, 226, 243

Vodou, 44, 54, 96–97

voluntary offering, of votives, 81

votives: Angenendt on offerings, 78; candle lighting of, 83; collection of, 90–92, 100; Inturrisi on, 87; *memorates*, 80; retail stores sale of, 43; Roberts on, 96; Saint Joseph altars as offerings of, 34; Salvatori on Italian, 79; as voluntary offerings, 81

vows, 31–33, 35–36, 77, 279n29; ex-votos as, 74–76, 80, 81–84; ex-votos as private, 82; public, 82; reciprocal giving partnership from, 34; Sicilian Americans dead relatives, 30, 37; Sicilian Americans powerful saints, 30; Teske and Sciorra on, 34. *See also* religious vows

Vrijhof, Pieter H., 4

Walker, Geraldine, 208–9
Walker, Stanley, 208
Watts, Jill, 163–64, 210, 244, 245, 292n4
Weisbrot, Robert, 207, 244, 245
Weisenfeld, Judith, x, xv, 237
Weiss, Richard, 269n12
Werfel, Franz, 85, 279n29
Wicca, 271n10; creative spirituality of, 11–12; retail stores, 43
Wildhaber, Robert, 59
women: African American, 164, 220, 291n45; faith response in adversity, 35; Peace Mission and, 147–48, 154, 155, 193, 198; Peace Mission influence, 166, 289n15; spirituality of Sicilian American, 34–38; Turner on altars for, 238. *See also* Dignity/Philadelphia; lesbian Catholics
women's religious crafts, 16, 18, 21, 25–26. *See also* hooked rugs; religious hooked rugs
Wood, Alan Jr., 183, 190
Woodmont, xiii, 154, 167, 224–27, 299n11, *p10*; Father Divine transformation theology and, 184–85; International Modest Code and visitors to, 300n28; Mother Divine at, 205, 211, 226, *p 11*; Mother Divine religious tourism development at, 234–35; as National Historic Landmark, 187, 235; Peace Mission aesthetic and, 186, 238; Price

as architect of, 183; religious foodways nonlinen napkins, 212, *p12*; restoration work in, 184–85, 190; Thomas on, 184. *See also* Shrine to Life

Yellow Flowers on a Purple Background scripture rug, of Sister Ann Ameen, *p2*

Yoder, Don, 59, 86, 145, 263n22, 269n12; on folk religion, 3; folk religion residualistic conception of, 3; on painted ex-votos, 85; on unified belief system, 7

Young, Serinity, 244

Zug, Terry, 21

ABOUT THE AUTHOR AND EDITOR

LEONARD NORMAN PRIMIANO was Professor of Religious Studies at Cabrini College and University from 1993 until his death in 2021. He held dual doctorates in religious studies and folklore from the University of Pennsylvania, and his influence registered internationally in both fields. A gifted educator, Primiano received the Kennedy Center/Stephen Sondheim Inspirational Teacher Award in 2014.

DEBORAH DASH MOORE is Frederick G. L. Huetwell Professor of History and Professor of Judaic Studies at the University of Michigan. She is the author and editor of a number of books, including *GI Jews: How World War II Changed a Generation* and *Walkers in the City: Jewish Street Photographers of Mid-Century New York*.

www.ingramcontent.com/pod-product-compliance
Lightning Source LLC
Chambersburg PA
CBHW071147070526
44584CB00019B/2696